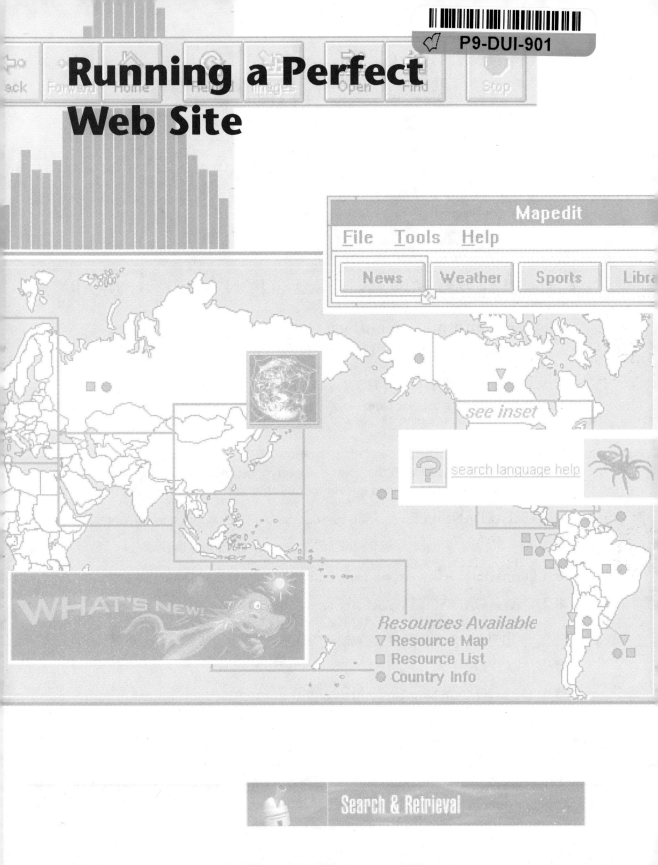

Running a Perfect Web Site

PLUG YOURSELF INTO...

THE MACMILLAN INFORMATION SUPERLIBRARY™

Free information and vast computer resources from the world's leading computer book publisher—online!

FIND THE BOOKS THAT ARE RIGHT FOR YOU!

A complete online catalog, plus sample chapters and tables of contents give you an in-depth look at *all* of our books, including hard-to-find titles. It's the best way to find the books you need!

- ● STAY INFORMED with the latest computer industry news through our online newsletter, press releases, and customized Information SuperLibrary Reports.

- ● GET FAST ANSWERS to your questions about MCP books and software.

- ● VISIT our online bookstore for the latest information and editions!

- ● COMMUNICATE with our expert authors through e-mail and conferences.

- ● DOWNLOAD SOFTWARE from the immense MCP library:
    - Source code and files from MCP books
    - The best shareware, freeware, and demos

- ● DISCOVER HOT SPOTS on other parts of the Internet.

- ● WIN BOOKS in ongoing contests and giveaways!

TO PLUG INTO MCP: ➔

GOPHER: gopher.mcp.com

FTP: ftp.mcp.com

WORLD WIDE WEB: **http://www.mcp.com**

Running a Perfect Web Site

David M. Chandler

with

Bill Kirkner

Jim Minatel

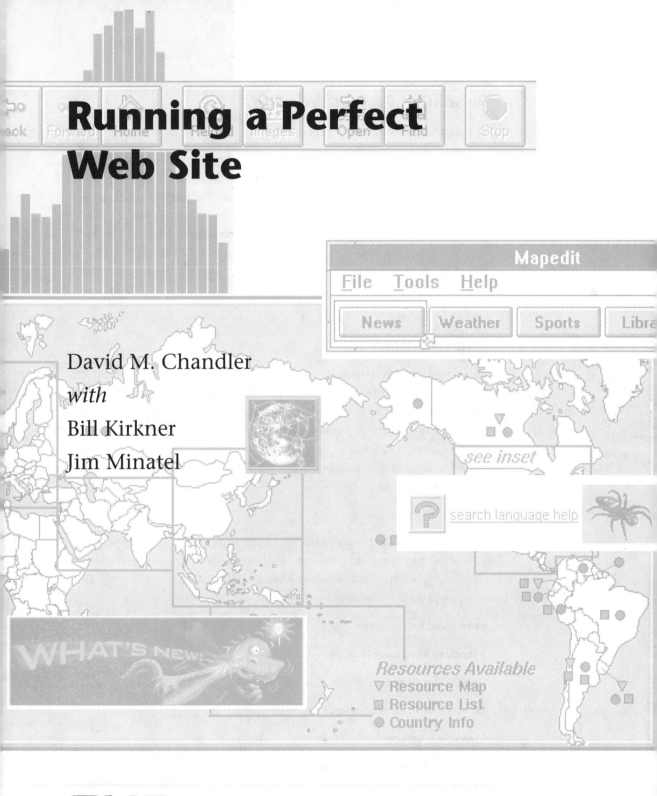

Mapedit

File Tools Help

News   Weather   Sports   Libra

see inset

? search language help

Resources Available
▽ Resource Map
■ Resource List
● Country Info

WHAT'S NEW!

Search & Retrieval

Running a Perfect Web Site

Library of Congress Catalog No.: 95-67672

ISBN: 0-7897-0210-x

98 97 96 95   6 5 4 3

Interpretation of the printing code: the rightmost double-digit number is the year of the book's printing; the rightmost single-digit number, the number of the book's printing. For example, a printing code of 95-1 shows that the first printing of the book occurred in 1995.

Publisher: Roland Elgey

Associate Publisher: Stacy Hiquet

Publishing Director: Brad R. Koch

Director of Product Series: Charles O. Stewart III

Managing Editor: Sandy Doell

Director of Marketing: Lynn E. Zingraf

Credits

Acquisitions Editor
Beverly M. Eppink

Product Director
Jim Minatel

Production Editor
Danielle Bird

Copy Editors
Noelle Gasco
Patrick Kanouse
Theresa Mathias
Julie A. McNamee

Technical Advisors
Jeff Bankston
Karl Laubengayer
Tim Parker

Figure Specialist
Cari Skaggs

Book Designer
Sandra Schroeder

Cover Designer
Dan Armstrong

Acquisitions Assistant
Ruth Slates

Editorial Assistant
Andrea Duvall

Production Team
Amy Cornwell
Chad Dressler
Karen Gregor
Barry Jorden
Daryl Kessler
Elizabeth Lewis
Stephanie Mineart
Kaylene Riemen

Indexer
Kathy Venable

Composed in *Stone Serif* and *MCPdigital* by Que Corporation

About the Authors

David M. Chandler is a World Wide Web enthusiast in Cedar Rapids, Iowa. He currently runs Internet at Work, an eastern Iowa Internet service provider also offering leased server space nationwide. Chandler previously managed Web servers for the Collins Avionics and Communications Division of Rockwell International. He has programmed computers since 1982 when he received a TI-99/4A as a gift. As a hobbyist, he enjoys learning new computer languages and building PCs. Chandler holds a degree in Electrical Engineering from the University of Kansas, and worked as a signal processing engineer in GPS before moving into the information systems field. When he's not at his computer, Chandler enjoys the mountains and flying as a private pilot. He can be reached via e-mail at **chandler@ins.netins.net**, and is available for Internet training and consulting. You can find Chandler on the Web at **http://www.netins.net/showcase/chandler/**. (Introduction, Chapters 1-9, and 11-15.)

Jim Minatel is a Product Development Specialist working for Que. His areas of expertise include computer graphics, the Internet, and multimedia. Before coming to Que, he developed college math texts and earned an M.S. in Mathematics from Chicago State University, in addition to a B.A. in Mathematicas and Physics from Wabash College. (Chapter 16 and WebmasterCD.)

Bill Kirkner first learned how to use a computer at the Boys' Latin School of Maryland on a set of spiffy TRS-80 Color computers at a time when 64K was considered a lot of RAM and an external 5 1/4-inch floppy drive was a quantum leap forward in technology. He first learned how to use the Internet as a consultant for the Academic Computing Service of Loyola College in Maryland, and he fondly remembers the days when you could still print a map of all the nodes on the Internet and post it on one wall. He has since earned his J.D. from the Georgetown University Law Center, and now works as a Technical Specialist for Walcoff and Associates, an Information and Technology Transfer contractor based in Fairfax, Virginia. Kirkner currently lives in the Dupont Circle neighborhood of Washington, D.C. (Chapter 10.)

Acknowledgments

I would first like to thank my wife, Vicki, who has patiently done more than her share of the work around the house while I was busy being an author. Secondly, I would like to thank Karl Laubengayer, the patient UNIX administrator who first got me into the Web and helped review this book. Thanks, also, to my management at Rockwell who supported this endeavor, including Randy Hillingsworth and Brian Wright. Special thanks go to Dave Lehman, who proofread the entire manuscript in a few nights. To Al Canton, author of *ComputerMoney,* thanks for responding to my questions as a total stranger on the Internet and giving me the confidence to pursue my first book contract. Thanks, also, to Mom and Dad, who taught me the meaning of Ecclesiastes 9:10 and who gave me a TI-99/4A in junior high which laid the foundation for everything I've done with computers to this day.

To the editors at Que: thanks for giving me the opportunity to write this book, I am especially grateful to Brad Koch for working with me to develop the outline, to Beverly Eppink for her professional support and encouragement, and Jim Minatel, whose insightful comments have made this book what it is. I was impressed with the Que team every step of the way.

David M. Chandler

Trademarks

All terms mentioned in this book that are known to be trademarks or service marks have been appropriately capitalized. Que Corporation cannot attest to the accuracy of this information. Use of a term in this book should not be regarded as affecting the validity of any trademark or service mark.

Contents at a Glance

Planning a Web Server

Setting Up a Web Server

Learning HTML

Applications

WebmasterCD

Contents

10 HTML Editors and Tools 251

11 Forms 291

14 Usage Statistics and Maintaining HTML   367

15 Database Access and Applications Integration   383

V Webmaster CD   395

16 Using WebmasterCD   397

Introduction

The World Wide Web is the most exciting development to hit the computer scene in years. Still in its infancy, it has attracted the interest of over two million people worldwide. Businesses, government institutions, universities, and organizations are flocking to the Web to promote their ideas and products. In less than two years, the Web has grown from nothing to the third largest source of traffic on the Internet (within months the Web may well be the single largest source).

Why are people so excited about the Web? What motivates people to spend $40 a month on a SLIP connection and spend countless hours downloading enormous graphics over slow modem connections? Surely TV requires less effort and is more entertaining. The answer is, in a word, discovery. The Web is a vast ocean of knowledge, hobbies, ideas, and topics of special interest. The daily discovery of new things stimulates the mind and expands horizons, unlike TV, which generally has the opposite effect. The World Wide Web blows away interactive TV and set-top converter boxes. No movies-on-demand test market has ever produced the enthusiastic response characteristic of the World Wide Web.

But the Web is much more than a technological innovation. It promises to be the catalyst for one of the greatest social revolutions the world has ever seen. The Web is an empowering tool. On the Web, everyone is equal. Products from the world's largest manufacturers receive no more or less attention than those of the smallest. The opinions of starving college students are as accessible as those of the highest government officials. Information is delivered directly into the hands of the people—unfiltered, uncensored, and previously unseen. The Web gives unprecedented visibility into government and public institutions. Every cause and political action group in America has a 24-hour voice on the World Wide Web, drowning out ABC, CNN, NBC, and CBS.

How does the Web give power to the people? It's free (or very nearly so)! Anyone with $40 a month not only has access to over a million pages of information on the Web but can also create a space on the Web. The Web thus gives small businesses the opportunity to compete with international corporations. It gives low-budget institutions the ability to engage in international public relations. It gives the underdog a voice.

When I first discovered the Web, I was excited. Partly, I was fascinated with the technology. But more importantly, I was (and still am) excited about the Web's potential. It is an incredible tool for publishing information. It's like a giant leaflet bomb in its ability to distribute information, but no one is inconvenienced in the slightest should they choose not look for the leaflets. The Web is the very spirit of the free market and free speech. It promotes open, honest, and fair competition. No one is excluded from participating, but no one has to participate, either.

Surprisingly, the Web does not have the feel of competition. Instead, it is characterized by cooperation: people helping people, giving some small part of themselves, as it were, back to the Net. I am continually amazed at the amount of time that knowledgeable and busy experts spend on the Net helping others to learn their particular field—people they've never met, who can offer little back, and who may even compete with them down the road. Without this cooperation, much of modern technology would never have come to pass, including the Web itself!

What This Book Is

This book is a comprehensive guide to creating your own World Wide Web presence and using Web technology internally. It's compiled from the writings and experiences of dozens of software authors, Web authors, and Internet strangers who took the time to answer questions on newsgroups. This book takes you all the way through learning what the Web can do to setting up your own server. It covers how to obtain your own Internet connection or lease space on a server, how to create Web pages and applications, and how to maintain your server. The final chapters are a reference for those wanting to use the Web for more advanced applications such as database access. Best of all, all the software you need to create a professional and successful Web site on either UNIX or Windows is included with this book.

Here's a brief overview of each chapter:

- Chapter 1, "Why the World Wide Web?," introduces you to the history of the Web and tells you what's made it popular and where it's going.

- Chapter 2, "An Introduction to Web Servers," presents how the Web can be used for everything from electronic books to powerful information searches and multimedia. It shows you how to use the Web for advanced applications and how to use the Web effectively with other Internet services such as News and e-mail.

■ Chapter 3, "Creating a Home Page on the Internet," presents the advantages and disadvantages of building your own server versus leasing space, how to find an Internet service provider, and what hardware and software is best for the job. Obtaining an Internet presence is easier than you might think.

■ Chapter 4, "Creating an Internal Web Server," tells you what's required to set up an internal Web server, including network, hardware, and software requirements. In addition, this chapter addresses document compatibility issues. Web technology is a powerful tool for sharing information—within a business or organization as well as with the outside world.

■ Chapter 5, "Getting Started with Web Servers," shows you how to install the software for UNIX and Windows that is included with this book and helps you get familiar with it.

■ Chapter 6, "Server Configuration," teaches you about all aspects of server configuration, including log files, document directories, MIME types, and security features. This chapter shows you that the server software included with this book is both flexible and powerful.

■ Chapter 7, "Managing an Internet Web Server," explains how to build a successful Internet Web server. It includes instructions on how to develop a fun and useful server, how to attract and keep visitors, how to protect your data, and how to promote your server. This chapter also lists popular features and overviews secure transactions.

■ Chapter 8, "Managing an Internal Web Server," describes how to maximize the effectiveness of your internal server. It explains how you can manage server content, provide useful features, and protect your internal network from hostile access. There is also a section on Internet firewalls.

■ Chapter 9, "Basic HTML: Understanding Hypertext," makes you aware that HTML is a simple yet rich language for creating Web pages. You learn everything you need to know about writing attractive and functional HTML documents, including how to use text and graphics features, use hypertext, and create clickable images.

■ Chapter 10, "HTML Editors and Tools," teaches you to create HTML using word processor templates and special editors and how to convert to HTML from other formats. Dozens of programs and templates have been developed to work with HTML.

■ Chapter 11, "Forms," gives you all the information you need about forms, which allow users to send data back to Web servers. You learn about all the elements of forms, including text boxes, check boxes and option buttons, pull-down menus, and push buttons. In addition, this chapter covers how data is sent to the server after it's been entered in a form.

■ Chapter 12, "Scripts," covers the programs that process form data and are the real power behind Web applications. You learn which scripting languages are best-suited to your needs, the general principles of scripting, and how to write scripts for UNIX and Windows. This chapter also explains how you can write secure scripts and server-side includes.

■ Chapter 13, "Search Engines and Annotation Systems," teaches how to write scripts to search simple text databases and how to efficiently search your entire server for information. It also covers systems for annotating Web documents.

■ Chapter 14, "Usage Statistics and Maintaining HTML," covers tools for analyzing usage data and tools for checking to see that your HTML files are all intact. This chapter helps you handle the maintenance activity involved once your server is up and running.

■ Chapter 15, "Database Access and Applications Integration," presents techniques for accessing data on various platforms. In addition, it contains resources for further information on World Wide Web development. You learn that the most advanced Web applications are those that communicate with relational databases.

■ Chapter 16, "Using WebmasterCD," provides a detailed overview of the contents of WebmasterCD and gives instructions on how to use it.

What This Book Is Not

This book is not an introduction to either the Internet or the World Wide Web. You should already have experience using a Web browser to use this book effectively.

This book is also not a programming reference for Visual Basic or perl, two of the languages used to develop Web tools and applications in this book. You can run the sample programs provided with this book without any knowledge of these languages, but customizing them requires some familiarity with the languages used.

Finally, this book is not an introduction to UNIX. If you want to run the UNIX Web server included with the book, you should already have some familiarity with the UNIX operating system.

WebmasterCD: Your One-Stop Web Resource

If all of this sounds like a good deal, hold onto your socks—there's more. This book includes an incredible CD-ROM called WebmasterCD (just inside the back cover). What makes it incredible is that it contains a tremendous variety of Internet and Web-based software programs for the Microsoft Windows environment and the UNIX operating system—everything from the Web server software discussed throughout the book and HTML authoring tools to e-mail, FTP, and news software for Windows. These resources will help you become a "Webmaster" in no time.

We've also included a large collection of useful documents about the Internet. You'll find all the RFCs, STDs, and FYIs on Webmaster. We've included lists of service providers, selected FAQs, examples of code and HTML from the book, and other documents of special interest.

Conventions Used in This Book

This book uses various conventions designed to make it easier to use. That way, you can quickly and easily learn to use the Web and how to run the perfect Web site.

With most Windows programs, you can use the mouse or keyboard to perform operations. The keyboard procedures for Windows software may include shortcut key combinations or *mnemonic* keys. In this book, key combinations are joined with plus signs (+). For example, Ctrl+X means hold down the Ctrl key, press the X key, and then release both keys. Some menu and dialog box options have underlined or highlighted characters that indicate mnemonic keys. To choose such an option using the mnemonic key, you press the Alt key and then press the indicated mnemonic key. In this book, mnemonic keys are set in bold: for example, **F**ile.

Commands and configuration options use special syntax to indicate options. Things inside brackets [ ] are optional. Items inside curly braces {} separated by a vertical bar are choices, like {high|medium|low}. Things inside angle brackets <> are HTML formatting tags. An ellipsis (...) indicates repetition.

The book uses several other typeface enhancements to indicate special text, as indicated in the following table.

Typeface	Meaning
Italic	Italic indicates variables in commands or addresses, and terms given definitions.
Bold	Bold indicates text you type and actual addresses for Internet sites, newsgroups, mailing lists, WWW pages, and more.
`Computer type`	This special type is used for commands (such as the DOS `COPY` or UNIX `cp` command). It also indicates sample HTML, program code, and names of directives and tags.

Tip

Tips suggest easier or alternative methods to execute a procedure.

Note

Notes provide additional information that may help you avoid problems or offer advice or general information related to the topic at hand.

Caution

Cautions warn you of hazardous procedures and situations that can lead to unexpected or unpredictable results, including data loss or system damage.

You'll also see the WebmasterCD icon (shown beside this paragraph) throughout the book in the margins. Where you see this icon, the text is discussing software or a document on WebmasterCD.

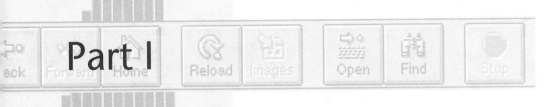

Part I
Planning a Web Server

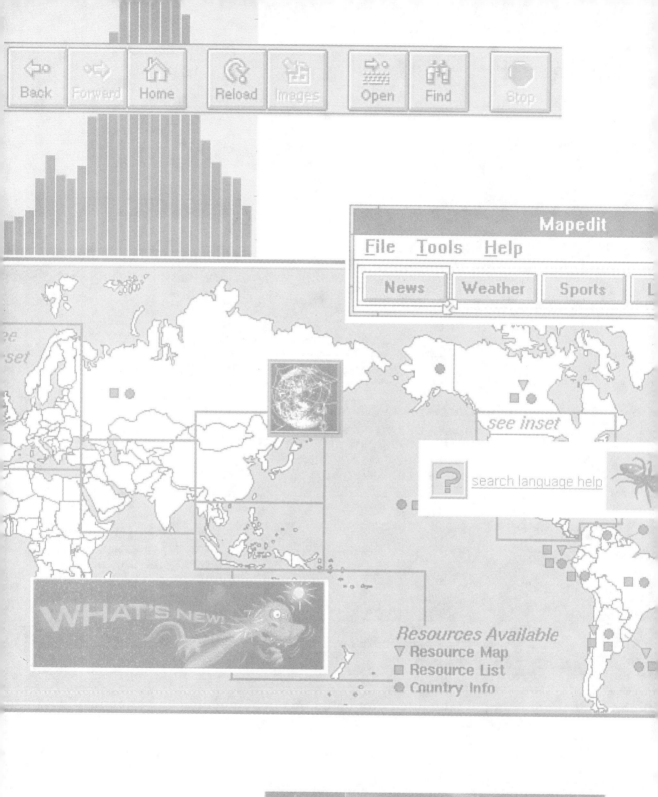

Chapter 1

Why the World Wide Web?

The World Wide Web is the fastest growing segment of the Internet. Its graphical interface and hypertext capabilities have caught the fancy of Internet users and the media like no other Internet tool in history. Businesses, schools, government, nonprofit organizations, and even individuals are flocking to the Web to promote themselves and their products in front of an audience spanning the entire planet. Because of the Web's popularity and its cost-effectiveness as a marketing tool, the World Wide Web is staged to become the electronic marketplace of the decade.

In this chapter, you learn

- How the Web was born
- Who uses the Web
- What makes the Web so popular
- How you can benefit from publishing on the Web

What Is the World Wide Web?

The World Wide Web is the first global interactive network. Although part of the Internet, it's radically different because it uses hypertext and graphics together to display information, allowing users to cross the globe with a single click of the mouse. The Web is accessible in 84 countries on all seven continents. The information available on the Web ranges from the esoteric to the absurd. Web sites are maintained by universities, companies, public institutions, states, cities, and even high schools. Powerful search engines allow rapid information location and retrieval, making the Web the ultimate tool for both research and interactive entertainment.

Like many previous Internet services, the Web uses client-server technology. The most significant benefit of this to Web users is that there are no platform incompatibilities. Any Web browser that follows Web standards can connect to any Web server that follows Web standards. A Windows Web browser can connect to a UNIX server and vice versa. This standardization makes the Web highly attractive for world-wide electronic publishing.

A Brief History of the Web

In only two years, the World Wide Web has grown into an international network comprising more than 10,000 information servers and an estimated two million users. The Web is growing at least twice as fast as the Internet itself, and is destined to become the largest source of traffic on the Internet.

The Home of the Web

The World Wide Web was invented at CERN, Europe's high-energy physics laboratory, which has long been involved in advanced computer technologies supporting scientific research. In 1989, CERN began developing the Web to enable physicists around the globe to communicate more effectively using hypertext. The first WWW software was publicly released in August 1991 by posting it to several Internet newsgroups. In February 1993, NCSA (National Center for Supercomputing Applications at the University of Illinois) published Mosaic, the now legendary graphical browser for the Web. Since then, World Wide Web servers have been created in most (if not all) of the 84 countries on the Internet. Table 1.1 lists countries with access to the World Wide Web.

> **Note**
>
> Network statistics for all countries on the Internet are updated monthly at **ftp:// nis.nsf.net/nsfnet/statistics/**.

Table 1.1 Countries with Access to the World Wide Web			
Code	**Country**	**Code**	**Country**
DZ	Algeria	KR	Korea, South
AQ	Antarctica	KW	Kuwait

Code	Country	Code	Country
AR	Argentina	LV	Latvia
AM	Armenia	LB	Lebanon
AU	Australia	LI	Liechtenstein
AT	Austria	LT	Lithuania
BE	Belgium	LU	Luxembourg
BM	Bermuda	MO	Macau
BR	Brazil	MY	Malaysia
BG	Bulgaria	MX	Mexico
CM	Cameroon	NL	Netherlands
CA	Canada	NZ	New Zealand
CL	Chile	NI	Nicaragua
CN	China	NO	Norway
CO	Colombia	PA	Panama
CR	Costa Rica	PE	Peru
HR	Croatia	PH	Philippines
CY	Cyprus	PL	Poland
CZ	Czech Republic	PT	Portugal
DK	Denmark	PR	Puerto Rico
EC	Ecuador	RO	Romania
EG	Egypt	RU	Russian Federation
EE	Estonia	SG	Singapore
FJ	Fiji	SK	Slovakia
FI	Finland	SI	Slovenia
FR	France	ZA	South Africa
DE	Germany	ES	Spain
GH	Ghana	LK	Sri Lanka

(continues)

Planning a Web Server

Table 1.1	Continued		
Code	**Country**	**Code**	**Country**
GR	Greece	SZ	Swaziland
GU	Guam	SE	Sweden
HK	Hong Kong	CH	Switzerland
HU	Hungary	TW	Taiwan
IS	Iceland	TH	Thailand
IN	India	TN	Tunisia
ID	Indonesia	TR	Turkey
IE	Ireland	UA	Ukraine
IL	Israel	AE	United Arab Emirates
IT	Italy	GB	United Kingdom
JM	Jamaica	US	United States
JP	Japan	UY	Uruguay
KZ	Kazakhstan	VE	Venezuela
KE	Kenya	VI	Virgin Islands

The Web's Phenomenal Growth

In January 1993, there were only 50 known Web servers in existence. Only 9 months later, there were over 500. Now, just 1 year later, more than 10,000 servers are on the World Wide Web. In less than 2 years, the Web has become the second largest source of traffic on the Internet. Table 1.2 and figure 1.1 show the growth of the Web relative to other Internet services on the National Science Foundation (NFS) backbone, which consists of high-speed trunk lines that carry Internet traffic from coast to coast.

Note

There are an estimated 10,000 WWW servers, not including many private servers used by businesses for internal communication. A list of all registered servers is available from **http://www.w3.org/hypertext/DataSources/WWW/Servers.html**.

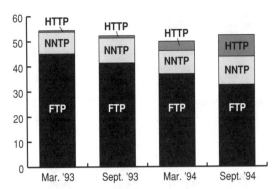

Percentage of
Total Byte
Traffic on the
NSF Backbone
Mar. '93 – Sept. '94

Fig. 1.1
This bar graph
illustrates the data
shown in table 1.2.

Table 1.2	Growth of World Wide Web Traffic		
Month	**FTP (File Transfer)**	**NNTP (UseNet News)**	**HTTP (World Wide Web)**
Percentage of Total Byte Traffic on the NSF Backbone			
Mar. '93	45.1	9.4	0.06
Sep. '93	41.3	10.0	0.90
Mar. '94	36.9	9.3	3.70
Sep. '94	32.5	11.2	8.60

Note

As of December 1994, Web traffic surpassed News to become the second-largest
source of byte traffic on the Internet. The top five sources are now FTP, HTTP (Web),
NNTP (News), SMTP (e-mail), and Telnet. Updated statistics are available from
ftp://nis.nsf.net/statistics/nsfnet/.

As table 1.2 illustrates, the World Wide Web is growing at an exponential
rate. The Internet is growing rapidly, too, but the Web is growing much
faster. In the first six months of 1994, the total number of bytes transferred
over the Internet's NSF backbone increased by 55 percent. By comparison,
WWW traffic almost tripled in the same time frame. It's true that much of
the growth is due to the initial development of the Web, but several factors
will cause the Web to continue to grow at an explosive rate. By 1996, it's
quite possible that the Web will account for more traffic than all other
Internet activity combined!

> **Note**
>
> The World Wide Web traffic in table 1.2 reflects only connections to World Wide Web servers. Web browsers can also connect to FTP (File Transfer Protocol), Gopher, and other types of servers. In addition, table 1.2 shows only WWW traffic on the NSF backbone. Web traffic between commercial entities is carried on a separate backbone.

The Future of the Web

In order to understand where the World Wide Web is headed, you need to know what's made it so popular to date.

A Graphical Interface to the Internet

The Web's graphical interface is at the heart of its success. Previous Internet tools required you to learn command-line sequences for making connections, transferring data, and viewing files. Graphical front ends have been developed for these programs, but none have come close to the power of WWW browsers, such as Mosaic and Netscape, with their simple hypertext operation. Unlike previous graphical front ends to the Internet, Web browsers make access to all Internet services transparent to the user. The user does not need to know which underlying service is used to retrieve data because the browser does all the work. Figure 1.2 illustrates how Web browsers can connect to a number of different Internet services.

The World Wide Web has done for the Internet what Microsoft Windows did for personal computers. In Mosaic, a single mouse-click can initiate a connection to a remote host on the Internet, transfer files containing formatted text and graphics via FTP, Gopher, or HTTP (the native Web protocol), and display the resulting page with hypertext links to many more sites (see fig. 1.3).

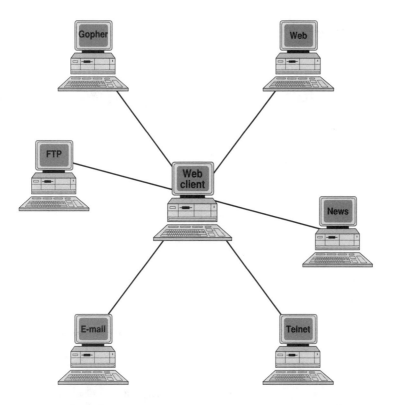

Fig. 1.2
Web browsers can connect to many Internet services, including FTP, Gopher, news, and Web servers. In addition, some browsers can support e-mail and Telnet.

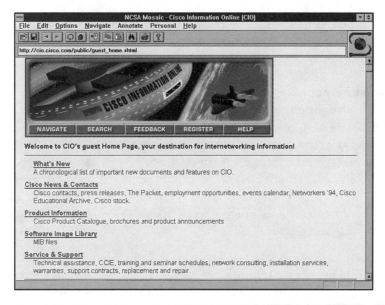

Fig. 1.3
NCSA Mosaic, a popular WWW browser allows point-and-click access to all major Internet services via hypertext links.

Table 1.3 lists some of the Internet services now graphically available through the World Wide Web.

Table 1.3 Internet Services Available from WWW Browsers	
Name	**Function**
E-mail	Electronic mail
FTP	File transfer
Gopher	Data searching and retrieval
News	Thousands of special interest forums
WAIS	Wide Area Information Search
Finger	Information on Internet users
Archie	Locating files
WHOIS	Who is ____? (Internet white pages)

The Internet Explosion

Besides the Web's graphical appeal, its popularity has benefited from increased public awareness of the Internet and the availability of dial-up Internet connections. These things make the Web accessible to homes and small businesses. Home consumer and business use will likely fuel much of the Web's growth for years to come.

Dial-Up Internet Access

Traditionally, getting a full connection to the Internet (as opposed to just e-mail) required a high-speed leased telephone line and expensive networking hardware. As a result, only businesses and large institutions could afford Internet access. This limited the Internet's usefulness for commercial purposes because home computer users could not get access, and businesses often restricted access except for e-mail. However, the introduction of high-speed modems and dial-up Internet access makes WWW access from home both possible and practical.

The Serial Line Internet Protocol and Point-to-Point Protocol (SLIP and PPP) are two commonly used schemes for transferring Internet data to a home computer over the regular phone system. This allows home users to obtain full Internet connections without having to purchase a leased line or expensive connecting hardware. Every SLIP or PPP user has a static or dynamically assigned IP (Internet Protocol) address that is used to send and receive data directly on the Internet. This means that SLIP and PPP users can do everything that users with faster leased line connections can do. This includes setting up an Internet server for FTP, Telnet, Gopher, and the World Wide Web. Figure 1.4 illustrates dial-up access via SLIP or PPP.

Note

"SL/IP" is equivalent to "SLIP." Both refer to Serial Line Internet Protocol; this book uses SLIP.

Note

Many dial-up services offer text-mode Internet access, which is usually cheaper than SLIP but can't support graphical access. However, a program called *The Internet Adapter* (TIA) emulates SLIP so text-mode users can have most of the benefits of true SLIP accounts. Information on other SLIP emulators is available in the newsgroup **alt.dcom.slip-emulators**.

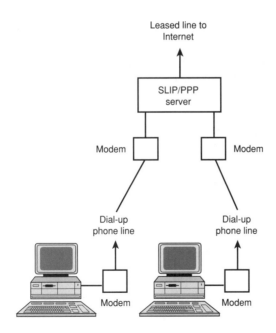

Fig. 1.4
This figure illustrates dial-up Internet Connection via SLIP or PPP. Users dial into a terminal server or modem bank, which forwards data to the Internet through a router.

Dozens of SLIP and PPP service providers have sprung up to meet the demand for affordable Internet access. Providers aren't limited to the coasts, either. Even in the rural Midwest, it's possible to find reasonably priced SLIP access. Iowa Network Services, for example, offers up to 250 hours/month SLIP service via a local telephone number for $40/month. This service is available in hundreds of small Iowa towns and includes free publishing space on an FTP, Gopher, and World Wide Web server.

High-Speed Modems

Without high-speed modems, SLIP and PPP would offer little benefit over text-mode Internet access. However, the introduction of 14.4 and 28.8 kbps (kilobytes per second) modems for under $200 has made full graphical access to the World Wide Web practical from home. Built-in data compression algorithms on newer modems and the CSLIP protocol (compressed SLIP) further accelerate graphical performance. As a result, many people getting on the Information Superhighway are signing up for SLIP connections rather than for traditional services such as CompuServe. Of course, the major online services all have plans to incorporate World Wide Web access, which will further stimulate the growth of the Web.

Built-in WWW Access

The last roadblocks to widespread home use of the World Wide Web are the difficulties of finding an Internet service provider and configuring a PC for SLIP or PPP. Thanks to the proliferation of Internet books, this is changing. But the event that will bust the floodgates of WWW access wide open is the introduction of WWW browsers built into the next versions of Microsoft Windows and OS/2. Not only is a Web browser built into OS/2 Warp 3.0 (see fig. 1.5), but it comes with a toll-free number to sign up for service via IBM's Advantis network. Windows 95 is expected to include a similar arrangement. This will bring fast, easy, and convenient WWW access to the average home computer user, providing even more incentive for businesses to adopt the World Wide Web as their electronic marketplace.

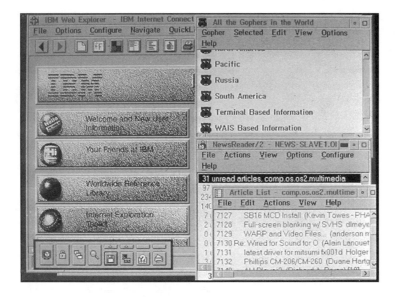

Fig. 1.5
IBM's Web Explorer incorporates the same functionality as Mosaic into the OS/2 environment.

Creating a Presence on the World Wide Web

Thus far, this chapter has discussed the growth of the Web only from a user's point of view. But what does it cost to publish on the Web? And just how easy is it? The Web may be accessible to users, but is it accessible to information providers? The answer is a resounding "Yes!" This is the final reason that the Web is poised for even greater growth.

It's Free!

Much of the reason for the Web's rapid growth is that the software necessary to set up a World Wide Web server is free. Organizations already connected to the Internet simply copy the necessary files from the Internet via FTP (or load them from Webmaster CD) and configure the software for their machines. An experienced system administrator can have a simple WWW server up and running in a day or so. Consequently, many large institutions with their own high-speed Internet connections already have WWW sites.

WebmasterCD

> **Note**
>
> Because the software is free, many companies are using WWW servers internally as a communication and workgroup tool on their existing computing networks. Chapter 4, "Creating an Internal Web Server" and chapter 8, "Managing an Internal Web Server" cover internal WWW servers in detail.

Even more important in terms of overall impact of the Web is the opportunity for small organizations without a lot of computer expertise or a lot of money (only the cost of the Internet connection) to establish a presence on the Web. Thanks to dial-up SLIP and PPP, the cost can be as little as $30 per month. Because the Web server software included with this book can run using a SLIP or PPP connection, any home computer enthusiast can run a World Wide Web server from home for a small monthly fee. In addition, some SLIP/PPP service providers allow customers to create their own Web pages on the service provider's Web server, making those pages more readily accessible from the Internet.

It's Easy

Developing your own pages for the World Wide Web doesn't require a degree in electrical engineering or five years of experience in network systems administration. If you can use a word processor or a simple text editor, you can create your own pages. Setting up and administering your own Web server is a little more difficult, but you can still accomplish it quickly and easily, thanks to well-documented software and to books like this one.

It's for Everyone

Because of low-cost Internet connections and free server software, even the smallest businesses can have the same presence on the World Wide Web as an international corporation. As consumers begin to use WWW search engines and directories just as they use the telephone yellow pages, small businesses will benefit from being listed right along with the big guys. This exposure will motivate more and more businesses to create a presence on the Web, which will in turn give more consumers a reason to start using the Web.

Because of its hypertext, graphics, and search capabilities, the Web is a great place to present product data. For example, a computer manufacturer interested in motherboards can locate several motherboard manufacturers, get an overview of their product lines, look at technical specifications for each product, evaluate testing procedures, and even obtain pricing, all from the common interface of the World Wide Web. Using the Web is faster and more convenient than dialing half a dozen bulletin board or fax-back services to obtain the same information.

Nonprofit organizations like consumer watchdog groups and political action groups can benefit from using the Web to distribute their information electronically. Important bulletins are available instantly, and items that are too lengthy to include in mass mailings are accessible on the Web. Voters, for example, can look up their representatives' voting records, see the issues currently before Congress, and even read the full text of bills and proposals. The Web enables organizations to maintain better contact with their members, providing more information on a more timely basis.

Note

Information on federal legislation is available from the Thomas project at the Library of Congress World Wide Web Home Page (**http://lcweb.loc.gov/**).

The Web has experienced terrific growth in the first two years of its existence. Fueled by applications in business, government, education, and research, all made available from home computers, the Web is poised to become the electronic marketplace and information source of the decade.

Chapter 2

Introduction to Web Servers

Before getting into the specifics of setting up and managing a WWW server, you should understand what the Web can do. This chapter gives you a broad understanding of WWW server technology and demonstrates how WWW can stimulate your imagination. The possibilities for using the Web are virtually limitless.

Because of the Web's cross-platform compatibility and easy graphical interface, it is rapidly becoming the choice for developing any type of information application that uses the Internet. This chapter gives you some idea of what you can do with the Web by looking at some of the most interesting, popular, and clever uses of the Web. You can combine any of the elements discussed here to make your own creative applications of World Wide Web technology.

In this chapter, you learn how to

- Enhance technical documents or publish electronic books with hypertext

- Create interactive maps and buttons with hypergraphics

- Incorporate multimedia into Web documents

- Use forms and scripts for global database applications

- Interact with the Web through UseNet and e-mail

- Protect Web servers for private use

Web Server and Client Capabilities

Any given capability of the World Wide Web depends on the Web server and the Web client. The *server* is the computer that makes information available to the Web. The *client* is the program that retrieves and displays information from Web servers. Not all servers support all features of the Web, nor do all clients. For example, some Web clients, such as early versions of Mosaic for Windows, don't support fill-in forms. Well-designed pages on the Web accommodate as many clients as possible. The following sections inform you if all clients or all servers do not support a capability.

Formatted Text and Graphics

All Web clients display pages constructed with *Hypertext Markup Language (HTML)*. HTML is by no means an advanced desktop publishing language, but it's a step up from pages of ASCII text in Courier font. Figure 2.1 shows a sample of some of the different text sizes and styles available. HTML supports bulleted, numbered, and nested lists. The HTML specification is constantly revised to support newer features. Newer browsers, such as Netscape, support some of these features, but HTML authors interested in achieving a common appearance should design for the least-capable browser. Older browsers might not support features such as tables, figures, and centering. If these features aren't available, the text will be a jumbled, formatting mess.

Fig. 2.1
HTML gives you a number of formatting options.

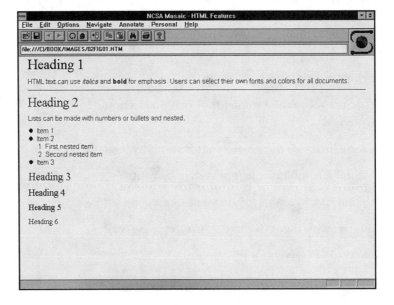

Besides text formatting, most browsers support inline graphics. However, many readers connecting to the Web over slow dial-up connections use text-only clients, such as Lynx, so graphics are not always available. As modems get faster and SLIP becomes more widely available, graphical browsers will replace most text-mode browsers. Figure 2.2 shows some possibilities for mixing text and graphics.

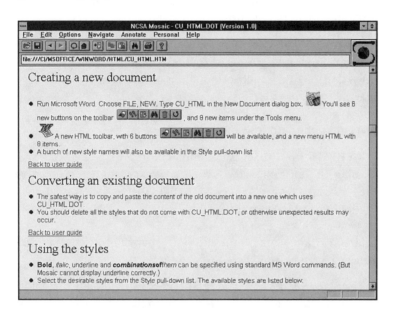

Fig. 2.2
Inline images can significantly enhance text.

Planning a Web Server

> **Note**
>
> Most early Web browsers supported the much-used *GIF* format for inline images because the *Graphics Interchange Format* has become a universal image standard on the Internet and dial-up bulletin board systems. Netscape also supports the newer *JPEG (Joint Photographic Experts Group)* standard for inline images, which uses a different compression algorithm than GIF.

Hypertext and Hypergraphics

Formatted text and graphics effectively present information; *hypertext* is the real key to the interactive nature of the World Wide Web. All Web clients support hypertext in some fashion. Hypertext can turn an otherwise lengthy and intimidating document into an interactive adventure. It's especially well suited for reference documents (which is why it was chosen at CERN as the fundamental protocol of the Web), technical documents, and any other material that users search more often than they read straight through.

Hypertext gets ideas across by reducing the amount of work required for authors and readers; it eliminates the need to restate facts. For example, prior to the World Wide Web, a scientist wishing to reference another document on the Internet might have written the following:

> In Lewis and Clark's excellent report on crossing the Mississippi River (available from ftp.lewis.net in /pub/expedition/crossing_the_miss.txt), Lewis describes the sandbar formations on the eastern and western sides ...

Using hypertext, the author would write:

> In <A HREF="ftp://ftp.lewis.net/pub/expedition/ crossing_the_miss.txt">Lewis and Clark's excellent report on crossing the Mississippi River</A>, Lewis describes the sandbar formations on the eastern and western sides...

This requires no more work for the author (perhaps a little less), but much less for the reader, who would see this:

> In <u>Lewis and Clark's excellent report on crossing the Mississippi River</u>, Lewis describes the sandbar formations on the eastern and western sides...

The reader simply clicks the underlined text and the referenced document appears. Previously, if the reader wanted to view the referenced document, it was necessary to run an FTP program, connect to ftp.lewis.net, change the directory to /pub/expedition, get the file "crossing_the_miss.txt," and then read the file in a text editor. Hypertext and the World Wide Web make this information much more convenient.

Electronic Books

People often use hypertext to create electronic books. A hypertext table of contents allows readers to proceed directly to an interesting section with a click of the mouse. This is particularly useful for reference works such as the one in figure 2.3. Hypertext is also useful for footnotes and other references. Because Web browsers can display or download graphics and other types of files, hypertext links can point to any kind of information, including sound and movies!

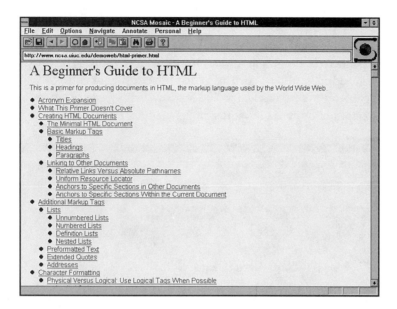

Fig. 2.3
Hypertext table
of contents in *A
Beginner's Guide
to HTML*.

Menus

People often use hypertext on the Web to display a menu of choices. You
can present menus in a variety of different formats, including numbered,
bulleted, and nested lists, which are all parts of standard HTML. Hypertext
menus point to Web pages and files all over the world, resulting in several
good Internet directories (see fig. 2.4). All Web browsers have a button or
command that returns to the previous page, making it very easy to try
several options on a menu in sequence.

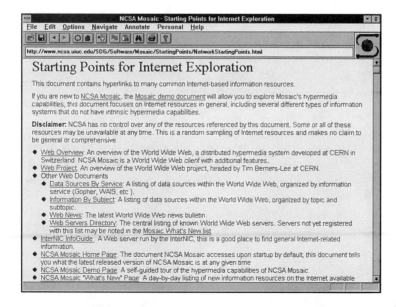

Fig. 2.4
NCSA's list of
Internet Starting
Points offers
convenient menu-
based Web
searching.

Hypergraphics

Hypergraphics are similar to hypertext, except that the user clicks images rather than text. In the simplest form, the user clicks a single graphic that has an associated link just like text. This allows the creation of button-like objects for more interesting pages, such as Sun Microsystem's page shown in figure 2.5. All graphical browsers support simple hypergraphics.

Fig. 2.5

You can use simple hyper-graphics to create push buttons and to make the page more appealing.

A more complex form of hypergraphic called an *imagemap* allows the user to follow different links depending on where the user clicks. This allows for the creation of button bars or toolbars (see fig. 2.6). All graphical browsers and most servers support imagemaps.

Fig. 2.6

This button bar was created using a single imagemap.

You can use imagemaps to create geographical maps, such as the world map of registered WWW servers shown in figure 2.7. When a user clicks a portion of the map, the server sends back another more local map or a list of WWW sites in the chosen region.

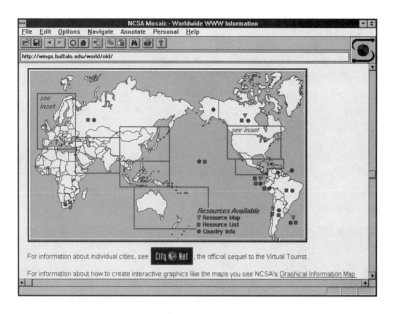

Fig. 2.7
WWW server
world map created
using imagemaps.

You also can use imagemaps to create interactive pictures (see fig. 2.8).
Another ideal use might be in the creation of company organizational charts.

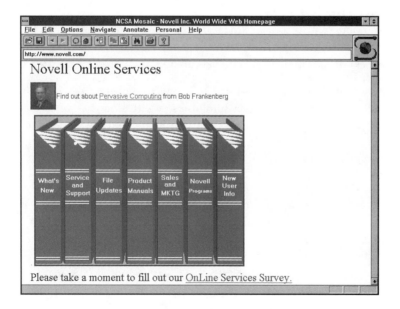

Fig. 2.8
Novell's interactive
bookshelf created
using an
imagemap.

Multimedia

The ability to seamlessly play sounds and movies is one of the most exciting aspects of the World Wide Web. A file sent by a Web server can be plain text, HTML, a WAV file (sound), an AVI file (video), or even a spreadsheet. When the browser receives a marked file, it launches the appropriate application to view the file, as defined by the user.

As with other aspects of the Web, multimedia capabilities are compatible across all platforms as long as multimedia files are in standard sound and image formats. Web servers send only raw data, and the browser launches the appropriate viewer.

> **Note**
>
> To identify the correct viewer for files sent via FTP or Gopher, Web browsers attempt to map the file extension to a list of viewers defined by the user. However, in a Web server transaction, files are sent with MIME (Multimedia Internet Mail Exchange) type information that is used by the browser in place of the file extension.

Sound and Movies

Any computer with a sound card and/or software to play videos can take advantage of multimedia on the Web. People use sound to convey a greeting at business sites or to demonstrate new albums at entertainment sites.

A speaker symbol usually accompanies sounds to indicate that the file to be received is a sound file. This is helpful to users with slow dial-up connections, because sound files are very large. On a 14.4 modem connection, 10 seconds of sound may take several minutes to download! Sound files are commonly in the AU (audio) format, which is compressed, but still large.

You can view movies, but you can't hear sound at the same time because movie files contain only picture information and sound files contain only audio information. Users commonly compress movies in the MPEG (Motion Picture Experts Group) or QuickTime formats; these files are even larger than sound files. A one-minute movie might take an hour to download on a 14.4 modem! Mosaic and similar browsers can't play sounds and movies by themselves. In order to take advantage of this capability, the user must have a program that can play the desired sound or video format. Fortunately, many such programs are published as freeware on the Internet. Figure 2.9 shows frames from Michigan State University's weather movies. Notice the large byte counts.

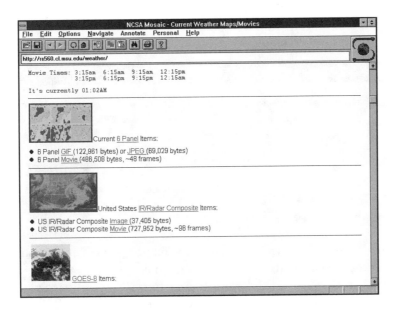

Fig. 2.9
Michigan State
University's
weather page
offers movies.

Planning a Web Server

Documents

Web browsers not only launch applications to play sounds and movies, they also accommodate any document format by simply launching the document's native application. For example, upon receiving a Windows Write file, the browser would launch Windows Write with the file inside. For this to work, the server must pass the correct information (MIME type) about the Write file and the client must be configured to launch Write.

Because Web clients exist for nearly every platform, only a few document formats are commonly used on the Internet to ensure compatibility. However, the ability to launch applications is particularly useful in an internal organizational setting. If a company has already standardized on a word processor and spreadsheet, for example, they can use a Web server as a database for all internal communications in those formats. When an employee clicks a document of interest, it automatically launches the correct application.

Programs

Because the Web can receive any file type, it's an ideal way to publish free software or shareware. Users can read all about a program, decide if they like it, and then click a link to download the program to disk. For example, on the NCSA Mosaic for Windows home page (**http://www.ncsa.uiuc.edu/ SDG/Software/WinMosaic/HomePage.html**), a link points to a list of multimedia viewing programs. You can download these programs directly.

Because of their size, programs are usually distributed as compressed ZIP files that the user must decompress.

> **Note**
>
> Some servers can send special information with compressed files and some browsers can use this information to automatically decompress them. This reduces the amount of time required to transmit large files and doesn't require any additional effort from the user.

Forms and Scripts

Fill-in *forms* on browsers allow users to send limited types of information back to the server. For instance, a user can sign up for a service, register for a conference, or enter search keywords using forms. Figure 2.10 is a sample search form on Lycos, a powerful Internet search engine.

Fig. 2.10

Lycos enables users to do full-text searches of over 1.5 million FTP, Gopher, and Web documents.

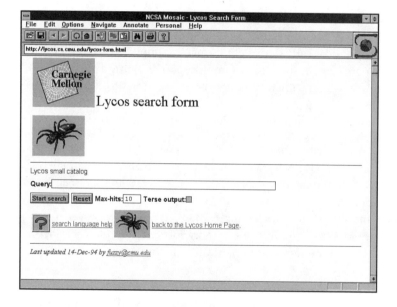

Forms can contain standard graphical user interface elements such as radio buttons, check boxes, text fields, and push buttons. Because they establish the basis for much commercial activity on the Web, all the new graphical browsers support forms. Lynx, a text-mode browser, also supports forms. Forms can't yet be used to transfer files from the client to the server, but this capability may eventually be added.

Scripts are programs that run on a server to process form input. Depending on the server platform, scripts can be in many different programming languages, and nearly all servers support scripts. You can use scripts to send e-mail, process data entered, search a database, or call other programs. Scripts and forms together make the possibilities of applications on Web servers virtually endless. People have even used forms and scripts to compose and display images via the World Wide Web (see fig. 2.11).

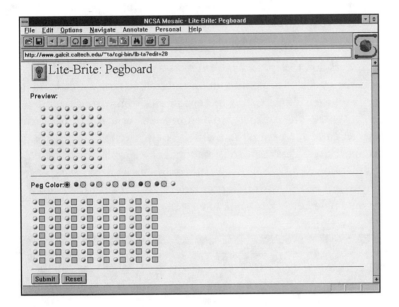

Fig. 2.11
The Lite-Brite page uses forms and scripts to bring new life to a familiar toy.

As mentioned previously, you can use forms and scripts to build databases and to communicate with other powerful databases such as Oracle and Sybase. You can make large amounts of existing data public without requiring a large translation effort. An excellent example of this is the STO Internet Patent Search System (**http://sunsite.unc.edu/patents/intropat.html**), which is continually upgraded to add more patent information. Many public and private databases currently distributed on CD-ROM could be put on the Web at a substantially lower cost, with the additional advantage of instantaneous data updates.

Interaction with News and E-mail

The World Wide Web promises to fulfill the vision of having one standard interface to the Internet. It must encompass two applications that have traditionally been run by themselves—news and e-mail. Many browsers, such as Lynx and Netscape, already incorporate many news and e-mail features.

Some, such as InternetWorks, have combined all common Internet services into a single interface.

News

Most Web browsers support direct reading of UseNet newsgroups; you don't have to go to a separate newsreader. There are links between related newsgroups on pages with specific interests. For example, a Web page discussing OS/2 might have a link to the OS/2 newsgroups. This helps users discover new newsgroups related to their interests and gives Web pages the ability to become one-stop information repositories.

Older browsers don't keep track of read messages, but newer browsers, such as Netscape, keep track of subscribed and unsubscribed groups, read and unread messages, and even allow posting to newsgroups from within the browser (see fig. 2.12). Also, the capability to read news inside a Web browser means that you can embed hyperlinks to useful Web sites in news messages; the user just has to click to access more information. For example, the proprietor of a new Internet flower shop might advertise on the newsgroup **rec.gardening** with a hyperlink to the flower shop's home page. Readers using a Web browser only have to click the link to visit the shop.

Fig. 2.12
Netscape's built-in newsgroup support.

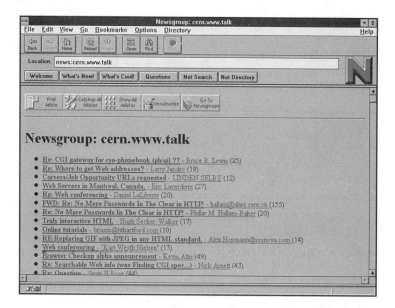

Note

Posting messages from within a browser is especially useful for setting up an internal company bulletin board system with one common interface for viewing documents, asking questions, and posting new information.

E-mail

Web browsers don't currently offer the features of a full-fledged mail program like cc:Mail, but newer browsers do allow users to send mail to a specified address using the browser. For example, a Web server administrator can set up a link that causes mail-capable browsers to send mail to report problems with the server or offer suggestions. The user doesn't have to remember an address because it's embedded in the hyperlink. The user just clicks the mail link, types a message, and sends the message. Figure 2.13 shows the built-in mail support in Netscape.

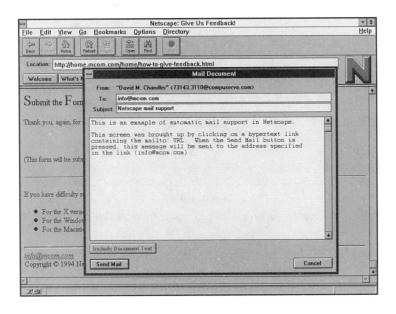

Fig. 2.13
Netscape's built-in mail support allows users to send Internet e-mail directly from the browser.

Browsers that don't have built-in mail support can still send e-mail messages using forms. The user types a message into a form and clicks a button to send the results to the server, which processes the message and sends it to the appropriate destination. This is a useful way for companies to obtain information about prospective customers. Users simply fill out an online form to enter a request for more information or for a follow-up phone call.

Security Features

The World Wide Web was originally designed as a tool for sharing information. It has become so useful for both company internal communications and commerce that some security features are required. There are three basic methods of enforcing security on the Web.

First, Web servers can prevent access from unauthorized addresses on the Internet. For example, a company running a private Web server may want to allow access only from other divisions. The company can restrict access to the whole server or to particular directories; server administrators can make some documents public but keep others private. They can allow or disallow addresses from an entire network down to a specific computer on the Internet.

Second, you can use password protection to prevent access to specific directories of information. You can restrict access to one user or to a group of users, each having a password. Most browsers remember the password after it's entered initially, so a user has to type the password only once during any session with the browser.

> **Note**
>
> Passwords aren't encrypted, so anyone who is eavesdropping on the Internet could discover the password. Chapter 5, "Getting Started with Web Servers," contains more detailed information about passwords and security.

Third, you can use data encryption to protect data passing from the server to the client and vice versa. This is an important issue for commerce, where it's important to be able to send credit card numbers over the Internet. Various proprietary and open security standards have been proposed; however, none have gained widespread acceptance. The Netscape browser implements one such standard when used with Netscape's Web server software; several large financial institutions already use it to offer secure credit card transactions via the Web.

Chapter 3

Creating a Home Page on the Internet

This chapter discusses various ways you can create a Web presence or a private bulletin board system using the Web. It describes many cost/feature trade-offs and makes recommendations for businesses and organizations. The first part of the chapter surveys the methods of establishing a presence on the Web; the second part of the chapter details how you can set up an external Web server. To learn how to set up an internal Web server, see chapter 4, "Creating an Internal Web Server."

Setting up an Internet Web server can be a complex undertaking. Setting up your own server requires the skills of both an experienced network systems administrator and telecommunications guru. This chapter does not attempt to teach you these trades; however, this chapter does familiarize you with the relevant terminology. For those less inclined to run their own server, this chapter also teaches you what you can expect when leasing space on a service provider's Web server.

In this chapter, you learn

- The advantages and disadvantages of creating your own Web server, leasing space on the Web, or using an existing FTP or Gopher server

- Which combinations of hardware and operating systems are ideal for various applications

- How to find an Internet service provider and what to look for in a provider

Establishing a Presence on the Web

There are several different ways to provide information on the Internet, and each one has advantages for different situations. This section reviews the three primary methods and discusses the trade-offs inherent to each.

Reviewing the Alternatives

By far the most flexible way to create a Web presence is to set up your own Web server. You can set up a server on everything from a $1500 PC with a dial-up SLIP connection to a dedicated UNIX workstation with a high-speed leased line connection to the Internet. Which type of hardware and connection you choose depends on your needs. When you create your own Web server, you depend on an Internet provider only to provide a connection to the Internet. Many providers do not get involved in security, programming, or content issues regarding your server. This setup is ideal if you use applications requiring complete control and flexibility. However, you may need more time to learn than you would if you leased space on the Web.

> **Note**
>
> If you want to run your own Web server but don't possess the necessary expertise, don't worry. Many Internet service providers and dozens of consultants can help you set up your own server and work out security and programming issues. Additionally, some graphic-design firms have begun to specialize in Web-content development.

A second way to establish a presence on the Web is to lease space. Many service providers now offer disk space on their Web servers for companies and organizations to lease by the month. Leasing gives you the capability to put information on the Internet without having to purchase a dedicated computer or expensive leased line connection to the Internet. The usual mechanism for putting information on a leased server is to upload files by FTP. Leasing space on the Web requires little knowledge of Web servers, security, and programming issues. However, the service provider has total control over how the server is used.

A third way to create a presence on the Web requires you to already have an FTP or Gopher server set up. You can create Web pages by placing HTML files on your existing server. Browser software, such as Mosaic and Netscape, can read your HTML pages just as if they came from a Web server (with a definite performance degradation). Using an existing FTP or Gopher server means you don't have to set up a new server. On the other hand, Web servers have capabilities above and beyond those provided by basic servers.

Comparing the Alternatives

Let's now take a more in-depth look at the advantages and disadvantages of each method of establishing a home page on the Web. The best choice for your application depends on a variety of factors that are examined in more detail in the following sections.

Setting Up Your Own Web Server

If you already have a dedicated Internet connection and a computer, you probably want to set up your own Web server. In certain situations you *must* set up a Web server; for instance, when you want to set up an internal bulletin board system. To run the server software, you can use any computer on a LAN connected to the Internet, including PCs, Macs, and workstations. It is possible to run multiple servers on the same LAN or to run one server and allow many people access to the files.

> **Note**
>
> If your LAN already has a dedicated connection to the Internet, setting up your own Web server on the LAN often appears to be the most economical and flexible method of establishing a presence on the Web. However, there are many hidden costs associated with systems administration that may make it more economical to lease space elsewhere.

Setting up your own Web server gives you complete control of the server's features. It enables you to use all features supported by your Web server, including forms and scripts, imagemaps, security, and MIME types for launching applications. Depending on your situation, this flexibility can be an advantage or a disadvantage. If you do not wish to concern yourself with the possibility of exposing private data on your LAN, the best option may be to lease space on an external Web server. This way, Web browsers never come into contact with your LAN. On the other hand, if you want to restrict access to certain sets of data on your Web server, you may have to set up your own Web server to be able to create your own custom configuration. In other words, leasing space provides more security for data on your LAN, but probably less for data on your Web server.

You can set up a basic Web server in a matter of minutes. Customizing the server and adding security features can take several hours, but servers generally come ready to run "out of the box." Once a server is running, however, maintenance effort can be considerable. Even for a small server with relatively static content, it is necessary to collect usage statistics and continually check documents for broken hyperlinks and out-of-date information.

Many tasks can be automated by running nightly maintenance programs, but these programs themselves need maintenance from time to time as new software versions come out and subtle changes are made to your server and network configuration.

Whether you run your own server or lease space elsewhere, creating new Web documents or converting from other formats takes time. This involves training in the necessary tools as well as the actual time spent writing documents. If several people are responsible for creating Web documents, yet more time is spent coordinating their efforts. Large companies tend to have several people creating graphics and Web text and at least one administrator whose sole job is to maintain the server. In all but the simplest cases, the cost of creating and maintaining Web pages is likely to exceed the cost of a high-speed Internet connection or leased space.

Table 3.1 summarizes the trade-offs inherent in creating your own server.

Table 3.1 Setting Up Your Own Web Server	
Advantages	**Disadvantages**
Can use all features	These take time to set up
Can control security	Requires knowledge of security
Can use internally	Requires careful configuration
Fast and efficient	Requires dedicated link and hardware

Leasing Space on the Web

Leasing disk space on a service provider's Web server is becoming an increasingly popular way for businesses of all sizes to get onto the Web. This method has benefits, especially for small businesses. It does have significant limitations, however, and is not always the most economical.

The main benefit of leasing space on the Web is that it does not require a dedicated, high speed connection to the Internet. Rather, the service provider has the fast connection and you simply upload files to the service provider's Web server to make them available to the Internet 24 hours a day, 365 days a year. You are saved the cost of an expensive leased line to the Internet. On the other hand, some service providers charge high rates for initial setup and a portion of their disk space and bandwidth—comparable to what you may spend to set up your own server.

> **Tip**
>
> Leasing space on the Web is particularly attractive for small businesses that cannot afford a high-speed Internet connection and dedicated server hardware.

A second benefit of leasing space on the Web is the additional exposure your Web site receives. Many service providers have adopted a shopping mall concept, where many different types of products and services are offered through their site. One of the most well-known is the Branch Mall at **http://www.branch.com** (see fig. 3.1). This may or may not be of benefit to your site, depending on the nature of your business. If you are using the Web as a marketing and sales tool, you likely will benefit. If you merely want to provide information electronically as a service, or in conjunction with a traditional marketing or public relations campaign, the benefit will not be as great. A service provider can charge organizations just to be listed on its Web page because of the resulting exposure. This is not yet common, however.

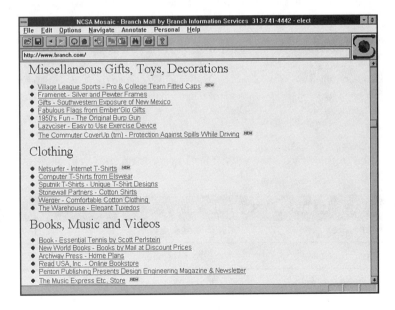

Fig. 3.1
The Branch Mall is a well-known Internet shopping mall.

A main disadvantage to leasing space on the Web is that the service provider has control over all aspects of the server. Because of data security concerns, your service provider can prohibit use of forms and scripts, imagemaps, and custom document types for launching applications. If all you want to do is raise public awareness of your company or organization on the Internet by putting simple pages on the Web, you do not need these capabilities, so this is not a problem. If you want to conduct sales transactions, such as order products and receive credit card numbers, you need to use forms and scripts, so your service provider must allow them.

An additional concern regarding service providers is that the service provider is responsible for ensuring good availability of its connection to the Internet. If you are running a mission-critical operation on a Web server, you may feel more comfortable having the responsibility to ensure your server's availability. The connection itself is not really at issue here because that always has to come from a service provider somewhere, but keeping your server up and running is. Most providers run several Web servers on one machine, either by creating separate directories for each customer or by running the server software multiple times under a multitasking operating system like UNIX. This allows them to charge less for the service than you would spend on a machine and a connection to the Internet. By sharing a machine, however, you become vulnerable to any system problems or crashes due to problems with other servers running on the same machine. In addition, if you share a machine with a Web site that suddenly becomes very popular, your server's speed and response time can suffer.

> **Note**
>
> Even though there are possible problems, a responsible service provider is better equipped to handle server issues and may therefore be the best choice for mission-critical work.

Table 3.2 summarizes the benefits of leasing space on the Web.

Table 3.2 Leasing Space on the Web	
Advantages	**Disadvantages**
Full-time connection	No control over server
Commercial exposure	May not be required or desirable
Economical monthly fee	Owning may prove better in the long run
Requires no server know-how	Service provider must be reliable

Using an Existing FTP or Gopher Server

This method of establishing a Web presence should really only be used as a stopgap measure until you can get a true Web server running. Nevertheless, if your site currently has only an FTP or Gopher server, and you are not a system administrator but would like to get on the Web, this is the way to go. It is advantageous from the perspective that you can begin publishing HTML documents without having to learn Web servers, but there are several disadvantages as well.

> **Tip**
>
> If FTP or Gopher is all that's available to you, you can still publish HTML documents with a Web "feel."

The main disadvantage to using FTP or Gopher for Web publishing is that data access is slower than from a Web server. Web servers use the HyperText Transfer Protocol (HTTP), which is specifically optimized for speed. Unlike FTP, which requires users to log in before transferring data, HTTP simply processes single requests for information. A document request comes in, and the server sends the file right back out. HTTP requires very little overhead. Because you can run multiple servers on the same machine, you are actually better off if you run both an FTP and an HTTP server than if you use an FTP server for both files and HTML publishing.

> **Note**
>
> In addition to speed concerns, FTP and Gopher do not implement many special features of Web servers, including forms and scripts, imagemaps, and configurable document types (MIME types). It is possible to enter keywords for simple searches using Gopher, but no other form of user input is possible.

Another key disadvantage to FTP and Gopher servers is that they are not as easy to find as Web servers. Many Web servers use the naming convention www.company-name.com to make themselves more visible on the Web. Consequently, users of Web browsers are not likely to look for your server using a Gopher or FTP address. In addition, many powerful Web search engines do not search files residing on FTP or Gopher servers.

Table 3.3 summarizes the trade-offs involved in using an existing FTP or Gopher server.

Table 3.3 Using an Existing FTP or Gopher Server	
Advantages	**Disadvantages**
Requires no setup	Slower and less efficient than HTTP
Works if HTTP not available	Cannot use Web server features
Uses familiar protocols	May be difficult to find on the Web

Leasing Space on the Web

A large number of companies offer leased space and a variety of other services, including home page design, HTML authoring, help with database and script applications, and server name registration, which creates a unique name for your page on the Internet as if you were running your own server.

Working with Leased Space

The most common arrangement for putting Web documents on a provider's server is via FTP. This is convenient because it means that the leased space provider can be located anywhere in the world as long as the customers have some form of Internet access, even a slow dial-up SLIP connection. Other providers accept floppy disks and files sent via e-mail. Some offer catalog conversion services where they take an entire hard copy product catalog, do all the necessary scanning and editing, and then put it on the Web.

Finding a Provider

Finding service providers on the Web is relatively easy. The National Center for Supercomputing Applications, which developed Mosaic, maintains a list of Web service providers at **http://union.ncsa.uiuc.edu/HyperNews/ get/www/leasing.html**. The Directory of WWW Service Providers at **ftp://ftp.einet.net/pub/INET-MARKETING/www-svc-providers** is another excellent resource containing Web consultants as well as service providers. This list is included as PROVIDER.HTM on WebmasterCD; table 3.4 summarizes the list. All providers in the U.S. who offer basic Web page serving and listed a Web address are included, along with the area codes they serve if local dial-up Internet access is also offered. Because the Web is growing so rapidly, it would be a good idea to check these lists often.

Table 3.4   WWW Service Providers

H = HTML Authoring/Web Application Development
C = CGI Script Processing
S = WAIS or other search capabilities offered
P = Prebuilt applications
Speed = Speed of service provider's connection to the Internet
Area = Area code(s) served in part or in whole by local dial-up
access. If no area code is listed, provider either offers
national dial-up access or none at all.

Name and URL	Services	Speed	Area
Computer Solutions by Hawkinson **http://www.mhv.net/**	HP	T1	914
Telerama Public Access Internet **http://www.lm.com/**	HCSP	T1	412
Quantum Networking Solutions **http://www.gcr.com/mall/**	HC	14K	
Internet Presence & Publishing, Inc. **http://www.ip.net/**	HCSP	T1	804
Computing Engineers, Inc. **http://www.wwa.com/**	HCSP	56K	312, 708
South Valley Internet **http://www.garlic.com**	CS	56K	408
Branch Information Services **http://branch.com**	HCSP	T1	313
APK, Public Access UNI*. **http://www.wariat.org**	HS		216
Internet Distribution Services, Inc. **http://www.service.com/**	HCSP	T1	415
Cyberspace Development, Inc. **http://marketplace.com**	HS	T1	
BEDROCK Information Solutions, Inc. **http://www.bedrock.com/**	HCS	T1	
Electric Press, Inc. **http://www.elpress.com**	HCSP	T1	

(continues)

Table 3.4 Continued			
Name and URL	**Services**	**Speed**	**Area**
Quadralay Corporation **http://www.quadralay.com/home.html**	HCSP	T1	
Downtown Anywhere Inc. **http://www.awa.com/**	HCSP	frac. T1	
Internet Marketing Inc. **http://cybersight.com/cgi-bin/imi/s?main.gmml**	HCS	T1	
The New York Web **http://nyweb.com**	HCSP	T1	
The Sphere Information Services **http://www.thesphere.com**	HC	56K	
The Computing Support Team, Inc. **http://www.gems.com/**	HCS	T1	
The Internet Group **http://www.tig.com/**	HCS	T1	
Lighthouse Productions **http://netcenter.com**	HP	115K	
Catalog.Com Internet Services **http://www.catalog.com**		T1	
Great Basin Internet Services **http://www.greatbasin.net/**	HCSP	56K	702
Net+Effects **http://www.net.effects.com**	HCSP	14K	
XOR Network Engineering **http://plaza.xor.com/**	HCS		
Flightpath Communications Digital Marketing, Inc. **http://www.digimark.net/**	HCSP HC	28K T1	
BizNet Technologies **http://www.biznet.com.blacksburg.va.us/**	HCSP	T1	
FINE.COM **http://www.solutionsrc.com/FINE/**	H	56K	206
Sell-it on the WWW **http://www.electriciti.com/www-ads/index.htm**	H	T1	
MicroSystems Internet Services **http://www.comnet.com/**	HCS	T1	801

Name and URL	Services	Speed	Area
RTD Systems & Networking, Inc. http://www.rtd.com/	HCP	T1	602
Atlantic Computing Technology Corporation http://www.atlantic.com/	HCSP	56K	
InterNex Information Services, Inc. http://www.internex.net/	HCS	T1	510, 415, 408
Teleport, Inc. http://www.teleport.com	56K		503, 206
ssSSNet, Inc. http://ssnet.com:8010/net/ssnhome.html	HCSP	56K	302, 610, 215
QuakeNet http://www.quake.net/	H	T1	415
Internet Information Services, Inc. http://www.iis.com	HCSP	T1	301, 410, 703
MicroSystems Internet Services http://www.comnet.com/	HCS	T1	801
CyberBeach Publishing http://www.gate.net/	HCSP	T1	305, 407, 813, 904
Primenet http://www.primenet.com/	HCP	T1	602
TAG Systems inc. http://www.tagsys.com/	HC	56K	
Internet Information Systems http://www.internet-is.com/	HCS	frac. T1	
Stelcom, Inc. http://www.webscope.com	HC	frac. T1	
A+ Marketing http://www.digimark.net/A+/	H	56K	
Coolware Inc. http://none.coolware.com/	HCS	56K	
IDS World Network Internet Access Services http://www.ids.net	HCSP	T1	401, 305, 407, 914

(continues)

Table 3.4 Continued			
Name and URL	**Services**	**Speed**	**Area**
SenseMedia Publishing http://www.picosof.com	H	T1	408
Home Pages, Inc. http://www.homepages.com	HCSP	128K	
TeleVisions Inc. http://www.tvisions.com	H	T1	
Internet Services Corporation http://www.netservices.com/	HCSP	T1	
EarthLink Network, Inc. http://www.earthlink.net	HC	T1	213, 310, 818
New Jersey Computer Connection http://www.njcc.com	H	56K	609
CTS Network Services http://www.cts.com	HCSP	T1	619
The Tenagra Corporation http://arganet.tenagra.com/Tenagra/tenagra.html	HCS	T1	

Cost

Prices range anywhere from 50 to 1500 dollars per month for a home page—considerably cheaper than obtaining your own connection but still not cheap at the high end. The wide price variation arises from differences in services offered. Some leased space providers offer "do-it-yourself" type services, whereas others offer turnkey solutions, including training. Most services charge an initial setup fee plus a monthly fee, but some charge commission based on number of accesses to your page or number of sales leads generated.

Connecting Your Own Web Server

In order to get your own Web server connected to the Internet on a dedicated line, you need an Internet service provider who offers leased line connections. It is possible to run a Web server on a dial-up modem connection via SLIP, but most applications require greater speed and availability. This section presents information both on obtaining a leased line and the required hardware.

Obtaining a Leased Line

Finding the least expensive leased line connection can be a tricky business. Service providers charge a monthly fee for Internet access at a certain speed, but the fee usually does not include the cost of the leased line from their site to yours; a phone company handles this connection. If the leased line goes outside your local telephone company's long distance service area (LATA), a long-distance company must provide the line. The local telephone companies on each end then charge a monthly local-loop fee to bring the line from a switching office to the business location at either end. Local-loop fees are often a significant portion of the overall charges. Providers usually help you obtain leased line cost estimates.

> **Tip**
>
> When checking out long-distance carriers for leased lines, be sure to look at smaller companies such as WilTel (**http://www.wiltel.com**) in addition to the giants AT&T, MCI, and Sprint. The smaller companies often have newer switching equipment and can provide better rates.

Finding the least expensive combination of a service provider's fee and a phone company's fee may take some shopping around. Like any free-market entity, phone companies price their lines based on demand. If a company has a lot of spare bandwidth, you're going to get a better price than where there's a waiting list. Consequently, it may actually be less expensive to lease a line from a service provider hundreds of miles away than from a local provider. Another factor to consider is that small local telephone companies often have more up-to-date equipment and spare bandwidth than the giants, often making the smaller services more attractive.

> **Note**
>
> The newsgroups **comp.dcom.telecom** and **alt.dcom.telecom** discuss telecommunications in general, including leased line connections to the Internet. Information about Internet service in general is available from CIX, the organization of commercial Internet providers, at **http://www.cix.org**.

Just because a service provider gives you a T1 connection doesn't mean you will always get T1 speed. Suppose your service provider has 20 T1 customers feeding into a single T1 connection to the Internet. You will then be competing with 19 other customers for the same T1 bandwidth! The same principle applies to your service provider's provider and so on; it is difficult to tell how fast your connection will really be. However, this is not necessarily a problem because Internet traffic is sent in short bursts (packets) rather than steady streams. On high-speed lines, it is common for customers to use only a tiny fraction (less than 5 percent) of the total bandwidth available to them. So as long as only one customer at a time sends packets, each customer has access to the full line speed. When packets are sent at the same time, customers see a temporary reduction in data throughput.

In order to accommodate many customers feeding off the same line while ensuring adequate speed for each, service providers monitor their Internet feed to make sure that only a fraction of the total bandwidth is being used. For example, if a service provider's Internet feed only has 25 percent utilization on average, it means that, on average, 75 percent of the full line speed is available to any individual customer who needs it. Feeding several customers off a single line is thus a very useful practice—each customer can transfer data very quickly in bursts when needed but can benefit from the lower cost of sharing an Internet feed with several other customers.

Note

Even if you obtained a leased line directly to the Internet backbone in the hope of achieving maximum throughput, your data is still slowed down by Internet traffic on the backbone itself and by the speed of the connection at the other end.

Reviewing Leased Line Speeds

Whether you're leasing space on the Web or setting up your own server, the speed of your connection is important. If you're leasing space, you need to know how fast your service provider's connection is because this speed determines the maximum speed at which your site can transfer documents. Particularly if your site contains large graphics, a slow connection will annoy many of your users. If you're setting up your own server, you will want a connection fast enough to handle your anticipated traffic and possibly provide Internet access for a local area network.

Note

Besides the speed of a service provider's connection, your total data throughput capability depends on how many customers are served by the provider, by the provider's provider, and so on all the way back to the Internet backbone. However, you don't need to know these numbers—responsible providers carefully monitor total throughput and tune their networks accordingly. If you're leasing space, the speed of the service provider's Web server is important, but don't try to second-guess your provider on machine specifications—if the server is responsive, that's all that counts.

Leased lines range in speed from 56 kbps. to 45 Mbps. The most common lines are 56K and T1, T2, and T3 or fractions thereof. Table 3.5 shows the most common lines and their speeds.

Table 3.5   Telephone Line Speeds

Name	Data Rate (kbps)
56K	56
ISDN	128
T1	1,544
T2	6,312
T3	44,736

56K

A 56K line is usually the most economical, but is not much faster than a 28.8 kbaud modem with data compression. If your site contains large files or graphics, delays in loading pages will be noticeable and multiple simultaneous connections will slow it to a crawl.

Note

While a 56K connection may not be ideal for heavy file transfer applications like a Web server, a single 56K line can provide basic e-mail and news services for thousands of users on a LAN.

A 56K connection to the Internet usually costs between $300 and $1000 per month for the Internet access itself. The leased line charges can run from $200 to $1000 per month, depending on how far away the service provider is. For 56K connections, the most expensive portion of the leased line charge is often the local-loop fee.

T1

A T1 is the most common connection, and provides enough bandwidth for dozens of Web servers and thousands of computers on a LAN, too. A large corporation can provide Internet access to thousands of LAN users on a single 256K link, which is only 1/6 of a T1. With a T1 connection, document transfers of several hundred kilobytes will appear virtually instantaneous on a similarly connected Web browser.

A T1 connection to the Internet costs between $1000 and $3000 per month for the Internet service itself, plus the leased line charges, which frequently exceed the cost of Internet access. Many phone companies and service providers also offer fractional T1 access, usually in multiples of 1/4-T1 or multiples of 256 kbps.

Note

High-speed leased lines are usually cheaper between major metropolitan areas. For example, a leased T1 from Cedar Rapids, IA (a city of 100,000) to a rural town 60 miles away costs the same as a T1 to another metropolitan area 200 miles away. Also, leased lines are often cheaper from locally owned telephone networks rather than the major carriers. A T1 from Cedar Rapids to Des Moines, for example, costs almost 5 times as much through a major long-distance carrier as through Iowa Network Services.

T2 and T3

T2 connections are typically used only inside the telephone system, so the next step up from a T1 for Internet access is a T3. A T3 connection is fast enough to serve hundreds of entire networks. T3 lines are used only by major Internet service providers and the Internet backbone itself.

Leased Line Alternatives

While leased lines are the oldest and most common way to connect to an Internet service provider, some providers offer service through ISDN, frame relay, cable, or wireless networks. All of these will play a larger role in future data communications than they do currently.

ISDN

ISDN stands for *Integrated Services Digital Network* and has recently become widely available, although the technology has been around for years. Unlike the other types of lines discussed here, an ISDN line is a dial-up rather than a dedicated line; usage is billed at an hourly rate ($1 to $2 per hour.) in addition to a monthly service charge. Because of the hourly rate, leased lines are more economical for full-time connections, but ISDN can be more economical for connecting to the Internet only a few hours per day.

ISDN service provides two channels, each of which can be used for voice or data. By combining both channels, it's possible to achieve a total data rate of 128 kbps. Internet service providers offering ISDN capability are beginning to pop up on the West Coast, but Internet service through ISDN is not widely available elsewhere. Basic ISDN service (not including Internet access) is available in over 80 percent of California through Pacific Bell for $23 per month.

> **Note**
>
> In some rural locations, ISDN is available from small local telephone companies that have purchased new digital equipment. Many of the giants do not offer ISDN yet.

Frame Relay

Frame relay is a relatively new technology that is used to link multiple locations more economically than running leased lines to each site. In frame relay, all sites connect to a central frame relay switch at the telephone company, forming a star network. The frame relay switch performs the same function as an expensive router which would otherwise be required to direct traffic to the right location. Like a router, the frame relay switch can handle lines at many different speeds, including 56K, fractional T1, and T1. If an Internet service provider already has a connection into a frame relay switch, customers need only obtain a local loop from the switch to their location.

Cable

Cable companies are beginning to provide Internet and other data services using their vast networks of existing high-bandwidth cables. To connect to a cable network, you need a cable modem—a card you can plug into a PC. Tests of these types of connecting devices are ongoing. In some areas, electric utility companies are competing with cable TV companies by running their own fiber optic cables to provide Internet and cable TV services.

Wireless

Wireless networks are still very new, but are expected to become the premier communication medium of the future, both for voice and data. Wireless is rapidly becoming popular because it offers freedom from cumbersome land lines and the government-granted monopolies that own them. In some areas, phone companies (notably PacBell) are raising rates on Internet service providers because the phone companies plan to offer their own Internet services. This practice may backfire on the phone companies as businesses go entirely wireless to avoid them. Thanks to spread spectrum and microwave frequency technologies, radio bandwidth is already virtually unlimited. New satellite networks and cheaper wireless communications hardware will eventually replace millions of miles of century-old copper.

Leased Line Hardware

Connecting a high-speed data line to your network requires solid networking knowledge, especially when dealing with security issues. Internet service providers will usually install and configure your system for you, but you may want to choose your own hardware. This section presents a brief guide to the necessary equipment.

> **Caution**
>
> You should be very careful choosing your hardware because it must be compatible with both your internal network and your service provider's equipment.

Routers

The centerpiece of a leased line connection is a router, which controls the flow of traffic between your internal network and the leased line. The same type of router is used to connect to the Internet as to a *Wide Area Network (WAN),* which uses leased lines to connect remote networks. WAN routers have Ethernet or Token Ring ports for connecting to your internal LAN and one or more high-speed serial (synchronous) ports for connecting to leased lines.

The Internet is based entirely on the TCP/IP protocol, so any router you choose must be able to route TCP/IP (nearly all can). To use Internet services, clients on your LAN must be able to talk TCP/IP. UNIX has built-in TCP/IP networking, as does Sun Microsystems' PC-NFS, which runs under DOS and Windows. However, users of most other networks will have to purchase TCP/IP software to run "on top of" their existing networks. See chapter 4, "Creating an Internal Web Server," for more in-depth coverage of TCP/IP software packages.

To connect to the Internet, your router must be able to handle speeds up to the leased line speed you're using. Almost all routers support serial connections up to T1 speed (1.5 Mbps). Some support serial connections all the way up to T3 (45 Mbps). Internet service is obtained by connecting your router to both a leased line Internet feed through the high-speed serial port and to your internal network through the Ethernet or Token Ring port, depending on which network protocol you use. Figure 3.2 illustrates a typical Internet connection.

Many network router vendors have released products designed specifically for Internet and WAN connectivity. These start in price around $2500 and typically feature one or two high-speed serial ports and one network port. Additional serial or network ports can often be added for an additional charge. There are many different protocols for making connections to other routers via leased lines; make sure that you choose a router that supports the protocol in use by your service provider. The most common protocol for leased line connections is PPP (Point-to-Point Protocol). Other protocols include HDLC, ISDN, frame relay, and X.25. Table 3.6 lists popular WAN router vendors.

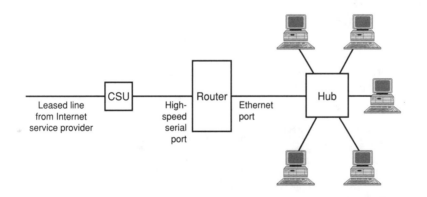

Fig. 3.2
This figure illustrates a typical Internet connection to a LAN.

Table 3.6 Routers for Internet Connectivity			
Vendor Name	**Product Line**	**Price**	**Contact Information**
Cisco	2500 Series	$2500+	**http://www.cisco.com**
Livingston	IRX Series	$2400+	**http://www.livingston.com**
Wellfleet	AN	$2300+	(800) 252-6926
Proteon	RBX	$2000+	(508) 898-2000

(continues)

Table 3.6 Continued			
Vendor Name	**Product Line**	**Price**	**Contact Information**
HP	Router PR	$3000+	**http://www.hp.com**
Motorola	BitRUNR CS	$2500+	**http://www.motorola.com**

Tip

Internet service providers can often sell networking equipment at a substantial discount from retail (up to 25 percent) through special agreements with vendors.

CSU/DSUs

High-speed data lines cannot be plugged directly into a router. The line must first be "cleaned up" by a Channel Service Unit/Data Service Unit (CSU/DSU), which converts the phone signals to data understandable by the router. CSUs are available for both 56K and T1 lines. T1 CSUs can usually be configured to service any data rate between 56K and T1, which is how fractional T1 service is obtained. Internet service providers usually require that you buy a CSU both for your end and their end of the connection. You can buy CSUs from networking consultants, many phone companies, and your Internet service provider. As with routers, check to see if your service provider has a preference for any particular brand. Typical prices are $250 to $800 for 56K CSUs and $1200 to $2500 for T1 CSUs.

Tip

If you plan to upgrade from a 56K to a T1 connection later on, you may want to purchase a T1 CSU right from the start to save the cost of additional hardware later on.

Installation

Service providers usually charge anywhere from $1000 to $3000 to set up your connection, including installation, configuration, and training. All the phone companies involved charge additional fees for circuit installation, ranging from $300 to $3000. If you don't want to mess with any of the hardware and phone issues yourself, most Internet service providers offer turnkey installations to spare you from the details.

Other services you should ask your provider about are domain name registration (www.your-company.com) and UseNet news. Most providers offer these, but some charge extra for them. When you sign up for service, make sure you understand what you are and are not getting so you won't be surprised when you get the first bill.

Official lists of leased line and other types of Internet service providers are available from **ftp://is.internic.net/infoguide/getting-connected/**. A list of leased line providers for the U.S. at the time of this writing follows.

Leased Line Providers in the United States

The following information is taken from the InterNIC Leased Line Providers List that is published by the InterNIC, a project of the National Science Foundation, and is reprinted here with permission. Some of the entries have been modified to reflect new information and addresses. For the latest information, follow the instructions provided to access the full list online.

```
===========================================================
InterNIC Information Services        E-mail: info@internic.net
General Atomics (GA)                 Phone: (619) 455-4600
P.O. Box #85608                      Fax: (619) 455-4640
San Diego, CA 92186-9784

===========================================================
Updated: 94/11/7
InterNIC Internet Service Providers List: Leased Line Only (United States)
```

Permission for noncommercial distributions is granted, provided that this file is distributed intact, including the acknowledgment, disclaimer, and copyright notice found at the end of this document.

This document is available at **ftp://is.internic.net/infoguide/ getting-connected/united-states/internic-us-provider-leased**. For more information regarding this document, please contact **provlist@is.internic.net**.

Adhesive Media, Inc.	Texas
Eden Matrix Online Service	(512) 478-9900 x200 (PHONE)
John Herzer	(512) 478-9934 (FAX)
adhesive-media@eden.com	
AlterNet	United States and International
alternet-info@uunet.uu.net	(800) 4UUNET3 (PHONE)

(continues)

Leased Line Providers in the United States

ACM Network Services
Angela Abbott
account_info@acm.org

United States
(817) 776-6876 (PHONE)
(817) 751-7785 (FAX)

American Information Systems
Josh Schneider
schneid@ais.net

Illinois
(708) 413-8400 (PHONE)
(708) 413-8401 (FAX)

ANS
Sales and Information
info@ans.net

United States and International
(800) 456-8267 (PHONE)
(703) 758-7717 (FAX)

APK Public Access
Zbigniew Tyrlik
support@wariat.org

Ohio
(216) 481-9428 (PHONE)

BBN BARRNet, Inc.
John Toth
info@barrnet.net

California, Nevada
(415) 528-7111 (PHONE)
(415) 934-2665 (FAX)

Beckemeyer Development
Sales
info@bdt.com

California
(510) 530-9637 (PHONE)
(510) 530-0451 (FAX)

CCnet Communications
Information
info@ccnet.com

California
(510) 988-0680 (PHONE)
(510) 988-0689 (FAX)

Centurion Technology, Inc
Joyce Blue
blue@tpa.cent.com

Florida, Texas, Ohio
(813) 572-5556 (PHONE)
(813) 572-1452 (FAX)

CERFnet
CERFnet Hotline
sales@cerf.net

Western United States and
International
(800) 876-2373,
(619) 455-3900 (PHONE)
(619) 455-3990 (FAX)

CICnet
Marketing and Sales Dept.
info@cic.net

Midwestern United States
(800) 947-4754,
(313) 998-6703 (PHONE)
(313) 998-6105 (FAX)

Leased Line Providers in the United States

Clark Internet Services
ClarkNet Office
info@clark.net

Northeastern United States
(800) 735-2258,
(410) 254-3900 (PHONE)
(410) 730-9765 (FAX)

Cloud 9 Internet
Scott Drassinower
scottd@cloud9.net

New York
(914) 682-0626 (PHONE)
(914) 682-0506 (FAX)

Supernet, Inc
Guy Cook
gcook@csn.net

Colorado
(303) 296-8202 (PHONE)
(303) 296-8224 (FAX)

Connix
Jim Hogue
office@connix.com

Connecticut
(203) 349-7059 (PHONE)

CRL Network Services
Sales
sales@crl.com (or) info@crl.com

California
(415) 837-5300 (PHONE)

CTS Network Services
Sales
support@cts.com

California
(619) 637-3637 (PHONE)
(619) 637-3630 (FAX)

CyberGate, Inc
Dan Sullivan
sales@gate.net

Florida
(305) 428-4283 (PHONE)
(305) 428-7977 (FAX)

DFW Internet Services, Inc
Jack Beech
sales@dfw.net

Texas
(817) 332-5116 (PHONE)
(817) 870-1501 (FAX)

Digital Express Group, Inc
John Todd
sales@access.digex.net

United States
(800) 969-9090 (PHONE)
(301) 220-0477 (FAX)

EarthLink Network, Inc.
Sky Dayton
info@earthlink.net

California
(213) 644-9500 (PHONE)
(213) 644-9510 (FAX)

(continues)

Leased Line Providers in the United States

The Edge
Tim Choate
info@edge.net
tchoate@edge.ercnet.com

Tennessee
(615) 455-9915 (PHONE)
(615) 454-2042 (FAX)

Escape (Kazan Corp)
Sales
info@escape.com

New York
(212) 888-8780 (PHONE)
(212) 832-0344 (FAX)

Evergreen Internet
Phil Broadbent
sales@libre.com

Arizona
(602) 230-9330 (PHONE)
(602) 230-9773 (FAX)

Florida Online
Jerry Russell
jerry@digital.net

Florida
(407) 635-8888 (PHONE)
(407) 635-9050 (FAX)

HoloNet
HoloNet Staff
support@holonet.net

North America
(510) 704-0160 (PHONE)
(510) 704-8019 (FAX)

Global Enterprise Services
Sergio Heker, President
market@jvnc.net

United States and International
(800) 35-TIGER (PHONE)
(609) 897-7310 (FAX)

IACNet
Devon Sean McCullough
info@iac.net

Ohio
(513) 887-8877 (PHONE)

ICNet
Ivars Upatnieks
info@ic.net

Michigan, Ohio
(313) 998-0090 (PHONE)

IDS World Network
Information
info@ids.net

Northeastern United States
(800) IDS-1680 (PHONE)

Innovative Data Services
Sales
info@id.net

Michigan
(810) 478-3554 (PHONE)
(810) 478-2950 (FAX)

INS Info Services
Customer Service
service@ins.infonet.net

Iowa
(800) 546-6587 (PHONE)
(515) 830-0345 (FAX)

Leased Line Providers in the United States

INTAC Access Corporation
Sales
info@intac.com

New Jersey
(201) 944-1417 (PHONE)
(201) 944-1434 (FAX)

InterAccess
Lev Kaye
info@interaccess.com

Illinois
(800) 967-1580 (PHONE)
(708) 498-3289 (FAX)

International Connections
Manager
Robert Collet
rcollet@icm1.icp.net

(ICM) International
(703) 904-2230 (PHONE)

The Internet Access Company
Sales
info@tiac.net

Massachusetts
(617) 276-7200 (PHONE)
(617) 275-2224 (FAX)

Internet Atlanta
Dorn Hetzel
info@atlanta.com

Georgia
(404) 410-9000 (PHONE)
(404) 410-9005 (FAX)

Internet Express
Customer Service
service@usa.net

Colorado
(800) 592-1240 (PHONE)
(719) 592-1201 (FAX)

Internet On-Ramp, Inc
Sales
info@on-ramp.ior.com

Washington
(509) 927-7267 (PHONE)
(509) 927-0273 (FAX)

Internetworks
Internetworks, Inc
info@i.net
ftp.i.net:/pub/internetworks

United States and Pacific Rim
(503) 233-4774 (PHONE)
(503) 614-0344 (FAX)

Interport Communications Corp
Sales and Information
info@interport.net
http://www.interport.net

New York
(212) 989-1128 (PHONE)

IQuest Network Services
Robert Hoquim
info@iquest.net

Indiana
(800) 844-UNIX,
(317) 259-5050 (PHONE)
(317) 259-7289 (FAX)

(continues)

Leased Line Providers in the United States

Kaiwan Corp
Rachel Hwang
sales@kaiwan.com

California
(714) 638-2139 (PHONE)
(714) 638-0455 (FAX)

LI Net, Inc
Michael Reilly
questions@li.net

New York
(516) 265-0997 x11 (PHONE)

Lightside, Inc
Fred Condo
lightside@lightside.com
http://www.lightside.com/

California
(818) 858-9261 (PHONE)
(818) 858-8982 (FAX)

Los Nettos
Joe Kemp
los-nettos-info@isi.edu

Los Angeles Area
(310) 822-1511 (PHONE)
(310) 823-6714 (FAX)

netMAINE, Inc.
Andy Robinson
sales@maine.net

Maine
(207) 780-6381 (PHONE)
(207) 780-6301 (FAX)

MCSNet
Karl Denninger
info@mcs.net

Illinois
(312) 248-8649 (PHONE)
(312) 248-9865 (FAX)

MichNet/Merit
Recruiting Staff
info@merit.edu

Michigan
(800) 682-5550,
(313) 764-9430 (PHONE)
(313) 747-3185 (FAX)

MIDnet
Network Inf Ctr
nic@mid.net

Mid-Western United States
(402) 472-7600 (PHONE)
(402) 472-0240 (FAX)

Minnesota Regional
Network (MRNet)
Dennis Fazio
info@mr.net

Minnesota
(612) 342-2570 (PHONE)
(612) 342-2873 (FAX)

MSEN
Owen S. Medd
info@msen.com

Michigan
(313) 998-4562 (PHONE)
(313) 998-4563 (FAX)

Leased Line Providers in the United States

MV Communications
Sales
info@mv.mv.com

New Hampshire
(603) 429-2223 (PHONE)

NEARNET
NEARNET Information Hotline
nearnet-join@near.net

Northeastern United States
(617) 873-8730 (PHONE)
(617) 873-5620 (FAX)

NeoSoft, Inc
Ed Ireland
jmw3@neosoft.com

Texas
(713) 968-5800 (PHONE)
(713) 684-5922 (FAX)

NetAxis
Luis Hernandez
luis@eliza.netaxis.com

Connecticut
(203) 969-0618 (PHONE)
(203) 921-1544 (FAX)

**NETCOM On-line
Communications Services**
Business or Personal Sales
info@netcom.com

United States
(800) 353-6600,
(408) 983-5950 (PHONE)
(408) 241-9145 (FAX)

netILLINOIS
Peter Roll
info@illinois.net

Illinois
(708) 866-1804 (PHONE)
(708) 866-1857 (FAX)

Network Intensive
Sales and Information
info@ni.net
http://www.ni.net/

California and New Mexico
(714) 450-8400,
(800) 273-5600 (PHONE)
(714) 450-8410 (FAX)

New Mexico Technet, Inc
Marianne Granoff
granoff@technet.nm.org

New Mexico and Navajo
Reservation (incl: AZ, UT,
CO Reservations)
(505) 345-6555 (PHONE)
(505) 345-6559 (FAX)

New York Net
Bob Tinkelman
sales@new-york.net

New York
(718) 776-6811 (PHONE)
(718) 217-9407 (FAX)

Northcoast Internet
support@northcoast.com

California
(707) 443-8696 (PHONE)
(707) 441-0321 (FAX)

(continues)

Leased Line Providers in the United States

NorthWest CommLink
Garlend Tyacke
gtyacke@nwcl.net

Washington
(206) 336-0103 (PHONE)
(206) 336-2339 (FAX)

Northwest Nexus, Inc
Information
info@nwnexus.wa.com
support@halcyon.com

Washington
(206) 455-3505 (PHONE)
(206) 455-4672 (FAX)

NorthwestNet
Member Relations
info@nwnet.net

Northwestern United States
(206) 562-3000 (PHONE)
(206) 562-4822 (FAX)

NYSERNet
Sales
info@nysernet.org

New York
(315) 453-2912 (PHONE)
(315) 453-3052 (FAX)

OARnet
Alison Brown
info@oar.net

Ohio
(614) 728-8100 (PHONE)
(614) 728-8110 (FAX)

Old Colorado City
Communications
L.S. Fox
thefox@oldcolo.com

Colorado
(719) 528-5849 (PHONE)
(719) 528-5869 (FAX)

Panix
New User Staff
info-person@panix.com

New York City, Nassau County in
Long Island, Jersey City, NJ
(212) 741-4400 (PHONE)
(212) 741-5311 (FAX)

Ping
Brett Koller
bdk@ping.com

Georgia
(404) 399-1670 (PHONE)
(404) 399-1671 (FAX)

Pioneer Global
Craig Komins or Brian Breen
sales@pn.com
http://www.pn.com

Massachusetts
(617) 375-0200 (PHONE)
(617) 375-0201 (FAX)

Planet Access Networks
Fred Laparo
fred@planet.net
http://www.planet.net

New Jersey
(201) 691-4704 (PHONE)
(201) 691-7588 (FAX)

Leased Line Providers in the United States

PREPnet
nic@prep.net

Pennsylvania
(412) 268-7870 (PHONE)
(412) 268-7875 (FAX)

Primenet
Clay Johnston
info@primenet.com

Arizona
(602) 870-1010 x109 (PHONE)
(602) 870-1010 (FAX)

PSINet
PSI, Inc
info@psi.com

United States and International
(800) 82PSI82,
(703) 709-0300 (PHONE)
(800) FAXPSI1 (FAX)

QuakeNet
Sales
info@quake.net

California
(415) 655-6607 (PHONE)
(415) 377-0635 (FAX)

The Rabbit Network, Inc
Customer Liaison Services
info@rabbit.net

Michigan
(800) 456-0094 (PHONE)
(810) 790-0156 (FAX)

Red River Net
Craig Lien
lien@rrnet.com

Minnesota, North and
South Dakota
(701) 232-2227 (PHONE)

Rocky Mountain Internet, Inc
Rick Mount
info@rmii.com

Colorado
(800) 900-RMII (PHONE)
(719) 576-0301 (FAX)

Scruz-Net
Matthew Kaufman
info@scruz.net

California
(800) 319-5555,
(408) 457-5050 (PHONE)
(408) 457-1020 (FAX)

SeaNet
Igor Klimenko
igor@seanet.com

Seattle
(206) 343-7828 (PHONE)
(206) 628-0722 (FAX)

Sibylline, Inc
Dan Faules
info@sibylline.com

Arkansas
(501) 521-4660 (PHONE)
(501) 521-4659 (FAX)

(continues)

Leased Line Providers in the United States

Sesquinet
Farrell Gerbode
info@rice.edu

Texas
(713) 527-4988 (PHONE)
(713) 527-6099 (FAX)

SIMS, Inc
Jim Sims
info@sims.net

South Carolina
(803) 853-4333 (PHONE)
(803) 762-4956 (FAX)

South Coast Computing Services, Inc
Sales
info@sccsi.com

Texas
(800) 221-6478 (PHONE)
(713) 917-5005 (FAX)

SprintLink
SprintLink
info@sprintlink.net

United States and International
(800) 817-7755 (PHONE)
(703) 904-2680 (FAX)

SURAnet
Kimberly Donaldson
kdonalds@sura.net

Southeastern US, South America, Puerto Rico
(301) 982-4600 (PHONE)
(301) 982-4605 (FAX)

Synergy Communications
Sales Deptartment
info@synergy.net

United States
(402) 346-4638 (PHONE)
(402) 346-0208 (FAX)

Telerama Public Access
Peter Berger
sysop@telerama.lm.com

Pennsylvania
(412) 481-3505 (PHONE)
(412) 481-8568 (FAX)

THEnet (Connectivity for education and government in Texas)
Frank Sayre
f.sayre@utexas.edu

Texas
(512) 471-2444 (PHONE)
(512) 471-2449 (FAX)

ThoughtPort Authority Inc
David Bartlett
info@thoughtport.com

National
(314) 474-6870,
(800) ISP-6870 (PHONE)
(314) 474-4122 (FAX)

Leased Line Providers in the United States

UltraNet Communications, Inc
Sales
info@ultranet.com

Massachusetts
(508) 229-8400,
(800) 763-8111 (PHONE)
(508) 229-2375 (FAX)

US Net, Inc
Services
info@us.net

Eastern United States
(301) 572-5926 (PHONE)
(301) 572-5201 (FAX)

VERnet
James Jokl
net-info@ver.net

Virginia
(804) 924-0616 (PHONE)
(804) 982-4715 (FAX)

ViaNet Communications
Joe McGuckin
info@via.net

California
(415) 903-2242 (PHONE)
(415) 903-2241 (FAX)

Vnet Internet Access, Inc
Sales
info@vnet.net

North Carolina
(800) 377-3282 (PHONE)
(704) 334-6880 (FAX)

West Coast Online
Christopher Ward
cward@wco.com

California
(707) 586-3060 (PHONE)
(707) 586-5254 (FAX)

WestNet
Lillian or Chris
staff@westnet.com

Western United States
(914) 967-7816 (PHONE)

WiscNet
Network Information Center
wn-info@nic.wiscnet.net

Wisconsin
(608) 262-4241 (PHONE)
(608) 262-4679 (FAX)

WLN
Rushton Brandis
info@wln.com

Washington
(800) DIAL-WLN,
(206) 923-4000 (PHONE)
(306) 923-4009 (FAX)

WorldWide Accesss
Kathleen Vrona
support@wwa.com

Illinois
(708) 367-1870 (PHONE)
(708) 367-1872 (FAX)

(continues)

Planning a Web Server

Leased Line Providers in the United States	
XMission	Utah
Support	(801) 539-0852 (PHONE)
support@xmission.com	(801) 539-0853 (FAX)

Acknowledgment and Disclaimer

This material is based on work sponsored by the National Science Foundation under Cooperative Agreement No. NCR-9218749. The Government has certain rights in this material. Any opinions, findings, and conclusions or recommendations expressed in this material are those of the author(s) and do not necessarily reflect the views of the National Science Foundation, General Atomics, AT&T, or Network Solutions Inc.

Choosing Your Server Hardware

If you decide to set up your own Web server, plan carefully when deciding what kind of system to run it on. Web servers have been ported to run on many different platforms, including UNIX workstations, Macs, and PCs; there are many possibilities. This section covers three of the most common platforms: a UNIX workstation, Microsoft Windows, and a PC running UNIX. Web servers can be run on many other systems, including VAX/VMS, NeXT, and OS/2. CERN (**http://info.cern.ch**), the home of the Web, maintains a list of all known server software.

UNIX Workstation

By far the most popular platform for running a Web server is a UNIX workstation like those made by Hewlett-Packard, Sun Microsystems, Silicon Graphics, and Digital Equipment Corporation. UNIX workstations have always been popular for Internet servers because they are powerful and have built-in TCP/IP networking.

Speed

A workstation is the fastest available Web server platform. Workstations usually include one or more high-speed RISC processors, a fast system bus, abundant RAM (16M to 64M is common), several gigabytes of SCSI disk space, and fast graphics. Workstations offer the very fastest performance available, and are highly scalable for future growth.

Security

Because UNIX is a true multiuser operating system, access to files on any machine on the network requires proper authorization. File rights can be assigned to an individual owner, a group of users, and the world at large. This makes it very easy to control content on a Web server. Other networking systems implement these capabilities, but in UNIX, they're built in.

Software

UNIX workstation users have the largest choice of server software available simply because the workstation is such a popular server platform. Choices include CERN's httpd, the NCSA httpd (both included with this book), and Plexus, a server based on the perl language. The Netsite Communications Server is a commercial offering from Netscape Communications Corp. (**http://www.mcom.com**) that offers security features when used with the Netscape Web browser. The price is $1500 for the nonsecure version.

WebmasterCD

Web Server Tools

If you plan to use forms and scripts, collect usage statistics, access databases, generate graphics on-the-fly, or do much of anything beyond plain-vanilla document serving, you need some good software tools. Because the Internet is heavily UNIX-based, you will find the widest variety of tools and utilities for this operating system. In addition, new tools are usually developed first for UNIX and then ported to other platforms. Besides Web server tools, UNIX users can benefit from thousands of public domain programs on the Internet, most of which are distributed with the source code.

Hardware

Workstations are available from a number of different vendors. All the major vendors have product information on the Web and are listed in table 3.7.

Table 3.7 Popular UNIX Workstation Vendors		
Name	**Operating System**	**Contact**
Hewlett-Packard	HP-UX	**http://www.hp.com**
Sun Microsystems	SunOS or Solaris	**http://www.sun.com**
Silicon Graphics	IRIX	**http://www.sgi.com**
Digital	OSF/1, Windows NT	**http://www.dec.com**

Note

Digital Equipment Corporation's workstations using the Alpha processor are unique among workstations because they can run not only DEC's OSF/1 UNIX but also Windows NT.

How much hardware you need for a Web server depends entirely on your application. The single factor that buys you the most speed is RAM, so get as much as you can afford. For a busy Web server with lots of graphics, 32M or even 64M is not too much. The CERN httpd supports caching disk files to RAM, which significantly improves Web server performance, so the more, the better. Many operating systems support disk caching natively, so your Web server can benefit from extra RAM even if it's not running the CERN httpd. Of course, the more applications you run as part of your Web server, such as database access scripts, the more RAM you'll want to support these applications.

Because UNIX workstations come with built-in SCSI support, you can pretty much add SCSI disk space as you need it. Even if you don't have a lot of graphics, at least 1 GB of disk space is recommended to start with because you'll probably want to store log files and search index information in addition to Web documents.

Cost

Workstations range anywhere from $5000 to $25,000, depending on the type of processor and amount of RAM and disk space. However, even a low-end workstation can handle heavy server loads because workstations are designed to move data fast. Because of the built-in multitasking capabilities of UNIX, it's possible to run Web-related applications like a search engine while still moving data along at a good clip. Because low-end to midrange workstations are already found throughout corporate America, companies can often start a Web server without any immediate hardware cost.

Microsoft Windows

While a UNIX workstation is the ideal Web server platform for speed and scalability, users more familiar with PCs and Windows can run Windows httpd on a PC. The economic advantages of this are obvious, as PCs are considerably cheaper than UNIX workstations. However, PCs are not as powerful, and UNIX's multitasking capabilities are superior to Windows', making UNIX ideal for applications where the server handles many simultaneous connections. Although a Windows machine can handle plain Web file transfers nicely, searches and other applications running in the background bog down a Windows PC.

Speed

Graphical operating systems like Windows consume tremendous system resources with the graphical interface alone. However, plenty of RAM can largely make up for the resources eaten by Windows and can be put to good work caching disk files or running background applications. If your Web server involves only simple file transfers (no scripts), you can get along nicely with Windows httpd. The server documentation claims that it can serve 25,000 documents per hour on a 486/66 with 8M RAM, but few details of the test were specified. When dealing with numerous long documents and large graphics files, performance can be much worse.

Security

Because Windows is not a multiuser operating system, anyone with physical access to a PC can modify or remove files on the hard drive. This is not, perhaps, a significant drawback but does increase the chances of internal information "leaking" onto the Web from an inside source, whether intentionally or accidentally. In addition, Windows applications are known to crash now and then. While this is not a security issue, per se, scripts should be treated with caution. To prevent loss of service, you should not run other applications in the background at the same time as the Web server.

Software

In addition to Windows httpd, a Windows user can run SerWeb, another public domain server in CERN's list of Web servers. If you're interested in free Web server code, you'll definitely want to check out SerWeb because Windows httpd does require payment for continued use. However, Windows httpd currently has the best feature set.

Web Server Tools

Tool availability is a definite drawback to the Windows server. Very few Visual Basic or DOS CGI scripts have been written to perform common Web server tasks. It is possible to modify perl or C programs intended for UNIX, but differences in the file system and graphical user interface can require extensive modification. Graphical programs that use the UNIX X Windows interface cannot be ported to Windows at all. As the Internet becomes increasingly popular and PCs become more powerful, Web server tools may be offered commercially, but commercial products are more likely to be geared to Windows NT.

Hardware

The chief advantage of running a Windows Web server is the cost of the required hardware. As mentioned previously, if only file transfers are required, a 486/66 with 8M RAM and a fast hard drive does the job. However, the server quickly bogs down if other applications are running simultaneously. To get good benefits from disk caching, 16M RAM is recommended. In order for other applications to run in addition to the Web server without having to go to the hard drive all the time, you probably need 32M RAM. For processor-intensive tasks like numerical calculations and transferring data between applications, you probably want a Pentium.

For disk storage, SCSI drives are recommended because they are easily expandable (up to seven drives on a single SCSI controller). This means you can always add space when you need it. In addition, Fast SCSI-2 drives can transfer data significantly faster than most IDE drives. An EISA or PCI SCSI controller is necessary to get the best performance out of SCSI drives. EISA is recommended as a mature and reliable technology that provides more than enough speed for disk transfers, but vendors seem to be dropping EISA support in favor of PCI.

Network cards don't have to be particularly fast for Web server applications for two reasons. First, standard Ethernet (10 Mbps) is over six times faster than a T1 leased line (1.5 Mbps), so a fast networking card simply gets you "nowhere, fast." Second, even the old ISA bus (8M per second equals 64 Mbps) can pump data faster than standard Ethernet, so EISA and PCI don't offer any improvement in networking speed over standard Ethernet unless they use the emerging 100 Mbps Ethernet standard. An excellent ISA Ethernet card is the 3Com 3C509.

Cost

A 486/66 PC with 8M RAM, 1 GB IDE hard drive, and a double-speed CD-ROM runs for less than $2000. For applications requiring more than basic file serving, you can pick up a 90 MHz Pentium PCI/ISA system with 16M RAM, a 1 GB SCSI-2 hard drive, and a quad-speed CD-ROM for $3500. Prices will, of course, be less by the time you read this. An ISA Ethernet card for either system runs $100 to $200. All in all, the Windows Web server can be a great deal for organizations wanting a simple Web presence without a lot of fancy features.

PC Running UNIX

For those already familiar with UNIX, a PC running some flavor of UNIX may be the most attractive option of all. The low cost of PC hardware combined

with the power of the UNIX operating system results in a very good price/
performance ratio. Popular versions of UNIX for PCs include SCO, BSDI, AIX,
and two freeware versions: Linux and FreeBSD.

Speed

By some estimates, a 486/66 running BSDI approximates a respectable 25
MIPS workstation in performance, and a Pentium 90 can achieve 70 MIPS
performance. Unencumbered by the Windows interface, PCs can really fly.
PCs use much of the same hardware as UNIX workstations, so the operating
system really makes a difference in speed. PCs and workstations differ primarily in their processors and graphics support; the EISA, PCI, and SCSI buses
are used in both. The hallmark of workstations used to be their RISC processors; however, the Pentium now incorporates many RISC-like features, bringing the two closer together. PC graphics have also approached workstation
graphics thanks to the PCI bus. In summary, PCs and workstations are rapidly
merging. Nowhere is this more evident than in Windows NT, which can run
either on an Intel platform or a DEC Alpha workstation.

Security

The same security benefits apply to PCs running UNIX as workstations running UNIX. Because of their low cost, UNIX PCs are often used in Internet
firewalls, which do not require much processing power, but definitely require
UNIX-based security features. Firewall software for DOS and Windows
machines is unheard of.

Software

PCs running UNIX can run all the same software as workstations, including
server software, as long as the source code is available for compilation. This
is the case with almost all UNIX-based freeware, including the NCSA httpd
included in this book. Because there are so many different UNIX platforms,
UNIX programs are frequently distributed as precompiled programs for the
most popular platforms along with the source code for compilation on other
platforms. For this reason, a C compiler is included with most UNIX systems.

The most popular PC UNIX version for Internet servers seems to be BSDI
(Berkeley Software Design, Inc.) because of its technical and networking support. In addition, almost all of the BSDI source code is available, although it
must be purchased, unlike Linux and FreeBSD. The list of BSDI customers at
http://www.bsdi.com is impressive and ever-growing. SCO (Santa Cruz
Operation) UNIX does not seem to be as popular for Internet connectivity
nor does IBM's AIX. Linux and FreeBSD are very popular, and both are

extensively supported on UseNet. Linux and FreeBSD distributions can be downloaded from the Internet or obtained on CD-ROM from several locations. Table 3.8 lists sources for various PC UNIX versions.

Table 3.8 Where to Get PC UNIX Versions		
Product	**Source Name**	**Contact**
FreeBSD	Walnut Creek CD-ROM	**http://www.cdrom.com**
Linux	Walnut Creek CD-ROM	**http://www.cdrom.com**
SCO	Santa Cruz Operation	**http://www.sco.com**
AIX	IBM	**http://www.ibm.com**
BSDI	Berkeley Software Design	**http://www.bsdi.com**

Web Server Tools

In addition to C programs, Web tools and other UNIX utilities are commonly distributed as perl programs. Perl itself is a C program which can be compiled on any UNIX system, so PCs running UNIX have access to the full spectrum of public domain programs and utilities developed for the UNIX environment. PC versions of UNIX come with X Windows just like their workstation cousins, so even the graphical programs can be run.

Hardware

Hardware requirements for a PC running UNIX are about the same as they are for a PC running Windows. You may be able to get by with a little less because UNIX requires less overhead than Windows. If you're running X Windows, however, you'll want the extra memory. Choosing hardware for a PC-based UNIX server can be a little tricky because new hardware vendors almost always write drivers for DOS and Windows before UNIX. Make sure you check your UNIX vendor's list of supported hardware before buying a system.

Cost

The hardware cost for a PC-based UNIX system is pretty much the same as that for a Windows-based Web server. The UNIX software cost can be significant, however. BSDI charges $545 for the first license (without the source) and SCO charges around $1000. Linux and FreeBSD are available on CD-ROM for $40, but these do not include formal technical support as do the others.

Chapter 4

Creating an Internal Web Server

Every company shares information among employees. Whether communicating company news and policies to an entire division or corporation, sharing engineering data among related product groups, or facilitating workgroup discussion, companies are looking for ways to increase productivity using computers. This chapter discusses how to plan a Web server to achieve this goal.

The focus of this chapter is to help you decide what you need to get your internal Web server up and running. Choosing the right hardware, software, and network can be confusing, but the material in this chapter shows you what you need.

In this chapter, you learn

- What kind of hardware and network is required

- Which browser features are most important

- How to solve cross-platform document format issues

The Company Bulletin Board

The model for many companies' electronic communication comes originally from the ubiquitous cork board on which important notices and information can be posted for all to see. More recently, dial-up or LAN-based bulletin board systems have been used to facilitate two-way discussion between workgroups. Dozens of specialized software packages exist that support group-based interaction. Older dial-up bulletin board systems used ASCII text as the basis of communication, allowing any computer with a terminal or communications program to use the service. Many more advanced programs exist, but use a proprietary data format and therefore require the purchase not only of a server, but also of client software for each computer on the network.

World Wide Web technology is not designed to be a full-fledged paperless work flow system, but it does provide a way for an organization to publish important documents for everyone to see. A World Wide Web server can be used in place of more expensive proprietary workgroup software or less featured ASCII text systems to accomplish many of the same workgroup goals.

An Information Publishing Tool

Most organizations have a sizable body of policies and procedures and other important documents that must be available to nearly every employee. Distributing these to everyone in written form is expensive and inefficient because of the time required to produce them. A Web server is an ideal way to make this kind of literature available online. It not only eliminates the waste of time and paper required to print and distribute documents, but it allows the use of hypertext and full-text searching to speed up the process of finding information tremendously.

Another common business need is a timely way to distribute company and industry news. Newsletters are time-consuming and always a day or two behind the news. Putting an electronic newsletter on a Web server, by comparison, allows instant updates and convenient searching of back issues for important items. In addition, this medium can be made interactive, allowing anyone to submit and publish their own news items (see the following mini-table).

Types of Information to Publish on a Web Server
Policies and procedures
Organizational charts
Searchable phone books
Business form templates
Business and financial information
Company and industry news

A Workgroup Tool

One of the biggest problems in a large organization is the duplication of effort that results from no one being aware of anyone else's efforts. A Web server solves this problem by allowing teams and departments in an organization to publish information about their past, current, and planned activities for their own use and for the use of others who might benefit.

Within a team or workgroup, a page on a Web server can serve as the central place for communicating important project news and as a repository for all documents relating to a project. Because Web servers use client-server technology, workgroup members spread across a wide geographical area can easily access the central database. Thanks to the security features in many Web servers, the Internet can tie together distant locations and save the cost of leasing dedicated lines between each location. See chapter 8, "Managing an Internal Web Server," and chapter 7, "Managing an Internet Web Server."

A major need in technical organizations is that of transmitting the knowledge possessed by one or more experts in a given technology or for a given product so that others can benefit. Typically, it is difficult to publish notes, memos, technical reports, trade studies, and so on in such a way that anyone looking for the information can find it. Using a Web server, however, it is possible to construct a central database capable of handling many document formats. The database can be full-text searchable so that the user can find information easily. Maintaining this kind of a database is invaluable for reducing product development cycles and for training new hires in technology.

In addition to simple document storage, search, and retrieval, you can use Web servers to create annotation systems for true workgroup interaction. Group members can create hypertext links to annotations in the body of a document, allowing convenient and productive discussion right in the document itself. Web servers offer tremendous flexibility for designing virtually any kind of workgroup system with a minimum of programming effort.

The following mini-table presents some uses of Web servers as a workgroup tool.

Uses of Web Servers in Workgroups
Track project status
Store project documents
Publish technical reports
Annotate shared documents
Disseminate departmental information

An Open Discussion Tool

A news server like those that form the structure of Internet newsgroups is a useful addition to an organizational Web server. Internet newsgroups allow anyone worldwide to join in informal discussion with other people interested in the same topics. In addition, anyone can post questions to the newsgroups in search of technical information or assistance of any kind. By applying this technology locally, an organization can inexpensively (the news server software is free) provide an organized communication medium in which all employees can participate.

> **Note**
>
> A popular news server is InterNetNews (INN) for UNIX, which is freely available from numerous FTP sites including **wuarchive.wustl.edu** in the directory "/packages/news/transport/inn." News servers for other platforms, such as OS/2, are forthcoming.

Organizations can benefit from setting up an internal news server to facilitate discussion on just about anything. Human resources departments can use an internal news server, for example, as a tool to assist in new hire orientation by allowing new hires to pose questions to more experienced employees. Workers in a certain field can discuss developments in that field on a newsgroup. Engineers looking for certain technical reports or information can post a question on the appropriate newsgroup and receive dozens of helpful pointers. Computer users struggling with a new software package can receive support from more experienced users or helpdesk personnel. The possibilities are really endless. Newsgroups are an effective way for thousands of people with the same interest to mutually further that interest. And newsgroups are a great productivity tool. By posting a question on a newsgroup, people can avoid several hours of research that might otherwise be required. See the following mini-table.

Possible Uses for an Internal News Server
Distribution of company and industry news
Posting of events such as network downtime
Hardware and software technical support
Support for procedural questions

Possible Uses for an Internal News Server
Workgroup discussions
Training of new employees
Hardware and software users groups

System Requirements

In order to set up a Web server, your network, Web server, and Web client(s) must meet certain requirements. This section tells you what you need to build a speedy server on your network and what you need to do to have all the features you want.

The Network

Unfortunately, it is not possible to set up a Web server on just any network without some additional software. This section discusses network protocol and speed requirements.

TCP/IP

TCP/IP, Transmission Control Protocol/Internet Protocol, is the language by which computers communicate on the Internet. All Web servers and clients use TCP/IP to communicate with each other. Although it is possible to use other network protocols, TCP/IP is designed specifically for fast, efficient communications across the Internet and local area networks.

It is possible to run Web applications such as Mosaic without TCP/IP, although you are limited to accessing local files or files on a connected local area network. Running locally, you can share hypertext information over the LAN but have none of the features of the Web itself. If you envision the Web as machines throughout the world, connected by a TCP/IP network, it is easy to see that your LAN would not be a part of the Web without TCP/IP and a connection to that network: the Internet. Viewing files on a LAN is usually too limiting for users, so TCP/IP and a connection to the Internet is almost a necessity for any Web site.

> **Note**
>
> While a TCP/IP network and connection to the Internet are desirable, organizations can still benefit from hypertext publishing without going to the expense of purchasing and configuring a TCP/IP network. Mosaic and other Web browsers have an option in the File menu to open local files. Using this option, you can view HTML documents stored on a common network drive regardless of the underlying network operating system.

What Is TCP/IP? TCP/IP is an *open networking protocol,* meaning that the technical description has been published and is available for anyone to implement. This has helped make TCP/IP the most widely used networking protocol in the world, with versions available for practically every hardware and software platform in existence.

TCP/IP is not a single protocol, but a suite of dozens of protocols dedicated to different tasks. All the protocols that make up TCP/IP use the "IP" of TCP/IP, the Internet Protocol, for sending packets of data. Because the vast majority of applications use TCP, the Transmission Control Protocol, for managing the communication of the packets, the protocol suite is usually called TCP/IP or just IP.

You are probably familiar with some of the TCP/IP applications: FTP (File Transfer Protocol) and Telnet, for example, and each has its own protocol. If you use UNIX workstations, you are probably aware of NFS (Network File System) and DNS (Domain Name System). Luckily, for most users, the details of the different protocols that make up TCP/IP are not important because they are transparent to all but network programmers and configuration managers.

The popularity of TCP/IP with the UNIX world has caused it to spread to every other computer platform that can be part of a LAN. There are public domain versions of important portions of TCP/IP for many hardware and software systems, and a thriving commercial business selling TCP/IP tools to the DOS and Macintosh market.

Because TCP/IP is not generally associated with PC-based LANs, there is some trepidation by users towards using the network protocol. Luckily, TCP/IP is not any more difficult to install and configure than Novell NetWare, Artisoft's LANtastic, and Microsoft's Windows for Workgroups. In some ways, because of the well-known behavior of TCP/IP and the number of expert users that are accessible through the Internet, TCP/IP is a better choice for a PC-based LAN than other protocols that require or use different types of computers or software.

The advantages of TCP/IP for a LAN operating system are simple: interconnectivity is possible for any type of operating system and hardware platform that you may want to add. Unfortunately, other network operating systems do not have this advantage. For example, it is difficult to add a Sun or HP workstation to a Novell NetWare network unless the Novell server is converted to run TCP/IP in addition to its native IPX (which is fully supported by the latest version of NetWare, reflecting TCP/IP's popularity).

A disadvantage to using TCP/IP for a network operating system is that it can be troublesome at times when many protocols from the family are internetworked. This usually only happens on very large networks where you may want to run several servers and directory processes.

Using TCP/IP as a Network Operating System. TCP/IP is used extensively as the default network protocol in the UNIX world, but adding PCs or Macintosh machines to a TCP/IP-based network requires TCP/IP software running on the smaller machines. TCP/IP software products for both PC and Macintosh machines are common and quite easy to use. When installed on a PC or Macintosh, TCP/IP lets users of those machines access other machines on the network as well as access the Internet and Mosaic. The Banyan VINES ™ Local Area Network operating system is one example. While older versions use a modified IP called VINES IP, the newer versions include standard TCP/IP.

There are two approaches to supporting TCP/IP on a PC or Macintosh: using it as the sole protocol, or combining it with other existing protocols such as Windows for Workgroups or Novell NetWare. If two protocols are to be supported, either a second network card can be added specifically for the TCP/IP network, or TCP/IP can coexist with the other network (assuming they can both use the same network card). Dedicated networks for each protocol remove any problems with conflicting network packets, but duplicate networks are more expensive and more trouble to install and maintain.

Many local area networks use more than one protocol at a time. Some may use a dozen or more. One group of computers may communicate via TCP/IP, another may use Windows for Workgroups and communicate using NetBEUI, and still another may use NetWare and communicate using IPX. In addition, some machines may use multiple types of packets. That is, they may send IPX packets to a Novell server and TCP/IP packets to a UNIX host.

This capability to use multiple protocols is due to clever design of the LAN, whether Ethernet, Token Ring, FDDI, or whatever. Each has information to tell a computer what type of packet is on the network (IP, IPX, and so on). The computer then deals with the packet accordingly.

The possible difficulty when using multiple protocols on a single host (sometimes called *piggybacking*) is how to configure the software. Each operating system has different mechanisms. In the PC environment, the NDIS (Network Device Interface Specification) or other device drivers can send out and receive packets of the appropriate types. The documentation for the software packages (NetWare, Windows for Workgroups) describe how to set up each specific package for this feature.

The alternative to piggybacking protocols is to configure the second network operating system to encapsulate its message within IP packets. This is a simpler system to implement in most cases, and allows a wider range of inter-connectivity options for hardware on the network. Many popular DOS and Macintosh network operating systems can be set to encapsulate their own packets within IP packets, although some still lack this capability.

Whenever TCP/IP is installed on a machine, it must be properly configured. The same information is required for all TCP/IP installations: the host name, IP address, broadcast address, subnetwork mask, and the names or addresses of routers (often called gateways) that may be involved in the network. Without this information, machines cannot communicate. This information is generally supplied by a network manager and entered into each machine by hand, or it may be downloaded over the network. For more in-depth coverage of TCP/IP, see Timothy Parker's *Teach Yourself TCP/IP in 14 Days*, published by Sams.

Commercial Versions of TCP/IP

There are several popular DOS and Windows implementations of TCP/IP available. Two of the most popular commercial products are ftp Software's PC/TCP and NetManage's Chameleon. A shareware version of TCP/IP for Windows, called Trumpet Winsock, is also in wide use, although it lacks many of the features of the commercial versions. For Macintosh users, the primary implementation of TCP/IP is called MacTCP.

All of the DOS and Windows-based TCP/IP products make changes to the AUTOEXEC.BAT, CONFIG.SYS, and Windows configuration files. The MacTCP product affects the kernel. Removing a TCP/IP product after installation can be somewhat troublesome, as the changes to the system are not always obvious. This is especially true when an existing protocol is overwritten or used in conjunction with TCP/IP.

NetManage's Chameleon. NetManage produces several TCP/IP-based software packages specifically for Microsoft Windows that are designed to provide a full set of TCP/IP utilities. NetManage's line of products includes a basic TCP/IP protocol stack called *Newt,* as well as a full TCP/IP application package called *Chameleon.* Use Newt when you need only basic TCP/IP functionality and plan to use other software for Web applications. Chameleon adds all the TCP/IP programs such as a Web browser, FTP, and Telnet (see fig. 4.1).

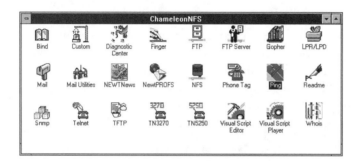

Fig. 4.1
The Chameleon Program Group includes icons for all the TCP/IP utilities a user can access.

NetManage's Internet products for Windows all use the WinSock standard DLL (Dynamic Link Library), but vary in support for modems, networks, and included client and server software (see table 4.1).

Table 4.1	NetManage Internet Products
Product	**Description**
Newt	Just the TCP/IP protocol stack (WinSock)
Chameleon	Newt plus a number of TCP/IP utilities such as Telnet and FTP
ChameleonNFS	Chameleon plus a client and server for Sun's NFS
Internet Chameleon	Chameleon plus a Web browser (dial-up only, no LAN support)
Chameleon/X	Chameleon with an X-Windows server
ChameleonNFS/X	ChameleonNFS plus an X-Windows server
Chameleon32/NFS	Chameleon for Windows NT
Chameleon/D	Chameleon for DOS and Windows

Chameleon is Windows-specific and not a part of a DOS TCP application. This means it has been optimized for better performance under Windows, but also means that TCP is not accessible for DOS-only applications.

Installation and configuration of Chameleon is not too difficult, although combining it with other protocols may require some manual editing of configuration files.

ftp Software's PC/TCP. The popular PC/TCP software package from ftp Software has become a de facto standard for DOS machines that want to run TCP/IP. PC/TCP runs under both DOS and Windows, with a Windows-specific version now available. PC/TCP provides all the TCP/IP functions to both DOS and Windows.

Because PC/TCP is both DOS- and Windows-compatible, configuration is a little more complex than a Windows-only based system. Although there is a menu-driven DOS configuration utility, PC/TCP requires a user to edit configuration files manually to set parameters for the network and IP addresses. When combined with a second network protocol, the process can become quite complex and more involved than novice users will want to undertake.

Trumpet Software International's Winsock. Trumpet Software's Winsock is a shareware TCP/IP protocol stack that works only within Microsoft Windows. Trumpet Winsock allows use of SLIP (Serial Line Internet Protocol), PPP (Point to Point Protocol) asynchronous (dial-up) access to the Internet, as well as networked TCP/IP support. Trumpet Winsock is not a complete TCP/IP set of utilities, providing only the protocol stack and a couple of diagnostic utilities.

Installing Trumpet Winsock generally requires a *packet driver* for the network interface. Packet drivers provide a standard software interface to Ethernet, Token Ring, and other networking cards. The documentation for Trumpet Winsock explains where to get packet drivers if you don't have one for your network interface card already. Installing a packet driver requires adding a line to your AUTOEXEC.BAT file. The Trumpet documentation provides very thorough instructions.

> **Tip**
>
> Many of these packet drivers are included on WebmasterCD.

Trumpet Winsock is simple to configure as long as you know the IP addresses of the machines to which you will connect or you can configure the asynchronous ports for SLIP or PPP (see fig. 4.2). You must invoke the protocol stack either manually or through a start-up icon every time you boot Windows. Running Winsock and another network protocol simultaneously can be troublesome.

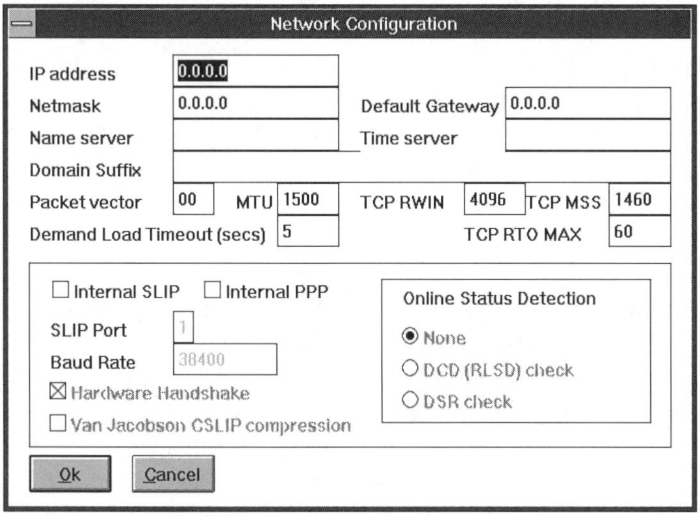

Fig. 4.2
Trumpet Winsock requests configuration information during installation.

Trumpet Winsock does not provide utilities such as FTP and Telnet; you must acquire them separately. Because it is shareware, a payment is expected if it is used beyond 30 days, but it is considerably less expensive than commercial TCP/IP products.

MacTCP. MacTCP is a commercial TCP/IP protocol stack for the Macintosh. You can use it as the only protocol on the machine, or it can coexist with another network. Using MacTCP, you can execute Macintosh versions of Mosaic, or you can X-Term into another machine and execute the Web browser there.

MacTCP is easy to install and configure, although you must know the IP addresses of machines that will be accessed through TCP/IP. Unlike many DOS and Windows TCP/IP products, MacTCP is solid and seldom causes a problem with configuration files.

> **Note**
>
> System 7.5 includes MacTCP 2.0.4. Previous versions of this were less stable but you can get upgrades from earlier versions free on the Net. The most current update is 2.0.6 and you can find it in the Info-Mac FTP archives (or any of the mirror sites) at **sumex-aim.stanford.edu** in the directory "/info-mac/Communication/MacTCP." The file name is "mactcp-206-updt.hqx."

Other Packages. There are a number of other TCP/IP packages for the PC and the Mac. Be careful that you select an appropriate package to use with a Web browser. NCSA Telnet is good, but some older packages do not allow you to add your own applications to their products easily (for instance, Netscape or Mosaic).

Speed

No minimum network speed is necessary to run a successful Web server. Most modern LANs are capable of at least 1 Mbps, which is fast enough to transfer several pages of hypertext almost instantaneously. Of course, if you have many users on the network, you can expect to see significantly less performance than that 1 Mbps data rate, but documents still appear very quickly. If you have any dial-up modems on your network that are used to form a WAN to another, remote network, data moves slowly over that link. Text is no problem, but graphics can take quite a while to download at 14.4 kbaud. The new 28.8 modems with compression should improve this considerably.

The Server

Because most LANs are capable of several megabytes per second, the Web server hardware itself is the single most important factor in determining performance. Several factors affect performance, including location on the network, disk space, and processor speed.

Network Location

No matter what kind of server hardware you choose, the server itself should be located near the center of the network to provide the fastest access to the greatest number of users. If the server is located on a busy subnetwork, data sent from the Web server to the main network can be bogged down by all the other traffic on the subnetwork. Figure 4.3 shows the recommended location of a Web server on a typical high-speed LAN.

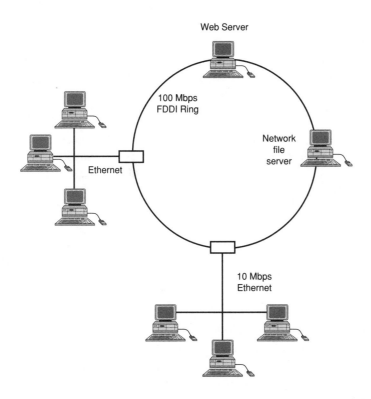

Web Server

100 Mbps
FDDI Ring

Network
file
server

Ethernet

10 Mbps
Ethernet

Fig. 4.3
Notice the
location of the
server in this
network.

Planning a Web Server

Disk Space

If you plan to allow many people in your organization to put files on the
Web server, be sure you have plenty of disk space. One hundred lines of
HTML take up less than 8K or so because HTML is actually 7-bit ASCII just
like plain text, but other types of document formats eat through your disk
much more quickly. Graphics are very disk-intensive; if you plan to use your
Web server to publish charts or drawings, look at a typical file size for planning purposes. Scanned images are the worst disk-eaters. A 10-page PostScript
document containing a scanned figure on each page can take up to 70M.

Note

Many scanning software packages save images in a TIFF format by default. However,
the GIF format is often up to three times smaller.

If you plan to run indexing software so you can do full-text searches on your
Web server, be sure to allow enough room for the index file. A full-text index
file for a body of HTML documents may be up to half the size of all the documents combined! In addition, keeping usage logs on a busy server can eat 10
or 20 megabytes per month.

Speed

As discussed in chapter 3, "Creating a Home Page on the Internet," the single most important factor in determining how long it takes a Web server to respond to a request is the processor speed. This is especially true if the server is performing searches, running scripts, or running any other program while the Web server is running.

Guidelines are difficult to establish because overall performance depends on so many factors, but on the whole, it's safe to say that a 486DX33 with a fast hard drive or equivalent Mac (any of the Quadra line for example) provides speedy responses on a network of several hundred users. If you have several thousand users, however, you need something more like an HP 715/50 UNIX workstation. UNIX is a robust multitasking operating system; a UNIX machine can very efficiently process requests from many users at the same time.

The Browser

Choosing a standard browser for your entire organization is desirable in order to ensure that all document features, such as forms, will be fully accessible from all browsers. This section will compare the capabilities of the most popular browsers: NCSA Mosaic, Netscape Communications Corp.'s Netscape, and Lynx from the University of Kansas. We'll also look briefly at several commercial products that include Web browsers as part of a suite of Internet tools. If you are setting up Web access in a corporate environment, you may find a commercial package to be the right solution as you can get technical support, documentation, and a level of service you are accustomed to with your other software applications.

Mosaic

NCSA Mosaic was the original graphical browser for Microsoft Windows, and is also available for the Mac and X-Windows (see figs. 4.4 and 4.5). It is free, but as such, comes with no technical support. However, in response to user feedback, NCSA has done a good job of working the bugs out in successive releases. All but the oldest versions support fill-in forms, allowing users to send data back to a Web server. Mosaic loads all text and graphics before displaying a page; this method works well in a LAN environment, but is slow over modem connections. Mosaic does, however, give users the option to turn off graphics to get around this difficulty.

A main drawback to Mosaic for Windows is that all but the earliest Windows versions require the 32-bit extensions of Windows to be loaded before Mosaic can run. This requirement was made in order to enable the use of common code between the Windows and Windows NT versions. It adds complexity to Windows, however, and therefore increases the chances for bugs. Other, non-Windows versions do not suffer this problem.

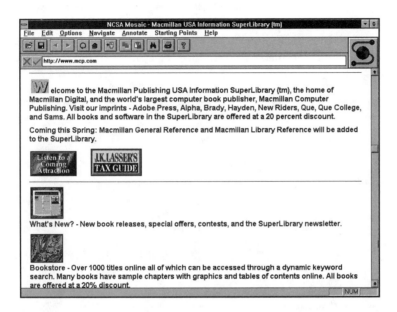

Fig. 4.4
This is part of the Macmillan home page in Mosaic for Windows.

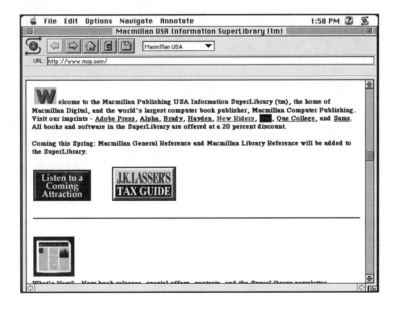

Fig. 4.5
This is part of the Macmillan home page in Mosaic for Mac.

Netscape

Netscape was developed by the Mosaic Communications Corp., which was started by Marc Andreessen, one of the original authors of NCSA Mosaic. Like Mosaic, Netscape is a free graphical browser for Windows and Mac. However, the license of the free, prerelease version prohibits commercial use. Version 1.0 is available for sale for commercial use, and will include technical support. Netscape is available for Windows, Mac, and X-Windows (UNIX). See figures 4.6 and 4.7.

Fig. 4.6
This is part of the Macmillan home page in Netscape for Windows.

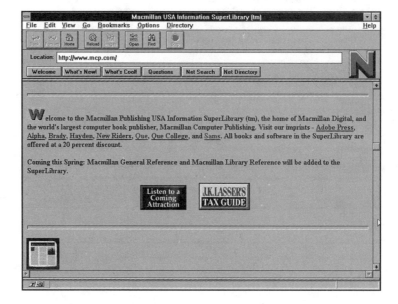

Netscape has many enhancements over Mosaic, the best of which is its ability to display text and graphics incrementally. Modem users can see something right away, then wait for more text and graphics if they choose. In addition, Netscape has a full-featured newsreader built-in that supports reading and posting to newsgroups from inside the browser. Mosaic can read groups, but does not allow the user to subscribe and unsubscribe to groups or to disregard messages that have already been read. Another Netscape enhancement is its support for the mailto feature, which sends Internet e-mail to an address specified in an HTML document. Because Netscape is a 16-bit rather than a 32-bit application, it is significantly easier to install.

Lynx

Lynx is a text-mode browser developed by the University of Kansas. It is useful for providing access to the Web from dumb terminals such as VT220s or from PCs without SLIP access to the Internet. Lynx runs mainly under VMS and UNIX, and is typically the fastest Web browser for modem use because these platforms are usually connected to the Internet via high-speed links. Lynx supports the mailto feature and has limited support for forms, but cannot display graphics (see fig. 4.8). Lynx's support for news is read-only as is Mosaic's.

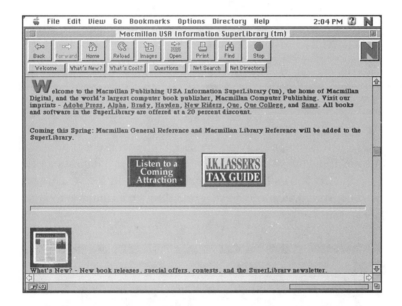

Fig. 4.7

This is part of the Macmillan home page in Netscape for Mac.

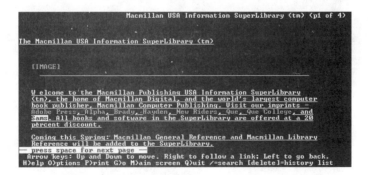

Fig. 4.8

This is part of the Macmillan home page in Lynx. Graphics have been replaced by text.

Table 4.2 summarizes the features of Mosaic, Netscape, and Lynx.

Table 4.2 Features of Mosaic, Netscape, and Lynx			
Feature	**Mosaic**	**Netscape**	**Lynx**
Cost	Free	Noncommercial free	Free
Technical support	No	Commercial version only	No
Graphical	Yes	Yes	No
Supports forms	Yes	Yes	Yes
Can post news	No	Yes	Yes
Can read news	Yes	Yes	Yes

InterAp

InterAp is a new commercial Windows-based Internet product from California software. It includes a Web browser (see fig. 4.9) in addition to a TCP/IP stack, e-mail software, and UseNet newsreader along with several other applications. All of the applications are accessed through a common toolbar called the InterAp Launch Pad.

Fig. 4.9

This is part of the Macmillan home page in InterAp Web Navigator.

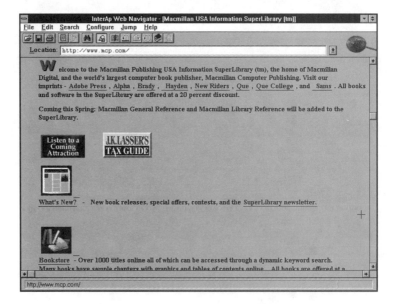

This suite will appeal primarily to business users who use Windows applications with OLE such as the Microsoft Office suite. InterAp has OLE 2 support to make it easy to integrate it with Word, Excel, Access and other OLE compliant products. It also includes a powerful scripting language to make it easy to automate Net activity.

You can get more information on this from their Web page at **http://www.calsoft.com** or from:

California Software, Inc.
3004 Ocean Blvd.
Corona del Mar, CA 92625
(714) 675-9906 Voice
(800) 830-3311 Sales

NetManage

The current version (4.0 or later) of the NetManage software discussed earlier in this chapter includes a Web browser called WebSurfer (see fig. 4.10). The main advantage of the various versions of this software is their completeness. In addition to the WebSurfer and TCP/IP, the dial-up version includes an FTP client and server, and Mail, News, Ping, Finger, Gopher, Archie, and Telnet clients.

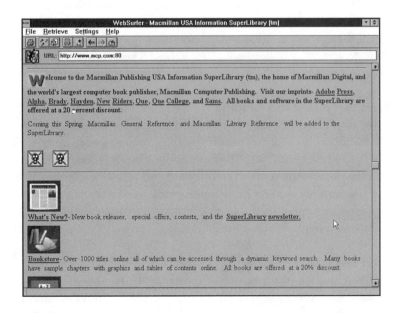

Fig. 4.10
This is part of the Macmillan home page in WebSurfer.

To find out more about NetManage, contact them at **http:// www.netmanage.com**

NetManage, Inc.
10725 N. De Anza Blvd.
Cupertino, CA 95014
(408) 973-7171 Phone
(408) 257-6405 Fax

Cross-Platform Compatibility

One of the most difficult issues involved in setting up an organizational Web server is finding a cross-platform document standard that has more features than HTML. This section presents some ideas on how to go about it.

Why Not HTML?

Presumably, when you set up your server, you are trying to make information available to everyone inside your organization, not just a few machines. Consequently, it is necessary to put all documents in a format that can be viewed the same way on all machines. The standard language of the Web, HTML, is ideal for this purpose. HTML supports very few formatting and graphics features and that makes it difficult to convert existing formatted documents. As the World Wide Web grows and more and more companies write HTML filters for their products, HTML will be modified to correct many present limitations, but this will not happen for at least a year. In the meantime, there are four alternatives.

Convert Everything to a Graphic

One way to get all the desired formatting and graphic features that HTML does not support is simply to create a graphic image of a page using a scanner or other electronic technique. All graphical Web browsers can read GIF files, so scanning images into GIFs would seem to be a plausible solution. However, this technique requires humongous amounts of disk space and does not allow the use of hypertext, full-text searching, or many other niceties of HTML. Consequently, it is not recommended.

Convert Everything to HTML

Many filters and templates exist for creating HTML documents with word processors. However, insisting that document creators always use this technique severely limits the kinds of documents that can be included because of the limitations of HTML. In addition, conversion requires an extra step that some users may not be willing to take in order to publish their documents. In that instance, everyone loses the benefit of being able to find and read a potentially valuable piece of work.

Convert Everything to PostScript

PostScript is a feature-rich, universal document standard. Nearly every word processor and operating environment includes the capability to generate PostScript files in order to print documents on PostScript printers. Consequently, it would seem that you could solve the document standard problem by launching PostScript viewing software from your browser. You can use a free program, GhostView, to view PostScript on several different platforms.

This scheme does work pretty well on fast UNIX workstations, but PostScript viewing on PCs and Macs is very slow. Consequently, it is not recommended. In addition, PostScript files containing scanned images or other graphics can be very large. PostScript also does not support the hypertext features of HTML.

On the positive side, commercial PostScript-related products such as Adobe Acrobat and Common Ground hold some real promise. Most of these support hypertext (although they do not support hypertext links to other Internet locations as does HTML), and can be created from standard PostScript files. These commercial solutions are available for a wide variety of operating systems, and the viewers are often free.

Use HTML, PostScript, and Native Formats

The only practical solution to the cross-platform problem at present is to use a combination of all the above. For example, you can allow Microsoft Word for Windows users to put Word documents on the Web server so long as they also create PostScript copies for UNIX viewing. Of course, users should use word processor templates and conversion filters to generate HTML wherever possible. Until the next iteration of HTML, this solution is acceptable only for documents without a lot of graphics.

This use of multiple formats is currently a particular headache for the maintainer of the data. Each form of the document must be created from the original. For instance, a document created in Microsoft Word must be saved as a Word file, printed to a file in PostScript and, potentially, stored as an HTML document. The HTML form can be created by using a program to convert the Word file to HTML or by using some Word macros to create an HTML document. Several HTML authoring programs and conversion utilities are discussed in chapter 10, "HTML Editors and Tools."

Part II

Setting Up a Web Server

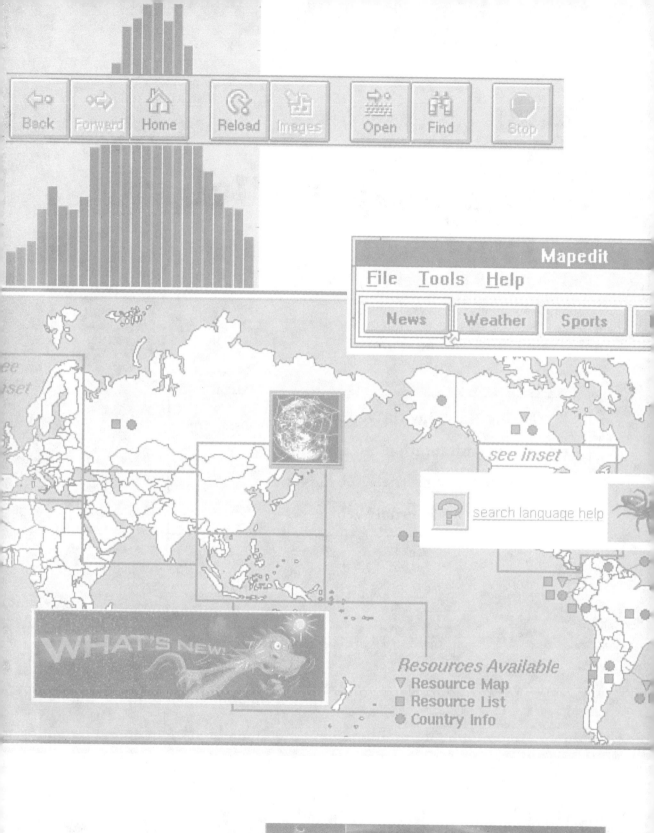

Chapter 5

Getting Started with Web Servers

This chapter takes you through the process of getting a Web server up and running for the first time under UNIX or Microsoft Windows. Both servers come with default configuration files that get your server up and running quickly. While the information in this chapter is geared primarily toward NCSA's UNIX server and a closely related Windows server, the principles and terminology you learn are generally applicable to any platform.

The information presented in this chapter shows you how to install and run the server for the first time. It does not cover many details of server configuration; these are included in chapter 6, "Server Configuration."

Specifically, you learn the following for both UNIX and Windows:

- How to install the server software included with this book

- How to start and stop the server

- How to use the server's command line options

- How to tune your system and troubleshoot common problems

- Where key files and directories are located

- Where to put your home page

Overview of Web Servers

NCSA (National Center for Supercomputing Applications) developed the UNIX server software included with this book. This Web server is one of the

WebmasterCD

most popular ones on the Internet. Since the original NCSA server for UNIX, various authors have ported the server to other platforms or based their work on NCSA's server. Table 5.1 lists these servers. This chapter focuses on the NCSA server and a closely related server, Windows httpd. Most of the principles and terminology covered here are the same for NCSA-based servers running on any platform.

Table 5.1 Servers Closely Related to NCSA's	
Platform	**Internet address**
UNIX	**http://hoohoo.ncsa.uiuc.edu/docs/Overview.html**
Windows	**http://www.alisa.com/win-httpd/**
OS/2	**ftp://ftp.netcom.com/pub/kfan/overview.html**
Mac	**http://www2.uth.tmc.edu/machttp_info.html**

Many other Web servers exist; the principles covered in the next few chapters are applicable to more than just the NCSA servers. You can obtain a list of popular Web servers from CERN at **http://info.cern.ch/hypertext/WWW/Daemon/Overview.html**. This page also contains information about writing your own server in C or perl. Table 5.2 lists free and commercial Web servers for various platforms.

Table 5.2 Free Web Servers for Various Platforms		
Product	**Platform(s)**	**Description**
CERN httpd	UNIX, VAX/VMS	Features proxy server and document caching
http://info.cern.ch/hypertext/WWW/Daemon/overview.html		
Global Access	SCO UNIX	Commercial from SCO
http://www.sco.com/Products/Datasheets/gap.html		
GN	UNIX	Combination Gopher/Web server
ftp://ftp.acns.nwu.edu/pub/gn/		
HTTP for VM	VM	Web server for IBM mainframes
http://ua1vm.ua.edu/~troth/rickvmsw/rickvmsw.html		

Product	Platform(s)	Description
HTTPS for NT **ftp://emwac.ed.ac.uk/pub/https/**	Windows NT	Runs as Windows NT service
NCSA httpd **http://hoohoo.ncsa.uiuc.edu/docs/Overview.html**	UNIX	All-purpose feature-rich server
Netsite **http://home.mcom.com/MCOM/products_docs/server.html**	UNIX	Commercial from Netscape Communications Corp.
Plexus **http://www.bsdi.com/server/doc/plexus.html**	UNIX	Server written in perl
WebWorks **http://www.quadralay.com/products/products.html#gwhis-server**	UNIX, Windows NT	Commercial from Quadralay

Windows httpd

WebmasterCD

Windows httpd is included with this book, and is one of the easiest Web servers to install. *HTTPD* stands for *Hypertext Transfer Protocol Daemon,* which is simply a type of information server that uses the HTTP protocol. It features simple installation and a wide variety of useful features, including:

- Low memory consumption and fast operation

- True multithreaded operation for supporting multiple simultaneous requests

- Ready to run "right out of the box"

- Compatible with nearly all Web browsers and Windows TCP/IP packages

- Automatic directory indexing for file serving

- Script support using DOS BAT files and Visual Basic

- Support for graphical usage statistics using VBStats

- Support for fill-in forms and imagemaps

- Built-in diagnostics

The only feature lacking in the Windows httpd that is found in the UNIX version of NCSA httpd (and the OS/2 port) is support for *server-side includes,* which allows HTML pages to include certain elements, such as date and time, that are generated on-the-fly. However, anything you can do with server-side includes you can also do with *CGI scripts,* which are supported by the Windows httpd. CGI scripts allow the Web server to interact with other applications, such as databases. Chapter 12, "Scripts," gives more in-depth coverage of server-side includes and CGI scripts.

NCSA httpd for UNIX

NCSA's Web server for UNIX was written first, and later ported to Windows and other platforms by various authors. The server source code and executables for several popular platforms are included in this book, along with an overview of the installation process. Most of the later material in this book covering scripts and advanced Web applications is based on the UNIX server because of the power of the UNIX operating system.

Getting Started with Windows httpd

This section is a tutorial on running Windows httpd, from copying the necessary files to starting the server. The next section contains detailed information on configuration.

Requirements

In order to use Windows httpd, your computer must meet certain system and network requirements. In addition, you should already be familiar with using Windows.

System Requirements

As discussed in chapter 3, "Creating a Home Page on the Internet," the recommended configuration for a busy Web server is at least a 486/66 with 8M RAM running Windows 3.1 or Windows for Workgroups. If you plan to use the Visual Basic script support built into Windows httpd, you must also have the Visual Basic run-time library VBRUN300.DLL, which is included on the WebmasterCD.

Network Requirements

In order to run any Web server and most client software, your computer must be configured to speak TCP/IP over a network or SLIP/PPP connection. If you can already run Mosaic, Netscape, or another browser that uses TCP/IP, no additional configuration is needed to run your Web server. If not, you will have to get one of these browsers running first. Information on how to do this is available in dozens of books, including *Using Mosaic* and *Special Edition Using the Internet,* Second Edition, from Que.

> **Note**
>
> Web servers require a true SLIP or PPP connection because your server must have its own IP address. You can't run a server using a SLIP emulator, such as the Internet Adapter or TwinSock. Programs that work with true SLIP/PPP connections include the shareware Trumpet Winsock (included on the WebmasterCD) and NetManage Chameleon.

If you're setting up a full-time Web server, you need a full-time connection to your Internet service provider. This can be a dial-up line, so long as the server is always connected (obviously, you only want to do this with a local provider). Dedicated access costs from $150 to $400 per month for a connection using 28.8 kbps modems. See chapter 3, "Creating a Home Page on the Internet," for more information on connecting to the Internet.

> **Tip**
>
> You can provide Internet connectivity to several machines on a network via a single dial-up connection by using a *dial-up router* such as the Rockwell NetHopper (**http:/ /www.rns.com/**). This makes a SLIP/PPP modem connection appear as a regular leased line to the Internet.

If you're setting up a part-time Web server for limited use, you don't need a full-time connection, but you do need a *static IP address* so that your server always has the same address. Some providers assign IP addresses dynamically, which means that your address changes every time you log into the service provider. This kind of connection is useful only for very limited experimental purposes because users must frequently be told the server's address.

Installation

Windows httpd is included on WebmasterCD.

WebmasterCD

> **Note**
>
> Windows httpd is free for personal and education use. It is included with this book for your convenience; however, by buying the book, you have not purchased the software in any way. No rights have been rented, leased, or assigned to you. For more information on WebmasterCD, see the license agreement and disclaimer opposite the CD at the back of the book. The Windows httpd license agreement is distributed with the software as LEGAL.HTM. Commercial users must pay a small fee after 30 days, which is described in the license agreement.

To install Windows httpd, follow these steps:

1. Create a new directory HTTPD on your hard drive (for example, C:\HTTPD). You must use this name for the installation.

2. Unzip the Windows httpd using your favorite file extraction utility and be sure to preserve the directory structure. If you don't preserve the directories, Windows httpd will not run correctly. If you use PKUNZIP, the command to use is `pkunzip d:\www\whttpd\whttpd14.zip c:\httpd -d` assuming WebmasterCD is in your D: drive and you are installing to C:.

   If you use a Windows based utility to unzip the files, be sure to preserve the directories. For example, in WinZip 5.5, you must select the Use Directory Names option in the Extract dialog box.

3. Edit your C:\AUTOEXEC.BAT file and add a line to set the TZ variable to your time zone. This line should include your time zone abbreviation, the number of hours from Greenwich Mean Time (GMT), and the abbreviation for daylight time in your zone if your state is on daylight time. For example:

   ```
   SET TZ=CST5CDT (Central Standard Time Zone)
   ```

   Table 5.3 lists time zone abbreviations in the United States. If you don't know the abbreviation for your locale, try one of these Web pages that offer interactive time zone information: **httpd//www.bsdi.com/date** or **httpd//hibp.ecse.rpi.edu/cgi-bin/tzconvert**.

Table 5.3 Settings for the Time Zone Variable in the United States	
Time Zone	**Setting**
Eastern Standard Time	EST4EDT

Time Zone	Setting
Central Standard Time	CST5CDT
Mountain Standard Time	MST6MDT
Pacific Standard Time	PST7PDT

You need to reboot for the AUTOEXEC.BAT change to take effect.

That's all there is to it. Your Web server is now ready to run.

Starting the Server

Assuming you have a SLIP or network connection to the Internet, simply follow these steps to start your server:

1. If you're using SLIP or PPP over a dial-up account, dial and log into your account as you normally would to run Mosaic or another browser. Make a note of your IP (Internet address, for example, **167.142.100.115**).

2. From the Windows Program Manager, create an icon pointing to C:\HTTPD\HTTPD.EXE.

   Tip

   You can quickly create an icon by dragging the file from File Manager into a Program Manager group.

3. To start the server, double-click the Server icon. The Server icon appears on your desktop showing the server initializing and then idle (waiting for connections).

   Tip

   If you plan to run your server whenever Windows is running, copy the WinSock and Server icons into the Program Manager Startup group. The WinSock icon should come first so Windows will start it first.

   Figure 5.1 shows Windows httpd after it's been opened.

4. To test your server, start your Web browser and open a connection to **http://<your IP>/** or **http://localhost/**. For example, if your IP is

167.142.100.115, select **F**ile, **O**pen URL in Mosaic (or another browser) and type **http://167.142.100.115/**. If your machine also has a name, you can use this as well, such as **s115.netins.net**. If your server is running properly, you see the label on the server icon indicate httpd_active (1), where 1 is the number of active connections.

Fig. 5.1

This is Windows httpd.

If the transfer is successful, you see the server's home page in your browser. Figure 5.2 shows the default server home page in Mosaic for Windows. By default, the server's home page is in C:\HTTPD\HTDOCS\INDEX.HTM. To learn how to write your own home page, see chapter 9, "Basic HTML: Understanding Hypertext."

Fig. 5.2

The default home page for Windows httpd appears if the transfer is successful.

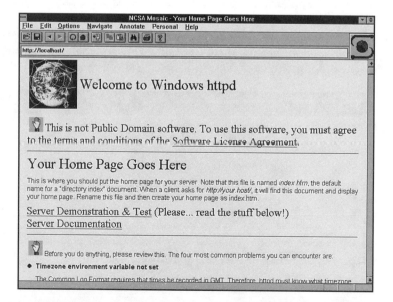

Stopping the Server

To quit running Windows httpd, double-click the Server icon and choose
Exit from the **C**ontrol menu. Alternatively, you can choose **C**lose from the
pop-up menu that appears when you click the Server icon.

> **Caution**
>
> To prevent Windows from locking up, always close all WinSock applications, like the
> Web server, before closing the WinSock program itself.

Troubleshooting and System Tuning

This section contains descriptions of many common problems and the appropriate solutions. If you are having performance problems with your server,
make sure the following items have been addressed.

Broken WinSock

A common problem with running Windows httpd is that some WinSock
software, which is at the heart of your TCP/IP connection, is not fully compliant with the Windows Sockets 1.1 standard used by Windows httpd. Fortunately, Windows httpd provides a workaround. Stop the server and restart it
by using the `-n` option on the command line `C:\HTTPD\HTTPD.EXE -n`. This
disables multithreaded operation, which means the server will answer only
one request at a time, but allows it to work with incompatible WinSock
programs.

To start the server with the `-n` option using the server icon, click the icon and
choose **F**ile, **P**roperties in Program Manager to edit the command line.

> **Tip**
>
> If you're using the shareware Trumpet Winsock version 2.0a, you probably need
> to use the `-n` option with HTTPD.EXE. In Trumpet version 2.0b, this is no longer
> necessary. If you're using version 2.0a, you should upgrade to 2.0b, which is on
> WebmasterCD.

Time Zone Not Set

The time zone must be set for proper access logging. Make sure your time
zone variable is set correctly in your AUTOEXEC.BAT file, as described in the
previous section.

CommandEnvSize

Certain pages in the documentation and applications you may write require DOS scripts. These will fail if you don't have enough DOS environment space for DOS sessions running under Windows. If you're having problems running DOS scripts, add this line to the [NonWindowsApp] section of your SYSTEM.INI file:

```
CommandEnvSize=8192
```

> **Note**
>
> For changes to your Windows SYSTEM.INI and WIN.INI to take effect, you must restart Windows.

Getting Started with NCSA httpd for UNIX

This section provides an overview of installing NCSA httpd. The installation varies from system to system, and probably requires system administrator (root) privileges. If you're not familiar with UNIX, you should find someone who is before attempting the installation. Failure to understand all the implications of various steps in the installation process can either cause the server not to run properly or, if the server is on a network, can cause serious security problems.

> **Note**
>
> NCSA httpd is in the public domain. It is included with this book for your convenience, but by buying the book, you have not purchased the software in any way. No rights have been rented, leased, or assigned to you. For more information on WebmasterCD, see the license agreement and disclaimer opposite the CD at the back of the book. The NCSA httpd license agreement is distributed with the software in the README file.

Requirements

NCSA httpd can run on any standard UNIX system connected to a TCP/IP network. Because TCP/IP networking capabilities are built into UNIX machines, virtually any UNIX workstation on a network can run a Web server. If your machine is already connected to the Internet, you can run a public Web server without any additional hardware or software. If you're not connected to the Internet, you can still run a Web server on your internal network for use as a company bulletin board system. See chapter 4, "Creating an Internal Web Server."

Hardware requirements depend on how much traffic your server must handle. A low-end workstation does fine as a simple document server, but more horsepower is required to run large numbers of scripts or other programs in the background. No matter what your application, be sure you have plenty of disk space for all the documents you might want to put on the server.

Installation

You can install NCSA httpd in one of two ways, depending on your system. If your system is one of the many popular UNIX systems listed below, the software has already been compiled and you can run it immediately. If your system is not listed, you need to compile the software before running it.

Precompiled Versions

If your machine is one of the several listed in this paragraph, you can obtain precompiled software from WebmasterCD or from NCSA's FTP site, which saves you the effort of compiling. If you don't have a C compiler, this is your only option. Precompiled executables of NCSA httpd for UNIX are available for workstations from:

SGI

DEC (MIPS and AXP)

IBM (RS/6000)

Sun

HP

All of these versions are on WebmasterCD. You can obtain version upgrades from **ftp://ftp.ncsa.uiuc.edu/Web/httpd/Unix/ncsa_httpd/ current/**.

If your UNIX machine is one of the platforms listed above, follow these instructions to install it:

1. Copy the software for your machine from WebmasterCD or from the NCSA FTP site.

2. Uncompress the software. (Example: `uncompress httpd_hp.tar.Z`.)

3. Unpack the software into its various directories using the `tar` command. (Example: `tar xvf httpd_hp.tar`.)

4. Edit the configuration files in the conf directory (see chapter 6, "Server Configuration"). You don't need to edit the configuration files to use the default settings.

5. Move the software into place by copying all the directories into the server root directory defined in the httpd configuration file. By default, ServerRoot is /usr/local/etc/httpd. (Example: `mv httpd_1.3 /usr/local/etc/httpd.`)

Caution

If you're installing the software on a network-connected machine, make sure you let your network administrator know what you're doing in order to avoid potential problems.

You have now successfully installed the server. Proceed to the section, "Starting the Server," to start the server on your machine.

Note

The documentation for NCSA httpd for UNIX is located online at **http://hoohoo.ncsa.uiuc.edu/docs/Overview.html**. You can also obtain a compressed version of all the documentation in HTML format from **ftp://ftp.ncsa.uiuc.edu/Web/httpd/Unix/ncsa_httpd/current/httpd_docs.tar.Z**.

Compiling

If precompiled software is not available for your machine or you feel more comfortable compiling the software for your particular machine, you can get the NCSA source code and make files from **ftp://ftp.ncsa.uiuc.edu/Web/httpd/Unix/ncsa_httpd/current/httpd_source.tar.Z**. Every platform has its peculiarities when compiling C code, so previous experience compiling C code on your platform is highly desirable.

To compile the server, follow these instructions:

1. Copy the source distribution to your machine from WebmasterCD or from the NCSA FTP site.

2. Uncompress the software. (Example: `uncompress httpd_source.tar.Z.`)

3. Unpack the software into its various directories using the `tar` command. (Example: `tar xvf httpd_source.tar.`)

4. Edit the make files (named "Makefile") in the src, cgi-src, and support directories. Follow the directions in the make files to specify the proper settings for your machine.

5. Compile the software by running the make files in each directory. (Example: `Makefile`.)

6. Edit the configuration files in the conf directory (see chapter 6, "Server Configuration"). You don't need to edit the configuration files to use the default settings.

7. Move the software into place by copying all the directories into the server root directory defined in the httpd configuration file. By default, ServerRoot is /usr/local/etc/httpd. (Example: `mv httpd_1.3 /usr/local/etc/httpd`.)

If all goes well, you are now ready to start the server.

Starting, Stopping, and Restarting the Server

Starting and stopping the server is the same as most other UNIX programs.

Starting the Server

To start the server, simply change to the server root directory and run the httpd executable. If you haven't changed any of the default settings in the configuration files, type:

```
cd /usr/local/etc/httpd
httpd
```

> **Note**
>
> To run the server in the default configuration, you must be root because, by default, the server runs on a protected port, port 80. To change the port, see chapter 6, "Server Configuration."

Stopping the Server

To stop the server, use the UNIX `kill` command. To do this, you must know the server's process ID (PID). By default, the server writes its PID to a file named "logs/httpd.pid" in the server root directory when started. If you're using the default settings, type:

```
cd /usr/local/etc/httpd
kill `cat logs/httpd.pid`
```

II

Setting Up a Web Server

Alternatively, you can obtain the PID by listing the active processes and searching for httpd. For example, this command will return the server's PID:

```
ps -ef ¦ grep httpd
```

To test the server, create an htdocs directory in the server root directory. Next, create a test document in this directory. The test document doesn't have to be an HTML file. For starters, just create a simple text file named "test.txt." The following example demonstrates how to create the htdocs directory and simple text file for the default configuration.

```
cd /usr/local/etc/httpd
mkdir htdocs
vi htdocs/test.txt
```

The final line in this example uses the vi editor to create the sample text file. You can replace it with your preferred editor.

After you've created the test file, open your browser and go to URL **http:// <your IP or machine name>/test.txt**. Your simple text file will be displayed. To begin writing HTML files, see chapter 9, "Basic HTML: Understanding Hypertext."

Restarting the Server

NCSA httpd provides a convenient way to restart the server without bringing it to a full stop. This is useful when you have made changes to the configuration files, which take effect when the server is restarted. To restart the server, use the kill -1 option:

```
kill -1 ´cat logs/httpd.pid´
```

This is the same as stopping and then starting the server again, but it's simpler and faster.

What's in the Server

This section gives you an overview of the files and directories that come with the server. NCSA httpd for UNIX and Windows httpd are very similar; the following discussion is applicable to both servers. In addition, servers for many other platforms are similar to the NCSA server, and therefore are configured similarly. This section explains the command line options and directory structures in both NCSA httpd for UNIX and Windows httpd. Chapter 6, "Server Configuration," explains server configuration in detail.

Files and Directories

This section contains information on the files and directories included as part of the Web server. Because Windows httpd and NCSA httpd are very similar, the files and directories common to both servers are covered first.

Files Common to NCSA httpd and Windows httpd

After you install the server, you will find several directories underneath the server root directory (C:\HTTPD or /usr/local/etc/httpd). These include:

- cgi-bin

- cgi-src

- conf

- icons

- logs

- support

The cgi-bin directory is where all scripts will be placed. NCSA httpd contains many sample forms and scripts to help you get started with forms and scripts. For more information on forms and scripts, see chapter 11, "Forms," and chapter 12, "Scripts."

The cgi-src directory contains source code used to implement script capabilities. You should not need to modify anything in this directory, but it may be a useful reference.

The conf directory contains all the server configuration files. These include:

- httpd.conf

- srm.conf

- access.conf

- mime.types

Under Windows, the configuration file names are truncated to conform to the DOS file-naming convention (eight characters and a three-letter extension maximum). *Httpd.conf* is the top-level server configuration file. It defines the server's name and port and points to other configuration files. *Srm.conf* is the server resource map. This provides information on the location and type of documents on the server. *Access.conf* defines who can access which directories on the server. Finally, *mime.types* associates file names with document types.

The configuration files are covered in detail in chapter 6, "Server Configuration." Before starting the server on a full-time basis, you should read the next chapter to make sure you understand all the implications of these files.

The *icons directory* contains images that may be useful to include in documents residing on your server. In the Windows version, these icons are used in the online server documentation. The icons directory also contains small GIF images that are used as file icons in server-generated directory indexes, which are covered in the next chapter.

The *logs directory* is the default location for both the error log and access log files, which record all accesses to the server. Chapter 14, "Usage Statistics and Maintaining HTML," covers log files.

The *support directory* contains several utility programs. *Htpasswd* converts document user names and passwords into a format readable by the server. Htpasswd is part of server access control, which is discussed in the next chapter. In the Windows version, the support directory also contains *WinCron*, which runs scheduled programs at specified times like the UNIX cron utility.

Additional Windows Files

In Windows httpd, four additional directories are created by default. These are listed below.

- CGI-DOS

- CGI-WIN

- HTDOCS

- VBSTATS

The CGI-DOS and CGI-WIN directories contain already written scripts that run under DOS and Windows, respectively. These can help you get started writing your own scripts. For more information on forms and scripts, see chapter 11, "Forms," and chapter 12, "Scripts."

HTDOCS is the top-level document directory by default. Normally, all HTML documents are placed under this directory. The documentation on the server itself is located in the HTTPDDOC subdirectory. By default, the server's home page is C:\HTTPD\HTDOCS\INDEX.HTM.

VBSTATS contains a utility to record and graph Web server usage statistics. For more information on usage statistics, see chapter 14, "Usage Statistics and Maintaining HTML."

Command Line Options

Both NCSA httpd for UNIX and Windows httpd can be started with command line options for various configuration and troubleshooting purposes. Two options are common to both platforms, and the rest are platform-specific.

Options Common to NCSA httpd and Windows httpd

The following options apply to both NCSA httpd and Windows httpd:

- `-d server_root_directory`

- `-f server_configuration_file`

Specifying `-d` followed by a directory name changes the location of the server root directory, which is where the server looks for the server configuration file by default. Under Windows httpd, this value defaults to C:\HTTPD. Under NCSA httpd, the default is /usr/local/etc/httpd.

> **Tip**
>
> The `-d` option is a convenient way to run multiple Web servers with different sets of configuration files and different documents. For example, you can run an internal and external Web server on the same machine by using the `-d` option to point to different sets of configuration files. To learn about running multiple Web servers on the same machine, read the "Advanced Security Topics" section of chapter 8, "Managing an Internal Web Server."

The `-f` option is similar to the `-d` option, but changes only the location of the server configuration file, not the entire server root directory. You can use this to test changes in one or more of the server configuration files without having to create an entirely new test directory.

Windows Options

Windows httpd has a few additional command line options that deal specifically with that operating system. These are listed as follows.

- ■ `-I DLL_name`

- ■ `-n`

- ■ `-r`

- ■ `-x 0xnnn`

This chapter's troubleshooting section discusses the `-n` option. The `-n` option disables multithreading to allow the server to run with network or SLIP software that does not meet the Windows Sockets 1.1 standard.

The `-r` option enables reverse DNS lookups, which causes the server to look up the name of each client that connects to the server using its IP address. By default, the server doesn't do this automatically. Reverse DNS lookups must be turned on if you're using name-based access control (see chapter 6, "Server Configuration") or if you want client names to appear in the log files (see chapter 14, "Usage Statistics and Maintaining HTML").

> **Note**
>
> VBStats, the usage statistics program that comes with Windows httpd, looks up address names when it's processing the usage log files, so you can still see address names even when the server `-r` option isn't turned on.

The `-I` option is used to load a DLL file (dynamic link library) when the server is started and keeps it loaded until the server is stopped. This option was designed for use with VBRUN300.DLL, which is used by servers using Visual Basic scripts. Without this option, the DLL is loaded and unloaded each time it is used, resulting in substantial overhead if it's used a lot.

The `-x` option is used for debugging, and is useful mainly for those very familiar with the HTTP and TCP/IP protocols.

UNIX Options

Besides `-d` and `-f`, there is only one other option under UNIX: `-v`. The `-v` option displays the current version of the server you are running

Chapter 6

Server Configuration

The previous chapter presented an overview of NCSA's server and Windows httpd. This chapter covers in detail all server configuration commands and how to use them, including those related to access control, directory indexing, and MIME types. The real power of the server is not visible at the surface. Like most other types of Internet servers, the capabilities of the server are determined by plain text configuration files that are edited by the server administrator. This chapter takes you step-by-step through each file and the wealth of possibilities.

Think of the server's four primary configuration files as a well-stocked toolbox. You can use as many or as few features as you like. If you want to get a plain-vanilla Web server up and running quickly, the configuration files require very little editing. However, the power is always there to add fancy features later.

In this chapter, you learn how to

- Set up the server's physical network parameters

- Serve documents from multiple directories

- Use and configure server-generated directory indexes

- Configure MIME types for launching viewers

- Implement password security and access control

Overview of Configuration

This chapter presents tutorials on using the server configuration files. These are at the heart of the server's real power and flexibility. The UNIX and Windows configuration files are very similar, but features available only in

Windows or UNIX are specifically noted. Table 6.1 lists the four primary server configuration files.

Table 6.1	Server Configuration Files	
UNIX	**Windows**	**Description**
httpd.conf	HTTPD.CNF	Primary server configuration file
srm.conf	SRM.CNF	Server resource map
access.conf	ACCESS.CNF	Security configuration
mime.types	MIME.TYP	Information on document types

General Principles

Making any server configuration change requires editing one or more of the server configuration files. All configuration files are simply plain ASCII text that you can modify in any text editor (Notepad, DOS EDIT, vi, and so on). All of the files follow these rules:

1. All files are case-insensitive ("ALL" is the same as "all").

2. Comment lines begin with the number sign (#). Comments must be on a line by themselves.

3. Except in the access configuration file, the order of statements is not important.

Note

File and path names in the configuration files must be given in UNIX format using the forward slash (/), even in the Windows version.

When you start the server, it reads the configuration files and loads them into memory for as long as the server is running. In order for changes made to the configuration files to take effect, you must restart the server (just the software, not the whole machine). This means that you can edit the files while the server is running without having any effect on the server. Only when the server is restarted do changes take effect.

Terminology

Many of the server configuration commands specify a path to a directory or file. This path can be one of two types, a physical or virtual path. In some cases, either can be specified.

A *virtual path* is the document path specified in a URL. In the URL **http://www.xyz.com/sales/intro.txt**, the virtual path is /sales/intro.txt. This may or may not correspond to an actual path on the server. One of the server functions is to map a virtual path to a physical path on the server. The *physical path* is the actual location on disk, such as C:\WINDOWS\MM.BMP (in Windows) or /etc/passwd (UNIX).

A physical path can either be absolute or relative. In Windows, *absolute paths* begin with a drive letter (like C:) or backslash (\). In UNIX, absolute paths begin with a forward slash (/). On both systems, *relative paths* begin with the name of a file or directory, like weddings/gowns/white.txt. Two special symbols can also be used in relative paths. A single dot (.) stands for the current directory, and two dots (..) means the parent directory. The previous example could also be written ./weddings/gowns/white.txt. The path ../birthdays points to the birthdays directory underneath the parent directory.

The Server Configuration File

The server configuration file is the main configuration file. By default, it resides in C:\HTTPD\CONF\HTTPD.CNF or /usr/local/etc/httpd/conf/httpd.conf. This is the starting place for configuration. It contains information about the server itself, the locations of log files, and the locations of other configuration files. This section shows you how to configure the server's primary configuration file.

> **Tip**
>
> It is a good idea to make backup copies of all configuration files before you begin editing.

Server Information

Several types of server information are specified in the server configuration file. These include parameters directly affecting the server's operation such as the server's port and timeout. Elements in the server configuration file used in error reporting include the server and administrator name.

II

Setting Up a Web Server

To define basic server information, you use the following directives:

- `ServerType` (UNIX only)

- `Port`

- `TimeOut`

- `User` (UNIX only)

- `Group` (UNIX only)

- `PidFile` (UNIX only)

- `ServerAdmin`

- `ServerRoot`

- `ServerName`

Setting the Server Mode (UNIX only)

You can run the UNIX server in one of two modes: standalone or inetd. In *standalone mode,* the server continues to listen for and process document requests as long as it's running. In *inetd mode,* the server is controlled by a program called inetd, which provides general Internet services under UNIX. In inetd mode, the server is started and stopped by inetd for each document request. To specify the server's mode, use the `ServerType` directive:

ServerType

Usage: `ServerType {standalone¦inetd}`

Example: `ServerType standalone`

Default: `standalone`

> **Tip**
>
> Running under inetd is not recommended because inetd must load the httpd program each time a new request is received, which is very inefficient.

Setting the Server Port

In order for your Web server to run properly, it must know what port to listen to for information. A *port* is somewhat like a CB channel, but it is implemented in software rather than physical channels. All Internet traffic to the server is carried on a single network cable; there are not really multiple channels. Every information packet contains a destination port number that is read by the receiving machine so that the data can be sent to the right program. Different types of Internet traffic are carried on different ports. Table 6.2 lists commonly used Internet ports. To set the server's port, use the `Port` directive:

Port

Usage: `Port number`

Example: `Port 80`

Default: `port 80`

The `Port` directive sets the port number that the server listens to for incoming requests. Most Web (HTTP) traffic is on port 80, but it is possible to set the port to any number from 0 to 65535. Ports under 1024 are reserved for the most common types of Internet traffic. In the UNIX version, only `root` can run the server on a port less than 1024. Experimental Web servers are often run on port 8080.

> **Note**
>
> Some network routers are configured by default to allow all incoming and outgoing Internet traffic on ports greater than 8000. It is very easy, therefore, for a PC or workstation on an internal network to bypass Internet security mechanisms by running a Web server on a high-numbered port. See chapter 8, "Managing an Internal Web Server."

Table 6.2 Commonly Used Internet Ports

Service	Port
FTP	21
Telnet	23
NNTP	119
SMTP	25
HTTP	80

(continues)

II

Setting Up a Web Server

Table 6.2 Continued	
Service	**Port**
Gopher	70
IRC	6667
Talk	517
Finger	79

Setting the Server's Timeout

All Internet data is sent in short bursts called *packets*. By breaking up each transmission into small packets, it is necessary to resend only a small amount of information (one packet) when there is a problem with the data transmission. Normally, a client receives a steady stream of packets from an Internet server. However, if the stream is interrupted for a significant time interval, the client or server can *time out* and abort the connection. To set the server's timeout interval, use the TimeOut directive:

TimeOut

Usage: TimeOut *seconds*

Example: TimeOut 30

Default: 30 seconds

The TimeOut directive is used primarily to facilitate more reliable connections over slow or busy links. TimeOut specifies the maximum time allowed between sending or receiving successive data packets. If, due to a busy or slow link, successive data packets are not sent or received within the allotted time, the server times out and reports an error. It may be necessary to set the timeout to 60 seconds to accommodate slow PPP or SLIP dial-up links on either the server or client end.

Setting the Server's User and Group (UNIX only)

In order for the server to be able to handle multiple document requests simultaneously, it runs a copy of itself for each separate document request. This is called *spawning child processes,* and the server itself is the parent. The child processes do not run under the same user and group names as the server itself, but rather as the user and group specified in the server configuration file. It is desirable to run the child processes as a nonprivileged user to prevent accidentally modifying any files, which could happen during script processing, for example.

To set the user name and group name under which the server processes documents, use the `User` and `Group` directives. In order to use these directives, the server must be run by `root` in standalone mode.

User

Usage: `User username`

Example: `User nobody`

Default: `User -1` (nobody)

The `User` directive specifies the user name under which requests for documents are processed. A special user name called `nobody` is often used for this purpose. As the name implies, `nobody` has no special privileges.

> **Note**
>
> In order for nobody to read documents and send them back to clients, documents must have world read access (and preferably not world write because this would allow anyone, including nobody, to modify files).

Group

Usage: `Group groupname`

Example: `Group webadmin`

Default: `Group -1`

The `Group` directive functions identically to the `User` directive, except that it specifies the group name under which requests for documents are processed instead of the user name. You can use the `Group` directive to do many of the same things as the `User` directive, limiting access to documents to a certain group rather than to a certain user. For example, all document authors can belong to a group `webauthor`. Because their documents are designed to be read only through the Web server, you can set the file permissions to allow group read but not world read access. You can then set the `Group` directive to `webauthor` to make the documents accessible through the Web server.

Logging the Server's Process ID (UNIX only)

When the Web server is started, it is given a process ID to identify it. You must use the process ID to stop or restart the server, so it is handy to keep a

II

Setting Up a Web Server

record of it. You can always obtain the process ID by looking for `httpd` in the list of active processes on the server machine (`ps -ef ¦ grep httpd`), but it is often more convenient to keep a record of the ID in a file. You can do this with the `PidFile` directive.

PidFile

Usage: `PidFile file`

Example: `PidFile dont_forget/where_is_the_pid.pid`

Default: `logs/httpd.pid`

Any time the server is started, it saves the process ID number in the file specified by `PidFile`. The specified path may be absolute or relative to the server root directory described by `ServerRoot`. To stop the server, you can simply type:

> **kill `cat *PidFile*`**

> ### Tip
>
> To restart the server without separate stop and start operations, use the `kill -1` command. This command causes the server to reread the configuration files, but to keep the same process ID.

Naming the Server

In certain kinds of document transactions, such as error reporting, the server reports its own name to the client. Normally, the server looks up the name of the server machine through system calls that use the Domain Name Service (DNS). If DNS is unavailable, however, only the server's numerical IP address is available. You can use the `ServerName` directive to specify a name for the server in this situation.

ServerName

Usage: `ServerName address`

Example: `ServerName www.xyz.com`

Default: httpd will look up the name through system calls

You can also use the `ServerName` directive to bypass DNS even if it's available. This allows the server to report a DNS alias instead of its real name. For example, a server's real name might be "ladybug.widgets.com," but is also known as "www.widgets.com" to DNS. When the server makes system calls to find its name, DNS returns the primary name, "ladybug," instead of the alias, "www." If you use the ServerName directive, you can override DNS and use www.widgets.com instead.

In addition to setting the server's name, you can set the name of the server administrator used for error reporting purposes. Typically, an e-mail address is given so users have someone to contact when errors occur. The ServerAdmin directive sets the name of the server administrator.

ServerAdmin

Usage: ServerAdmin *address*

Example: ServerAdmin webadmin@www.xyz.com

Default: None

The address specified in ServerAdmin does not have to be an e-mail address, but this is often the most convenient method of receiving error reports. This way, if a client requests a document to which access is forbidden or experiences some other problem, the server returns an error to the browser containing the server administrator's e-mail address. The user can then direct questions to the administrator via e-mail.

Locations of Other Configuration Files

Because the server configuration file is the main configuration file, it defines the locations of all the other configuration files, including the global access configuration file, server resource map, and MIME types configuration file.

You can specify the names of these files as absolute system paths or relative to the server root directory by using the ServerRoot directive.

ServerRoot

Usage: ServerRoot *directory*

Example: ServerRoot /testweb/httpd

Default: /usr/local/etc/httpd (UNIX), C:\HTTPD (Windows)

The ServerRoot directive specifies the path to the top-level directory containing the configuration, support, and document directories and files. You can override this directive with the -d command line option.

The following directives define the locations of the other configuration files:

- `AccessConfig`

- `ResourceConfig`

- `TypesConfig`

AccessConfig

Usage: `AccessConfig` *file*

Example: `AccessConfig /private/access_control.conf`

Default: `conf/access.conf` (UNIX), `CONF/ACCESS.CNF` (Windows)

The `AccessConfig` directive points to the global *access configuration file,* which defines allowable access to all server documents and features. The specified path may be absolute or relative to `ServerRoot`.

ResourceConfig

Usage: `ResourceConfig` *file*

Example: `ResourceConfig /admin/srm.conf`

Default: `conf/srm.conf` (UNIX), `CONF/SRM.CNF` (Windows)

The `ResourceConfig` directive points to the *server resource map file,* which defines where documents are located and controls special document-related options. The specified path may be absolute or relative to `ServerRoot`.

TypesConfig

Usage: `TypesConfig` *file*

Example: `TypesConfig /admin/mime.types`

Default: `conf/mime.types` (UNIX), `CONF/MIME.TYP` (Windows)

The `TypesConfig` directive specifies the location of the *MIME type configuration file,* which associates file extensions (TXT) with MIME (Multimedia Internet Mail Exchange) types reported by the server. The specified path may be absolute or relative to `ServerRoot`.

Locations of Log Files

NCSA httpd for UNIX and Windows httpd can log every document access and every error. You can use several different utilities to collate and graph these statistics after they are collected. See chapter 14, "Usage Statistics and Maintaining HTML."

Two directives specify the locations of log files:

- ErrorLog

- TransferLog

ErrorLog

Usage: ErrorLog *file*

Example: ErrorLog /errors/web.err

Default: logs/error.log

The ErrorLog directive specifies the location of the file that records server errors, including:

- Documents that could not be found

- Timeouts due to slow communication links

- Connections that have been interrupted

- Script errors

- Invalid configuration files

The path to the file specified in the ErrorLog directive can be absolute or relative to the server root directory as specified by ServerRoot. For more information on the error log file, see chapter 14 "Usage Statistics and Maintaining HTML."

TransferLog

Usage: TransferLog *file*

Example: TransferLog /access/web.log

Default: logs/access.log

The TransferLog directive contains the path to the *server access log,* which records all documents transferred from the server. The file can be an absolute path name or relative to ServerRoot. For each transfer, the access log records the date and time, remote host name or IP address, and the name of the document requested. For more information on the transfer log file, see chapter 14, "Usage Statistics and Maintaining HTML."

> **Note**
>
> On a busy server, the transfer log can grow large very quickly—up to several mega-bytes per day. In order to conserve disk space, you can disable the transfer log by specifying that the log file be written to /dev/null, the UNIX equivalent of a black hole.

Identity Checking

One final directive in the server configuration file does not fall neatly into any other category. You can use the `IdentityCheck` directive to determine the user names of those accessing server documents.

`IdentityCheck` (UNIX only)

Usage: `IdentityCheck {on¦off}`

Example: `IdentityCheck off`

Default: `off`

The `IdentityCheck` directive determines whether the server will attempt to find the user name of the remote client for every document requested. The remote user name is only available if identd is running at the remote site. Unless you really need to know user names, leave this option off as it requires considerable overhead.

> **Caution**
>
> Remote identity checking is intended to be for information purposes only. It is not secure.

Example Server Configuration File

The following server configuration file for Windows demonstrates how you can use all the relevant directives together.

> **Note**
>
> The example files in this chapter will work for Windows httpd 1.4 and the previous release, version 1.3.

```
#-------------------------------------------------------------------
#
#    HTTPD.CNF
#
# Main server configuration for NCSA WinHttpd V1.3 (Windows)
#
# NOTE: path defaults are relative to the server's installation
#       directory (ServerRoot). Paths should be given in Unix
#       format (using '/').
#
# Bob Denny <rdenny@netcom.com> 13-Aug-94
#
# Modified by David M. Chandler 26-Jan-95
#
#-------------------------------------------------------------------

# ServerRoot: The directory the server's config, error, and log files
# are kept in. This can also be specified on the startup command line.
#
# Format: ServerRoot <path>
#
ServerRoot c:/httpd/

# ServerAdmin: Your address, where problems with the server should be
# e-mailed.
#
# Format: ServerAdmin <email addr>
#
ServerAdmin webadmin@xyz.com

# ServerName allows you to set a host name which is sent back to clients for
# your server if it's different than the one the program would get (i.e. use
# "www" instead of the host's real name). Make sure your DNS is set up to
# alias the name to your system!
#
# Format: ServerName <domain name>
#
ServerName www.xyz.com

# Port: The port the server listens to. 80 is standard for Web
# servers.
#
Port 80

# Timeout: The timeout applied to all network operations. If you are on
# a slow network, or are using a SLIP or PPP connection, you might try
# increasing this to 60 sec.
#
# Format: Timeout nn     (seconds)
#
Timeout 45

# ErrorLog: The location of the error log file. If this does not start
# with / or a drive spec (recommended!), ServerRoot is prepended to it.
#
# Format: ErrorLog <path/file>
```

```
#
ErrorLog logs/error.log

# TransferLog: The location of the transfer log file. If this does not
# start with / or a drive spec (recommended!), ServerRoot is prepended
# to it.
#
# Format: TransferLog <path/file>
#
TransferLog logs/access.log

# AccessConfig: The location of the global access configuration file.
#
# Format: AccessConfig <path/file>
#
AccessConfig conf/access.cnf

# ResourceConfig: The location of the server resource map.
#
# Format: ResourceConfig <path/file>
#
ResourceConfig conf/srm.cnf

# TypesConfig: The location of the MIME types file.
#
# Format: TypesConfig <path/file>
#
TypesConfig conf/mime.typ
```

MIME Types

Multimedia Internet Mail Exchange (MIME) types provide a way for Web
browsers to automatically launch a viewing program associated with the file
received. For example, the server MIME types file maps an image file in the
JPEG format that has the extension JPG to type "image/jpeg." This type is
then sent to the browser, which you can configure to launch a JPEG viewer
when it receives a file of type "image/jpeg." You can use MIME types to
launch word processors, spreadsheets, or any program that resides on the
client's machine, as well as to launch multimedia viewers.

The MIME Types Configuration File

A list of registered MIME types is contained in the MIME types configuration
file that comes with the server. By default, this file is named
"C:\HTTPD\CONF\MIME.TYP" (Windows) or "/usr/local/etc/httpd/conf/
mime.types" (UNIX).

Each line in the MIME types file contains one MIME type/subtype and a list
of file extensions to map to that type. Image, audio, and video types launch
their respective multimedia viewers. Text types are for documents written in

plain text, but can also be interpreted using formatted tags (like HTML). Application types are defined for most everything else. Subtypes containing x- are experimental types. The following is the standard MIME types file that comes with NCSA httpd.

```
# Edited by Bob Denny <rdenny@netcom.com>
# 07-May-1994
# Per comments received from Kevin Altis
#
application/activemessage
application/andrew-inset
application/applefile
application/atomicmail
application/dca-rft
application/dec-dx
application/mac-binhex40
application/macwriteii
application/msword              doc
application/news-message-id
application/news-transmission
application/octet-stream        bin
application/oda                 oda
application/pdf                 pdf
application/postscript          ai eps ps
application/remote-printing
application/rtf                 rtf
application/slate
application/mif                 mif
application/wita
application/wordperfect5.1
application/x-csh               csh
application/x-dvi               dvi
application/x-hdf               hdf
application/x-latex             latex ltx
application/x-netcdf            nc cdf
application/x-sh                sh
application/x-tcl               tcl
application/x-tex               tex
application/x-texinfo           texinfo texi txi
application/x-troff             t tr roff
application/x-troff-man         man
application/x-troff-me          me
application/x-troff-ms          ms
application/x-wais-source       src
application/zip                 zip
application/x-bcpio             bcpio
application/x-cpio              cpio
application/x-gtar              gtar
application/x-shar              shar
application/x-sv4cpio           sv4cpio
application/x-sv4crc            sv4crc
application/tar                 tar
application/x-ustar             ustar
application/x-lzh               lzh
application/x-gzip              gz
```

```
audio/basic                      au snd
audio/x-aiff                     aif aiff aifc
audio/wav                        wav
image/gif                        gif
image/ief                        ief
image/jpeg                       jpeg jpg jpe
image/tiff                       tiff tif
image/x-cmu-raster               ras
image/x-portable-anymap          pnm
image/x-portable-bitmap          pbm
image/x-portable-graymap         pgm
image/x-portable-pixmap          ppm
image/x-rgb                      rgb
image/x-xbitmap                  xbm
image/x-xpixmap                  xpm
image/x-xwindowdump              xwd
message/external-body
message/news
message/partial
message/rfc822
multipart/alternative
multipart/appledouble
multipart/digest
multipart/mixed
multipart/parallel
text/html                        html htm
text/plain                       txt log
text/richtext                    rtx
text/tab-separated-values        tsv
text/x-setext                    etx
video/mpeg                       mpeg mpg mpe
video/quicktime                  qt mov
video/msvideo                    avi
video/x-sgi-movie                movie
```

Creating New MIME Types

In some cases, you may wish to create a new MIME type in order to automatically launch an application not defined in the standard configuration file. This is frequently useful on an internal Web server, where the appropriate viewer application for the new type is available on the network. However, it is less useful on a public Web server because browsers have to be specially configured for your new type. Typically, this means you have to tell users what the new type is and provide the viewer application. This is time-consuming and inconvenient; therefore, use new MIME types sparingly on public Web servers.

You can use one of several methods to create new MIME types for document types not defined in the default MIME types configuration file. You can edit the MIME types file directly but this is not recommended. A better method is to use the AddType directive in the server resource map (covered in the next section) to create a new MIME type for all documents on the server.

In addition, you can add MIME types for files only in certain directories by using the `AddType` directive in *local directory access configuration files*. The "Local Directory ACFs" section later in this chapter covers this type of file.

> **Note**
>
> Do not modify the MIME types file provided with the server, because you might accidentally modify standard MIME types. If you do edit the MIME types file directly, be sure to mark all changes with comments so that you can find them later.

The Server Resource Map

The server resource map file controls server content-related features, including the location of document directories, MIME types for launching viewers, and automatic directory indexing features. By default, the server resource map is located in C:\HTTPD\CONF\SRM.CNF (Windows) or /usr/local/etc/httpd/conf/srm.conf (UNIX).

Establishing Document Directories

By default, all documents are served from a single directory tree called the *document root,* which is defined by the `DocumentRoot` directive. However, it is possible to serve documents from many other directory trees defining aliases to these directories in the server resource map.

You can create simple directory aliases using the `Alias` directive, which maps a virtual path to a physical path on the server. You also can use the `Alias` directive to define directories containing executable scripts. Use the `Redirect` directive to serve documents from locations on other servers; `Redirect` redirects requests for documents in a given directory to another location. In addition, you can serve documents from users' personal directories on a network with the `UserDir` directive.

The following directives apply to document directories and scripts:

■ `DocumentRoot`

■ `Alias`

■ `ScriptAlias`

■ `WinScriptAlias`

■ `OldScriptAlias` (UNIX only)

■ Redirect

■ UserDir

By default, all documents are served from a single directory tree specified by the DocumentRoot directive. As far as the Web server is concerned, the document root directory is the highest level directory possible. Users of the server cannot specify a higher-level directory using the .. relative path that normally points to parent directories. This is vital for security, because all Web server security mechanisms are built upon the notion that documents are located only in those directory trees explicitly defined in the server resource map.

DocumentRoot

Usage: DocumentRoot *directory*

Example: DocumentRoot /usr/local/etc/httpd/testdocs

Default: /usr/local/etc/httpd/htdocs

The document directory is the directory in which the server looks when it receives a URL without any path information, like http://www.xyz.com/home_page.html. Only one DocumentRoot may be specified in the server resource map. You can define additional directory trees with the Alias directive.

Creating Aliases

You can serve documents from directory trees outside the document root directory by defining aliases to them with the Alias directive. An *alias* maps a virtual path in a URL to a physical path on the server.

Alias

Usage: Alias *virtual_path physical_path*

Example: Alias /sales /usr/local/finance/sales/data

Default: none

The Alias directive provides a way to serve documents from directories other than the document root directory. By default, the server looks for documents in the root directory only. Using aliases allows other virtual directories to be created. In this example, if a request was received for http://www.xyz.com/sales/march.gif, the server would look for /usr/local/finance/sales/data/march.gif. You can define as many aliases as you like in the server resource map.

> **Tip**
>
> In addition to serving documents from directories other than DocumentRoot, aliases can be used to shorten long path names. For example, "/xyzcorp/a1division/finance/data/sales" can be shortened to just "/a1sales" by defining an alias.

Aliases can point only to directory trees accessible on the server. This includes all drives physically located on the server and those accessible via a network. Aliases cannot be used to point to other servers. This is the function of the `Redirect` directive.

Redirect

Usage: `Redirect virtual_path new_URL`

Example: `Redirect /data/finance http://xyz.finance.com/data`

Default: none

The `Redirect` directive is similar to the `Alias` directive, but causes URLs beginning with the specified path to be redirected to a new location, which can be any other site on the Internet. The `Alias` directive defines an alias for a physical path, whereas `Redirect` defines an alias to a virtual path, which can be any valid URL.

> **Tip**
>
> If a document has moved, use `Redirect` to point to the new location so that browsers and HTML files at other sites on the Internet do not all have to be updated to point to the new location.

Establishing Script Directories

Closely related to document aliases are *script aliases,* which define directories containing executable scripts instead of documents. When the server reads a document from a script directory, it attempts to run the file rather than sending it on to the client. Script directories are defined with several variations of the `ScriptAlias` directive, depending on which environment the scripts are written for.

ScriptAlias

Usage: ScriptAlias *virtual_path physical_path*

Example: ScriptAlias /cgi-bin/ /usr/local/etc/httpd/cgi-bin/

The ScriptAlias directive is used to define a directory as containing executable CGI (Common Gateway Interface) scripts rather than files to be sent to the client. It also creates a virtual path to the specified directory just like the Alias directive. Files in script directories are not sent to the client. Instead, they are executed and the resulting output is sent to the client. You can define multiple script directories. For more information about scripts, see chapter 12 "Scripts."

WinScriptAlias (Windows only)

Usage: WinScriptAlias *virtual_path physical_path*

Example: WinScriptAlias /WIN-CGI/ C:/WINDOWS/CGI/

Default: none

The WinScriptAlias directive is identical to the ScriptAlias directive except that it identifies directories containing Windows scripts rather than DOS scripts. You can define multiple WinScriptAliases.

OldScriptAlias (UNIX only)

Usage: OldScriptAlias *virtual_path physical_path*

Example: OldScriptAlias /cgi-bin/ /etc/httpd/ncsa/cgi-bin/

Default: none

The OldScriptAlias defines directories that contain the older NCSA-style scripts instead of CGI scripts. Multiple script aliases can be defined.

> **Note**
>
> The OldScriptAlias is provided for purposes of backward-compatibility, but all new scripts should be written for the Common Gateway Interface (CGI), as this has become the universal Web standard.

User Directories

In addition to serving documents out of the document root directory and aliased directories, it is possible to serve documents out of private user directories. A single directive, `UserDir`, is used to define a name for all user directories.

UserDir

Usage: `UserDir directory`

Example: `UserDir webdocs`

Default: `UserDir public_html`

> **Note**
>
> The long file name "public_html" is difficult to work with on Windows systems. On networks with both UNIX and Windows users, you should set `UserDir` to something mutually agreeable such as "webdocs."

The `UserDir` directive provides a way for documents to be served from users' home directories on a network. This directive is applicable on any networked system for which user profiles are defined in the /etc/passwd file. For example, suppose that the `UserDir` directive specifies webdocs. To use this capability, user `john_doe` creates a new webdocs directory underneath his home directory (as specified in /etc/passwd). When the server receives a request in the form /~john_doe/about_john.html, it looks for the file called "about_john.html" under John's webdocs directory. Only one `UserDir` may be specified in the server resource map.

> **Tip**
>
> The `UserDir` directive is a convenient way to allow users at any networked institution to publish their own personal pages on the Web. You can also use User directories to test HTML documents before releasing them to the server's main document tree.

MIME Types and Encoding

As discussed in a previous section of this chapter, MIME types provide a way to launch viewers and applications from within a Web browser. The server implements this by sending MIME type information with each document.

Defining MIME Types

Normally, the server uses file extensions to map documents being served to their appropriate MIME types. If a file has no extension or an extension that cannot be found in the MIME types file, the server sends the default MIME type, text/html. In certain instances, you may wish to change the default MIME type. You might want to do this, for example, if you have many formatted plain text documents without extensions. To avoid renaming all the documents to end in TXT, you can simply change the default MIME type to text/plain so that the documents are viewed correctly in Web browsers. Change the default MIME type with the DefaultType directive.

DefaultType

Usage: DefaultType *type/subtype*

Example: DefaultType text/plain

Default: text/html

The DefaultType directive in the server resource map specifies the default MIME type for all documents on the server. In UNIX, it is also possible to specify a default MIME type for all files in a directory in access configuration files local to each directory. A later section of this chapter, "Access Control," covers access configuration files.

> **Tip**
>
> If your server contains many nonHTML files that have no extension, it is important to use the DefaultType directive to specify the correct document type. Otherwise, the server assumes they are HTML files (type "text/html").

You can create MIME types that are not currently registered in the MIME types configuration file with the AddType directive. In general, you should not add new MIME types unless absolutely necessary because of the work involved in configuring clients for new MIME types. This is especially true on public Web servers. Like the DefaultType directive, the AddType directive can be used to add a MIME type just for one directory by placing it in a local directory access configuration file. For more information about these files, see the later section, "Local Directory ACFs."

AddType

Usage: AddType *type/subtype* {*extension¦file¦physical_path*}

Example: AddType application/msword doc

Default: none

Using the `AddType` directive is the preferred method of adding MIME types to the server (as opposed to editing the MIME types configuration file). All documents having the specified extension are mapped to the specified type. The extension argument can be a file name or full path name to a single file as well as a file extension. For example, the statement `AddType image/jpeg sat001.dat` maps all files named "sat001.dat" to type "image/jpeg." The statement `AddType image/jpeg /pictures/earth_view/sat001.dat` maps only the file "sat001.dat" to type "image/jpeg." Any number of these directives may appear in the server resource map.

A capability similar to MIME types is *encoding,* in which the server can mark compressed documents as being encoded in a specified format. Browsers that support automatic decoding can then use the encoding type information to automatically decode the file when it is received. You indicate encoding types with the `AddEncoding` directive.

AddEncoding

Usage: `AddEncoding encoding extension`

Example: `AddEncoding x-gzip gz`

Default: none

You can use the `AddEncoding` directive to conserve bandwidth on a busy network; however, few clients currently support automatic decoding, so it is not commonly used.

> **Note**
>
> You can achieve automatic decoding using MIME types even on clients that do not support the HTTP encoding extensions. The types "application/zip" and "application/x-gzip" (x means experimental) are already defined in the standard MIME types file. To automatically uncompress ZIP files, users simply configure their browsers to run PKUNZIP after receiving files of type "application/zip."

Directory Indexing

Directory indexing is a powerful Web server feature that enables the server to function somewhat like an FTP server. When the server receives a document request containing only a directory name, it can automatically generate a hypertext list of all files in the specified directory, complete with dates, sizes, descriptions, and icons. Figure 6.1 shows a directory index. You can also include information about the directory listing above (UNIX only) and below the directory index.

Fig. 6.1

An automatic directory index can include file information as well as file names.

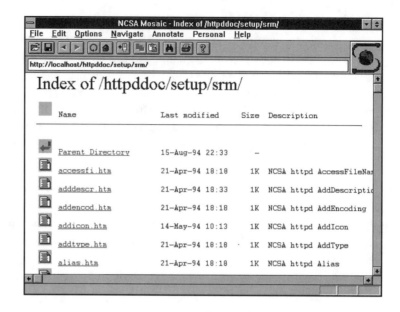

Types of Directory Indexes

A simple directory index contains only the names of files in the requested directory. You can create more detailed indexes by turning on *fancy indexing,* in which file size and date information is displayed along with file names. In Windows, you turn on fancy indexing with the FancyIndexing directive.

FancyIndexing

Usage: FancyIndexing {on¦off}

Example: FancyIndexing on

Default: on (Windows), off (UNIX)

The FancyIndexing directive controls whether automatically generated directory indexes contain icons, file size and date information, and descriptions as well as file names. If FancyIndexing is off, only file names are listed.

> **Note**
>
> In automatically generated directory indexes, files are listed alphabetically. Unfortunately, there is no way to list files by size or date.

On both UNIX and Windows systems, it is possible to control individual elements of a fancy index using the directives in the next three sections.

In addition to displaying server-generated directory indexes, you can configure the NCSA Web server and Windows httpd to display a prewritten index. A *prewritten index* can be any Web document having the name specified in the `DirectoryIndex` directive. If a prewritten index file is present in a directory, it is displayed instead of a server-generated index.

DirectoryIndex

Usage: `DirectoryIndex file`

Example: `DirectoryIndex index`

Default: `index.html`

The `DirectoryIndex` directive specifies a file name to look for when a client sends a directory URL to the server. This is usually an HTML file, but does not have to be. `DirectoryIndex` provides a convenient way to establish a standard for locating top-level descriptions of Web documents. For example, suppose a company has assigned directories to various departments on an internal Web server. If each department creates a home page with the name specified by `DirectoryIndex`, information from a given department is easy to find. Only one `DirectoryIndex` directive is permitted in the server resource map.

> **Note**
>
> UNIX-based network operating systems such as PC-NFS map UNIX file names that do not conform to the DOS convention (eight characters plus a three-letter extension) into awkward-looking names in DOS. Consequently, on systems with both UNIX and Windows users, you should set `DirectoryIndex` to a name that is easily accommodated on both platforms, such as "index.htm." If the UNIX users rebel at being limited by DOS users, perhaps just "index" will be acceptable. Because there is no extension, however, make sure that the default document type (`DefaultType`) is set to "text/html," or whatever format used by the index files.

Including Directory Information

It is often useful to include general information about a directory along with the list of files generated by the server. The NCSA server and Windows httpd support this by including the contents of a README file in a directory index, if one is present. The name of the README file is defined in the `ReadmeName` directive.

II

Setting Up a Web Server

ReadmeName

Usage: ReadmeName *file*

Example: ReadmeName readme

Default: none

If a file having the name defined by the ReadmeName directive is present in a directory, it is included as a footer to the directory listing. The file can either be plain text or HTML, depending on the extension. In this example, if the server found a file named "readme," it would display the file as plain text at the bottom of the index. If it found a file named "readme.html," it would display it as HTML. Only one ReadmeName directive is allowed.

On the UNIX server, it is also possible to include information before the directory listing. This is possible using the HeaderName directive.

HeaderName (UNIX only)

Usage: HeaderName *file*

Example: HeaderName header

Default: none

The HeaderName directive works just like ReadmeName, except that the included file is displayed before, rather than after, the directory index. Only one HeaderName directive is allowed.

Adding Icons and File Descriptions

Icons in front of file names make indexes more attractive and allow file types to be identified quickly. To add icons to a directory index, you can specify a default icon and any number of additional icons. You can define the default icon with the DefaultIcon directive.

DefaultIcon

Usage: DefaultIcon *virtual_path*

Example: DefaultIcon /icons/default.gif

Default: none

Only one default icon is permitted in the server resource map.

Tip

The default icon should be the same size as all other icons used in the directory to achieve a consistent appearance for all files.

You can define icons in three ways: for all files having a certain extension or extensions, for all files having a certain name, or for exactly one file matching a specified path. Add icons with the AddIcon directive.

AddIcon

Usage: AddIcon *virtual_path* {.*extension*¦*file*¦*physical_path*} ...

Example: AddIcon /icons/image.gif .gif .jpg .bmp .pcx

Default: none

The file type specified in the AddIcon directive can either be an extension, a file name, or the full path to a file. You can add icons to directories using the special keyword ^^DIRECTORY^^. In addition, you should specify a blank icon for the keyword ^^BLANKICON^^. The blank icon appears as a placeholder at the beginning of the line containing column labels and should be the same size as the other icons to preserve correct column alignment. You can define multiple icons in the server resource map.

Note

Unlike the other directives that use file extensions (AddType and AddEncoding, for example), AddIcon requires a leading dot (.) before the extension.

The UNIX server allows you to specify an additional element in the AddIcon directive. This element specifies text to appear in place of an icon on nongraphical browsers. In place of the virtual path to the icon file, you can use an expression in the form (ALT,virtual path), where ALT is any three-letter text abbreviation for the icon.

The UNIX server provides two additional ways to define icon types: by MIME type and by encoding type. These are defined with the AddIconByType directive and the AddIconByEncoding directive, respectively.

AddIconByType (UNIX only)

Usage: AddIconByType `virtual_path type/subtype`

Example: AddIconByType /icons/image.gif image/*

Default: none

The AddIconByType directive functions like the AddIcon directive except that icons are displayed according to a file's MIME type as specified in the MIME types configuration file or AddType directives. The type specification in the AddIconByType directive may contain wild cards, as in the example.

AddIconByEncoding (UNIX only)

Usage: AddIconByEncoding `virtual_path encoding…`

Example: AddIconByEncoding /icons/gzip.gif x-compress *zip

Default: none

The AddIconByEncoding directive functions like the AddIcon directive except that icons are displayed according to a file's encoding type as defined in an AddEncoding directive. You can specify multiple encoding types for each icon, and you can use wild cards in the encoding type, as in this example. You also can use this directive to define multiple icons.

In both the UNIX and Windows servers, file icons can be considered informational only or can actually be part of the hypertext links to the files. To make icons part of the hypertext links, use the IconsAreLinks directive.

IconsAreLinks

Usage: IconsAreLinks {on¦off}

Example: IconsAreLinks on

Default: off

If IconsAreLinks is on, the user can click either on the file name or its icon. On the UNIX server, the IconsAreLinks option is available as an option under IndexOptions

Besides icons, files listed in a directory index can contain descriptions. You can add descriptions for files of any name or type with the AddDescription directive.

AddDescription

Usage: AddDescription `"description" {extension¦file¦physical_path}`

Example: AddDescription `"Microsoft Word document" doc`

Default: none (UNIX) or HTML title (Windows)

By default, the Windows server uses a document's title (as specified by the HTML `<TITLE>`...`</TITLE>` construct) as its description. The UNIX server only does this if `ScanHTMLTitles` is included in `IndexOptions`. You can specify multiple descriptions in the server resource map.

On the UNIX server, you can control many index options with a single directive. This includes some options that are not available under Windows, such as the capability to suppress file size and date information in a fancy index. On the UNIX server, you can specify index options with the `IndexOptions` directive.

IndexOptions (UNIX only)

Usage: IndexOptions `options`

Example: IndexOptions FancyIndexing IconsAreLinks ScanHTMLTitles

The available options are:

- FancyIndexing
- IconsAreLinks
- ScanHTMLTitles
- SuppressLastModified
- SuppressSize
- SuppressDescription

The last five options apply only if you specify `FancyIndexing`.

Caution

On UNIX systems, you should not use the `FancyIndexing` directive with `IndexOptions`. If you do, the server will not start due to an invalid configuration file error. Instead, use the `IndexOptions` directive to turn `FancyIndexing` on or off.

Excluding Files from Indexes

By default, a directory index displays all files in the directory. However, in many cases it is not desirable to provide a link to the parent directory (..) or to any configuration files in the directory. You can exclude these from the directory index with the `IndexIgnore` directive.

IndexIgnore

Usage: `IndexIgnore {extension¦file}`

Example: `IndexIgnore CNF #HACCESS #README #README.HTM ..`

Default: . (the symbol for the current directory)

You can specify files to be ignored by extension or file name. In this example, all configuration (CNF), access configuration (#HTACCESS), and #README files are to be ignored, along with the parent directory (..).

Tip

It is useful to ignore access configuration files to prevent unauthorized users from learning about your access control mechanisms. Ignoring files specified by the `ReadmeName` directive prevents redundancy, because these files are displayed as the index footer.

Configuring Resources Per Directory

You can apply most of the directives in the server resource map to individual directories as well as globally. This way you can specify different MIME types and directory index information for each directory. You can do this in either the global or local access configuration files, which also contain access and security information as the name implies. The `AccessFileName` directive in the server resource map specifies the name of the local access configuration file in each directory.

AccessFileName

Usage: `AccessFileName file`

Example: `AccessFileName #htaccess`

Default: `.htaccess`

The `AccessFileName` directive sets the name of the access configuration file (ACF) in each directory. You can use ACFs to override global access settings if permitted in the global access configuration file. Only one `AccessFileName` is permitted in the server resource map.

Tip

Be sure to exclude local access configuration files from automatic directory indexes to prevent possible security problems. Do this with the `IndexIgnore` directive.

Example Server Resource Map

A sample server resource map file for the Windows server follows.

```
#-----------------------------------------------------------------------
#
#    SRM.CNF
#
# Server resource configuration for NCSA WinHttpd V1.3 (Windows)
#
# NOTE: path defaults are relative to the server's installation
#       directory (ServerRoot). Paths should be given in Unix
#       format (using '/').
#
# Bob Denny <rdenny@netcom.com> 13-Aug-94
#
# Modified by David M. Chandler 26-Jan-95
#
#-----------------------------------------------------------------------
#
# DocumentRoot: The directory out of which you will serve your
# documents. By default, all requests are taken from this directory, but
# aliases may be used to point to other locations.
#
DocumentRoot c:/httpd/htdocs

# =======================
# Aliasing and Redirection
# =======================
#

# Aliases: Add here as many aliases as you need, up to 20. One useful
# alias to have is one for the path to the icons used for the server-
# generated directory indexes. The paths given below in the AddIcon
# statements are relative.
#
# Format: Alias fakename realname
#
Alias /icons/ c:/httpd/icons/

# ScriptAlias: This controls which directories contain DOS server
#              scripts.
#
# Format: ScriptAlias fakename realname
```

```
#
ScriptAlias /cgi-dos/ c:/httpd/cgi-dos/
ScriptAlias /cgi-bin/ c:/httpd/cgi-dos/

# WinScriptAlias: This controls which directories contain Windows
#                 server scripts.
#
# Format: WinScriptAlias fakename realname
#
WinScriptAlias /cgi-win/ c:/httpd/cgi-win/

# Redirect allows you to tell clients about documents which used to exist in
# your server's namespace, but do not anymore. This allows you to tell the
# clients where to look for the relocated document.
#
# Format: Redirect old_path new_path

# UserDir is the name of user directories referenced with the ˜username URL.
#
# Format: UserDir directoryname

# =========================
# MIME Content Type Control
# =========================
#
# DefaultType is the default MIME type for documents which the server
# cannot find the type of from filename extensions.
#
# DefaultType text/html
DefaultType text/plain

# AddType allows you to tweak MIME.TYP without actually editing it, or to
# make certain files to be certain types.
#
# Format: AddType type/subtype ext1
#
AddType application/msword doc

# AddEncoding is like a MIME type but tells clients about compression type
# rather than MIME type
#
# Format: AddEncoding encoding extension
#
AddEncoding x-zip zip

# =============================
# AUTOMATIC DIRECTORY INDEXING
# =============================
#
# DirectoryIndex: Name of the file to use as a pre-written HTML
# directory index. This document, if present, will be opened when the
# server receives a request containing a URL for the directory, instead
# of generating a directory index.
#
DirectoryIndex index.htm
```

```
# The server generates a directory index if there is no file in the
# directory whose name matches DirectoryIndex.

# ReadmeName is the name of the README file the server will look for by
# default.  The server will first look for name.htm, include it if found,
# and it will then look for name.txt and include it as plaintext if found.
# NOTE: Do not include an explicit extension; it is an error.
#
# Format: ReadmeName name
#
ReadmeName #readme

# IndexIgnore is a set of filenames which directory indexing should ignore
# Here, I've disabled display of our readme and access control files,
# plus anything that starts with a "~", which I use for annotation HTML
# documents. I also have disabled some common editor backup file names.
# Match is on file NAME.EXT only, and the usual * and ? meta-chars apply.
#
# WARNING: Be sure to set an ignore for your access control file(s)!!
#
# Format: IndexIgnore name1 name2...
#
IndexIgnore  ~* *.bak *.{* #readme.htm #haccess.ctl

# FancyIndexing: Whether you want fancy directory indexing or standard
#
FancyIndexing on

# AddIcon tells the server which icon to show for different files or
# filename extensions. Four-letter extensions are acceptable, as Windows
# 95 will allow long filenames.
#
AddIcon /icons/text.gif    .html   .htm    .txt    .ini
AddIcon /icons/image.gif   .gif    .jpg    .jpe    .jpeg   .xbm    .tiff
.tif    .pic    .pict    .bmp
AddIcon /icons/sound.gif   .au     .wav    .snd
AddIcon /icons/movie.gif   .mpg    .mpe    .mpeg
AddIcon /icons/binary.gif  .bin    .exe    .bat    .dll
AddIcon /icons/back.gif    ..
AddIcon /icons/menu.gif    ^^DIRECTORY^^
AddIcon /icons/dblank.gif  ^^BLANKICON^^

# DefaultIcon is which icon to show for files which do not have an icon
# explicitly set.
#
DefaultIcon /icons/unknown.gif

# IconsAreLinks: Whether the icons in a fancy index are links as
# well as the file names.
#
IconsAreLinks off

# AddDescription allows you to place a short description after a file in
# server-generated indexes. A better place for these are in individual
# "#haccess.ctl" files in individual directories.
#
# Format: AddDescription "description" filename
```

```
#
AddDescription "Recent sales figures" sales.dat

# AccessFileName: The name of the file to look for in each directory
# for access control information. This file should have a name which is
# blocked from appearing in server-generated indexes!
#
AccessFileName #haccess.ctl

## END ##
```

Access Control

Access configuration files (ACFs) allow or deny permission to use various server features based on Internet address or password security. For example, a whole server can be locked out to all Internet addresses, allowing only internal use. A subscription Internet service can allow access from only paying customers by allowing requests only from their IP addresses. A sensitive document or script can be password-protected so that only authorized users have access.

In addition to providing security, you can use access configuration files to modify features in the server resource map on a per directory basis. This is possible because there are actually two types of access configuration files: the global access configuration file and per directory (local) access configuration files. The next section covers the global access configuration file and its capabilities. The section "Local Directory ACFs" at the end of the chapter explains local directory ACFs.

The Global Access Configuration File

The global access configuration file is the master file. It determines the permissions and features allowed in each directory. The global file also determines the permissions and features that local directory ACFs can override. By default, the global ACF is located in C:\HTTPD\CONF\ACCESS.CNF (Windows) or /usr/local/etc/httpd/conf/access.conf (UNIX).

The global file is broken up into sections for each directory in question. By default, all permissions are wide open. If this is not your intended configuration, you must describe the permissions for each controlled directory tree in a separate section of the global ACF.

Each section of the global ACF can contain directives that enable or disable various security features. These security features include the ability to disable potentially dangerous server features, restrict requests based on IP address, require user authorization, and disallow per directory overrides. In addition, the global ACF can contain directives that allow certain document and index capabilities defined in the server resource map to be implemented on a per directory basis.

Sectioning

The global ACF uses a *sectioning directive* named Directory to break up the file into one section for each controlled directory.

Directory

Usage: <Directory *physical_path*>...options...</Directory>

Example: <Directory /usr/local/etc/httpd/htdocs>
             Options None
             </Directory>

Default: none

A pair of Directory tags designates a section of the ACF. All directives contained between the Directory tags apply to the specified directory and all subdirectories. Every <Directory> tag must be accompanied by a corresponding </Directory> tag, and nested sections are not permitted.

Caution

Every controlled directory hierarchy must be called out specifically in the global ACF. A common oversight is to protect the document root directory, but to overlook directories accessible via aliases and script aliases. These are not protected under the auspices of the document root directory because the global ACF is based on real paths, not virtual paths.

Disabling Potentially Dangerous Server Features

The UNIX httpd allows several potentially dangerous operations that can be controlled by the global access file. These include using server-side includes, implementing automatic directory indexing, executing CGI scripts, and following symbolic links.

Automatic directory indexing is potentially dangerous because people can use this feature to search directories for files you really don't want them to see. If this feature is disabled, they have to guess the names of any files not specifically mentioned in accessible HTML files.

Server-side includes allow the server to automatically insert certain elements such as date and time in HTML documents each time the document is

II

Setting Up a Web Server

requested. One server-side include option, exec, is particularly dangerous because it can run any program accessible from the server. For more information on server-side includes, see chapter 12, "Scripts."

Executing CGI scripts is as dangerous as using server-side includes because, like the exec function, scripts can execute any program accessible to the server. Scripts are discussed in detail in chapter 12, "Scripts."

Symbolic links are dangerous because they can point to files outside directories protected by the global ACF. Symbolic links are a feature of the UNIX environment, and do not apply to Windows.

> **Tip**
>
> You can use symbolic links to create two names for a file. For example, if you want the file "home_page.html" to also be accessible under the name "index.html," you need to link these two files using the command: ln -s home_page.html index.html.

You can control each of these potentially dangerous operations with the Options directive, which you can place in each section of the global ACF.

Options

Usage: Options {None¦Indexes¦All} (Windows), *options* (UNIX)

Example: Options Indexes FollowSymLinks IncludesNoExec

Default: All

Under Windows, only the Indexes option is available. Table 6.3 lists the elements available under UNIX. If Indexes is turned off, automatic directory indexes are disabled. However, prewritten index files specified by DirectoryIndex are always allowed.

Table 6.3   Options Available Under UNIX

Name	Description
None	Disallow all options
All	Allow all options

Name	Description
Indexes	Allow server-generated directory indexes
Includes	Allow all server-side include functions
IncludesNoExec	Allow server-side includes except exec
ExecCGI	Allow CGI scripts to execute
FollowSymLinks	Follow all symbolic links
SymLinksIfOwnerMatch	Follow links only if the destination file has the same owner as the link itself

Tip

The SymLinksIfOwnerMatch option under UNIX ensures that links can only be made to files with the same owner. This prevents someone authorized to create files in a document directory from linking to files created by another user, and thus helps ensure that only authorized users can create documents.

Restricting Access by IP Address

In many cases, it is necessary to restrict access to a directory or perhaps an entire server to only certain IP addresses. You can do this with the Limit directive, which uses a paired tag format similar to Directory.

Limit

Usage: <Limit {GET¦PUT¦POST} ...>...options...</Limit>

Default: Open to all addresses, no passwords required

The Limit directive occurs inside a pair of Directory tags and limits access to files in the specified directory tree. The first Limit tag specifies what kind of access is restricted. GET access is the most commonly used and includes all document requests from the directory. PUT access is not yet implemented in the NCSA servers. POST access means posting form data to the server for script processing. Limit supports four options inside the pair of Limit tags: Order, Deny, Allow, and Require. Order, Deny, and Allow are discussed here, and Require is discussed under user authorization.

Deny

Usage: `Deny from {host(s)¦all}`

Default: No hosts are denied

The `Deny` directive refuses the type of access specified in the `Limit` directive to the specified host(s). A *host* can be a full or partial host name or IP address or the keyword `all`.

Examples:

```
Deny from 127.0.0.1
Deny from 127.0
Deny from racecar.ncsa.uiuc.edu
Deny from .uiuc.edu
Deny from all
```

Allow

Usage: `Allow from {host(s)¦all}`

Default: All hosts are allowed

The `Allow` directive allows the type of access specified in the `Limit` directive to the specified host(s). A host can be a full or partial host name of IP address or the keyword `all`.

Examples:

```
Allow from 142.167.100.115
Allow from 142.
Allow from 142.167.
Allow from monkey.zoo.stlouis.com
Allow from all
Allow from .stlouis.com
```

Order

Usage: `Order {deny,allow¦allow,deny}`

Default: `deny,allow`

The `Order` directive specifies in what order `Deny` and `Allow` directives are evaluated. This is very important when a host occurs in both `Allow` and `Deny` directives because of wild cards. By default, the order is deny, then allow.

Caution

The order in which `Deny` and `Allow` directives appear in a `Limit` section has no bearing on the order of evaluation. This is determined strictly by the `Order` directive.

Examples:

```
<Limit GET>
Order deny,allow
Allow from 167.142.
Deny from all
</Limit>
```

In this example, only host addresses beginning with 167.142 are allowed. All others are denied.

```
<Limit GET>
Order allow,deny
Allow from 167.142.
Deny from all
</Limit>
```

In this example, GET access is denied to all hosts, even though 167.142. is specified in an Allow directive. Why? Because the Allow directive is evaluated first, but then all hosts are denied!

> **Tip**
>
> One or more spaces between allow and deny in the Order directive results in a server configuration error.

Requiring User Authorization

Besides restricting access by IP address, directories can be password-protected by requiring a valid user name and password combination. If a directory is protected, users need authorization to access any file in that directory. Access can only be restricted on a per directory (not per file) basis.

The following directives apply to user authorization:

- AuthType

- AuthName

- AuthUserFile

- AuthGroupFile

- Require (in a Limit section)

In order for password protection to be enforced, an access configuration file must contain all of the above directives except AuthGroupFile, which is only necessary when allowing access to a group of individuals.

The AuthType directive specifies the kind of authorization in effect for the directory. Currently, only the Basic type is implemented.

AuthType

Usage: AuthType Basic

Default: none

The AuthName directive specifies the reason for requiring access. The name is displayed on the user's browser when the user is asked for a user name and password, and gives some indication as to why authorization is necessary. Of course, if you to want to keep unauthorized users totally in the dark, you can specify AuthName Secret or something equally unclear to potential users. The specified name may contain spaces, as in the example.

AuthName

Usage: AuthName *name*

Example: AuthName Policy Working Group

Default: none

In order to enforce password security, the Web server needs a list of acceptable user names and passwords. These are contained in a password file, or authorized user file, specified by the AuthUserFile directive.

AuthUserFile

Usage: AuthUserFile *file*

Example: AuthUserFile /webaccess/working_group/passwd

Default: none

The AuthUserFile specifies a physical path to a user authorization file containing user names and passwords of authorized users.

User authorization files are created with the htpasswd utility included in the Web server support directory. To create a new password file, type **htpasswd -c file username**, where *file* is the name of the file to create and *user* is the user name to add. Htpasswd will then ask you to create and verify the user's password. To add a user to an existing file or to change a user's password, simply omit the -c option.

> ### Caution
>
> Passwords created with `htpasswd` are totally unrelated to network login and system passwords. They are stored in encrypted format on the server; someone reading the `AuthUserFile` cannot obtain passwords. However, when passwords are transmitted from client to server they are only UUEncoded. Users can employ programs called *sniffers* to detect certain types of traffic on the Internet. It is unlikely, but not impossible, for someone to capture your password by sniffing password traffic and UUDecoding it. Consequently, you should choose a password for Web authorization that is unrelated to any other password you may have.

In addition to requiring a single user name and password, NCSA httpd and Windows httpd can require membership in a group of authorized users. To implement group security, you must create a user authorization file as usual containing names and passwords. This can be a new file or an existing one. In addition, you must create a group authorization file that lists the members of each group. The location of the group authorization file is defined by the `AuthGroupFile` directive.

AuthGroupFile

Usage: `AuthGroupFile file`

Example: `AuthGroupFile /webauth/working_group.pwd`

Default: none

The `AuthGroupFile` directive defines groups of users whose user names and passwords are stored in a user authorization file. Group files are plain text files that have the following format on each line:

        `Group:user1 user2 user3 user4 ...`

You can define multiple groups in one group file.

The previous directives have merely set up the locations of files to be used in password protection. The directive which actually enforces this protection is the `Require` directive, which occurs in a `Limit` section and requires that all accesses to files in the restricted directory be accompanied by a valid user name and password.

Require (in a Limit section)

Usage: `Require {user¦group} name`

The `Require` directive pulls together all the other authorization directives to enforce user authorization. If an individual is specified, `Require` looks for that user's information in the `AuthUserFile` specified for the directory. If membership in a group is required, `Require` checks to see that the user has a valid user name and password as specified in `AuthUserFile` and that the user is in the specified group as listed in `AuthGroupFile`.

Examples:

```
<Directory /usr/local/etc/httpd/htdocs/secrets>
AuthType Basic
AuthName Secrets
AuthUserFile /usr/local/auth/user.auth
AuthGroupFile /usr/local/auth/group.auth
<Limit GET>
Require user Dickens
</Limit>
</Directory>
```

In this example, any user attempting to access a file in the secrets directory is asked to provide authorization for `Secrets`. If the user enters user name `Dickens` and the correct password in `AuthUserFile`, access is granted.

```
<Directory /usr/local/etc/httpd/htdocs/more_secrets>
AuthType Basic
AuthName More Secrets
AuthUserFile /usr/local/auth/user.auth
AuthGroupFile /usr/local/auth/group.auth
<Limit GET>
Order deny, allow
Deny from all
Allow from .hp.com
Require group Wise
</Limit>
</Directory>
```

In this example, a user attempting to access a file in the more_secrets directory would be asked to provide authorization for `More Secrets`. In order for access to be granted, the user's user name must appear in group `Wise` in `AuthGroupFile` and the user name and password must be valid in `AuthUserFile`. In addition, the user's IP address must end in "hp.com" or else access is denied.

Local Directory ACFs

Local directory ACFs allow most Web server features to be applied to individual directory trees. This includes features pertaining to MIME types, directory indexing, and security. The name of the Access Configuration File in each directory is given by the `AccessFileName` directive in the server resource map. Local ACFs can use all the same directives as the global file with the exception of `Directory` and `AllowOverride`.

Security Features

Local ACFs provide a more convenient way to edit security and document features on a per directory basis than editing the global access configuration file. In addition, through the use of the `AllowOverride` directive, the administrator who maintains the global ACF can grant permission in the global ACF to use some or all of the features of local ACFs. This way, you can preserve essential security, but control less dangerous features such as indexing in each directory.

> **Note**
>
> Directives appearing in access configuration files, whether the global ACF or per directory ACFs, apply recursively to all subdirectories.

Document and Indexing Features

You can specify many of the directives in the server resource map in the global and local directory ACFs. This allows you to modify various document and indexing options for each directory. The server resource map directives that you can include in ACFs are listed below:

- `DefaultType` (UNIX only, directory ACFs only)

- `AddType`

- `AddEncoding`

- `ReadmeName`

- `DefaultIcon`

- `AddIcon`

- `AddDescription` (Directory ACFs only)

- `IndexIgnore`

Disabling Local Directory ACFs

The administrator of the global ACF can selectively disable features in the local directory ACFs using the `AllowOverride` directive in each directory section. This directive can only appear in the global ACF.

AllowOverride

Usage: AllowOverride *options*

Example: AllowOverride FileInfo Options

Default: All

The `AllowOverride` directive allows local directory ACFs to override some or all of the settings in the global ACF. You can specify any of the following options:

- None

- All

- Options (indexes, includes, and so on)

- FileInfo (AddType, AddEncoding)

- AuthConfig (AuthType, AuthName, AuthUserFile, AuthGroupFile)

- Limit (Order, Deny, Allow, Require)

Note

In order to give authors of documents on your server the capability to password protect their document directories, you must allow both the AuthConfig and Limit directives in local ACFs. Be aware, however, that this also gives document authors the capability to use the access control provisions of the Limit directive to restrict or unrestrict access from Internet addresses.

Example Access Configuration Files

Examples of both global and local ACFs are included below.

Global ACF

```
#-----------------------------------------------------------------------
#
#   ACCESS.CNF
#
# Global access configuration for NCSA WinHttpd V1.3 (Windows)
#
# Bob Denny <rdenny@netcom.com> 13-Aug-94
#
# Modified by David M. Chandler 30-Jan-94
#
#-----------------------------------------------------------------------
#
```

```
# The following access configuration establishes unrestricted access
# to the server's document tree. There is no default access config, so
# _something_ must be present and correct for the server to operate.
#
# This should be changed to whatever you set ServerRoot to.
#
<Directory c:/httpd>
Options Indexes
</Directory>

# This should be changed to whatever you set DocumentRoot to.

<Directory c:/httpd/htdocs>

# This may also be "None", "All", or "Indexes"

Options Indexes

# This controls which options the #HACCESS.CTL files in directories can
# override. Can also be "None", or any combination of "Options",
# "FileInfo", "AuthConfig", and "Limit"

AllowOverride FileInfo

# Controls who can get stuff from this server.

<Limit GET PUT POST>
order deny,allow
deny from all
allow from 167.142
</Limit>

</Directory>

# You may place any other directories you wish to have access
# information for after this one. Be sure to include your script
 directories!
```

Local ACF

A sample local access file is also included so you can see the differences
between local ACFs and the global ACF. Note the absence of Directory tags.

```
#------------------------------------------------------------------
#
#   #HTACCESS
#
# Local access configuration for NCSA WinHttpd V1.3 (Windows)
#
# David M. Chandler 30-Jan-94
#
#------------------------------------------------------------------
#
# Define a MIME type for Interleaf files in this directory.
AddType application/interleaf pl
#
```

```
# Define a footer file to be included in the directory index.
ReadmeName about_interleaf
#
# Restrict access to users in group NeedToKnow at interleaf.com
AuthType Basic
AuthName Private
AuthUserFile /accts/webadmin/user.auth
AuthGroupFile /accts/webadmin/group.auth
<Limit GET>
Order deny,allow
Deny from all
Allow from .interleaf.com
Require group NeedToKnow
</Limit>
```

Chapter 7

Managing an Internet Web Server

Operating a public Web server is a fun and exciting endeavor. With the many hypertext, graphics, and fill-in forms, only your imagination limits the possibilities of creating a fun and informative site. This chapter gives you lots of practical ideas, tips, and tricks for creating a rewarding site. It includes tips on avoiding some of the potential pitfalls of running a public Web server.

Many of the topics addressed in the next chapter are also applicable to running an Internet server. These include managing server content and many security topics. To get a thorough understanding of running either an internal or Internet Web server, you should read both chapters. This is especially important where security is concerned because many companies run both an internal and Internet Web server and need to keep the data separate.

In this chapter, you learn

- How to use hypertext and graphics effectively

- How to make your site accessible to all browsers

- Popular and useful server features

- How to make your site accessible to users not on the Internet

- How to protect your image and data

- Popular ways to draw attention and keep readers coming back

- How to advertise your server

Putting the Web to Work for You

Many newcomers to the Web are tempted to take existing literature and simply translate it to HTML to create Web pages. There is nothing wrong with this approach, but it doesn't take full advantage of the possibilities of HTML for turning large quantities of paper into a fun and interactive journey. The following sections teach you how to make the most of your server's capabilities.

Think Convenience

Imagine a traditional product catalog, similar to the dozens of mail-order computer software and supply catalogs you probably receive each month. This is obviously only a subset of the types of things you can put on the Web, but the principles can be generalized. Traditional print catalogs suffer from limited space and poor organization that make them cumbersome, if not difficult, to use. The Web brings freedom from many of these limitations, allowing all forms of advertising, public relations, and public service to focus more attention on reader convenience. You can use the Web to overcome those traditional limitations.

Think Big

Traditional print advertising limits space to keep costs down. Therefore, it is only possible to present a limited amount of information about any given product or service. Readers usually want to know as much as they can about products before purchasing.

The Web easily overcomes space limitations. Even a relatively small hard disk (200M) can contain far more information than appears in most catalogs. This means that you are free to present all the information potential customers might want. Also, by using hypertext, you allow readers to choose what aspects they want to read more about. The end result is reader convenience: more information with less effort. The readers choose exactly what they want to know.

The Web's increased capacity for information also means that readers no longer expect to see the same five-line product sales pitches they read in print catalogs. Consequently, you need to put more effort into developing Web-based advertising. However, in some respects, the Web makes this easier. For example, traditional print catalogs often put symbols next to products indicating awards and reviews. On the Web, you can make these symbols hyperlinks to the full text of the award or review on a magazine publisher's Web server. *PC Magazine*, for example, already has a good sampling of its articles published on a Web server at **http://www.pcmag.ziff.com/** (see fig. 7.1).

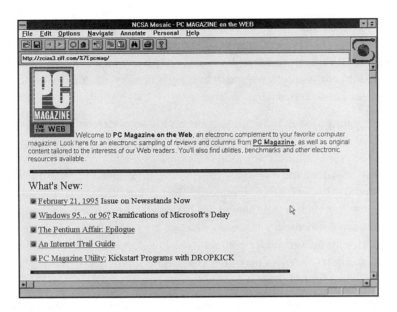

Fig. 7.1
PC Magazine offers much of its publication online along with the useful *PC Magazine* utilities.

Think Fast

Probably the most cumbersome aspect of using traditional catalogs is the amount of time required to find an item of interest. Many catalogs do not include indexes, so you have to read every word on every page to find your item. Even if an index is included, what happens if you can't remember the exact name of a product, or how to spell it, or who makes it?

The Web's search capabilities put an end to tedious hunting for information. Web servers usually have a search option on the home page, if not on every page, that you can use to find information anywhere on the server. Electronic searches excel at partial searches. Can't remember the full product name? No problem. Can't remember who makes it? No problem. Want to find out who makes it? No problem. And, unlike print catalogs, Web searches do not require you to flip through 30 unnumbered pages. Everything is a click or a keystroke away. Finally, a Web-based search can turn up more information than a traditional index because you can search the full text of a catalog, not just product or manufacturer names.

As you plan what to put on your server, seriously consider including an easily accessible, full-text search. Your readers will appreciate it, and it will also reduce demand on your server because readers can go directly to what they're looking for. It will all cost less than a direct mail campaign.

Think Multimedia

Print literature can present only two kinds of information: text and pictures. This makes it difficult to sell items you have to hear, such as audio CDs; items that are inherently interactive, such as computer software; and items you have to see in motion, such as videos.

Because graphical Web browsers support multimedia viewers, use the Web to present sound and video in addition to text and graphics. Entertainment companies, for example, put sound clips from new albums on the Web. Corporations are including voice greetings. Sound files can be large, but even a short sound bite can convey important information. Video is not yet as popular because it is even larger than audio. However, compression standards such as MPEG can condense a 3-minute video to a 10- or 15-second download on a network connection. Wider availability of low-cost ISDN, 28.8 kbaud modems, and alternative data networks from cable companies may finally make video practical for home users.

As you're designing your Web site, make the most of the Web's multimedia capabilities. Don't be tempted to use multimedia just because it's available, but do take advantage of it when information is best conveyed this way. Remember, also, that even though many Web users do not have high-speed networks with sound and video capabilities, the ones who do will appreciate your extra effort.

Think Sales

In any sales endeavor, the real key to success is closing the sale quickly. If purchasing is inconvenient, consumers are less likely to purchase right away and might think less of the company in the future. This is particularly a problem for companies that sell through regional distributors. When you call the toll-free number, you're asked for your ZIP code or area code or some such thing and referred to your regional distributor, who does not have a toll-free number. You then call the distributor, who gives you another phone number that is answered by a machine. Mail-order catalogs make purchasing fairly easy by printing the toll-free number on every page, but you still have to flip to the front, or the back, or the middle of the catalog to find the shipping and return policies.

The Web offers freedom from these inconveniences. You can put any information you want the reader to have, such as hyperlinks to sales contacts, purchasing policies, and a full-text search, on any page you want. If you want to refer potential customers to a local distributor, use a point-and-click map or an index by state. Better yet, when readers click the map, take them directly to the distributor's page on the Web. Surprisingly, many companies that published catalogs on the Web still don't include these features. Many require readers to return to the home page first, and then tunnel down through several documents looking for purchasing information.

The ultimate in sales convenience is allowing customers to make purchases right on the Web, without having to call a toll-free number, hold for five minutes, and then dig back through the catalog to find the desired product number. When customers find something they want to buy, they should be able to click the Buy button, enter a shipping address and payment method, and be finished. Automated sales is not only convenient for Web users, but also requires much less overhead on the vendor's part. That means lower prices for everyone.

Note

Many companies are concerned about the possibility of criminals sniffing Internet traffic to find credit card numbers and personal information. However, standards such as secure HTTP and new encryption techniques promise to eliminate this concern and throw the Internet's doors of commerce wide open. In the meantime, some companies simply require customers to preregister by phone or mail and then use their assigned customer number for all purchases.

Developing an effective Web server requires careful planning for user convenience. No longer limited by space and format constraints, Web-based advertising should allow customers to quickly and easily find all the information they need and move right into the purchase. The principle of user convenience applies not only to advertising, but to any publicity effort. Convenience encourages users to visit again and leaves a positive impression.

Develop a Theme

Large corporations spend hundreds of thousands of dollars designing and promoting their corporate images. This can include a logo, consistent typeface, and a slogan. They do this to create a desired image in your mind, obviously, but also to associate clearly the company with its products or services. When you see the golden arches, you know what's underneath the sign. Conversely, when you want a quick hamburger, you can quickly and visually identify all the nearby alternatives.

Creating a Lasting Impression

Most of the Web users who visit your site will not buy something on the spot. If you offer particularly appealing products, they might make a note of your site to come back to later. But more likely than not, their attention will be lost as they link away to the next site. How can you create an impression strong enough that they will remember your company and products later on?

Suppose you recently looked at several computer catalogs. You now want to buy a particular scanner and remember seeing it, but can't remember where. You pick up your catalogs and begin paging through them. You probably remember seeing a picture of the scanner, because pictures tend to stick better than words. Unfortunately, catalogs are usually so cluttered with disjointed, full-color photos that your chances of finding the picture again are slim. If the catalog was designed well, you might remember something about the format of the page on which you saw the scanner. If you see a similarly formatted page, you instantly know you have the right catalog. Otherwise, you have to go through each catalog again.

As you develop your Web site, develop a consistency that will help people remember where they saw a product. Use a consistent logo, color scheme, slogan, or even text. In fact, slogan- and text-based elements are highly recommended because many browsers are not graphical. The use of textual elements can be more effective than graphics if used properly. For the catalog example, a black-and-white catalog on newsprint might have been most effective because all the flashy color catalogs look alike.

By prominently displaying your organization's name, slogan, and possibly your Web address on every page, users can always return to your site. Even if your Web address is not in the usual Web address format (www.company-name.com), users can use one of the powerful Web-based search engines to look for your company name or slogan.

Tip

If your Web address is hard to remember, it is even more important to include it or some other easily remembered textual element on every page. There are no graphical search engines on the Web, so even if you have a clever graphic, users will not be able to find your site again unless they remember a searchable element.

Creating a Distinctive Atmosphere

In addition to creating a lasting impression, consistent use of textual and graphical elements helps create a sense of atmosphere at your Web site. Atmosphere is just as important on the Web as it is at a physical storefront or office location. Because hypertext can take you around the world and back in a matter of seconds, it is easy to become disoriented—every Web page can appear as just another screen full of text. Consistent use of unique elements at your site helps create a sense of "virtual presence." Similar to a physical storefront or restaurant, customers will buy from your site or visit just to window shop because of the atmosphere.

Some examples of sites that effectively convey a distinctive atmosphere are CISCO, which makes networking hardware, and Netscape Communications, the developers of the Netscape browser.

Netscape Communications Corp. conveys a welcoming atmosphere through its Mozilla character (Mozilla was Netscape's original name), who appears in different scenes on many pages. Figures 7.2 and 7.3 show Mozilla on the Welcome and What's New pages.

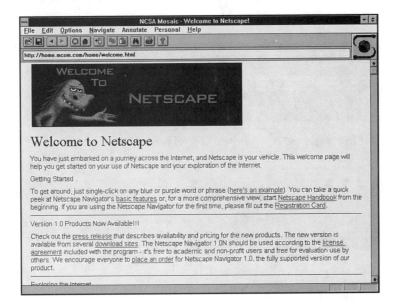

Fig. 7.2

Netscape Communications Corp.'s Mozilla gives a friendly welcome.

II

Setting Up a Web Server

Fig. 7.3

Mozilla shows off more of his personality.

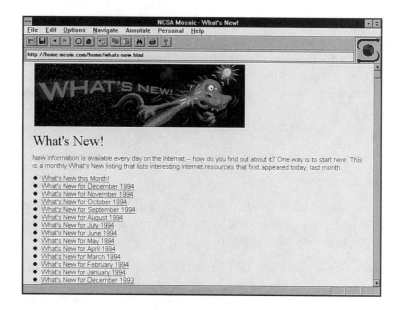

CISCO developed a space theme on its pages that includes graphics related to page functions (see fig. 7.4 and fig. 7.5).

Fig. 7.4

Search the CISCO universe with its built-in telescope.

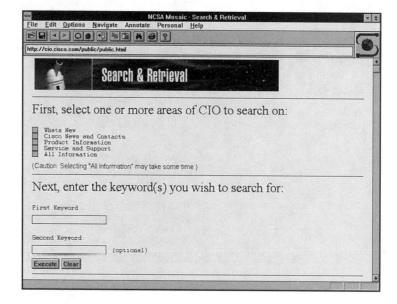

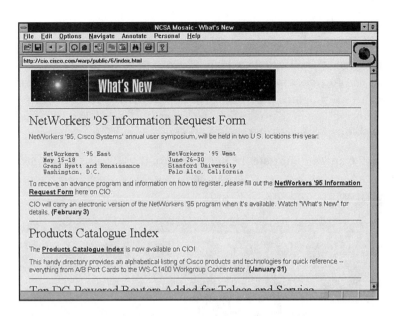

Fig. 7.5
What's on the
horizon at CISCO?

Make it *Functional*

A successful Web site should be both easy and fun to use. As a rule, people do not like to shop where aisles are crowded and lines are long, or where salespeople are unfriendly and the atmosphere is dull. In many ways, electronic commerce is well ahead of traditional business in this regard. Companies such as CISCO and Netscape Communications Corp. illustrate that point.

Creating a positive and fun image is not limited to using clever graphics. Anything on the lighter side helps. You can use quotes, jokes, or cartoons. You can offer a cool Web Site of the Day or links to other fun places. At one large company, the developer of the company's internal Web server credits much of the project's success to the color weather map that updates hourly. Be creative. When people start having fun at your site, they quickly spread the word.

Please Don't Tease the Lions: Accommodating All Browsers

As you develop your site, keep in mind that the Web can be accessed through many different browsers on many different platforms over many different types of connections. In some cases, users of lesser-known or less-capable browsers feel quite left out and even put out when Web sites don't accommodate them. For instance, text-mode users are forever begging Web authors to not rely exclusively on graphics to convey information. The following guidelines will help you make your site accessible to all.

Use the *ALT* Tag with All Graphics

For text-only browsers such as Lynx, HTML does provide a way to convey meaning even though graphics are not visible. By using the ALT tag, you can specify text to appear in place of the graphic. This replacement is essential on pages that use graphics as buttons. Without the ALT tag, text-only users just see a bunch of boxes that say [Image]. Chapter 9, "Basic HTML: Understanding Hypertext," discusses the ALT tag in more detail.

Figures 7.6 and 7.7 illustrate the importance of the ALT tag. Figure 7.6 shows the Iowa Network Systems page as it appears in Mosaic. Figure 7.7 shows the page as it appears in Lynx.

Fig. 7.6

For graphical browsers, Iowa Network Systems offers buttons to go to various areas.

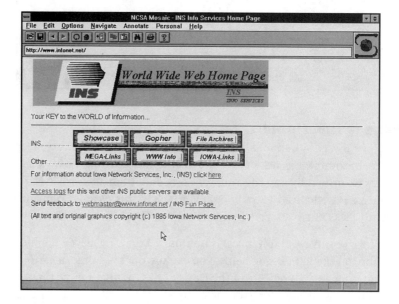

A slightly more difficult case is when one graphic contains multiple buttons, such as an imagemap (see chapter 9, "Basic HTML: Understanding Hypertext"). In this case, text-only browsers see only a single [Image] box. To solve this problem, simply provide an alternate text menu with the same functionality as the graphical menu. If you want to put the text menu at the bottom of the page—to keep it from detracting from the imagemap—you can use the ALT tag in the imagemap to give directions for finding the text menu.

```
┌─────────────────────────────────────────────────────────┐
│ ▭                  PROCOMM PLUS for Windows        ▼ ▲  │
│ File  Edit  Scripts  Communication  Window  Help        │
│ ┌──────┐ Rapid Dial:      Script File:                  │
│ │      │ INS          ↓ ↗ ins      ↓                     │
│ └──────┘                                                │
│                                   INS Info Services Home Page │
│                                                         │
│    INS Info Services -=- World Wide Web Home Page       │
│                                                         │
│    Your KEY to the WORLD of Information...              │
│    ──────────────────────────────────────────────────  │
│                                                         │
│    INS............... [Showcase×... ] [Gopher...... ] [File Archive ] │
│    Other............. [MEGA-Links.. ] [WWW Info.... ] [IOWA-Links.. ] │
│                                                         │
│    For information about Iowa Network Services, Inc., (INS) click here. │
│    ──────────────────────────────────────────────────  │
│    Access logs for this and other INS public servers are available. │
│                                                         │
│    Send feedback to webmaster@www.infonet.net / INS Fun Page │
│                                                         │
│    (All text and original graphics copyright (c) 1995 Iowa Network │
│    Services, Inc.)                                      │
│                                                         │
│ Commands: Use arrow keys to move, '?' for help, 'q' to quit, '<-' to go back │
│    Arrow keys: Up and Down to move. Right to follow a link; Left to go back. │
│    H)elp O)ptions P)rint G)o M)ain screen Q)uit /=search [delete]=history list │
│ Alt- │ 1-DOS │ 2-Host │    │    │    │    │    │    │   │
│ CONNECT 14400/ARQ to INS                    online  00:00:45 │
└─────────────────────────────────────────────────────────┘
```

Fig. 7.7
Text-only users
can still browse
this page effec-
tively without the
graphic buttons.

Text-only browsers are probably going to be around for a long time; dial-up
access to the Internet is much faster for text-only browsers than graphical
browsers. A text-only browser usually runs on a machine with high-speed
Internet access and only the text screen is sent via modem to the user.
Because the browser actually runs on the host, connections and data transfers
are accomplished much quicker than when all data goes directly to the user,
as in a SLIP connection. This is true even when the data being presented
contains no graphics. So don't think that text-mode browsers are a thing of
the past. If you do, you'll hear from all the disgruntled users.

Be Kind to 14.4

Many people now enjoy running graphical Web browsers at home via a SLIP
or PPP connection. However, modem speeds are bearable at best for graphical
access. Although 28.8 kbaud modems will soon replace 14.4 modems, large
graphics will still take a minute or two to transfer. Users appreciate a small
number of small graphics (less than 10K). If you do use large graphics or lots
of small graphics, simply let dial-up users know so they can turn off inline
graphics before they initiate the link.

> **Note**
>
> Although most people purchasing new modems for Web access will choose 28.8 modems, most department store computers come with a cheap 2400 or 9600 baud faxmodem, or at best 14.4, so it will be a while before 28.8 modems are in the majority.

New browsers, such as Netscape, partially eliminate the graphics size problem by loading text first and then graphics. However, there are other types of large files that can pose problems. In particular, you should always indicate a sound, video, or other large file so that dial-up users know what to expect. Displaying a file size next to the link is very handy; it allows users to figure out how long the transfer takes and whether it's worth the wait.

Indicate File Types

Most browsers can only view text, HTML, and a handful of graphics formats. To handle other file types beyond these, viewers must be configured. A browser that isn't configured interprets any type of document as HTML or text. In some cases, the browser crashes. At best, it represents wasted time and possibly a puzzled user. Many users don't take the time to or don't know how to look at a link's URL before they activate the link; you can't count on users figuring out document type by file extension. Consequently, always use graphics or text to indicate something about the nature of the link.

On a related note, don't post documents intended for public access in non-standard or proprietary formats, such as Microsoft Word, WordPerfect, Excel, Quattro Pro, and so on. Many users do not have these programs, and they might not even be available on their platform. Few true cross-platform languages exist. ASCII and HTML are excellent, of course, but they're a little feature-shy. Choosing Postscript is excellent, but viewers are very slow and somewhat difficult to install on personal computers. Proprietary cross-platform solutions such as Adobe Acrobat may hold some promise. Many of these viewers are free, but the user must still obtain and install them.

Try Several Browsers

There are numerous platforms on which to access the Web, and most platforms also have many different browsers that have different sets of capabilities. For example, many browsers don't allow fill-in forms, which are often used in searches. To accommodate these browsers, it's common to provide a separate search page containing a hypertext alphabetical index of the searchable data.

Besides differences in browser capabilities, it's impossible to control spatial relationships and textual appearance using HTML. HTML uses logical styles—not physical fonts and sizes—and users can define a given logical style to be any font they choose. Furthermore, HTML text automatically conforms to the size of the browser window, and users can browse in a window of any size. The best way to have a consistent appearance is to try several browsers using their default settings, but even this produces mixed results. For example, the default header 2 style in Mosaic for Windows is a much larger font than in Mosaic for X Windows.

So what's the answer? You just have to get used to users making your page look however they like it, and learn to convey information without counting on spatial relationships. This can be a hard sell to desktop publishers and graphic designers whose bread and butter is visual appeal. Corporate "logo police" can also have a difficult time accepting deviations from the approved corporate image.

Popular and Useful Features

Here are some ideas for things to include at your Web site. Many of these are already commonplace on the Web, and others are hybrid ideas based on several different related concepts. This is not a how-to section—just ideas, but references to how-to information are presented where possible.

Press Releases and News

Many Web sites offer press releases about the company or organization. They are usually presented in a hypertext, chronological index (see fig. 7.8). Currently, many of these are plain text files in standard press release format. While this is useful for people who want to find out what's going on in your organization, the possibilities with HTML are even greater. You can include graphics, links to related releases, sound clips, video, and more. You also can provide a search facility for finding things in old releases.

Many media organizations insist on electronic releases rather than hard copy—they don't have to retype everything. In a sense, a Web site is a press release in itself. When the media wants to know about your business or organization, using the Web is a convenient way to get that information. Of course, the media still has to make the effort to come get information on your Web server, whereas press releases are usually unsolicited. How can you meet both goals?

II

Setting Up a Web Server

Fig. 7.8

Press Releases at
Lockheed Missiles
& Space Co.
are organized
chronologically
and are fully
searchable.

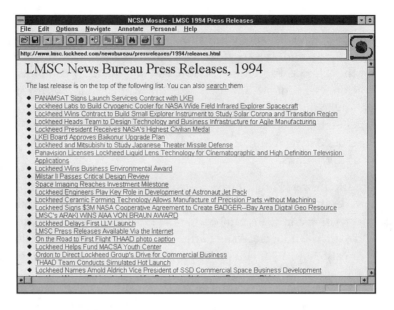

If you intend to distribute press releases automatically, consider using e-mail. By constructing an address list of the intended news organizations, you can drastically reduce time spent copying and addressing envelopes by sending releases via e-mail. Your e-mail releases can then point to your Web server for additional information.

To take it a step further, if several people in your organization need to send releases to the same list of places, you can set up list server software. This software retransmits all mail received at the list server address to all the recipients. Many list server packages also allow new recipients to add themselves to the list by e-mailing a special message to a subscription address. By advertising this capability on your Web server, you can pick up new recipients of your news automatically. You can use this same technology to send out newsletters to your interested customers. Mailing lists are commonly used on the Internet to form discussion groups where all mail sent to the list is sent to all recipients. Chapter 13, "Search Engines and Annotation Systems," discusses list servers in more detail.

An alternative way of providing news which may require less maintenance of HTML files is simply to set up an Internet news server and create a new newsgroup at your site just for press releases and news. The advantage of a news server is that once you post news, newsreaders (Web browsers) automatically handle the formatting and presentation of the articles in chronological order. You simply include a link on your Web page to your press release newsgroup and Web browsers can read all the articles in the group. Chapter 9, "Basic HTML: Understanding Hypertext," contains more information on the news: URL. Chapter 13, "Search Engines and Annotation Systems," discusses the relative merits of using mail or news for distributing information.

What's New (and What's Old)

A What's New list of some kind is a must on every server to allow users to quickly find new information without having to search your entire server. Perhaps equally important, however, is a What's Old feature, which allows users to discover what's on your server in a logical or fun manner. This might be a hypertext tour or overview of what's on your server, or a game that takes users to a new place every time.

The idea of discovering the Web via a game was pioneered by the University of Kansas Campus Internet Association (KUCIA) with the creation of URouLette at **http://kufacts.cc.ukans.edu/cwis/organizations/ kucia/uroulette/uroulette.html**. Every time you spin the wheel, you are taken to a random site anywhere on the World Wide Web. Because of the Web's immensity, this is a fun and semipractical way to discover what's on the Web. The same thing can be applied locally on your server.

Product Selection Guide

If your company offers many closely related products, it may be useful to offer a product selection flowchart or configuration guide. This can simply be a graphical flowchart or a series of questions in a form. For example, an industrial control firm might use a form to determine the proper type of controller to recommend to a customer.

If HTML forms capability is too limited for your application, you can distribute a small program written in the language of your choice for several different operating systems. Users simply download the program, run it, and then use the results to make purchasing decisions. Using a macro language, you can even have your custom program command a browser to download an updated data file from your server.

Forms to E-mail Processing

Using forms or the mailto: URL (discussed in chapter 9), you can allow Web users to send e-mail directly from their browser. This way, users do not have to remember, type in, or even copy an e-mail address. You might use this capability to allow users to submit feedback or request further information from sales. By specifying different addresses, mail can be routed automatically to the right people inside your company. Not all browsers support the `mailto:` URL, so forms may be a better choice to reach the widest audience. Chapter 12, "Scripts," tells you how to use forms to send e-mail. Chapter 9, "Basic HTML: Understanding Hypertext," discusses the `mailto:` URL.

Accommodating Users without Internet Access

Although full Internet services are common in the workplace, many smaller businesses and home users have e-mail-only connections to the Internet through an online service. Ideally, you want these people to have access to your Web site so you don't have to duplicate information on another system, such as a dial-up BBS. You can provide dial-up access to your Web server that behaves just like a dial-up SLIP connection to the Internet. Users without Internet access can then dial up via modem, run SLIP software and a Web browser (both of which are free), and use your Web site.

To do this, you need to set up a SLIP server on one of your machines. This is the same software that Internet access providers run to provide SLIP services. If you have a PC or workstation running UNIX, you can use free SLIP server software available on the Internet. If you run OS/2, IBM's TCP/IP kit includes a SLIP server. Setting up SLIP servers is by no means a plug-and-play operation, but it saves you time by not requiring you to maintain both a Web server and a dial-up BBS.

Caution

Operating a SLIP server can give any dial-up user full access to the Internet, not just to your Web server. This can make your site very popular in a hurry, but nobody would be looking at your Web server. To prevent this, you need to configure the SLIP server, or your network routers and a proxy server, to disallow all Internet traffic from the dial-up SLIP addresses except to your Web server. In addition, configure your routers or a firewall to prevent the dial-up users from getting access to your internal network. See chapter 8, "Managing an Internal Web Server."

Protecting Your Data and Your Image

This section deals with two different aspects of protecting your Web server: protecting your graphics and files from being copied, and protecting your server from hostile or accidental damage.

Copyrights and the Internet

After you invest considerable time developing a unique atmosphere at your Web site, make sure no one can copy your efforts. The problems of stolen software and plagiarism are magnified many times on the Internet because of the ease with which materials can be copied electronically. Unfortunately, there isn't an easy answer.

The Internet was built with the intent to make information freely available. Indeed, thousands of programmers and document authors give selflessly of their time to write programs and utilities, read newsgroups, and publish frequently asked question lists (FAQs) for everyone to read and freely copy. Huge volumes of material on the Internet are not copyrighted, or they have notices placing them in the public domain.

Because of the Internet's origins, many people assume that everything on the Internet is in the public domain. This is not true. However, you can't technically keep people from copying documents that are copyrighted—just as it's impossible to keep people from running to the copier. Anything you can view on a Web page can be copied. For graphics, even with the most clever protection schemes, all it takes is a screen capture program to make a local copy. If you are really worried about protecting your look and feel, including graphics, layout, and so on, you must seek competent legal counsel.

Your Server Can Be Used Against You

There *are* plenty of things you can do technically to keep people from misusing or abusing your Web server. Here are some of the common pitfalls.

Hide Your Logs and Configuration Files

If any directories or capabilities on your server are restricted to certain users or IP addresses, make sure you don't allow public access to your configuration files. To see your access configuration files, a user just has to guess a few popular names or look at a directory index—if you didn't use the `IndexIgnore` directive to keep these files from being displayed. Seeing the configuration files does not necessarily mean that a user can "break in" to unauthorized areas of your server, but it can certainly provide clues. And a user smarter than you are might look at your configuration files and see holes immediately. If you intend your server to be a public server, of course, you don't need to worry about unauthorized use.

It is important to hide your access and error logs if other machines on your network access the public Web server. Hiding your logs is easy—just don't place them in any publicly accessible document directory (see chapter 6, "Server Configuration," for more information on establishing document directories). Every access shows up in the logs, so mischievous people can use the information in the logs to find out the names and/or addresses of machines on your network. When they have those addresses, they can wreak havoc on your systems. Even if you don't access your own Web server internally, it's good to hide your logs so other people's organizations are not exposed. To illustrate this, go to a popular Web search site, such as WebCrawler, and search for the last part of your own Internet address (company.com or a1.company.com). If you were using the Internet a lot, your address shows up in several access logs around the world. These are public and therefore indexed by the Web search engines. This happens most often not with the raw logs themselves, but in usage statistics.

A Note about E-mail

If you allow users to send e-mail through their Web browsers to obtain feedback or request more information, make sure they can only send mail to predefined addresses rather than specifying an address of their choosing. Why? If you use forms and some form of the UNIX sendmail program to send the mail, the mail will arrive at its destination showing that the author is your Web server (such as daemon@www.company.com) instead of the Web user who actually wrote the message. This may confuse, annoy, or shock the reader, depending on what your Web user wrote.

In reality, there are dozens of easy ways to "forge" e-mail, so don't be too concerned about this one. However, abusing form-based e-mail is probably one of the most obvious ways to the casual user. In general, you should never trust the origins of e-mail, anyway. It's really no different than writing someone else's return address on any envelope you send. There is no security required or enforced in either system. Thankfully, people don't go around writing other people's return addresses on envelopes all the time. There's no reason they couldn't, but they just don't. It's the same with e-mail.

Data Validation

If your site uses scripts for forms processing, be sure to check for loopholes in your scripts that might cause unusual results. This is just an application of good programming practice. You can have a script, for example, that allows a user to type a value between 1 and 100. What happens if the user enters 200? Does your script make the user try again, does it just die quietly, or does it use the erroneous input in a system command which then impairs some aspect of your system?

> ### Caution
>
> Before you implement any scripts on an Internet Web server, make sure you read the section on writing secure scripts in chapter 12, "Scripts."

Scripts are the most dangerous aspect of running a Web server. For example, it is quite possible to embed UNIX system commands in a form's text field by using the proper syntax. In the course of processing the form data, the script executes the embedded commands. In general, it isn't a good idea to allow the public to execute programs on your machine. To protect against this, screen user input for embedded commands before performing any operation on the input, or simply remove any potentially dangerous commands from the server. This may be an unlikely scenario, but it isn't impossible.

One final note on scripts and data validation. As you will learn in chapter 11, "Forms," form data is sent to the server just like any other document request (URL). A user who knows a little about how scripts and forms work can easily edit a URL to make it look as though it was generated by a form, but actually wasn't. In essence, the user can take your intended form, change anything in it, and post data based on the revised form to your script rather than data based on the original. This just means that you can't rely on forms for data validation. The validation must occur in the script itself.

If You Build It, They Will Come

After you've built your Web server, how do you draw attention to it? People won't start coming automatically; this section discusses publicity pointers. First, you need to know what thing on your server will draw attention. Second, you need to know how to actively promote your server.

Give Back to the Net

In any business, word of mouth advertising and networking plays a large role in overall exposure. When you offer a superior product or service, people pass the word quickly to their friends and neighbors, coworkers, and so on. The same thing happens on the Net, only word spreads even faster through e-mail and Internet newsgroups.

What kind of Web site generates enthusiasm that spreads itself all over the world? Basically, any site that has something free to offer as well as advertising. The Internet was built on freebies and cooperation. The amount of perfectly legal free software on the Internet is unbelievable. Similarly, why individuals would volunteer their time and expertise to answer thousands of questions on Internet newsgroups is equally amazing. But that's part of Internet culture. If you want to receive the benefits of Internet exposure, you have to give something back to the Net. Here are some popular things to offer.

Free Software

Free software is an excellent way for your site to get noticed. General purpose, free software certainly draws attention. But better yet is software related to your field. If your company sells astronomical supplies, for example, you could offer an astronomy screen saver containing planet photos. If your company offers financial services, you could offer a program to assist in simple home financial decisions. If your company is an engineering or scientific organization, there are probably already dozens of free programs distributed around the Internet to do various types of calculations related to your field. Collect them and make your site the clearinghouse for these kinds of programs, and you will have a steady stream of visitors as the word goes around.

A Free Service or Database

In addition to free software, people will come to your site for information they can't find anywhere else (or have to pay for elsewhere). For example, a stock broker might offer a stock charting service or mutual fund database. Why would you want to give away this data? Simply put, if you don't, someone else will—and they'll get all the credit. A single benevolent company or institution could dry up the demand for certain kinds of information services overnight by offering the same data for free on the Web! To use this particular example, some students at MIT have already created a decent set of Web pages to track popular stock offerings. Had a commercial company done that, they could have received a lot of good publicity that could have led to enormous sales of related products, such as the actual stocks.

Tutorials and How-To Information

Another popular type of free offering on the Net is information on new technologies, topics of public interest, or general information related to your product or service. For example, Rockwell Network Systems (**http://www.rns.com**/), which makes networking hardware, has some great white papers on the Internet, connecting to the Internet, and LAN remote access. This kind of information demonstrates that your company or organization is knowledgeable in your field and that you stay on top of developments. In short, it positions your company as an industry leader.

Fun Stuff

As mentioned earlier, a good sense of humor is always a drawing card for the Internet community. Include a "purely-for-fun" link somewhere in your Web site with pointers to interesting and humorous activities you discovered on the Web. People always appreciate finding something they didn't know was there. If you update your fun stuff daily, people are more inclined to frequently connect to your site to see what's new. Fun stuff doesn't have to be related to your work, either. Maybe you're a small business owner and you're interested in gardening. Include links to your favorite gardening sites on the Web. Perhaps only a few of your customers will be interested in gardening, but they will be glad to know that you are, too, and will frequent your business more often. The Web is often as toy-like as it is business-like, so go ahead and have some fun.

Actively Promoting Your Server

While your Web site's intrinsic qualities are certainly important in garnering interest on the Internet, you must also expend some small effort to let people know about your site. Here are several different methods of making your server well-known.

Complementing Traditional Advertising

For starters, you should put your Web address on all of your standard literature and advertising right along with your phone number and e-mail address. If you already enjoy a widespread market reputation, this is the quickest way to garner interest among those who already read your ads.

Name Recognition on the Web

A simple way to draw in people without even advertising is to choose a name for your Web server that is easy to find and remember. The most popular naming convention is www.company-name.com. Anyone wondering if Microsoft is on the Web would only need to try **www.microsoft.com** to find that they are indeed. If your company name is already well-known, this is an excellent technique. Universities follow similar conventions, like **www.iastate.edu** (Iowa State) or **www.uiowa.edu** (University of Iowa).

Internet Shopping Malls

Many Internet providers offer a shopping mall concept. When you buy Internet service or Web space through these providers, your storefront is listed prominently in the mall. Your site immediately benefits from the publicity the mall receives, and customers who visit other stores on the mall can see your store, also.

The What's New List

NCSA, Netscape Communications Corp., and O'Reilly and Associates Global Network Navigator got together to offer a single What's New page for the entire World Wide Web. Entries are currently pouring in at the rate of four hundred per week, so there is a two-week delay before publication. You can view the What's New list, as well as add your own entry, at **http://www.ncsa.uiuc.edu/SDG/Software/Mosaic/Docs/whats-new.html**.

UseNet

An easy way to advertise your Web site is to post it to relevant Internet newsgroups. However, be very careful here. Advertising on newsgroups is generally unwanted, and has been abused in the past. You should only post to immediately relevant groups, and only if your site can offer some value to the newsgroup (not just the other way around). Some newsgroups were created just for this purpose, such as **comp.infosystems.announce**. It's appropriate to announce all new Web sites here.

Internet Directories

There are many directories of Internet servers, some more complete than others. There is an excellent directory of directories at **http://home.mcom.com/home/internet-directory.html**. Some of the more popular directories are listed here, as well. One of the most comprehensive directories of Web servers is Yahoo at **http://akebono.stanford.edu/yahoo**. Yahoo is organized by subject, is fully searchable, and contains over 13,000 entries. It's a very popular Internet resource.

Search Engines

Somewhat similar to Internet directories, Internet search engines allow you to search for any subject matter on the Web. However, search engines are unique because they automatically roam the Web day and night, reading and indexing several thousand documents per day. Many search engines not only search for document titles, but also for words inside documents. The idea of a full-text index of the World Wide Web is almost unimaginable, but it is being done.

In many cases, search engines can find you even if you don't tell them where you are. This happens when a site that is currently known to the search engine contains a link to your site. Of course, the best way to make sure you're noticed is to tell the search engine that your site exists. Most search engines can add new sites.

A very popular and thorough engine is Lycos at **http://lycos.cs.cmu.edu/**.
An excellent list of other search engines is available at **http://
home.mcom.com/home/internet-search.html**. The best approach
is to make your server known to all engines.

Tip

Because many search engines sort by number of occurrences of the search word, pick
a few key words describing your site and make sure they appear frequently on one
page.

Final Pointers for Success

If you apply the principles in this chapter, you will soon have a thriving site
on the Web. To put on the finishing touches, follow these last few pointers.

Don't Release Unfinished Pages

Due to the relative novelty of the Web, it's still common to see pages with
sections marked "Coming Soon" or "Under Construction." This may be
acceptable in moderation, but large numbers of these can create the appearance that your site is not finished, so people won't bother coming back. If
you plan to add lots of new features, wait until they're ready, and then tell
the world about them.

Make It Look Like You're Home

The Web thrives on novelty. Update your site frequently to keep people
coming back for new information. This takes a lot of work, but can be very
rewarding. Let people know that you're really committed to using what the
Web has to offer.

Have Fun!

This has already appeared twice in this chapter for good reason. The Internet
has become what it is because people have had fun doing it. Programmers,
who spend countless hours working on code to give away on the Net, do it
because they enjoy it. Home users who had to struggle with the Internet
before *The Complete Idiot's Guide to the Internet* did so because they enjoyed it.
And people will continue to use the Web because it's fun. So sit back and
think of the craziest thing you can offer to the world of the Web. My all-time
favorite is the Amazing Fish Cam at **http://home.mcom.com/fishcam/**,
where the programmers at Netscape Communications Corp. point a camera
at their fish tank and publish the resulting images on the Net every minute or
so. Who says you can't have a fish tank in your office?

Chapter 8

Managing an Internal Web Server

This chapter discusses several aspects of running a private Web server inside your organization. Running an internal server requires careful attention to document control, document formats, and security. In addition, running an internal server means that everyone on your LAN will be using a Web browser, which requires you to think carefully about Internet access issues.

The first section of this chapter presents ideas for features to make your server as useful as possible. The second section deals more with complex networking and security issues that require a good understanding of networking and operating systems. If you do not have the necessary experience, or don't understand the concepts presented here, ask a consultant or system administrator for help.

In this chapter, you learn how to

- Manage content and structure

- Include several useful features

- Protect your server from outside access

- Protect your LAN from viruses and outside access

- Run a server accessible from specific outside clients

- Create a "private" network via the Internet

Managing Server Content

As you begin setting up your internal server, you need to think about content issues right away. A poorly structured Web server can make information harder, rather than easier, to find. Will you allow all users to place files in all directories, or will all information have to go through an approval process? Will you have an organized hierarchy of information? How will new categories be added to the hierarchy? Can all users edit files, or only the authors? Can server administrators edit all files? The answers to these questions are different for every situation. The following sections discuss aspects of content management so you can choose the best solution for your needs. As you read this section, you may want to refer to chapter 6, "Server Configuration," to see how to configure server directories in the server resource map.

Putting Documents on the Server

You can place files on a Web server in one of two ways. You can either copy files to the server directly over a network or, if you are running an FTP server in addition to a Web server, you can put files on the server using FTP. For internal Web servers, copying files directly is usually the most convenient method. This allows authors to save files directly to a network drive seen by the Web server. In either case, the server administrator must have a good understanding of the underlying file system, and from the very beginning must work to develop a logical document structure.

> **Note**
>
> Future browsers and servers may support the HTTP PUT method, which will allow browsers to copy local files to the server.

Although the NCSA httpd and Windows httpd don't include a document management system, they do provide the directory index file feature, which simplifies the creation of organized data structures. See chapter 6, "Server Configuration."

Directory Index Files

Theoretically, a Web server can present an organized hierarchy of documents to users even though all files are located in a single, large directory. This is possible because the document hierarchy presented to readers is strictly dependent on the nature of the hypertext links inside the documents. However, such a system would be difficult to manage.

It is generally useful to maintain a close correspondence between the structure of hypertext links inside documents and the structure of the directories containing those documents. You can conveniently use the directory index file feature to do this. For example, if the server `DirectoryIndex` directive specifies that index files should be named "index," a file with this name in any directory will be served when just the directory name is requested from the server. By consistently using this feature, you will always know the name of the home page in each directory without having to examine the hypertext link structure on your server.

> **Note**
>
> Even though the server knows to use the directory index file automatically, it still requires some diligence on the part of the administrator to ensure that this practice is consistently followed by users.

Structure

Depending on the size of your organization and the nature of your server, there may be anywhere from 1 to 10,000 people who need to place files on your server. How can you accommodate everyone's needs while still maintaining some sense of order and organization on your server? The answer to this question really depends on another question: "Who can put files on your server?" You can choose from several different schemes including open access, centralized control, or distributed control.

> **Note**
>
> The right solution for your organization might be a combination of several methods. Following any one scheme too strictly just for the sake of consistency is self-defeating. Do what best meets your needs.

Open Access

Under this model, anyone can place files anywhere on your Web server. This includes creating directories and subdirectories, new files, modifying existing files, and so on. Figure 8.1 is a diagram of the open access model.

The open access model is very easy to administer and allows users to develop documents quickly. This scheme is most appropriate for situations when the Web server is used simply to place documents in a common location. For example, a user might want to place a paper on the Web server for review by peers and then notify co-workers of its location.

Fig. 8.1

The open access model allows anyone to place files on the Web server directly without requiring anyone else's permission.

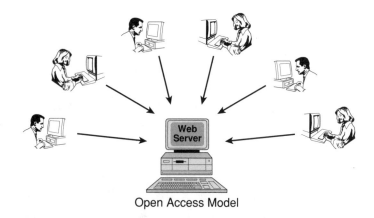

Open Access Model

Caution

The open access model can quickly lead to chaos in a large organization. No one would be able to find anything because of the lack of structure. An alternative might be to allow users to place files only in certain directories by allowing users to create new files in predefined directories but not to create their own directories.

Centralized Control

Under this model, all materials placed on the Web server must be approved through a site administrator (see fig. 8.2). This scheme enforces strong structure and ensures that only materials deemed appropriate by the administrator(s) are placed on the server.

Centralized control is good for a small organization where only one or two people know how to create documents on the server. However, in large organizations, centralized control tends to produce a giant bottleneck, severely impeding productivity.

Note

A variation on centralized control might be to control only the main document structure or a few directories, but to allow all users to create and maintain their own personal directories. To create user directories, use the `UserDir` directive in the server resource map.

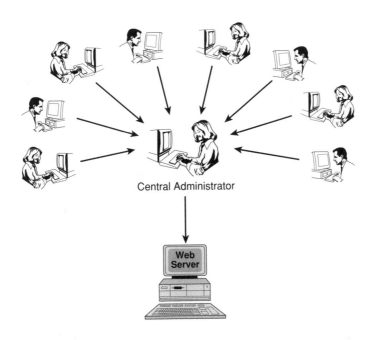

Fig. 8.2
The centralized control model requires all documents to be approved through a central authority.

Distributed Control

Under this scheme, one central administrator delegates control of subdirectories to various developers. Each developer controls one or more directories and can help users create documents in those directories. Figure 8.3 illustrates the distributed control model.

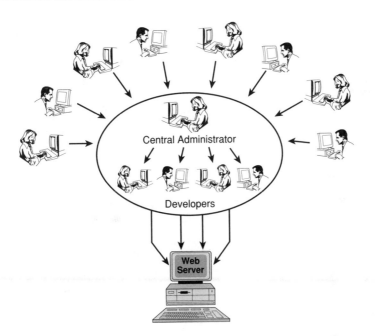

Fig. 8.3
The distributed control model has several levels of authority and is similar to most management structures.

The distributed control model is appropriate for an organization of any size, because it's easy to scale. Because control of each directory is delegated downward through the organization, the central administrator can give more attention to server technical issues rather than spend time approving documents. In this sense, the system is self-maintaining. Users who want to add documents to the server simply contact the developer handling the appropriate section.

> **Note**
>
> Because local developers are likely to be more accessible than a central administrator, distributed control allows users to put files on the Web server with a minimum of effort—while still maintaining an organized information hierarchy.

Controlling File Permissions

The only way to put files on a Web server is to copy them to the document root directory tree or to other directories created using the `Alias` directive in the server resource map. Servers and browsers currently do not support the HTTP PUT method, which allows clients to transfer files to the server. The HTTP GET method, which is used in ordinary document requests, only allows the client to retrieve files from the server. (See chapter 12, "Scripts," for more information on HTTP methods.) Because files are not placed on the Web server through a Web client, the mechanism used to control documents put on the server is that of system file permissions. The Web server software doesn't play a part in who can put documents on the server. This section describes typical permissions used in conjunction with the schemes described earlier.

Understanding File Permissions

Under UNIX and most network operating systems, files can be protected from various types of access. Typically, everyone can read a file, but only a file's owner or a select group of people have permission to modify the file. Various systems are used to assign these rights. This section discusses the UNIX file system because most other systems are derived from or closely related to it.

> **Note**
>
> DOS and Windows do not support any file security by themselves. Anyone with physical access to a machine can read, create, or destroy files on the machine. In order to create file permissions on DOS and Windows machines, you need a network operating system. Besides providing better security, a network operating system

allows users to place files on the server from anywhere on the network. The capability to restrict file permissions is built in to UNIX and Windows NT because these are true multiuser operating systems.

In a nutshell, assigning file access rights means controlling who can do what to a file.

The "who" consists of the following:

- An individual owner of the file (owner)

- A group of users having access to the file (group)

- Everyone else (world)

The "what" consists of the following types of privileges:

- Permission to view and copy the file (read)

- Permission to modify or delete the file (write)

- Permission to run or execute the file (execute)

Note

Execute privileges are not relevant to documents on Web servers because the server only needs read privileges to see and display the file. The exceptions are script files, which the server must actually run.

When applied to directories, read, write, and execute privileges have special meanings. These are:

- *Read.* Required to see a listing of all files in the directory

- *Write.* Required to create new files in the directory

- *Execute.* Required to read and execute files in the directory

Note

Directory read and execute privileges are similar, but not identical. Read privilege gives permission to see a directory listing, even though all files in the directory are not readable themselves. Execute privilege is required to read or write any file in the directory, even though the file itself is readable or writeable.

II

Setting Up a Web Server

File rights are now discussed with reference to the control schemes mentioned previously. Because file rights are really the only control mechanism you have over server documents, it's important to think carefully about setting up file rights.

> **Note**
>
> In addition to basic group, world, and owner rights, UNIX and many other operating systems support *Access Control Lists (ACLs),* which allow you to further refine who can do what to files. ACLs can be useful, but knowledge of ACLs is by no means necessary to run any kind of Web server.

The Implications of File and Directory Ownership

First, you need to understand what it means to own a file. Under UNIX and most other network operating systems, a file's owner controls permissions to the file. Only an administrator (such as UNIX root) can override the file rights assigned by the owner. The owner can assign read, write, and execute privileges for the owner, group, and world categories. In addition, the owner can transfer control of the file to a new owner or assign a new group.

> **Note**
>
> Different types of UNIX respond differently to attempts by the owner to change a file's group. Under HP-UX, a file's owner can change the file's group to any group. Under SunOS, a file's owner must belong to the file's group.

Because a file's owner has the most important rights to the file, the implementation of any control scheme rests largely on determining who can own files and directories. Directory ownership is especially important because a directory's owner determines whether all users, some users, or no users can place new files in the directory.

Typical File Permissions

As mentioned previously, the implementation of any control scheme rests primarily on directory permissions. File ownership and rights are not as significant because users can only create files in directories for which they have permission. However, you need to consider several other important factors when determining allowable file rights.

All files on the Web server have more or less the same rights—only the owners vary. Typical rights look like this:

- Owner: read, write, execute

- Group: read

- World: read

Using these rights, only a file's owner has the exclusive right to modify the file, but everyone else can read it. Under UNIX, these rights would show up in a directory listing as rwxr—r— and could be assigned by using chmod 744 or chmod o=rwx,g=r,w=r. The procedure for changing file permissions is different on every network operating system. Some systems require you to type commands on the command line; others use interactive programs.

> **Note**
>
> A file must be readable to the Web server program for it to be visible to Web clients. The easiest way to do this is to make all files world-readable. In UNIX, document requests are processed by the user named in the User directive in the server configuration file.

A slight variation on the typical file rights shown previously might be used to allow multiple users to modify the same file or to allow administrators to edit all files. You can do this by creating a group with the desired users and then giving the group write permission to the file as follows:

- Owner: read, write, execute

- Group: read, write, execute

- World: read

> **Tip**
>
> It's easy to get system file permissions confused with the server's access restrictions. When a client requests a server document, the server does not know who the requesting user is. As long as the server can read a file, anyone with access to the server through a Web browser can read a file. Consequently, if files must remain private to certain groups, you have to use both system file permissions and server access control features to adequately protect the private files.

II

Setting Up a Web Server

The following sections discuss how directory permissions can be modified to support the control models.

Open Access

Under this model, all users have write access to all directories. Directory rights look like this:

- Owner: read, write, execute

- Group: read, write, execute

- World: read, write, execute

Caution

World read and write access means that anyone in the world who can connect to your machine can exercise these privileges. Users don't need to be authorized users of your system to exercise world privileges (although they normally have to be authorized users to connect to your system). If you allow any type of anonymous login, anyone can read and copy world-readable files. Similarly, anyone can modify world-writeable files.

If you want to allow only users in certain groups to create new files and directories, use these permissions:

- Owner: read, write, execute

- Group: read, write, execute

- World: read

Centralized Control

Under a centralized control scheme, the central administrator owns all directories and reserves all rights to place files in those directories. The directory permissions look like this:

- Owner: read, write, execute

- Group: read

- World: read

A listing of the server root directory shows that the central administrator owns all directories, as shown in table 8.1.

Table 8.1 Ownership of Directories Under Centralized Control	
Directory	**Owner**
general_news	topdog
business_news	topdog
finance	topdog
standards	topdog
engineering	topdog

Caution

Centralized control makes it difficult to publish documents because you always need someone's approval. This defeats one of the main puposes of running an internal Web server—to make it easy to share documents. Therefore, use the centralized control scheme only where it is absolutely vital to ensure data security.

Distributed Control

The distributed control scheme uses the same directory permissions as central control, but many different people can own directories, as shown in table 8.2.

Table 8.2 Ownership of Directories Under Distributed Control	
Directory	**Owner**
general_news	tjyoung
business_news	mrchandl
finance	ryoung
standards	kdemares
engineering	kelauben

II

Setting Up a Web Server

> **Note**
>
> Even though developers or administrators own directories, individual users can own files in those directories so that they have exclusive rights to modify their own files. To implement this, directory owners simply create files for users and then change ownership of those files to the users. In UNIX, you do this with the chown command.

Useful Features

Once you've established a basic document structure for your server, you can begin adding features that enhance the usefulness of your server.

News

Many large organizations, in particular, suffer from a chronic lack of communication between departments and divisions. Depending on how sophisticated you want to get, you can write scripts to allow anyone to submit their own news items via fill-in forms, or simply give a few people authorization to edit the news files.

> **Tip**
>
> Writing scripts to create a news "database" allows users to read current items and to search old news. This can be useful for finding dates and times of upcoming events, for example.

A very simple way to provide news access is to use the news: URL in HTML to point to an in-house news server running InterNetNews (INN) or another popular server. Figure 8.4 shows news from a news server presented in Mosaic. If you use Netscape or another browser with similar news features, you can read and post news items through the same browser interface used to read documents. For more information on news servers, see chapter 13, "Search Engines and Annotation Systems."

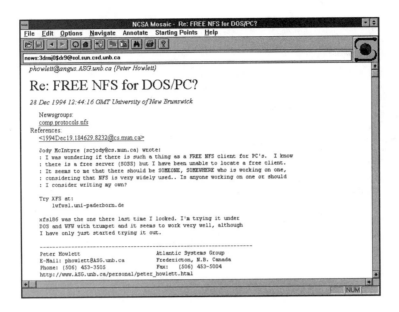

Fig. 8.4
Reading news
through a Web
browser is often
more convenient
than switching
to a separate
newsreader
program.

What's New and What's Old

When your Web server really takes off and people begin adding files daily,
you will need to have a way to find out what's being added to the server. You
can require users to submit "What's New" items for each new item they create, but that's really unnecessary. A better approach is to write a script that
searches the server directories each day or night and looks for new files. These
can then be presented in a hypertext index (see fig. 8.5). A program that does
this is covered in the "Finding What's New" section of chapter 14, "Usage
Statistics and Maintaining HTML."

In addition to finding out what's new on your server, you need to provide a
way for new users to explore the system and discover "what's out there." You
can do this through a hypertext guided tour or a list of the major categories
of information available. For a little more pizzazz, try a "page of the day" or
"random location" feature like URouLette discussed in the "What's New (and
What's Old)" section of chapter 7, "Managing an Internet Web Server."

II

Setting Up a Web Server

Fig. 8.5

An automatically generated What's New list can automatically use HTML document titles as descriptive names in the hypertext index.

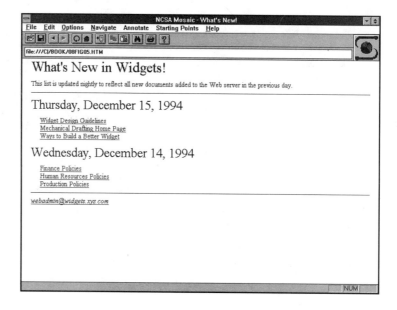

Search Capabilities

A search engine is perhaps the most important tool for finding information when your server becomes large. You can use a simple but powerful search engine such as ICE to create a full-text index of your server each night. (ICE is discussed in the section "Searching an Entire Web Server" in chapter 13, "Search Engines and Annotation Systems.") Once the index is built, the search interface allows users to search the entire contents of your server or just certain sections. Any search script should present search results in a convenient hypertext format. Figure 8.6 shows the results of an ICE search.

Company Policies

A Web server is an ideal location to place hypertext versions of corporate or institutional policies for everyone to read. Online versions of policies are instantly accessible to everyone and are fully searchable; it's easy to find the right policy quickly. In addition, you can distribute policy updates immediately. By putting policies on a Web server, you also eliminate the cost of copying and distributing thick policy books. This fact, combined with the cost savings to policy users in not having to waste time hunting for things, can probably pay for a nice workstation on which to run the server. Figure 8.7 shows a sample policy index.

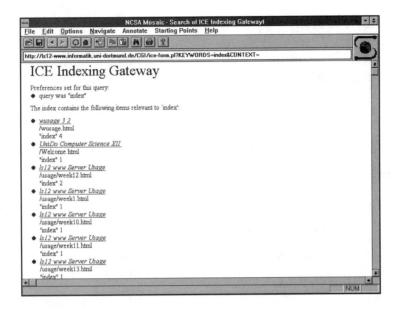

Fig. 8.6
ICE presents
search results
in a convenient
hypertext index.

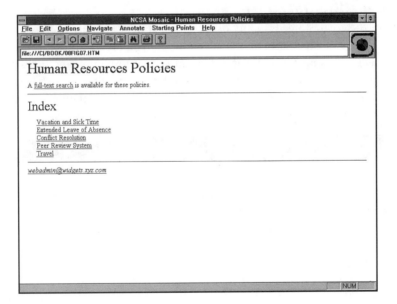

Fig. 8.7
An internal policy
index is a more
convenient place
to look for
information than
a thick manual.

II

Setting Up a Web Server

Project (Workgroup) Pages

Project pages are a fantastic way for teams, departments, and workgroups to share information with other team members and with the organization at large. An engineering project page, for example, might contain the following items:

- Project history, funding, and progress

- Index of working documents

- Links to Internet resources such as standards documents

- Drawings, design reports, and test data

- Engineering design tools and software

- A gateway to a project newsgroup or mailing list

- Customer feedback

Knowledge Database

One of the greatest needs in any organization is the capability to transmit the knowledge and experience of one generation of employees to the next. This knowledge can range from technical expertise to information about customers and sales contacts. As employees accumulate knowledge, it can be entered in a database via fill-in forms or simple text files. Everyone then can access the information for browsing, searching, and retrieval.

> **Tip**
>
> Knowledge databases are very useful for training new hires, reducing duplication of effort across the organization, and maintaining continuity when employees leave the organization.

You can organize a knowledge database in several different ways. You can use a series of fill-in forms in which users enter important data. Alternatively, you can use a page listing important reports, study results, and lessons-learned papers in a variety of different document formats. To be really useful, users should be able to search the database by:

- Author

- Date and time created

- Subject

- Keywords

- Full-text

You can implement a Web interface to a database in several different ways. For simple applications, use simple forms and scripts that work with a text-oriented database (see the section on "Searching Simple Databases" in chapter 13, "Search Engines and Annotation Systems"). For more complex applications, such as those requiring a full relational database, implement scripts that access a separate relational database. Relational database techniques are presented in chapter 15, "Database Access and Applications Integration."

Protecting Your Data from Outside Access

If you want to develop an internal Web server, you need to protect your data from outside access via the Internet. This is guaranteed to be one of management's top concerns, along with concerns about the cost of and appropriate use of outgoing Internet access. The next several sections deal with protecting your data from intruders and accidental or intentional leaks from the inside.

The following sections discuss three ways to protect your internal sever from outside access (from minimum to maximum effectiveness):

- Hide your server

- Restrict access via software

- Use screening routers

Hiding Your Web Server

Hiding your server as used here simply means making it less visible, not invisible. To make it invisible, read the sections on software configuration and router security.

Caution
The following three techniques do nothing to prevent discovery of your internal data. They simply make it less likely to be discovered.

Run Your Server on a Nonstandard Port

Most Web traffic is carried on port 80, and all Web browsers assume this port if none is specified in a Web address. Consequently, an easy way to prevent your server from being accidentally discovered is to run it on a different port. Port numbers range from 0 to 65,535. There are plenty of numbers to choose from; however, many port numbers under 1024 are reserved for common Internet protocols. If you run the server on any port other than 80, make sure it doesn't conflict with other Internet services. For a list of common services and for more information about the `Port` directive, see chapter 6, "Server Configuration."

Give Your Server an Unusual Name

In addition to running your server on a nonstandard port, you can give it an unusual name. Don't name it "www.company-name.com"—that's extremely obvious. Don't be afraid to give it a really weird name such as "fjwicnmvb." Browsers can be configured to load your home page by default without the users worrying about the name. Better yet, don't name your server at all. Browsers can access servers by their IP addresses as well as by their names.

Don't Let Your Server Show Up in Anyone's Logs

Even if you give your server the most unusual name and port number, you can blow it all by letting it show up in log files on the Internet. This happens if you run Mosaic on the same machine as your server. In that case, the log files kept for many Internet sites will clearly show accesses by your server. Because some Web administrators make their log files public (either intentionally or accidentally), Web search engines index many of these log files. Someone searching the Internet for "your-company-name.com" can then see the names of several of your machines.

> **Note**
>
> As long as you have more rigorous security measures in place such as address screening, it doesn't matter if your private server shows up in Internet logs. Your access control measures prevent anyone from seeing your data. (The next section covers address screening.)

Restricting Access Through Software

NCSA's server software includes very flexible security features, as described in chapter 6, "Server Configuration." The simplest way for you to restrict access to your server is to use the `Limit` directive to deny access to all Internet addresses. This is effective and simple to set up.

Caution

Restricting Web server access through the server software only prevents people from accessing data on your network through your Web server. It does not close any other security holes you may have that allow access to the raw data.

Preventing Access Using Routers

Routers screen traffic between your network and the Internet. You can configure routers to block traffic based on port numbers and source and destination addresses, among other things. The best way to ensure that no one gets into your internal Web server is simply to configure the router to block all traffic to and from the Internet on your Web server's port number. Even better is to block Internet traffic anywhere on your network except through a gateway known as a *proxy* or *SOCKS server*. Better still is to set up a complete firewall.

Tip

Using routers to screen Internet traffic is the safest and one of the most secure ways to prevent external access. It doesn't require full-scale implementation of a firewall—but that's even better.

Because all routers are different, you can't assume anything about what your routers do and don't do. Many routers are configured by default to allow all traffic on all ports. Some are not capable of screening. Some screen only ports numbered less than 1024 or less than 8000. Consequently, make sure you understand what your router actually does before counting on it to provide all your internal security.

Why Port 8001?

As you use the Web, you may notice a few Web servers that run on port 8080 or 8001. These sites may use the high-numbered ports because the routers at these sites do not or cannot screen high-numbered port traffic. By convention, port 8080 is used for experimental servers.

Note

A useful way to test your router's configuration is to get an Internet account with a public access provider in your area and then to try breaking into your site from there.

Protecting Against Internal Leaks

Because Web servers are so easy to set up and are available on common platforms such as Microsoft Windows, it is entirely conceivable that someone in
your organization could set up a server for experimental or malicious purposes. Your only defense against this is router security. Blocking Web traffic
only (port 80) is not sufficient because Web servers can run on any port.
Consequently, you have to block all Internet traffic on every port; however,
this prevents all Internet access. To allow Internet access and prevent users
from running their own servers, you must set up a proxy server or firewall as
discussed under "Advanced Security Topics" later in this chapter.

Protecting Your LAN

One of the consequences of running an internal Web server is that everyone
in your organization now has a Web browser, which makes access to the
Internet easier than ever before. Because the Internet is frequently portrayed
as all fun and games, you may be tempted to disallow all Internet access to
protect against viruses and other types of attacks on your network. However,
the growing wealth of business and technical information available on the
Internet means that you can lose valuable business information by shutting
off Internet access entirely. How can you minimize the risks of Internet access
while still reaping the benefits?

Understanding the Risks

There are basically two types of risks to your LAN that are consequences of
allowing Internet access. You can minimize both risks through education and
technical solutions.

The most significant risk is that of users unwarily downloading viruses that
can then spread to other machines on the network. To mitigate this risk,
check every executable program for viruses before you run them. Protecting
against this risk is largely a matter of user education because there are no
strictly technical solutions that can completely eliminate this risk.

A second significant risk is that of an outsider gaining access to your network
through any one of a number of security back doors. You can minimize this
risk by funneling all Internet access through one or two machines called
proxy or SOCKS servers.

User Education

Regardless of any technical measures you employ to control Internet access, user education is your first and strongest line of defense against virus attacks. Network administrators lose a lot of sleep over the thought of users down-loading viruses from the Internet that can then spread to the entire network. This is most likely to happen for one of three reasons:

- Users don't understand viruses and the virus risk

- Users don't know how to check for viruses

- Users assume that protective measures have already been taken by network administrators

The third item is common in organizations where Internet access has previously been off-limits, and then is suddenly opened up. Users assume that the administration would not let them do anything potentially harmful and therefore take no protective measures on their own. It is impossible for administrators to inspect and approve every file and document brought in from the Internet in a large organization and there aren't programs that can detect viruses before they reach a destination machine on your network. Programs like Microsoft Anti-Virus and PCTools Anti-Virus can automatically check for viruses in the background, but you must run these programs on every machine on the network. You must teach users simply to check all downloaded files for viruses before running them.

All three reasons for failure to check for viruses are entirely preventable through education. Central network administration and technical solutions alone cannot solve all of your problems. Anyone using the Internet must be aware of the virus risk and how to protect against it.

Technical Solutions

Proxy and SOCKS servers force all Internet traffic through one or two gateway machines, thereby reducing the number of machines open to attack. You use screening routers to disallow all Internet traffic except from the gateway machines. The proxy and SOCKS gateways receive requests from authorized clients on the network and relay the data outside. Many Web clients such as Mosaic and Netscape have built-in proxy support, and Netscape also has SOCKS support. You can find more information on proxy and SOCKS servers in the section "Firewall Implementation" later in this chapter.

Advanced Security Topics

This section presents information on advanced security topics that build on previous discussions in this chapter. These topics include running both an internal and external Web server, running a semiprivate Web server, creating a network of private Web servers between divisions, and setting up an Internet firewall.

Running Both Internal and External Servers

Security is a big issue if you run both an internal and an external (public) Web server and need to keep the two separate. This section presents several strategies and recommendations for keeping internal and external data separate.

One Machine, Two Directory Trees

The simplest approach to running both an internal and an external Web server is simply to create aliases to two separate directory trees: one for internal use and one for external use. You can then use the `Limit` directive in the server access configuration file to allow only internal addresses permission to access the private data tree.

Caution

Running one Web server with two directory trees is the most dangerous method of providing both internal and external access. You should only use it when absolutely necessary for cost reasons or when your internal data is not that important.

This scheme is workable, but very risky. First, you must be extremely careful and make sure all back doors to your private files are closed. Remember that there are two types of access configuration files: the global file and per directory files. If you're not careful, a user can create a local access configuration file that overrides the settings in the global access file. To prevent this, edit the global access configuration file to prohibit per directory overrides of the global access settings (the `AllowOverride None` directive is the safest way to do this). Chapter 6, "Server Configuration," explains global and local access configuration files.

Caution

Don't forget: You must define restrictions for every aliased directory in the global access configuration file—including script directories, not just the document root. By default, all directories are unprotected.

This method is dangerous because both sets of data are being served from the same machine. If an internal or external user manages to compromise the server, your internal data (and possibly your entire network) can then be exposed. This is especially of concern if your server uses scripts either internally or externally. Because scripts allow you to send data to the server, there is more potential for problems.

If you're going to use this method, make sure you do one of the following:

■ In the global access configuration file, disallow access to all private directories, including all aliased directories, using the Limit directive in each directory section.

■ Disable per directory overrides of the Limit directive using the AllowOverrides directive in the global access configuration file.

One Machine, Two Ports

Under this method, you can actually run two servers on the same machine, but on different ports. The external Web server usually runs on port 80 because this is what most users expect. The internal server can run on any port of your choice (from 0 to 65535).

This method is slightly preferable to running only one server because you can specify two separate document roots. In addition, you can exclude aliases to private directories on the internal server entirely from the external server's resource map. Put together, these two measures ensure that a user cannot reference data from one server to the other. However, your internal data and network are still vulnerable if the machine running the servers is compromised.

Caution

For the internal and external document directories to be entirely separate, neither one can be a subdirectory of the other.

If you must use the multiple port technique for separating internal and external data, make sure you do all of the following:

■ Create two separate server root directories, including separate configuration files and separate document directories. Use the -d or -f command line options when starting the server to tell the server where to find its document root directory and/or configuration files.

- Disable per directory overrides of the `Limit` directive using the `AllowOverrides` directive in the global access configuration file.

Two Machines on the Same Network

A slightly better method than the previous two schemes for providing information both internally and externally is to run your internal and external Web servers on two separate machines. For example, if one machine is compromised through the use (or abuse) of scripts, the other machine is not compromised (although it could be, depending on the nature of the attack). If the external server simply crashes, the internal server is still fine. However, if an intruder gains privileged access to the external server, the intruder can then use the server to attack other machines on the network.

> **Caution**
>
> In a UNIX environment, if an intruder manages to get privileged access to a machine (the machine believes the intruder is an authorized user), the intruder can then attack other machines on the network that trust the compromised machine. For example, the `rlogin` command can be used to log into another machine without a password simply because the calling machine is in a list of trusted hosts (the file "/etc/hosts.equiv"). To protect against this type of attack, remove the external server machine from all trusted host lists on the network.

The same caution applies to this method as to the others. Because both machines have potential access to the same files via the network, you must take precautions to ensure that only the public files are accessible externally. However, you eliminate the risk of crashing both the internal and external servers at the same time because they're two separate machines.

Two Machines on Opposite Sides of a Firewall

Having an Internet firewall is the best way to ensure internal data security, both on the internal Web server and the internal network at large. Under this scheme, files on your internal network are not physically accessible from the external server, and the firewall prevents an attack on the external server from spreading to the network.

The safest way to serve data both internally and externally using WWW technology is to run an external server outside a firewall. In order to put data on the external server, you can't simply copy files over the network because the external server is not on the internal network. The safest way to put data on the external server is to load it from floppy disks or a tape drive; this way, the external server does not need any connection to your internal network. A more convenient method is to run an FTP server on the external Web server. To put files on the Web server, authorized users supply a correct user name and password to the FTP server and then transfer the files. To prevent internal leaks, only a few users (and possibly only a few machines) should be able to put data on the external server.

Firewall Implementation

The *firewall* gets its name from the familiar physical mass that prevents the spread of fire in a burning building. An Internet firewall prevents an Internet virus attack or other type of attack from spreading to your internal network. Conceptually, an Internet firewall is like tinted glass. You can see out from the inside, but the outside can't see in.

> **Note**
>
> Firewalls are often viewed by internal users as restrictive because they prevent users from gaining access to the Internet. The exact opposite is actually true. Without a firewall, the only way to prevent unwanted Internet traffic is to shut off Internet access altogether. With a firewall, you can filter unwanted traffic. While it's true that you can implement firewalls to restrict Internet access, this is only a consequence of trying to keep the bad guys out.

There are many possible firewall philosophies. This section describes only one of the more conservative approaches to firewall implementation. This approach assumes that all traffic not expressly permitted is prohibited. You must implement every firewall according to the needs of the specific network protected; it's impossible to generalize to all firewalls.

A conservative firewall approach is to require that all data from the Internet must pass through a narrow and heavily guarded gate before it can be accepted into the internal network. Frequently, you can accomplish this by running mail and other public Internet server applications outside the firewall on bastion hosts and by requiring interactive traffic from inside the firewall to pass through proxy and/or SOCKS servers (see fig. 8.8). *Bastion hosts* are special-purpose computers that run the minimum software necessary to do their function.

Fig. 8.8
A firewall requires all Internet traffic to the internal network to pass through gateway servers.

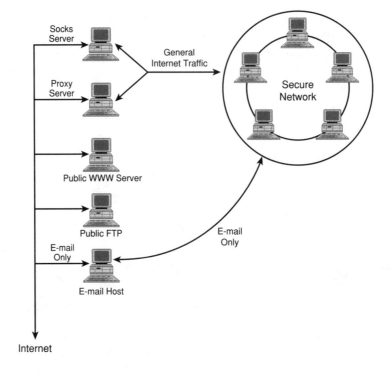

Bastion Hosts

A bastion host closes security loopholes and back doors by running the bare minimum software necessary to do its job. For example, the e-mail bastion host runs only a mail program. It removes all other software and nonessential parts of the operating system from the machine. This way, a potential attacker cannot use other software (such as a compiler) on the machine in an attack.

> **Note**
>
> Bastion hosts are typically used to run public Internet servers such as e-mail, anonymous FTP, Web, DNS, and so on. Bastion hosts can also create log files of all activity on the host.

You can implement a bastion host by forcing all Internet traffic related to the host application (such as e-mail) to pass through the host before it can be accepted internally. You can do this by using a combination of hardware routers and firewall software. Use routers to allow only certain types of traffic (based on the port number) to or from certain machines (based on

IP address). For example, you can configure a router to allow only mail traffic (port 25) into the mail host outside the firewall. The router also ensures that only mail traffic from the mail host is allowed inside the firewall.

Proxy and SOCKS Gateways

You use proxy and SOCKS servers to reduce the risk of an outside attack on a network by allowing Internet traffic through only one or two machines on the network. You use routers to shut off all Internet traffic except from the proxy and SOCKS servers, and all other machines on the network must funnel Internet traffic through those servers. By shutting off Internet access to all but one or two machines, fewer machines are open for possible attack.

Both types of servers simply pass Internet traffic from an internal network to the Internet. A *proxy server* passes all requests from authorized addresses. A *SOCKS server* is one type of proxy server that passes requests accompanied by proper user authorization.

> **Note**
>
> SOCKS servers require proper user authorization to send requests to the outside world, whereas proxy servers only screen requests by the client's address. Both types of servers can log all Internet activity passing through the server.

To access the Internet on a network using a proxy or SOCKS server, Internet application programs must be capable of communicating with these servers. An application capable of using SOCKS is said to be *SOCKSified*. Many UNIX-based Internet tools are SOCKSified, but this is less common on other platforms.

A popular proxy server for use with Web clients is the CERN httpd (included on the WebmasterCD and available at **http://info.cern.ch/hypertext/ WWW/Daemon/Status.html**). In addition to functioning as a Web server, the CERN httpd acts as a proxy for HTTP, FTP, Gopher, and WAIS requests from Web clients. Other proxy servers and clients are typically available in firewall toolkits.

You can get more information on how to SOCKSify servers and clients from **ftp://ftp.nec.com/pub/security/socks.cstc**. Beginning with version 2.17, CERN httpd offers SOCKS as well as proxy support.

Firewall Toolkits

Programs have been written to eliminate potential security problems with nearly every Internet service. Collections of these programs are available as firewall toolkits. One popular toolkit, the TIS Firewall Toolkit from Trusted Information Systems, is freely available on the Internet at **http:// www.tis.com/**. The TIS Web site contains many excellent papers on firewalls as well as a commercial toolkit. Other commercially available firewalls include Digital's SEAL, Sun's Firewall-1, and Raptor Eagle.

Setting up a firewall requires practical experience with UNIX and TCP/IP networking. Fortunately, firewall assistance is often available from your hardware vendor and there are many consultants who can help in firewall installation. If you feel uncomfortable with setting up your own firewall, you should strongly consider hiring a consultant or commercial firewall provider to assist you—the security of your entire network depends on it.

Running a Private Web Server

World Wide Web technology is a convenient way to communicate not only with the public at large, but also with specific individuals and groups of people using the Internet infrastructure. For example, you can provide proprietary data to customers or dealers by using a Web server on the Internet and eliminating the need to invest in a separate communications network. This section describes methods you can use to prevent unauthorized access of your private data.

You can use many of the techniques available for protecting an internal server to run a private Web server accessible only by authorized users on the Internet. However, in this case the internal network is the Internet itself, which is anything but private. Therefore, you must take additional precautions— encrypt your data, for instance.

Hiding the Server

As a very minimum security precaution for protecting private data, run the private server on a port other than the default port 80. By making the port number known only to authorized users of the private server, you eliminate the possibility that your data will be discovered by accident. However, this method alone does nothing to actually prevent access to your private data; further techniques are necessary.

Address Screening

By running your private server on a nonstandard port, you can use your routers to filter out all traffic on that port from unauthorized addresses. If you are providing data to product dealers, for example, simply allow traffic only from your dealers' Internet addresses. This eliminates the possibility of public discovery of your data.

Password Security

Another way to prevent unauthorized access to your private server is to require valid user names and passwords for each private directory. Passwords are set up using the `Auth` and `Limit Require` directives in the access configuration files, and are described in detail in chapter 6, "Server Configuration." Most browsers remember passwords during each session so that users don't have to reenter their password to see each new document.

Caution

Running on a different port, using address screening, and enforcing password security only prevent unauthorized users from accessing data via your server. However, data is transmitted to authorized users over the Internet "in the clear," so sniffers on the Internet can still see and record data sent to authorized users. *Sniffers* are the software equivalents of illegal bugs or wiretaps. Protecting against them requires encryption.

Encryption

Data encryption techniques are the only guaranteed way to protect private data. Several different options are available for transmitting encrypted data. You don't necessarily need a military-class encryption algorithm (unless you're transmitting military secrets!). The purposes of encryption are to scramble data so that keywords are not obvious to potential sniffers. Depending on the sensitivity of your data, you may want to use stronger encryption algorithms so that anyone wanting your data has to go through a lot of work to decipher it.

A simple way to merely hide data from keyword sniffers is to UUEncode sensitive data. UUEncode and UUDecode are available on most UNIX machines, and are built into many programs such as the shareware WinCode. UUEncode and UUDecode were originally intended for converting 8-bit binary files to 7-bit text files for transmission over networks. However, you can UUEncode any file to produce a gibberish-looking result. No keys are required—this is strictly a scrambling technique. A sample of UUEncoded text follows.

```
M1G)I9&%Y+"!397!T96UB97(@,C,L(#$Y.30@,3<Z-3,@15-4#0H-"E9E<G-I
M;VX@,"XY,BXV#0H-"E1H:7,@:7,@86X@3DY44"!N97=S<F5A9&5R(&90<B!-
M:6-R;W-O9G0@5VEN9&]W<R`S+C$@@;R@5VEN9&]W<R].."X@(%EO=0T*8V%N
M('5S92!I="!T;R!R!R96%D(&%N9"!P;W-T(%5S96YE="!N.97S+"!A;F;F0<V5N
M9"!E;6%I;"!"`H=%FEA(%--5'`@;W(@34%022D-"@T*4F5Q=6ER960;G1S.@T*
M#0I&;;W(@%5TE.4.4T]#2%$#2R`H&=C$C9N("!O<B!H:H:67(I(&8-.O7!L:66%N="!40U``0
```

> **Caution**
>
> UUEncoding files is *not* encryption. An encoded file looks like gibberish, but no codes or keys are required to decode the gibberish—just a freeware or shareware program that does UUDecoding, such as WinCode.

Several industrial-strength encryption algorithms are available. PGP (Pretty Good Privacy, which is actually much better than its name) is becoming a popular Internet standard, and is free for noncommercial purposes. RSA is a commercial algorithm, and must be licensed as such for all uses.

At any rate, raw algorithms don't do much good unless your Web server and browsers can support automatic encryption and decryption. This eliminates the hassle of having to run a separate decryption program for each document transferred via the Web. At present, the main contender for secure transactions is Netscape. It can conduct secure transactions in conjunction with the Netsite Commerce Server, which runs for about $5,000. The encryption technique employed by Netscape is the Secure Sockets Layer (SSL) and has been proposed as an open standard on the Internet; however, Netscape Communications Corp. can charge for it because free servers or clients using SSL have not been written.

Dial-up SLIP Connections

An alternative to encryption for keeping your data from public view is to run a SLIP server and allow authorized users to connect to your private Web server on dial-up lines. This keeps your data out of view of the Internet entirely. A drawback to this method is that you can only use password security to protect your data because the caller's Internet address is always that assigned by your SLIP server. If you really want to, you can use CallerID to figure out who was calling the SLIP server, but passwords are probably sufficient for most applications.

Connecting Divisional Web Servers via Internet

Corporations and other geographically distributed businesses are beginning to use the Internet infrastructure to communicate company private data. This saves the expense of leased lines between regional offices; however, unless encryption is employed, it is not completely secure. This section presents a few considerations for setting up a network of private Web servers to communicate data between divisions.

Address Screening

You can configure routers and server access configuration files to allow Web server traffic only from authorized Internet addresses (other company locations). This is a simple and effective way to restrict data access. Each division's Web server allows traffic only from the other divisions.

A potential problem with address screening is that a proxy server at an authorized address can potentially forward requests from unauthorized locations if the proxy server was not configured properly. To mitigate this risk, configure divisional Web servers to accept requests only from a single proxy or SOCKS server at each division.

> **Caution**
>
> Like any private Web server application, access can be restricted, but data is still transmitted "in the clear" to authorized users. Only encryption is sufficient for airtight protection of data transmitted over a public network.

Hardware Encryption

Software-based encryption is difficult to implement in an internetworking scenario because each program used to transmit data over the network must have built-in encryption. Fortunately, several vendors offer bridges and routers that perform encryption at a hardware level. These routers allow the secure transmittal of data to another site using the same bridge or router for decryption.

Hardware encryption is transparent to your application programs; you don't have to modify your Internet applications. By setting up encrypting routers at each divisional location, you establish a network of private Web servers without modifying either Web server or client software to support encryption. Until a wider variety of Web servers and clients support software encryption, hardware encryption is your best choice for maintaining a private network.

> **Caution**
>
> Hardware encryption does not eliminate the need for access control measures, such as address screening, because encrypting routers can still allow unencrypted traffic to and from the Internet just like any router. Hardware encryption only guarantees that data can be passed safely between two or more protected sites.

II

Setting Up a Web Server

Part III

Learning HTML

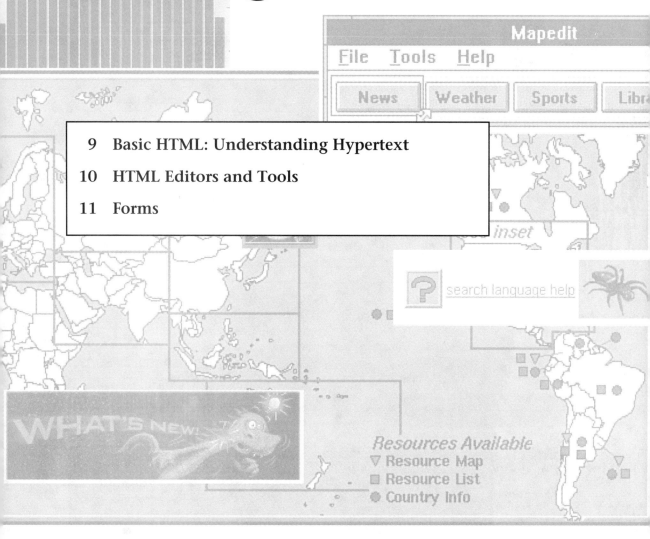

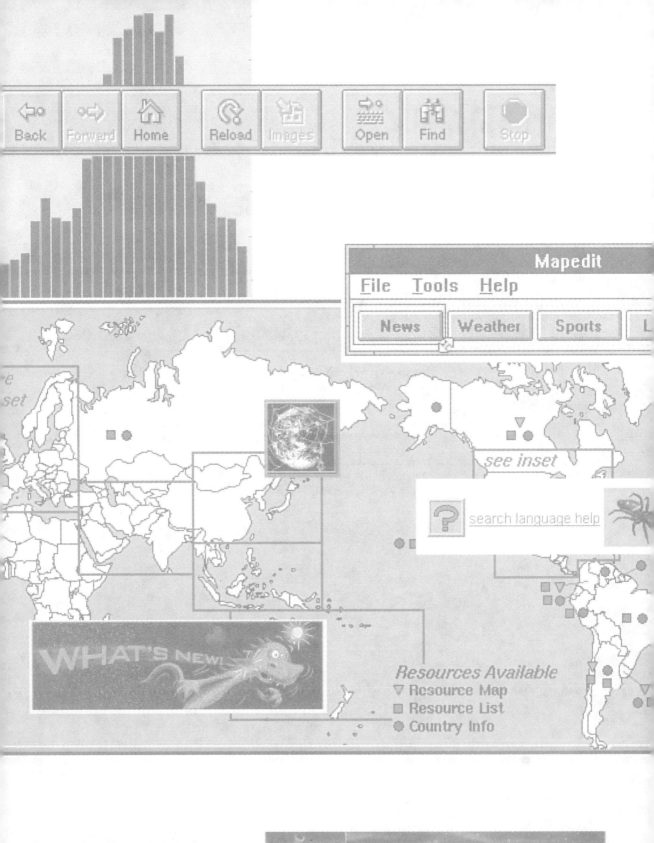

Chapter 9

Basic HTML: Understanding Hypertext

At the heart of every Web page is the *Hypertext Markup Language,* a page description language with built-in hypertext capabilities. Although it falls far short of having full-fledged formatting capabilities like a word processor or desktop publishing language, HTML at least allows for nicer formatting than plain, Courier font ASCII text.

The present version of HTML, otherwise known as *HTML 2,* is most commonly used. Most clients support this version, but a few, such as Netscape, support additional features, such as blinking text, that are not in any HTML specification. Most of this chapter covers standard HTML. *HTML 3* (formerly HTML+), which is still being formulated, includes more formatting features, such as centered text, tables, figures, and equations. HTML 3 promises to make strides toward a universal document format that is both compact and rich in formatting.

In this chapter, you learn the basics of HTML, including how to

- Use logical styles
- Use headings, lines, and lists
- Include images
- Use hypertext and hypergraphic anchors
- Link to other documents
- Create point-and-click imagemaps

Introduction

HTML is unique in the world of document formats. It is a simple, text-based language that you can nevertheless view in a variety of fonts on any platform. You can use it with text-only clients, such as Lynx, on a VT220 terminal or with fully graphical clients such as Mosaic on advanced graphical workstations. Although HTML is a very new language, more than a million public documents already use it, as estimated by the Lycos Web searcher.

History

The first version of HTML, HTML 0, was developed at CERN beginning in 1990 and is largely out of use today. HTML 1 incorporated inline images and text styles (highlighting) and was the version of HTML used by most of the initial Web browsers. HTML 2 is the current standard and should be issued as an Internet RFC (Request For Comments) by the time you read this. HTML 3, formerly called HTML+, will incorporate tables, figures, equations, and other more advanced formatting features.

ASCII-Based

HTML is simply ASCII text with formatting codes that specify different fonts and styles. It is very similar to older word processors that require insertion of formatting tags to specify bold, underlined, or italicized type. You can write or edit HTML using simple text editors because the language is ASCII-based and compact. Only a handful of formatting tags are commonly used and commonly supported, which makes all the available features easy to remember. The following example of HTML is taken from the NASA home page on the Web. Figure 9.1 shows the page as it appears in Mosaic for Windows, and figure 9.2 shows the page as it appears in Lynx, a text-based browser.

```
<html>
<head>
<title>NASA Information Services via World Wide Web</title>
</head>

<body>
<h2>National Aeronautics and Space Administration</h2>
<img src="http://www.nasa.gov/images/nasaban.gif" alt="[NASA Logo]">
<h3><i>World Wide Web (WWW) information services</i></h3>

<hr>
<a href="http://www.nasa.gov/nasa/nasa_hottopics.html"><b>* Hot Topics *
</b></a>......... NASA news and subjects of public interest
<br>
<hr>
```

```
<b>
<a href="http://nctn.hq.nasa.gov/nsp/nsp.html">NASA's Strategic
Plan</a>, Specific <a
href="http://www.nasa.gov/nasa/nasa_strategies.html">
NASA Strategies & Policies </a>
<p>
<a href="http://www.nasa.gov/hqpao/hqpao_home.html">NASA Public Affairs </a>
<p>
<a href="http://www.nasa.gov/nasa_online_education.html">
NASA Online Educational Resources</a>
<p>
<a href="http://www.nasa.gov/nasa/nasa_subjects/nasa_subjectpage.html">
NASA Information Sources by Subject </a>
</b>
<br>
<hr>
<a name="USA">
<b>NASA Centers (click on a center's name for its home page):</b></a>
<a href="http://www.nasa.gov/cgi-bin/imagemap/newusa">
<img src="http://www.nasa.gov/images/newusa.gif"
alt="[Map of NASA Centers]" ismap>
```

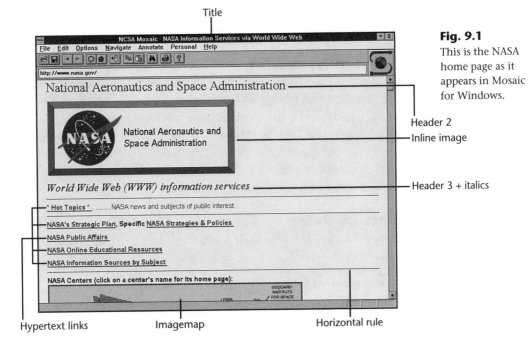

Fig. 9.1
This is the NASA home page as it appears in Mosaic for Windows.

Fig. 9.2

This is the NASA home page as it appears in Lynx, a text browser.

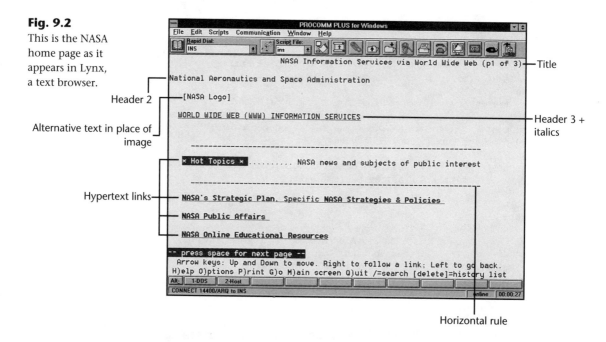

Title

Header 2

Alternative text in place of image

Header 3 + italics

Hypertext links

Horizontal rule

Platform-Independent

All of HTML's formatting features specify logical rather than physical styles. For example, the heading tags, which normally indicate larger font sizes, do not specify which fonts to use. Instead, browsers map logical styles to actual fonts available on that browser. This allows Macs to view files written on PCs and vice versa. The disadvantage to this approach is that it is impossible to control the exact formatting of any HTML document because users can choose their own fonts and styles to go with each HTML style.

Formatting Rules

Web browsers follow three basic rules when presenting HTML. These are listed and discussed below.

- White space is ignored.

- Formatting tags are not case-sensitive.

- Most formatting tags occur in pairs.

White Space Is Ignored

Because a document's text can be in any user-chosen font and a browser window can be of any size, normal HTML text is automatically word-wrapped to fit inside the user's window. When you view an HTML document, carriage returns at the ends of lines do not correspond to where they occur in a text editor. In fact, browsers ignore all white space (tabs, extra spaces, and carriage returns). Figure 9.3 illustrates this fact. Note that word wrapping does not occur where it does in the ASCII listing and that the browser ignored the extra spaces between The and End.

```
<TITLE>HTML Sample</TITLE>
<H1>HTML Sample</H1>
This is a sample of HTML
which illustrates that
browsers automatically fit
lines to the size of the
viewing window, regardless of
where word wrapping occurs
in the HTML file.
<P><HR><P>
<I>The        End</I>
```

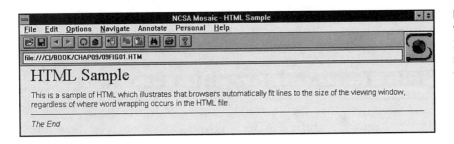

Fig. 9.3
This formatted HTML demonstrates ignored white space.

Tags Are Not Case-Sensitive
You can write all HTML formatting tags in upper, lower, or mixed case. When you are editing native HTML, it is sometimes easier to read documents when formatting tags are all in uppercase because they stand out more on the page.

Tags Occur in Pairs
With only a few exceptions, HTML formatting tags always include a beginning and an ending tag, with the text to be modified in-between. For example, to specify that a line of text appear in bold, you write:

```
<B>This text will appear in bold</B>
```

The closing tag is always preceded by a slash. The exceptions to this rule are the <P> (paragraph),
 (line break), and <HR> (horizontal rule) tags, which occur by themselves. Future versions of HTML may require that <P> tags occur in pairs, so you may want to use them that way now to ensure future compatibility.

III

Learning HTML

Document Structure

An HTML document consists of two parts—a head and a body. The *head* contains information about the document, such as the title. The *body* contains the document itself. The head and body are distinguished by the use of the <HEAD> and <BODY> tags, which are very similar to the <Directory> directive in the global access configuration file discussed in chapter 6, "Server Configuration." The <HEAD> and <BODY> tags occur in pairs, and enclose their respective portions. The structure is as follows:

```
<HEAD>
Elements contained in the header
</HEAD>
<BODY>
Text of document
</BODY>
```

Use of the <HEAD>...</HEAD> and <BODY>...</BODY> tags is not required because no tags can appear in both head and body sections; no confusion is possible. Use of these elements is considered the best style, however, and may be required in future versions of HTML.

Plain Text and Graphics Features

This section covers just the "Markup Language" portion of the Hypertext Markup Language. Features unrelated to hypertext fall into several categories:

- Header elements

- Headings

- Text styles

- Lines, paragraphs, and line breaks

- Lists

- Special characters

- Images

Header Elements

The document header has only two commonly used elements. These elements are listed and described below:

- Document title: <TITLE>...</TITLE>

- Document address: <BASE="*URL*">

Giving the Document a Title

Syntax: `<TITLE>...</TITLE>`

The title tags are used to enclose a document's title. The title is not displayed in the main document window but typically above the document body. In Mosaic for X-Windows and older versions of Mosaic for Windows, the title is displayed in a special title window above the document. More recent versions of Mosaic for Windows and Netscape display the title in the application's title bar. Lynx displays the title at the top of the page.

WebmasterCD

Title information is used in other ways, as well. Searches and What's New lists use document titles when generating a hypertext list of documents. If a document does not have a title, it will not show up correctly in hypertext lists that use titles. In addition, Windows httpd, one of the servers included with this book, places document titles in the description field of a fancy directory index. NCSA httpd for UNIX can be configured to do the same. You don't have to use the `<TITLE>` element, but you are strongly encouraged to do so.

Including a Document Address

Syntax: `<BASE="URL">`

Use the `<BASE>` tag to specify a document context so that relative paths in the document are correct when the document is read out of context. Browsers keep track of document context when reading documents online. However, when a browser attempts to display a local file, such as a document saved in an online session, it does not know the document's address and thus cannot find relative links inside the document. This typically means that inline images and links to subdocuments do not work correctly.

The `<BASE>` tag allows the document author to include its address (URL) so that browsers reading the document out of context can use the links in the document. `<BASE>` isn't a required element, but its proper use makes it easier for users to make local copies of your document, thereby reducing demand on your server.

Headings

HTML supports six heading styles, which are used to make text stand out by various degrees. These are numbered one through six, with `<H1>` being the largest. Figure 9.4 shows how the six heading styles are rendered in Mosaic for Windows by default. Users may, of course, specify any combinations of fonts or styles they choose. In Mosaic, you do this by choosing **O**ptions, **C**hoose Font.

III

Learning HTML

> **Note**
>
> The menu command may vary depending on which release and platform version of Mosaic you use.

Fig. 9.4
HTML headings help separate sections of a document.

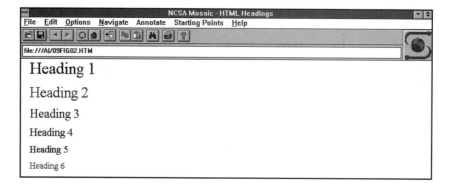

> **Note**
>
> Heading styles usually apply to an entire line of text, even if the heading tags enclose only one or two words on the line.

Text Styles

HTML supports two types of text styles: physical styles and logical styles (or highlighting). *Physical styles* are actual font attributes, such as bold, underline, and italics. *Logical styles* indicate the meaning of text; you can configure these styles in the browser to use any typeface and size desired.

> **Note**
>
> According to the HTML specification, browsers are not required to support any text styles. Do not assume that any given style is available in all browsers. In some browsers, for example, the underline style is reserved for displaying hyperlinks.

Creating Bold, Italicized, and Underlined Text

The physical styles supported by HTML are bold, italics, underline, and typewriter (fixed-width font). Table 9.1 lists these styles.

Table 9.1 Physical Styles in HTML	
Name	**Tag**
Bold	`<B>...</B>`
Italics	`<I>...</I>`
Underline	`<U>...</U>`
Typewriter	`<TT>...</TT>`

Figure 9.5 shows these styles as rendered by Mosaic for Windows with the default fonts. Note that underline is not available because it is used for hyperlinks.

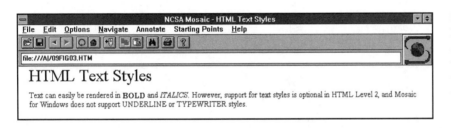

Fig. 9.5
HTML text styles are used to make text bold, italicized, underlined, or a fixed-width.

> **Note**
>
> The HTML specification allows nesting of physical text styles; not all browsers support this.

Using Logical Styles

Logical styles can be interpreted by browsers however the user chooses. Table 9.2 lists the common logical styles and their meanings and typical renderings. Closing tags are required for all logical styles, but have been omitted in the table to save space. To create a closing tag, just add a slash before the tag name, like `</ADDRESS>`.

III

Learning HTML

Table 9.2 Logical Styles in HTML		
Style Name	**Tag**	**Typical Rendering**
Address	<ADDRESS>	Italics
Block quote	<BLOCKQUOTE>	Left and right indent
Citation	<CITE>	Italics
Code	<CODE>	Fixed-width font
Definition	<DFN>	Bold or bold italics
Emphasis	<EM>	Italics
Keyboard	<KBD>	Fixed-width font
Sample	<SAMP>	Fixed-width font
Strong	<STRONG>	Bold
Variable	<VAR>	Italics

Figure 9.6 illustrates many of the logical styles supported in Netscape. The corresponding HTML follows:

```
<TITLE>HTML Logical Styles</TITLE>
<H1>HTML Logical Styles</H1>
<HR>
We would like to <EM>emphasize</EM> that payment must accompany
<STRONG>all</STRONG> document requests.
According to <CITE>Corporate Policy 42-A-1</CITE>:<BR>
<BLOCKQUOTE>Documents can only be released from the company when
accompanied by appropriate payment in the form of a check or money
order.</BLOCKQUOTE><P>
Fill out your request as in this example:<P>
<SAMP>Introduction to Standards</SAMP><BR>
<SAMP>Document #15226</SAMP><BR>
<SAMP>$425.00</SAMP><P>
Be sure to include the appropriate <VAR>document number</VAR>.<P>
<HR>
<ADDRESS>John Q. Public<BR>
jqpub@nowhere.com</ADDRESS><P>
```

Emphasis   Strong   Citation

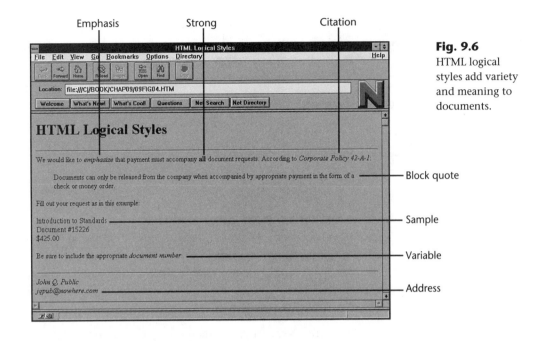

Fig. 9.6
HTML logical
styles add variety
and meaning to
documents.

Block quote

Sample

Variable

Address

Creating Tables and Aligning Text

Syntax: `<PRE>...</PRE>`

Some kinds of text, such as tables, require an exact relationship both horizontally and vertically between lines of text. HTML 2 does not support tables directly, but it does support preformatted text, which renders text in a fixed-width font and does not ignore carriage returns, tabs, or spaces as does normal HTML. A block of preformatted text begins with `<PRE>` and ends with `</PRE>`. The browser displays all text between `<PRE>` tags exactly as it appears in the HTML file. Figure 9.7 shows an example of preformatted text. The corresponding HTML is listed here, as well.

```
<TITLE>Pre-formatted Text</TITLE>
<H1>Course Timetable, Spring 1995</H1>
<PRE>
Course      Description        Days      Time
------      ----------------   ----      ----------
CS210       Intro. Op. Sys.    TR         3:30- 5:00
CS211       Beginning PASCAL   MWF        1:30- 2:30
CS314       Compiler Design    TR        10:30-12:00
CS451       Advanced UNIX      MWF        8:30- 9:30
</PRE>
```

III

Learning HTML

Fig. 9.7
You can use preformatted text to create tables.

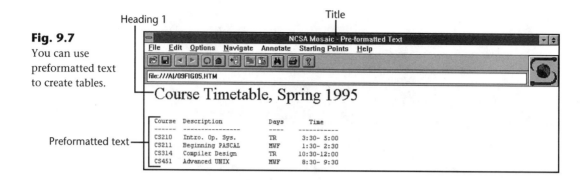

Lines, Paragraphs, and Line Breaks

HTML currently supports only one line style—a single horizontal line across the entire width of the browser window. A line is created with the <HR> (horizontal rule) tag. No closing tag is necessary. Figure 9.8 includes an example of a horizontal line.

The <P> tag is used to indicate the start of a new paragraph. It, too, occurs by itself under the current version of HTML, but may be required in HTML 3. Paragraphs are separated by a blank line. To start a new paragraph without the extra line of separation, use the <BR> tag (line break). Figure 9.8 shows the difference between paragraphs and line breaks. The corresponding HTML follows:

```
<TITLE>Lines, Paragraphs, and Line Breaks</TITLE>
<H1>Lines, Paragraphs, and Line Breaks</H1>
HTML text can be broken up vertically by several different
means.  Whitespace is ignored, so formatting tags must be
used to cause breaks in the text.<P>
This is the beginning of a new paragraph.  Note the extra
space between this paragraph and the last.  To eliminate
the extra space, use a<BR>
line break.
<P><HR><P>
```

Fig. 9.8
Lines, paragraphs, and line breaks set off sections of text.

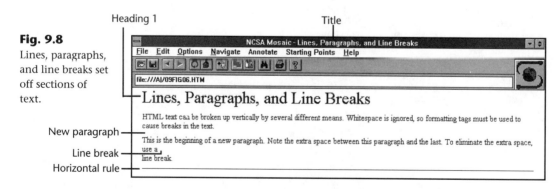

Lists

HTML supports several types of formatted lists for data presentation. All lists require a pair of tags indicating the type of list and a tag beginning each list item. Table 9.3 lists the five types of formatted lists.

Table 9.3 Formatted Lists in HTML		
Type	**List Tag**	**Item Tag(s)**
Ordered	`<OL>...</OL>`	`<LI>`
Unordered	`<UL>...</UL>`	`<LI>`
Menu	`<MENU>...</MENU>`	`<LI>`
Directory	`<DIR>...</DIR>`	`<LI>`
Description	`<DL>...</DL>`	`<DD>,<DT>`

All lists have the common characteristic that list items are indented some-what from the left. This indentation makes it easy to distinguish between normal text and listed items. In an ordered list, the browser automatically inserts item numbers. This numbering makes it easier to rearrange list items later on. An unordered list uses bullets rather than numbers to mark items. Menus and directories are very similar to unordered lists, but not all browsers support them well. Description lists are handy for presenting terms and defi-nitions. Figure 9.9 illustrates the many types of lists available in HTML.

> **Note**
>
> If a browser does not support a given HTML feature, text created using the feature just shows up as normal text.

The HTML text used to generate figure 9.9 follows:

```
<H3>Description List</H3>
<DL>
<DT><I>Description list</I>
<DD>A list containing terms and/or descriptions.
<DT><I>Description term</I>
<DD>A term being defined in a description list.
</DL>
<H3>Ordered List</H3>
<OL>
<LI>This is the first item.
<LI>This is the second item.
```

```
</OL>
<H3>Unordered List</H3>
<UL>
<LI>This is the first item.
<LI>This is the second item.
</UL>
```

Fig. 9.9
Ordered, unor-
dered, menu, and
description lists
enhance text.

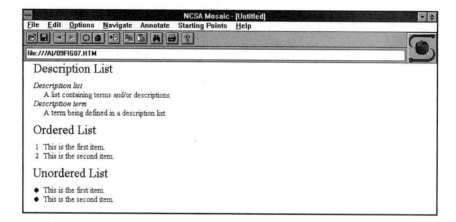

Note

You can nest lists inside other lists (see fig. 9.10). The HTML text for this figure
follows.

```
<H3>Tasty Fruits</H3>
<UL>
<LI><H4>Iowa Fruits</H4>
<OL>
<LI>Apples
<LI>Grapes
</OL>
<LI><H4>Florida Fruits</H4>
<OL>
<LI>Oranges
<LI>Grapefruits
</OL>
</UL>
```

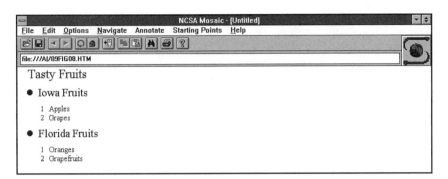

Fig. 9.10
You can create
a full outline
structure with
nested lists.

Special Characters

Because many characters have special meanings in HTML, it is necessary to
use special character sequences when you intend for special characters to
show up as normal characters. You can also use special character sequences
to produce foreign language characters and symbols.

Using Characters with Reserved Meanings

Because the less-than (<), greater-than (>), and quotation mark (") characters
are used in HTML formatting tags, the characters themselves must be represented differently. The ampersand (&) is used in these special sequences, so it
also must be represented differently. Table 9.4 lists all the special character
sequences in HTML.

Table 9.4 Special Character Sequences in HTML		
Sequence	**Appearance**	**Meaning**
&lt	<	Less than
&gt	>	Greater than
&amp	&	Ampersand
&quot	"	Quotation mark
		Nonbreaking space

Creating Comments

It is possible to include comment lines in HTML that do not show up in
browsers. The format for a comment is as follows:

```
<!-- Everything in here is part of the comment. -->
```

Note

Server-side include commands embedded in HTML use the same character sequence as comments. This is so that the server-side include commands do not show up even when a server does not support server-side includes. Documents utilizing server-side includes must have the extension SHTML; avoiding this extension eliminates all confusion with normal comments. For more information about server-side include commands, see chapter 12, "Scripts."

Creating Foreign Language Characters

HTML uses the ISO-Latin1 character set, which includes foreign language characters for all Latin-based languages, as the name implies. Like the other special character sequences in HTML, these sequences begin with an ampersand (&) followed by a written-out description of the character and a semicolon (;). The semicolon is necessary to indicate where the character description ends and normal text resumes. Table 9.5 lists all the foreign-language sequences available.

Table 9.5   Foreign Language Characters in HTML

Character	Sequence
Æ,æ	&AElig,&aelig
Á,á	&Aacute,&aacute
Â,â	&Acirc,&acirc
À,à	&Agrave,&agrave
Å,å	&Aring,&aring
Ã,ã	&Atilde,&atilde
Ä,ä	&Auml,&auml
Ç,ç	&Ccedil,&ccedil
Ð,´	&ETH,&eth
É,é	&Eacute,&eacute
Ê,ê	&Ecirc,&ecirc
È,è	&Egrave,&egrave
Ë,ë	&Euml,&euml

Character	Sequence
Í,í	&Iacute,&iacute
Î,î	&Icirc,&icirc
Ì,ì	&Igrave,&igrave
Ï,ï	&Iuml,&iuml
Ñ,ñ	&Ntilde,&ntilde
Ó,ó	&Oacute,&oacute
Ô,ô	&Ocirc,&ocirc
Ò,ò	&Ograve,&ograve
Ø,ø	&Oslash,&oslash
Õ,õ	&Otilde,&otilde
Ö,ö	&Ouml,&ouml
ß	&szlig
Þ,þ	&THORN,&thorn
Ú,ú	&Uacute,&uacute
Û,û	&Ucirc,&ucirc
Ù,ù	&Ugrave,&ugrave
Ü,ü	&Uuml,&uuml
Ý,ý	&Yacute,&yacute
ÿ	&yuml

Creating Other Special Symbols

You can reference any ASCII character in an HTML document by including the ampersand (&) and pound sign (#) followed by the character number in decimal and a semicolon (;). For example, to include the copyright symbol (©) in an HTML document, you write:

```
When you see this symbol &#169;, don't copy the page!
```

> **Tip**
>
> Windows users can use the Character Map program that comes with Windows to see the codes for all ASCII characters.

Images

Without the visual appeal of inline images, it is doubtful that the World Wide Web would have become as popular as it has so rapidly. Graphical Web browsers such as Mosaic can automatically display images in the GIF format inside documents. GIF (Graphics Interchange Format), originally developed for CompuServe users, was chosen as the WWW standard because it is compact and one of the most popular graphics formats. Every graphics-capable platform offers tools for editing and converting GIFs.

> **Note**
>
> Netscape can also display images compressed using the JPEG standard (JPG), but this is not part of standard HTML. Netscape gives users the option to display all images inline or in an external viewer.

You must save images as separate files even though they are referenced and displayed inside an HTML document. To include an inline image, use the `<IMG>` tag.

Syntax: `<IMG SRC="URL">`

Inline images always begin at the left side of the browser window, although future versions of HTML may allow centering. For example, to include a caution symbol next to some warning text, the HTML might look like this:

```
<IMG SRC="/icons/stop.gif">Formatting a disk erases its contents.
```

Figure 9.11 shows this HTML as it appears in a browser.

You can modify the `<IMG>` tag by several attributes (see table 9.6).

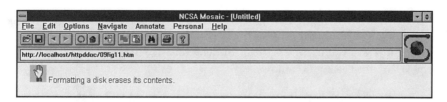

Table 9.6   IMG Tag Attributes

Attribute	Description
SRC="*URL*"	Location of the image file
ALIGN={TOP ¦ MIDDLE ¦ BOTTOM}	Location of text next to image
ALT="*text*"	Text to show instead of image
ISMAP	Used to make imagemaps

The SRC attribute tag contains a URL to the desired image. Because URLs can point anywhere, you can reference images on remote servers as well as your local server. Browsers can load images from a server running any protocol supported by the browser, including FTP and Gopher.

Note

Because browsers can load images from any server on the Internet, browsers establish separate server connections for each image in a document, even if all images are on the same server. For small images, it takes more time to establish the connection than to transfer the image data. Therefore, avoid numerous small images.

The HTML Graphics Format

Support for inline images as single files allows convenient reuse of graphics on your server because you can set up a common graphics library, or directory, for all documents on the server. On the other hand, the fact that graphics must be separate files, and GIF files at that, is one of the most difficult aspects of converting documents from any other format into HTML because of the time and effort required to separate all the graphics.

III

Learning HTML

The ALIGN attribute controls the location of text to the right of an inline image. By default, text appears at the bottom of an inline image. Figure 9.12 shows how you can use the ALIGN attribute to change the position of text. The HTML for this figure follows.

```
<IMG SRC="/icons/stop.gif" ALIGN="TOP">Formatting a disk erases its
contents.
```

Fig. 9.12

The ALIGN attribute changes text position relative to the image.

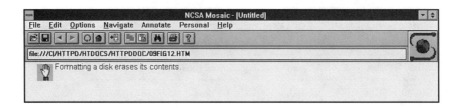

The ALT attribute specifies text to be shown in place of an image in text-only browsers. Including the ALT attribute tag is a courtesy to dial-up and dumb terminal users; don't overlook this courtesy. For example, to include text-only support in the previous example, the line would look like this:

```
<IMG SRC="/icons/stop.gif" ALIGN="TOP" ALT="STOP">Formatting a disk
erases its contents.
```

In Lynx, this line would appear as:

```
[STOP]Formatting a disk erases its contents.
```

Use the ISMAP attribute to create point-and-click imagemaps. Imagemaps are discussed at the end of this chapter.

Tip

You can use even small images to add variety to documents. A popular technique on the Web is to create bulleted lists using small colored balls for the bullets. Each different-colored bullet is a separate GIF file and each GIF file is loaded only once. Browsers remember each image loaded so that the image can be used many times in the same document. Depending on the browser's cache settings, it may also remember the image for use in other documents.

Note

One of the most frequently asked questions on the World Wide Web newsgroups is: "How can I create transparent GIFs?" Because many browsers allow users to set the background color, the background color of the image may be different than that of the browser window. A solution to this problem is to create GIFs with transparent backgrounds. In order for this to work, the browser and GIF creation tools must be able to support transparent GIFs. On the PC, LView Pro is one program that can create transparent GIFs. Both UNIX and Windows users can use a program called *Giftrans* to create transparent GIFs from existing images. Information about Giftrans and transparent GIFs is available from **http://melmac.corp.harris.com/transparent_images.html** and the World Wide Web FAQ.

Hypertext and Hypergraphics

Now to the other half of the Hypertext Markup Language—the hypertext part. A hypertext reference is very simple. It consists of only two parts: an anchor and an address, or URL. The *anchor* is the text or graphic that the user clicks to go somewhere. The *address* points to the document that the browser will load when the user clicks on the anchor.

Anchors

In HTML, an anchor can be either text or a graphic. Text anchors usually appear underlined and in a different color than normal text on graphical browsers and in bold on text-only browsers such as Lynx. Graphic anchors (hypergraphics) usually have a border around them to distinguish them from plain graphics.

Creating Hypertext Anchors

Any text can be a hypertext anchor in HTML, regardless of size or formatting. An anchor can consist of a few letters, words, or even lines of text. The format for an anchor-address pair is simple:

```
<A HREF="URL">text of the anchor</A>
```

The letter A in the <A HREF> tag stands for "anchor," and HREF stands for "hypertext reference." Everything between the <A HREF> and </A> tags is the text of the anchor, which appears underlined or bold, depending on the

III

Learning HTML

browser. The next section discusses the address. The following example shows a hypertext reference and how it would be displayed in a browser.

```
<A HREF="info/fruits.html">Information about fruits</A>
Information about fruits
```

Note

Other formatting codes can be used in conjunction with hypertext anchors. For example, to cause a text anchor to appear in the level 3 heading style, you write:

```
<A HREF="URL"><H3>text of the anchor</H3></A>
```

The order of nesting formatting codes is not important. It's also possible to write:

```
<H3><A HREF="URL">text of the anchor</A></H3>.
```

Creating Graphic Buttons

You can use hypergraphics to create button-like effects and provide a nice alternative to clicking plain text. The format for a graphic anchor is the same as a text anchor. However, instead of putting text between the <A HREF> and </A> tags, you reference an inline image. Figure 9.13 shows a hypergraphic.

```
<A HREF="/homepage.html"><IMG SRC="images/stop.gif"></A>Stop now
and return to the home page.
```

In this example, when the user clicks the hand, the browser returns to the home page as specified in the URL.

Fig. 9.13
Hypergraphics create button-like objects.

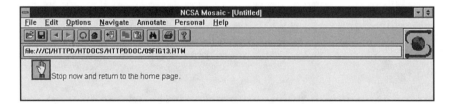

Tip

If text or images used in hypertext anchors don't seem to be working right, check to see that the document address in the <A HREF> tag is completely enclosed in quotes. Omitting the final quotation mark is a common and easy mistake.

Addresses (URLs)

A hypertext address is called a *uniform resource locator,* or URL. The URL scheme is a way of compactly identifying any document on any type of Web-compatible server anywhere in the world. The URL consists of four parts: a protocol, Internet address, port, and file name. With the exception of the News protocol, the general format for a URL is as follows:

```
protocol://internet_address:port/file name
```

In addition, you can optionally specify search or query information after `file_name` when sending data to a search or script. This is covered in chapter 11, "Forms."

Protocol

The protocol indicates what type of Internet service is requested. In order to use a given protocol, both the client (browser) and Internet server must be able to speak that protocol. The most common is HTTP, which is spoken by all Web servers and clients. In addition, almost all browsers support FTP, Gopher, Telnet, and news. Some also support WAIS. Some fictional examples of URLs using these protocols follow:

http://www.somewhere.com/WWW/product_info.html

ftp://ftp.internet.stats/last_month/statistics.txt

gopher://gopher.government.gov/reports/income_tax.txt

telnet://fedworld.gov

news:sci.alchemy.nuclear

mailto:sales@widgets.com

Note

The news URL is substantially different than the others because it does not specify an Internet address or file name. Instead, it simply names a newsgroup. The name of the news server must be made known to the browser when you initially configure the browser.

III

Learning HTML

Where to Get News

In order for you to read Internet news through a Web browser, you have to be able to connect to a news server, which continually receives messages over the Internet and stores them locally for a short time (usually about two weeks). Newsfeeds cost money, and for this reason, no news servers are publicly available on the Internet. If your site wishes to take full advantage of Internet news, you must obtain a newsfeed from your Internet service provider or obtain authorization to connect to your provider's news server.

The mailto: URL allows you to send electronic mail to the specified address directly from your browser. The mailto: URL is supported by Netscape, Lynx, and others, but it isn't supported by all browsers.

Port

The port is an optional URL element. If the port is omitted, the default port for the specified protocol is assumed. For more information on port numbers, see chapter 6, "Server Configuration."

Address

The address portion of a URL is simply the name or number of an Internet server. This address can be either the familiar named dot notation (like ftp.ncsa.uiuc.edu) or a number sequence (like 127.0.0.1).

Note

You can reference other machines on your network simply by specifying the name of the local machine without the full address. For example, a URL to a document on a local server named "web_server" might be http://web_server/finance/quarterly_report.html. The full path of your organization's name is not required.

File Name

The document path, or *file name,* is the same as that used by DOS and UNIX systems alike, although the slash is forward (/) rather than backward (\) for DOS users. Each slash goes down to the next subdirectory having the specified name, and the path ends in a file name with an extension (such as TXT or HTML). It is also possible to specify a path to an entire directory simply by ending with the directory name and a trailing slash (/). For example, to see the contents of the fruits directory on an FTP server, you can use

```
ftp://ftp.healthy.com/fruits/
```

A powerful shortcut when developing a web of documents on your server is to use relative rather than absolute paths. You can omit the protocol and address and simply begin the document address in the hyperlink with a relative path. For example, if you're working on a file called "fruits.html" on your Web server and want to link to "banana.html" in the same directory, the link is simply:

```
<A HREF="banana.html">Information on bananas</A>
```

If the file is in a subdirectory named "yellow_fruits," start with the name of the subdirectory:

```
<A HREF="yellow_fruits/banana.html">Information on bananas</A>
```

> **Note**
>
> Some Web documents about HTML refer to absolute and relative paths as fully qualified and partially qualified.

You can also specify a relative path to a document in higher-level directories using "..", the symbol for the parent directory. For example, this reference points to a file named "about.html" in the parent directory:

```
<A HREF="../about.html">About yellow fruits</A>
```

Even if a document is in an entirely separate directory tree but still on the same server, you can omit the protocol and Internet address by beginning the file name with a slash (/). This references the server's document root directory, from which subdirectories and aliased directories can be referenced (see chapter 6, "Server Configuration"). For example, if your server has a separate directory tree named "bananas" underneath the server document root, you write:

```
<A HREF="/bananas/banana.html">Information on bananas</A>
```

> **Note**
>
> In addition to providing a typing shortcut, use of relative path names is highly recommended for making document trees more portable. This way, you can remove or rename entire directory trees without having to edit each HTML file in the directory to change link names.

III

Learning HTML

Imagemaps

Inline images can act as graphical buttons when they are made into hypergraphic anchors. In addition, you can subdivide images into regions using imagemaps. Imagemaps allow a single GIF image to contain several "hot regions." Depending on where in the image the reader clicks, different links are followed. This technique can be used to create graphical buttons and interactive maps.

How Imagemaps Work

An *imagemap* is actually a single hypergraphic that links to a server script. When a reader clicks the image, the mouse coordinates relative to the image are sent back to the imagemap script. The script then looks in the corresponding map file to decide which hyperlink to follow based on the mouse coordinates.

Creating Imagemaps

In order for imagemaps to work, several configuration steps are necessary. First, your browser must support imagemaps. All of the popular graphical browsers do this; no special browser configuration is required, so this is easy. Second, certain imagemap support files must be present on your server. Third, you must create the graphic and define the coordinates of the various regions. This discussion is specifically for UNIX systems, but the same principles apply to the Windows httpd.

Configuring NCSA httpd for Imagemaps

Both the NCSA httpd and CERN httpd feature imagemap support, although there are slight differences. This book discusses primarily NCSA's imagemap feature, but differences are noted. NCSA httpd requires two files for imagemap support. The first is a script called *imagemap,* which must be compiled for your machine and placed in the cgi-bin directory. This script is automatically placed in the cgi-bin directory when you install NCSA httpd for UNIX.

Note

The imagemap script usually goes in the cgi-bin directory but you can put it in any CGI script directory that has been created using the `ScriptAlias` directive (see chapter 6, "Server Configuration").

Second, you need write permission to the imagemap.conf file in the server's conf directory. This file maps image names, which you create, to their associated map files. If you do not have write access to this file, your administrator has to add a line to this file for each new imagemap created. The format of the imagemap.conf file is simple:

```
image_name : physical_path
```

The path to the map file is not a URL. It's the physical path on your system. A sample imagemap.conf is included below.

```
homepage : /top/homepage.map
buttonbar : /top/buttons.map
usmap : /top/countries/us.map
```

Creating an Imagemap

You can use any image-editing program or GIF conversion tool to make the GIF file itself. The most difficult part of making an imagemap is mapping image coordinates to corresponding actions.

The present version of the imagemap script handles coordinate regions that are rectangles, circles, and polygons. Windows httpd also has experimental support for ellipses. A map file defines these regions. Each line in a map file defines one "hot spot" region, like this:

```
rect url upper_left(x,y) lower_right(x,y)
circle url center(x,y) edge_point(x,y)
poly url vertex1(x,y) vertex2(x,y) vertex3(x,y) ...
```

Note

The CERN imagemap facility uses the keywords rectangle, circle, and polygon instead of NCSA's rect, circle, and poly. In addition, the format of the map file is slightly different.

Each line defines one region and its associated URL. Rectangular coordinates are in the order (x,y), with (0,0) being the upper-left corner. The first line of a map file is the default, which specifies what action to take if the coordinates are outside any defined region. A sample map file follows that divides a 400×200 rectangular box into four equal "buttons."

III

Learning HTML

```
default /top/homepage.html
rect /box/upper_left.html 0,0 199,99
rect /box/upper_right.html 200,0 399,99
rect /box/lower_left.html 0,100 199,199
rect /box/lower_right.html 200,100 399,199
```

Note

Virtual buttons in a map file can also point to full URLs on other servers. For example, a map file can contain:

```
rect ftp://ftp.internic.net/ 0,0 199,99
```

With most image editors, including Windows Paintbrush, LView, and xv (UNIX), you can turn on a feature to display the current mouse coordinates at all times. You can use this to help you locate coordinates for the map file. Better yet, there is a program called *Mapedit* that you can use to draw rectangles, circles, and polygons directly on the GIF image. Mapedit will automatically create the corresponding map file for use with NCSA or CERN httpd. Mapedit runs on both UNIX and Windows systems. Fig. 9.14 shows Mapedit for Windows. Mapedit for both UNIX and Windows is available on WebmasterCD. You can obtain information about changes and new versions from **http://sunsite.unc.edu/boutell/mapedit/mapedit.html**.

Note

Mapedit is free for educational and nonprofit use, but commercial users must pay a fee after 30 days. By purchasing this book, you have not purchased Mapedit in any way. No rights have been assigned, rented, or leased to you. For more information on the WebmasterCD license agreement, see the description opposite the back cover. For more information regarding the Mapedit license agreement, see the documentation on WebmasterCD.

Fig. 9.14

Mapedit lets you draw rectangles, circles, and polygons on an existing image and automatically creates the map file.

Linking to the Imagemap

After you create a map file for an image, you must make it an anchor to include it in an HTML file, like this:

```
<A HREF="/cgi-bin/imagemap/buttonbar"><IMG SRC="buttons.gif"></A>
```

The hypertext reference must contain the URL to the imagemap script followed by a slash (/) and the name of the map defined in the imagemap.conf file. The actual picture is then included with the <IMG SRC> tag.

For this example to work, there must also be a line in the imagemap.conf file pointing to a map file for the imagemap "buttonbar." That line might look like this:

```
buttonbar : /top/buttons.map
```

Note

The CERN httpd includes a slightly different version of the imagemap script called *htimage* that eliminates the need for the imagemap.conf file. Instead, htimage allows you to specify a URL to the map file directly. Using htimage instead of imagemap in the previous example, you would write:

```
<A HREF="/cgi-bin/htimage/top/buttons.map"><IMG SRC="buttons.
gif"></A>
```

Tip

You can use CERN's htimage script even if you run the NCSA httpd.

In summary, there are only three steps to creating point-and-click images.

1. Create the map file.

2. Create an alias to the map file in imagemap.conf (if you're using the NCSA httpd).

3. Make the image a hypergraphic anchor in an HTML document.

III

Learning HTML

Chapter 10

HTML Editors and Tools

It's easy to write an HTML document. After all, the main document is nothing but ASCII text, and much of that is often the plain-language text that you're trying to communicate on the page. The tricky part is getting the proper tags in the right place to make your text and images come out looking like you want them to. Browser programs are very literal in the way that they interpret HTML, so errors in your HTML syntax make your page look very unusual. You need to take extra care to ensure that your page comes out looking like you planned.

Because HTML documents are all ASCII code, originally Web documents were written with simple text editors, such as the Windows Notepad, or Pico or emacs for UNIX. As people began writing longer and more complex documents, many turned to their favorite word-processing programs (which can save documents in plain ASCII text) and wrote macros and tools to help them.

As the Web has expanded, dedicated HTML editing programs (similar to word processing programs, but designed to produce results for the screen and not the printed page) began to appear. These programs allow Web page creators to more quickly format their text into proper HTML format by allowing authors to have codes placed automatically around text at the click of a toolbar button. The popularity of these editors has driven developers to produce dozens of new editors, filters, and utilities, all aimed at making a Web author's life easier (as well as ensuring that the Hypertext Markup Language is properly used).

As you can see, there are many ways you can write your HTML documents; you can use your favorite line editor, a word processor, or a dedicated HTML tool. The choice of which system to use depends on personal preference and your confidence in your use of HTML.

Because many HTML-specific tools have checking routines or filters to verify that your documents are correctly laid out and formatted, they appeal to new writers of Web documents. They also tend to be friendlier and more graphically based than nonHTML editors.

On the other hand, if you're a veteran programmer or writer, you may want to stick with your favorite editor and use a filter or syntax checker afterwards. Luckily, there are ample tools available for whichever approach you take.

This chapter looks at five types of applications that are useful in developing HTML documents:

- Plain text editors

- Tools and macros for word processing programs

- Stand-alone HTML authoring tools

- Tools, converters, and filters for importing other types of documents into HTML

- Utilities to help maintain links in HTML documents

Note

One of the best sites to look for new editors and filters is CERN. Through the WEB, connect to **http://info.cern.ch/WWW/Overview.html**. Also useful is the NCSA site, accessible through the Web at **http://www.ncsa.uiuc.edu/SDG/Software/ Mosaic/Docs** where the document "faq-software.html" contains an up-to-date list of offerings. You can also find a good index of HTML editors from Yahoo at **http:// akebono.stanford.edu/yahoo/Computers/World_Wide_Web/ HTML_Editors/**.

Many of the editors discussed in this chapter are included on WebmasterCD.

Plain-text Editors

You can use any ASCII editor to write HTML pages. The tags necessary to indicate special effects that a Web browser should show are only combinations of ASCII characters (such as <BLINK> at the beginning of text that's supposed to blink and </BLINK> at the end). In contrast, most word processing programs embed special binary codes in the text to indicate changes in font styles or the location and format of graphics. Because hypertext authors know the HTML codes, they can write in various formatting effects as easily as they can enter sections of text.

This simplicity can be extremely useful. Many veteran HTML authors rely on a simple plain-text editor as they tweak specific points on any given page. Plain-text editors have the advantage of taking up less memory, which allows experienced authors to open up multiple Web browser programs simultaneously to see how their page looks in each format. (Although a code for something to be bold is read by Cello, Mosaic, and Netscape as bold, the way bolded text appears may vary slightly with each browser.)

The major annoyance with plain-text editors is that HTML codes are not treated as complete units. You have to edit each and every keystroke in the HTML code, whereas many editor programs treat the code as an entire entity. In a plain-text editor, getting rid of the code combination <B> and </B> around text requires deleting each keystroke. Some of the dedicated editors recognize the combination and eliminate the whole code (and even delete its companion code on the other side of the text).

Nevertheless, you will probably need to use a simple editor sometime; become familiar with at least one, even if it's not what you usually use to compose your HTML files. The next section takes a look at a few of the most commonly used plain-text editors.

Pico, emacs, and vi Editors for UNIX

Many users familiar with the UNIX system recognize one or more of these editors. Pico, emacs, and vi are each different plain-text editing programs commonly found on large UNIX systems. Users who have net access primarily through a UNIX shell account may be compelled to use one of these editors to edit files that are stored on the UNIX system.

You can use all three editors to edit HTML files, as all three can create a file in standard, ASCII-only text format. Nevertheless, this is pretty much the hard way to go about editing your HTML files. Even if you don't have an add-on for editing HTML on your word processor, you may want to edit your files there, save them in ASCII format, and then upload them to your UNIX system.

III

Learning HTML

Of course, if you're a veteran at editing code on these editors, you can write macros to insert the correct tags where you need them. To some extent, how you choose to use any plain-text editor is largely a matter of personal preference.

Of the three, Pico is easily the most user-friendly. Pico provides a menu of common editing codes on the bottom of the screen. Moreover, many users who are familiar with the PINE mail program will recognize that Pico looks very much like the PINE text editor. Just remember that while using Pico that the symbol ^ represents the Ctrl key on most PCs.

Notepad for Windows

You can use Notepad to edit HTML documents, as long as the documents are not too long. Notepad has a file size limit; any particularly complex HTML document probably exceeds its capacity.

One advantage that Notepad has is that it creates files in ASCII format. This capability saves you the step of translating the file from a word processor format into ASCII that is necessary if you use some of the add-on templates for word processors.

Notepad can also prove useful if you just need to make a quick tweak on a document that's already mostly edited. You may be able to open the HTML document in Notepad and make the minor adjustment without having to go through the hassle of opening your word processor and activating the proper template.

Tip

If you use a plain-text editor for most of your HTML authoring, it's a good idea to check the syntax in your documents before putting them on the Web. To check the syntax, use a program with HTML filtering, such as Quarterdeck's HTML Authoring Tools for MS Windows.

HTML Editing Tools for Use with Word Processors

Because many people are already familiar with the editing features of their favorite word processor, many HTML authors have turned to creating specialized macros and tools that take advantage of the properties of the word processing programs to make editing HTML even easier. Now, even developers are getting into the act, and produce programs designed explicitly as add-ons for commercial word processors.

For whatever reason, be it the strong use of Styles or an easy, powerful macro language, Microsoft's Word seems to be the word processor of choice for those writing HTML editing tools; the vast majority of these types of tools are written expressly for Word for Macintosh or Windows. It is, perhaps, this obvious demand in the Word market that has compelled Microsoft to release its own package of utilities for using Word on the World Wide Web.

Microsoft Internet Assistant for Microsoft Word

Internet Assistant is a no-cost add-on offered by Microsoft for Word for Windows that turns Word into a Web Browser and includes styles, toolbars, and tools for authoring HTML.

> **Note**
>
> The following information is based on the beta test version of this software. It is expected that by the time this book reaches publication, Microsoft will have formally released the official version of this product. References to some menu items or toolbars may be different as a result.

> **Note**
>
> You can find a copy of Internet Assistant under the "What's New" heading of Microsoft's Home Page on the World Wide Web. The URL is **http://www.microsoft.com/**. Microsoft will also ship a copy on floppy disk to registered owners of Word 6 for a shipping and handling charge of $5. Call (800) 426-9400.

In addition to turning Word into a functional Web Browser, Microsoft's Internet Assistant for Word provides two ways to create documents for use on the Internet. First, this add-on offers a set of tools for editing HTML documents, primarily in the form of an extensive set of styles to be applied to text and the ability to drag and drop links to other documents.

Second, Microsoft has created a viewer Word document that allows Word-format documents to be placed directly on the Web. When the user opens a link to one of these documents, he can activate his Word viewer and look at the document. Users who have Microsoft Word would theoretically be able to treat the document as any other Word document, including copying text and graphics to use in other documents.

III

Learning HTML

Installing Internet Assistant on your System

After downloading the file, the installation of the Internet Assistant is fairly easy. If you have installed a Microsoft program yourself, this process should be familiar.

> **Note**
>
> In the beta version we looked at, the installation procedure was not as easy as we had hoped it would be. Several people who worked on this book experienced unexplainable crashes.

1. Make sure that the Internet Assistant self-extracting archive is in a temporary directory.

2. Execute the self-extracting archive by double-clicking the archive file from the Windows File Manager. When the file has finished extracting, press Enter to return to Windows.

3. Execute the setup.exe file. Simply double-click the file name from the Windows File Manager. (You may need to choose **W**indow, **R**efresh to see the files that you extracted.)

4. Choose OK on the first installation screen to proceed with the Internet Assistant installation. (If you want to stop the installation, choose **E**xit Setup.)

5. The next three screens show you the Internet Assistant license agreement. Click **C**ontinue on the first two screens, and Agree on the final screen to begin the installation.

6. The next screen lets you specify the directory where Internet Assistant is installed. The default is a directory called "internet" under your Word 6 directory. You can browse your local disk to specify a different directory.

7. Before Internet Assistant installs the Web browsing component, it brings up a screen asking if you have Internet access. Click **Y**es to install the Internet browsing software if you have Internet access.

8. The progress of the installation is shown on a linear graph. Once the installation is complete, you will receive a message telling you that installation was successful.

9. To exit the setup program, choose OK in the dialog box.

10. The installation of the Internet Assistant software is now complete. You can remove the temporary directory where you unpacked the software if you want; it is no longer needed.

Using Internet Assistant to Edit HTML

After you install Internet Assistant, you will find that you have access to two new templates, called HTML.DOT and WEBVIEW.DOT. Opening a new file using the WEBVIEW template causes Word to act like a Web Browser, whereas activating HTML.DOT provides a set of styles and tools for editing HTML.

To open a new document using the HTML template:

1. Open the File menu and choose New. A dialog box with a list of templates appears.

2. Select HTML and choose OK. When the new document opens, you see a new toolbar with several regular Word functions removed.

In the example presented in figure 10.1, both the Standard and Formatting toolbars are open. Keep in mind that you can customize these toolbars, like all of the toolbars in Word. You can add buttons and rearrange their order; your tools may look different than those in figure 10.1.

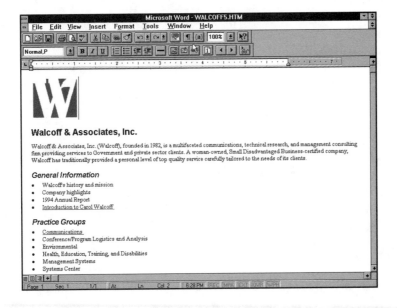

Fig. 10.1
Internet Assistant lets you edit HTML using standard Word tools.

III

Learning HTML

Table 10.1 lists the new Internet Assistant Tools.

Table 10.1	Internet Assistant Tools	
Tool	**Name**	**Description**
	Copy Hyperlink	Copies URL information on the open document to the clipboard so it can be pasted into another document.
	HTML Hidden	Toggles HTML tags to either visible or hidden.
	Numbered List	Tags text to appear as a numbered list.
	Bulleted list	Tags text to appear as a bulleted list.
	Horizontal Rule	Places horizontal line between sections of document.
	Picture	Places a graphic image into the page.
	Bookmark	Stores URL information on an open page to the Bookmark list.
	Hyperlink	Creates a hyperlink by placing anchor information and visible text into the page.
	Title	Opens dialog box to create title and header information.
	Go Back	Jumps back to the previous Hypertext document.
	Go Forward	Follows link to the next Hypertext document.
	Switch to Web Browse View	Closes editing tools and opens Web browsing tools.

If you want to edit an existing HTML document, Word will automatically open the HTML template when you select a document with an HTM extension. (Nevertheless, in the beta version that we looked at, Word didn't present an option to select HTML documents in its Open Document dialog box.)

As you type in the text of your Web Page, you can mark it for specific text effects such as bold or italic using the standard Word tools. Word will automatically translate those effects into HTML tags. You can also format text in HTML modes such as Strong or Preformatted by using the styles available under the HTML template. You can select a style using the Styles tool in the formatting toolbar, or you can open the F**o**rmat menu and choose either **S**tyle or Style **G**allery.

Entering Special Characters Using Internet Assistant

Internet Assistant also provides a way to place special codes such as diacritical marks, copyright and trademark symbols, or other special punctuation. To access these special characters, open the **I**nsert menu and choose **S**ymbol. A dialog box with listings of special characters appears (see fig. 10.2). Double-clicking the name of any specific character places it in the text where the I-beam cursor is located.

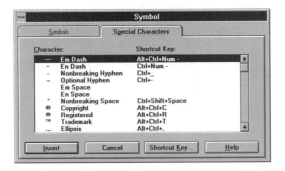

Fig. 10.2
Special characters and symbols can be inserted through this dialog box.

Handling HTML Codes Not Supported by Internet Assistant

There are also several HTML tags and effects that Internet Assistant does not accommodate through styles or tools. To enter these additional tags (or any extra HTML code), open the **I**nsert Menu and choose **H**TML Markup. A dialog box with a large window for entering direct HTML code appears (see fig. 10.3). The entered text is handled and displayed as HTML code without ever being translated into Word format.

Fig. 10.3
You can enter HTML tags that aren't supported by the tools in Internet Assistant through this dialog box.

III

Learning HTML

Creating Forms Using Internet Assistant

Internet Assistant has some fairly extensive features for creating interactive forms. You can begin a form by opening the **I**nsert menu and choosing the For**m** Field option. This causes Internet Assistant to enter the HTML tags that surround a form. A Forms toolbar and a dialog box appear to help you create the form field (see fig. 10.4).

Fig. 10.4

Internet Assistant has several tools for editing forms.

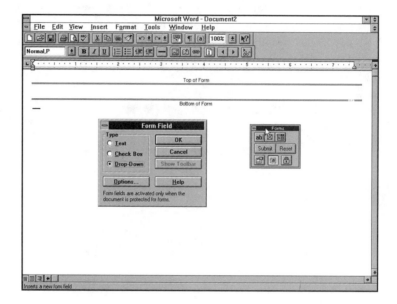

If you've created forms in Microsoft Access, you may recognize the look of some of these form tools. The Forms toolbox gives you point-and-click access to creating click-boxes, pull-down list boxes, and text boxes. This toolbox also provides a standard Reset button. When you place a field in the form area, additional dialog boxes open up to help you create the necessary choices for a pull-down list box or other controls to help make the form work. You can even add help text that may appear in the browser's status bar. You can also link form fields to macros to help automate the exchange of data.

Linking a Web Page to a Database

If you open the **I**nsert menu, you see an option called **D**atabase, which, if used by itself, lets you insert a database table (or a table of query results) into the text of an HTML document. This is useful if you need to put tabular data online in its tabular format, but it is probably not a good way to create an effective and exciting Web document. The **I**nsert, **D**atabase option has much more potential to be used as an element in macros that could then be linked to your interactive forms. See the section "Windows Database Servers" in chapter 15, "Database Access and Applications Integrations."

By combining the forms that you create with macros using the **I**nsert, **D**atabase option, you can create HTML documents that provide dynamic responses to searches whose terms are specified by the user viewing your Web page. This allows you to make the information contained in your databases available to a much wider audience, and increases the utility of your documents.

Saving Documents in HTML Format

Word Internet Assistant saves documents in HTML format by default. The resulting document is then ready to be used on your Web Server. This is a contrast to many of the third-party templates discussed in this chapter, which require you to translate the document from Word DOC format into ASCII/HTML text.

Using Word Documents on the World Wide Web

Along with the HTML editing tools, Microsoft has released a viewer that allows people who do not own Word to view Word documents from the World Wide Web. This means that authors can use the various formatting tools and special design capabilities of Word to design documents that exceed the capability of HTML. Users who own Word can treat the online document as any other Word document, and can consequently take advantage of features such as Word's capability to interact with other Microsoft products, such as Access or Excel.

Unfortunately, people who don't have Word probably can't take advantage of all of these capabilities. This means that if you design a Web page in Word, even though everyone may be able to get a viewer to look at the document, some percentage of the audience will be unable to fully interact with the document unless they invest in additional Microsoft products. There are potentially two negative side effects to this. First, if the majority (or even a large percentage of Web pages) were designed in Word format, more people would eventually be compelled to use one company's products to interact with the Web. This could eventually have the effect of giving a large percentage of control of the future of the Web to a single company. The opposite could also be true; people who don't want to deal with the Microsoft family of software products could stay away from your site in droves, knowing that they wouldn't have full accessibility.

III

Learning HTML

Nevertheless, this capability presents new options for the Web page designer, who can now incorporate functional links to databases and spreadsheets into their documents. The capability to drag-and-drop components will undoubtedly help to spur the creativity of at least some Web authors. This creativity may force the rest of the Internet community to come up with other ways to accomplish the same kinds of tasks through a revised and expanded HTML.

> **Note**
>
> You can find a link to a copy of the Word Viewer for people without Word on the same Web page with the Internet Assistant under the "What's New" heading of Microsoft's Home Page. The URL is **http://www.microsoft.com/**.

Quarterdeck's WebAuthor

Quarterdeck recently released a commercial package of HTML Authoring Tools for use with Microsoft Word 6 for Windows called WebAuthor.

> **Note**
>
> The information in this section was based on our evaluation of a beta version of Quarterdeck's WebAuthor for Word for Windows; the final version may look slightly different, as Quarterdeck changes or adds features. Quarterdeck plans to release a version of WebAuthor for Macintosh soon. It's expected that the look and feel of those tools will be much like the Windows version, so even though these instructions are Windows-oriented, they also may be helpful for Macintosh users.

Setting up Quarterdeck's WebAuthor for Windows is relatively simple; it comes with a fairly standard INSTALL program. This creates a program group that contains a Windows-standard help file and a Write document with release information. The main body of the tools is not apparent, however, until you open Microsoft Word.

To activate WebAuthor, open the **T**ools (Alt+T) menu. An option called **H**TML Authoring should appear at or near the bottom of this menu (see fig. 10.5). Choosing this option opens the HTML Authoring Tools dialog box.

A problem that you may experience is that when you try to open WebAuthor, it may say that your GIF Graphics Converter is not installed, and that you need to install it from my Word Setup disks as soon as possible.

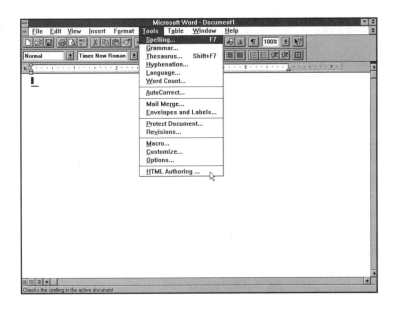

This sounds more complicated than it actually is. If you ran a complete installation of Word (or office), you've probably already installed the proper filter. If you haven't, the first time that you try to open WebAuthor, a dialog box informs you that the filter isn't installed (see fig. 10.6).

Quarterdeck's WebAuthor requires you to have the CompuServe GIF filter installed in order to be able to take advantage of the WYSIWYG interface for your HTML documents. But you don't need to belong to CompuServe to get it; it actually comes with Word, and is available as one of the options that you can install. You probably just skipped it when you initially installed Word.

No need to panic; it's easy to install the filter. Despite the fact that there are lots of steps, the following procedure is actually pretty simple:

1. Run your Word Setup program (or your Office Setup program, if your copy of Word is part of the Microsoft Office suite of programs).

III

Learning HTML

2. When you're in the setup program, choose Add/Remove.

3. Next, select Converters, Filters, and Data Access and click Change Option.

4. This brings up a list of different types of filters for different types of text and video. The CompuServe GIF option is the only one you need to worry about; make sure that it's selected, and then click OK, and feed it the required disks, as prompted.

After you activate WebAuthor, you should see a box that provides several options (see fig. 10.7). You can Create a New HTML Document (Blank), in which case Word opens a new document where you can start from scratch. You can Import and Convert an Existing HTML Text File, in which case the tools take an HTML file and convert it to Word format so that you can edit it. Or you can Open a Word Document (HTML Original) for Editing to change the document to an HTML file. One of the things that you can't do is take a document that's already open and turn it into HTML. You'll need to save and close the document and reopen it in WebAuthor if you want to modify it as an HTML document.

Fig. 10.7
You're given several options after you choose HTML Authoring from the Tool menu in Word.

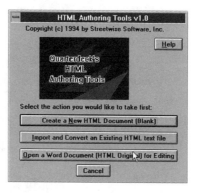

Opening and Editing a New File
If you open a new file, when you get the blank screen, notice that there are some notable differences to the toolbars. According to Quarterdeck, the different toolbars remove some of the Word functions that are almost exclusively designed for print features. Likewise, some additional tools (more relevant to processing HTML) appear. WebAuthor helpfully provides tooltips to help you identify the new tools. *Tooltips* are the little labels that appear when you let your pointer sit on top of a tool for more than a second. Table 10.2 is a quick synopsis of the new tools presented by WebAuthor.

Table 10.2	WebAuthor Tools	
Tool	**Name**	**Description**
	New	Opens a new Word document based on your default template, like its regular Word counterpart.
	New HTML	Opens a new HTML document.
	Open	Opens a directory containing both Word and HTML documents.
	Open from HTML	Opens a document in hypertext format as a Word document.
	Save	Saves a file; you can choose from a number of formats. HTML is *not* an available format, but you can save the file as a DOS file.
	Save to HTML	Saves a Word document as an HTML document. As you work, your document is in Word format; you need to save it to HTML format before you can place it on the Web.
	Document View Toggle	Changes the view of the document; gives you several options as to the type of editing screen you can work on.
	Style	Specifies the appearance of text on your page.
	Format Character	Specifies one of the standard HTML character formatting types (such as Strong, Citation, or Emphasis).
	Anchor Manager	Specifies anchors on your page.
	Image Manager	Specifies graphics in your page design.
	Form Manager	Inserts the basic codes necessary for having a form in your document.
	List	Creates lists on your page; specifies the type of list you want to create.
	Insert Symbol	Enters special codes, such as the Copyright or Trademark symbol.

For the beginning user, this collection of tools speeds up the editing of many types of HTML documents.

III

Learning HTML

Opening an Existing HTML File

If you choose to open an existing HTML file, Authoring Tools asks if you want the program to filter the existing document (see fig. 10.8). This helpful step checks the syntax of your existing file for errors and displays the errors, along with some good fixes. Using this option provides you with the HTML Editing toolbar.

Fig. 10.8

When you open an HTML document created by another editor, WebAuthor asks if you want to check the existing tags.

Note

The filtering feature is particularly useful if you've been editing your HTML documents in some other fashion, such as with a plain-text editor. The filter catches mistakes in syntax that you might not otherwise notice (including some cases where types of markers are incompatible with each other). This feature is particularly nice because some of these errors may be transparent to the author and the user (they don't necessarily show up on the page), but may confuse the browser programs, and eventually lead to errors.

It may take a minute or two for Authoring Tools to revise your document so that it's in the proper format, but the wait may be worth it. What you end up seeing isn't exactly WYSIWYG, but it's closer than you'd get using a plain-text editor (see fig. 10.9).

WebAuthor also enters some markers that help show what the effects of certain codes will be. Hypertext links show up in green; click them to open up a dialog box that shows their destination (see fig. 10.10).

Unfortunately, WebAuthor doesn't let you directly edit the text labels for anchors; that is, if you try to click-position your I-beam bar on the label, it selects the whole label. If you need to edit the label for a link, click the Anchor Manager tool. The Anchor Definition dialog box appears (see fig. 10.11). Clicking the Next button provides you with an opportunity to change the visible text. It also seems to be impossible to give a label a special effect (such as italics or bold) and still have WebAuthor treat it as an anchor.

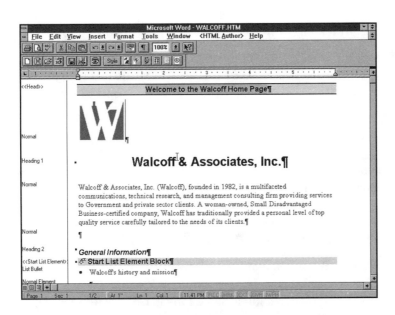

Fig. 10.9
The almost-WYSIWYG view of a page in WebAuthor.

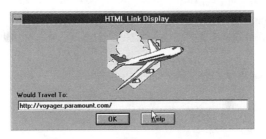

Fig. 10.10
Clicking high-lighted links displays the URL to which the text is linked.

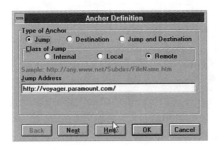

Fig. 10.11
Specify the URL to be connected to an anchor in the Anchor Definition dialog box. Clicking the Next button lets you edit the anchor text.

III

Learning HTML

Opening a Word Document (HTML Original) for Editing

If you've been editing an HTML document in Word, but haven't yet saved it in HTML format, this option opens the document and brings up the appropriate HTML editing toolbar. By contrast, if you've written a Word document that you want to convert to HTML format, this option doesn't make that automatic conversion (nor does it bring up the HTML toolbars).

Your best bet for doing this sort of conversion is to follow this process:

1. Save the Word document in MS-DOS Text format. To do this, open the File menu and choose Save As. Select MS-DOS Text as your file type, and use HTM as your file extension when you name the file.

2. This allows you to open up the file as an HTML file when you start Authoring Tools.

When you create a document with Authoring Tools, it saves the file as a Word document until you explicitly save it in HTML format. The Word format includes embedded binary codes, which are unreadable to Web browsers. Therefore, when using Authoring Tools, you need to be sure to save the file as an HTML document, otherwise it's worthless on the Web.

You should be able to tell that documents are saved in the appropriate format if Word saves them with an HTM extension. If Word saves the document with a DOC extension, it's still in Word format. Go back into the document and resave it in the appropriate format before trying to use it on the Web.

> **Note**
>
> Suggested retail price for Quarterdeck's WebAuthor is $149.95. You can get more information about WebAuthor by calling (310) 392-9851. You can also check Quarterdeck's Internet Web site at **http://www.qdeck.com/**; or you can send an e-mail request to **info@qdeck.com**. You can also write to Quarterdeck at Quarterdeck Office Systems, Inc., Pico Boulevard, Santa Monica, CA, 90405.

The ANT Template for Word

The ANT template is a low-cost shareware program designed to help edit HTML documents that works with Word for Windows for the Macintosh. With ANT's toolbar you can edit a document and insert the appropriate HTML codes. ANT also reads your document's formatting and converts styles (where possible) to equivalent HTML tags. Another big plus of the ANT_HTML template is that it works with all of the international language versions of Word, giving an added degree of flexibility to authors who create multilanguage versions of their pages.

Unfortunately, ANT_HTML can't incorporate the tags created in another program the way that Quarterdeck's Authoring Tools can. It's also somewhat fussy during installation, at least under Windows.

Installing ANT

To install ANT, copy all of the ANT files into a subdirectory. Then open a document called ANT_INST.DOC in Word. This opens a document with an install button (see fig. 10.12).

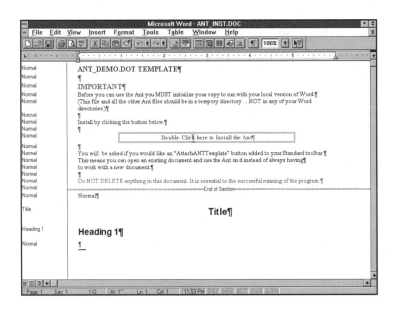

Fig. 10.12
Opening the file ANT_INST.DOC reveals this document. Click the button to install the ANT template.

When you click the install button, ANT installs itself in Word. A dialog box asks you if you want to add ANT to your standard Word toolbar. If you choose Yes, a tool with an A appears on your regular toolbar. If you have an open document, clicking the A tool reveals the ANT toolbar (see fig. 10.13 and table 10.3).

III

Learning HTML

Table 10.3 The ANT Toolbar

Tool	Name	Description
	Convert and Save	Changes the document from Word into HTML.
	The Ant	Gives information about the ANT_HTML template.
	Check styles for HTML codes	Reads Word styles and converts to HTML equivalents.
	Hidden Text	Hides or reveals HTML tags.

(continues)

Table 10.3 Continued

Tool	Name	Description
A	Address	Places HTML Address tags.
N	Normal	Marks text as plain text.
T	Title	Places HTML Title tags.
	Pre	Places HTML tags to maintain text exactly in its format as created by the author.
S	Styles	Activates dialog box of styles to be applied to text.
1 6	Head 1-6	Places HTML tags for the first six levels of headings.
	Horizontal Rule	Places a tag for a horizontal line to appear on the page.
⟨P⟩	P	Marks the end of a paragraph.
BR	BR	Makes a break.
	GIF	Activates a dialog box for inserting a GIF image in the document.
	Placeholder	Enters a placeholder image where a graphic image will later be placed.
→	URL	Links selected text to a specific URL.
	Local Anchor Ref	Creates a link to another section of the Web document.
	Local Anchor	Marks an area that can be linked to within Destination the Web document.
	Description List	Marks selected text Entry as a description list.
	Numbered List	Marks selected text as a numbered list.
	Unnumbered list	Places tags to mark text as an unnumbered list.
	Form Entry	Creates several types of tags for HTML forms.
	Ant to HTML demo	Transforms demonstration Word document into WYSIWYG format.

The A Tool

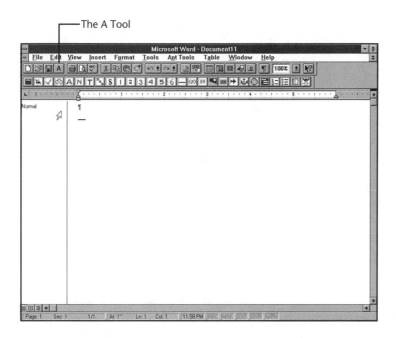

Fig. 10.13
Clicking the tool
marked A reveals
the ANT toolbar
beneath your
standard Word
toolbar.

Using ANT to Place HTML Tags

When you open a new document, Word prompts you to select a template for the document's format. At this point, you should select the ANT_HTML template if you want to use ANT.

Clicking the A tool reveals the ANT toolbar. The ANT toolbar features fairly extensive tooltips that tell you what each tool does. Most of the tools are designed to insert tags around a particular piece of text. To get ANT to place the appropriate tags, follow these steps:

1. Highlight the text you want to tag.

2. Click the appropriate tool.

3. The appropriate tags should be entered on either side of the text.

Unfortunately, ANT doesn't recognize the tags as entire entities. To remove a tag, you must delete each character in the tag one at a time. Furthermore, you must be careful to remove the companion tag (if one exists).

Using the ANT-HTML Template in Style Gallery

ANT also installs a style template that contains many of the standard HTML formats. Using these styles, you can quickly link sections of text to the appropriate format. When you apply a specific style, the text, as it appears

III

Learning HTML

on-screen, appears with the attributes of that particular HTML style, but the HTML codes don't appear.

If you save a document created using the ANT_HTML styles in ASCII (MS-DOS) format, the resulting document contains the proper HTML codes.

Changing a Word Document into an HTML Document with ANT

If you've created a Word document that you'd like to translate into HTML format, ANT can help make some of the conversion simpler.

The Check Styles for HTML Codes tool causes ANT to check the open document's styles to see if there are formatting codes that have an HTML equivalent. ANT tags words that are bold, italicized, or underlined with the appropriate HTML codes.

Because the original document was formatted for the printed page, you will probably still have to go back and reformat some of the document.

> **Note**
>
> If you've created a document using the ANT_HTML template styles, clicking the Check Styles for HTML Codes tool reveals all of the HTML codes (see fig. 10.14 and 10.15). To hide these codes again, click the Hidden Text tool.

Fig. 10.14
This Web page was created using ANT styles.

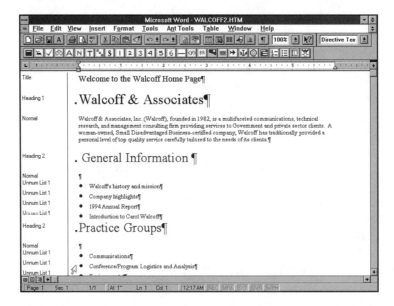

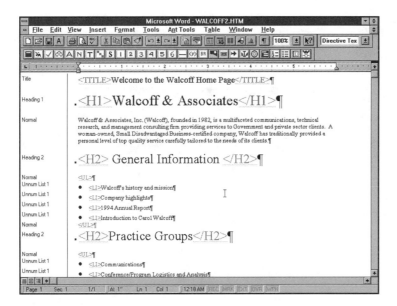

Fig. 10.15
This is the same page with HTML tags revealed.

Saving Your Word Document in HTML Format

The documents that you create using the ANT templates are in Word format as you create them (regardless of whether you're using the styles or the toolbars to enter the appropriate tags). To use these documents on the Web, you need to save them in ASCII format. To do this, you can either click the Convert and Save tool, or you can use the standard Word commands.

To save the file as you would in Word, open the File menu and choose Save As. When the Save As dialog box opens, select ASCII (or MS-DOS) as your File Type, and then enter a file name and click OK.

Clicking the Convert and Save tool brings up a dialog box with two options (see fig. 10.16). The first option allows you to run a basic filter over the document that adds appropriate formatting tags where necessary. The second option allows you to skip the filtering process, and save the file directly as an ASCII file.

> **Note**
>
> You can obtain ANT_HTML by anonymous FTP from **ftp.inet.net** in the EINet/pc directory. The latest version is usually available as ANT_DEMO.ZIP.

III

Learning HTML

Fig. 10.16
When ANT converts your document to HTML, it can check your tags and formatting.

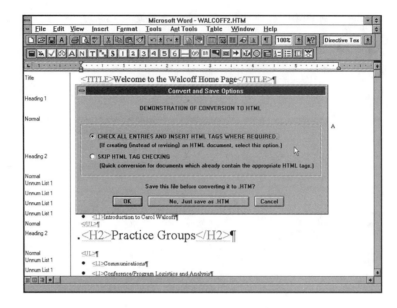

CU_HTML

CU_HTML, named after the Chinese University of Hong Kong where it was created by Kenneth Wong and Anton Lam, is a template-based add-on for Word 2 and Word 6.

CU_HTML comes with installation instructions in an HTML format. Use your browser to open the cu_html.htm file (see fig. 10.17). If your browser's not working, just open the Word document "CU_HTML.DOC."

Fig. 10.17
CU_HTML comes with installation instructions in HTML format that can be read using a Web browser.

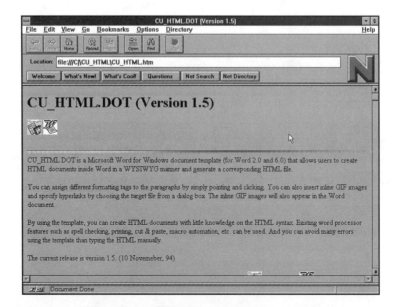

After you install CU_HTML's files, you can select the CU_HTML template when you open a new document in Word.

If you choose this template, a bunch of styles equivalent to HTML tags are loaded. There's also an extra menu item, **H**TML (see fig. 10.18). This menu item also provides you with some options for tagging text, mostly for linking text in the document to other files (such as graphics or other hypertext links). For tags to format text, open the Format menu and select Styles (or Style Gallery). CU_HTML provides tags for most of the basic HTML text formatting functions.

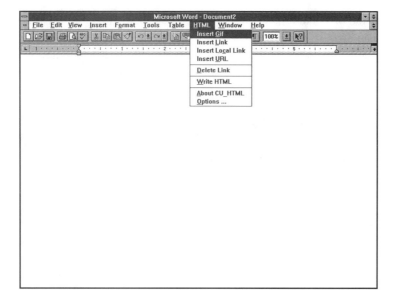

Fig. 10.18
CU_HTML creates a new menu item, called HTML, that gives the user access to several useful HTML editing tools.

CU_HTML requires that you save a copy of the file before it lets you put tags on anything. So after you open a new document, save it. This allows you to insert GIF files.

After you've entered text, you can use the options under the HTML menu to format links to other files. You can link to a graphics file with the Insert Gif option, or another locally stored HTML file with Insert Link. You can create a link to another section of your Web document with Insert Local link, or link to another document on the Web with Insert URL.

Like most of the templates for Word, CU_HTML creates files in Word format. You must be sure to save the completed document in HTML format before you try to use it on the Web. To do this using CU_HTML, open the **H**TML menu and choose **W**rite HTML.

Note

You can obtain CU_HTML from the Chinese University of Hong Kong by anonymous **FTP from ftp.cuhk.hk.** It's stored in the directory "/pub/www/windows/util." The file name is usually "cu_html.zip"

GT_HTML Template for Word

GT_HTML is a simple template designed to provide some access to HTML tags to Word for Windows users.

Installation of the template is simple; just copy the template into your templates subdirectory for Word. If you activate the template when you open a new document in Word, you have the ability to add two new toolbars. These toolbars give you the ability to apply HTML tags to highlighted text (see fig. 10.19).

Fig. 10.19
When you install GT_HTML, you have the option of turning on two small toolbars to help you edit HTML.

This template doesn't provide the sort of WYSIWYG view of the HTML document. However, the Browser tool will activate a browser to view the document as it's being created.

Another button allows you to hide all of the HTML codes so that you can see the plain text, as it should appear on the completed page. The HTML Save tool allows you to automatically save the Word document in HTML format, eliminating the need to use the Save As feature in Word.

What this template doesn't do is provide a lot of preset styles for formatting text. In fact, the only styles supported are three levels of Headers. Nevertheless, this template will meet your needs if you need to create some basic, information-only pages for your Web site.

Stand-alone Editors for HTML

Beyond the templates for word processors, some stand-alone editors are designed completely for the purpose of editing HTML documents. This section covers some of the most common stand-alone editors for HTML.

Alpha and BBEdit Extensions: HTML Text Editors for Macintosh

Alpha is a text editor for the Macintosh that has an HTML extension for the insertion of tags into a document. This lets you use Alpha as a default text editor, as well as an HTML authoring tool. Except for the HTML pull-down list of tags, Alpha behaves as any other editor with no checking of tag locations or validity.

BBEdit is similar to Alpha in that it is a general-purpose editor with an HTML menu item containing tags. Again, there is no validity checking for inserting tags at the correct location. Both Alpha and BBEdit are freeware.

> **Note**
>
> To obtain Alpha HTML extensions, use anonymous FTP to **cs.rice.edu** and check the /public/Alpha/contrib directory. Several versions of the extensions are usually available.
>
> BBEdit extensions can be obtained from Macintosh archives, such as the Info-Mac archives at **sumex-aim.stanford.edu** in the \info-mac\text directory. Using WWW, try **http://www.uji.es/bbedit-html-extensions.html**.

HTML.edit and SHE: HyperCard Editors for Macintosh

HTML.edit is freeware that is written in HyperCard for use on the Macintosh. (HTML.edit doesn't require HyperCard to execute.) However, this does present a somewhat strange interface to the first-time user. It's necessary to read the accompanying help or documentation files to understand the basic processes.

III

Learning HTML

HTML.edit is a feature-heavy editor that allows you to insert HTML tags in simple text files. Special characters (nonEnglish text characters and graphics) are available with automatic conversion to the HTML code. Links are supported in a process that is fast and simple. Among its added features, HTML.edit has automatic insertion of paragraph tags and an indexing feature for generating a table of contents.

SHE (Simple HTML Editor) is another freeware Macintosh package based on HyperCard, but this one does require HyperCard to execute. SHE is a simple editor that uses a menu for HTML tags (although not all tags are provided) or a small toolbar that has the six most commonly used tags.

SHE is not really useful for larger documents, as it lacks the features needed for working with more than a single page or two. With larger files, SHE has an annoying habit of truncating anything that exceeds a size limit (unspecified, but this seems to depend on system memory available for HyperCard). There's no warning generated by SHE when truncation occurs, so this can be a very annoying problem.

> **Note**
>
> To obtain a copy of HTML.edit, try a Macintosh archive like the Info-Mac archives at **sumex-aim.stanford.edu** in the directory "\info-mac\text." Several other sites also carry copies in their Macintosh directories.
>
> To obtain SHE, use anonymous FTP to **ericmorgan.lib.ncsu.edu** and check for the /Public/simple-http-editor.hqx file. The program is also available on some Macintosh archives. On WWW, try **http://info.cern.ch/hypertext/WWW/Tools/SHE.html**.

HTML Assistant

WebmasterCD

HTML Assistant is a pretty thorough HTML editor for Microsoft Windows. Like most of the stand-alone editors, it inserts HTML tags around highlighted text and links to images and other URLs through a dialog box in which you insert the appropriate code into the HTML document.

Unlike several of the other editors, it incorporates a full set of tools aimed at supporting the creation of forms, and provides a menu option that translates MOSAIC.INI files and Cello bookmark files into HTML files that can be used as personal home pages.

Furthermore, HTML Assistant allows you to build files of URLs, so that you can pull up URLs that you use repeatedly at the click of a button.

Tags at the Click of a Button

HTML Assistant has a huge toolbar that sports most of the common HTML tags. The organization of the toolbar separates tags into particular types; tags that adjust the appearance of text are grouped together, as are the tags that link the document to other files (see fig. 10.20).

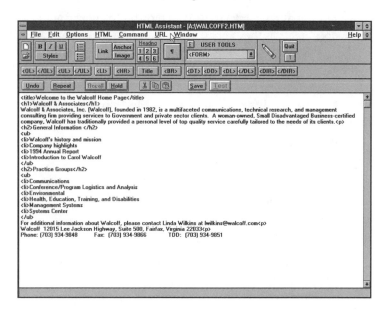

Fig. 10.20
HTML Assistant has a huge toolbar that puts access to tags at the author's fingertips.

The toolbar also has drop-down lists in which the user can create tags for other functions that aren't otherwise supported on the toolbar. This is where HTML Assistant stores most of the forms-related tags.

If the toolbar is taking up too much of your desktop, it can be hidden by opening the **O**ptions menu and then toggling the option Hide Lower toolbar. (The toolbar can be restored in the same fashion.)

HTML Assistant has a button for repeating a tag, a function that can be particularly useful when you prepare HTML documents with lists, or for inserting standard icons next to links to other files (such as a standard audio icon next to the links for each of a series of WAV or AU files).

Some Additional Helpful HTML Assistant Features

One of the useful features of HTML Assistant is the ability to create files of URLs that you can call up while creating an HTML text document. This is particularly helpful if you're creating a Web site that requires references to certain key index pages.

III

Learning HTML

Like some other editors, HTML Assistant has the ability to save MOSAIC.INI files and Cello bookmark lists as HTML files. The MOSAIC.INI translator even retains the menu structure of your original Hotlists from Mosaic. (Mosaic refers to its bookmark files, or its lists of frequently used sites as *Hotlists,* which are stored as part of the MOSAIC.INI file.)

HTML Assistant can also be linked to a Web browser to allow you to view your HTML documents as they appear when translated by the browser. After you link the browser to HTML Assistant, you can activate the browser by clicking the Test button on the toolbar.

HTML Assistant Pro and Some Liabilities in the Shareware Version

You can find a shareware version of HTML Assistant on the net that contains the features most HTML editors need to create some fairly sophisticated Web pages.

Unfortunately, the shareware version has a file size limit of 32K. You can create larger files by editing the file in pieces in HTML Assistant, and then by stitching the pieces together in a word processor or an editor with an ability to handle larger files.

HTML Assistant Pro is the commercial version of the software. It doesn't have a file size limit and has more complete support for the Expanded Character set, as well as a feature called the Automatic Page Creator, which works like a Microsoft-style wizard to create an HTML page.

> **Note**
>
> As of January 1, 1995, the price for HTML Assistant Pro was US $99.95, plus postage and handling ($10 in North America, $15 elsewhere). To order a copy of HTML Assistant Pro, contact Brooklyn North Software Works at 25 Doyle Street, Bedford, Nova Scotia, Canada, B41 1K4, or fax (902) 835-2600.
>
> You can get a copy of the freeware version of HTML Assistant from many of the Windows Utilities and WWW Utilities archives. Set your Archie client to look for a file called "htmlasst.zip." One site that carries HTML Assistant is the Chinese University of Hong Kong (anonymous FTP at **ftp.cuhk.hk**). HTML Assistant is stored with several other HTML editors in the /pub/www/windows/util directory.

HTML Editor

HTML Editor is a combination of a text editor and a WYSIWYG editor for Macintosh that allows you to view an HTML document in its finished form.

HTML Editor supports tags through buttons and pull-down menus. It also allows you to change styles and add customized tags.

> **Note**
>
> HTML Editor is available through anonymous FTP from **cs.dal.ca** in the giles directory. The current version is called "HTML_Editor_1.0.sit.hqx." The documentation file is available as "HTML_Editor_Documentation.html."

As you enter tags, text is reformatted to match the tag characteristics. With HTML Editor, you can use a Preview button to hide tags or to call your favorite Web browser. Unlike HyperCard-based editors, there is no file size limit with HTML Editor, and it reads existing files without a problem. The only disadvantage to HTML Editor is a lack of print output.

HTMLed

HTMLed is a great little shareware HTML editor for Microsoft Windows. Running the HTMLed program opens up a simple editing screen with a menu bar and toolbar (see fig. 10.21). Even though it looks pretty basic, this program has a lot of useful features.

WebmasterCD

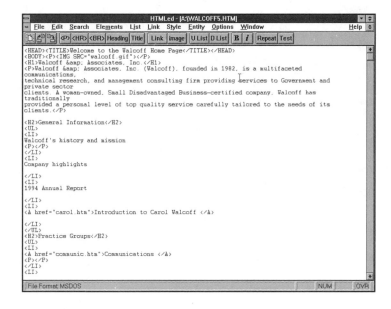

Fig. 10.21
HTMLed contains a wealth of useful features, particularly if you're working in several languages.

III

Learning HTML

HTMLed Toolbars

Toolbars are probably one of the best features of this program. Instead of depending on icons, developer Peter Crawshaw has chosen to either put the tag itself or the plain-English name for the tag (or type of tag) on the buttons. This requires novices to know a little more about HTML code, but it's probably for the best.

Clicking the Link or Image tool brings up a dialog box into which you enter the appropriate file name or URL. Once a URL is entered in the dialog box, it is saved in a list that can be used to pull up the same URL if you need to create a link to it in other locations throughout the document.

If you're tagging a set of text items that need the same tag (such as items in a list), you might find the ability to repeat a tag useful. HTMLed provides both a toolbar button and a menu item (Ele**m**ents, **R**epeat Last Markup) for repeating tags.

Furthermore, HTMLed provides a few extra toolbars that are particularly useful for heavy-duty HTML authors. The first is a Headings toolbar, which allows you to click a tool and automatically format text with the appropriate Header tag. A second toolbar, called the Common Tags toolbar, provides a tool for inserting 15 common tags. The Extended Character toolbar provides access to 62 characters beyond the standard ASCII set, such as accented vowels, which are particularly useful when creating the other-than-English language versions of your Web pages. Figure 10.22 shows these toolbars.

Fig. 10.22

HTMLed features three "floating" toolbars that you can activate if you need them, and easily shut off if you don't.

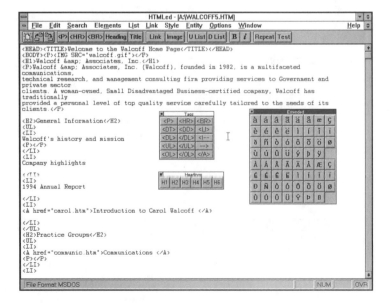

You can also create your own custom button bar by entering a brief description of the tag and the keystrokes that comprise the tag that it should enter.

Some Interesting HTMLed Menu Items

The HTML menu bar breaks down standard tags into fairly easy-to-understand groupings. You can find the standard divisions of an HTML document under the Elements menu. One option, Standard Document Outline, drops in the opening and closing codes, as well as the tags for the head and body sections of your HTML document.

The List menu provides access to tagging styles for each of the major types of lists. The Style menu allows you to tag text with most of the HTML text styles.

There are some punctuation marks, letter formats and other common text items for which HTML must use special codes. These include greater than and less than (><), and the ampersand (&), which HTML uses as part of tags or other extended codes. The Entity menu provides access to these text extended text elements and codes by providing the proper code in HTML format.

There's also a very smart set of menu items for providing diacritical marks. This is a particularly slick set of tag controls because it reads the letter that you're trying to place the diacritical mark on and then assigns the appropriate HTML code. Furthermore, it won't let you place an accent or other diacritical mark on a letter that's not supposed to have one.

Configuring HTMLed

Under the **O**ptions menu, there's a Setup option. The Setup dialog box allows you to specify whether you want HTMLed to display Extended characters as they will appear or as they are coded in HTML. You can also choose to have several of the special toolbars appear every time you start the program.

HTMLed also provides an option for linking the editor to Mosaic so that you can test your HTML files with the browser before putting them on the Web. In the Setup dialog box, there's an option for specifying the path of your Web browser. This links your browser to the Test button on the Standard toolbar and to the **T**est HTML Document option under the **F**ile menu.

Other Features

HTMLed also has a few other fairly useful features. One feature under the Options menu (Convert MOSAIC.INI to HTML file) does just that—it enables you to turn your MOSAIC.INI file into an HTML file (thus turning all of your favorite links into a personal home page.) HTMLed also allows you to save files in a variety of formats: as a DOS, UNIX, or plain-text file (without the HTML tags included).

All in all, this is a pretty sharp editor that should prove particularly useful for new HTML authors and users with some experience. HTMLed doesn't cover some of the tags for forms and other advanced HTML features that some of the other editors do, but it's useful for the vast majority of your HTML editing needs.

> **Note**
>
> You can get a copy of HTMLed via anonymous FTP from **ftp.cuhk.hk**. In the /pub/www/windows/util directory, you'll find HTMLed saved as htmed10.zip (later versions may increase the number), along with several other programs and templates for editing HTML.

HoTMetaL

WebmasterCD

HoTMetaL is an HTML editor created by NCSA and distributed by SoftQuad for Microsoft Windows and for X-Windows running under UNIX. The first thing you need to know about HoTMetaL is that it's very big. The files take up about 5M of disk space, and require about 3M of memory to run.

The second thing that you need to know is that HoTMetaL is probably the strictest editor with respect to requiring absolute adherence to HTML syntax rules. In some respects, it's like riding a bike with training wheels—you're guaranteed not to make any mistakes, but you're not likely to be able to use it to do the cool stuff that more experienced authors are doing.

As an example, HoTMetaL doesn't recognize any of the so-called HTML2 tags (such as Center and Blink) that are supported by Netscape. Documents containing these codes can't be opened by HoTMetaL. Likewise, older HTML documents or HTML documents with *nested* tags (an italic tag inside of an anchor, for example) are often rejected. Many files created in editors other than HoTMetaL can't be imported to this editor.

> **Tip**
>
> It is possible to turn Rules Checking off, if you're trying to create a document that uses newer standards than those contained in your Rules file. Check under the **M**arkup menu for the option Turn Rules Checking Off, or try Ctrl+K.

But HoTMetaL does provide an exceptionally good interface for people who are first learning how to write HTML documents. There's a certain amount of enforced precision that comes from working in HoTMetaL that encourages good authoring practices down the road. All of HoTMetaL's templates are in perfect HTML form, complete with all HEAD and BODY tags intact and properly placed (see fig. 10.23).

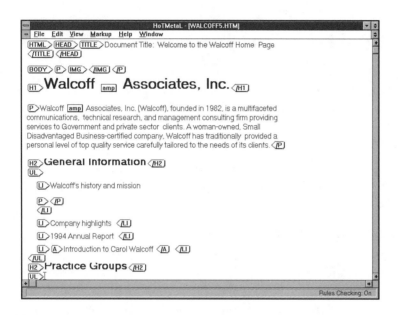

Fig. 10.23
HoTMetaL provides an easy-to-understand interface with HTML tags indicated as big labels.

HoTMetaL provides quite a few templates of standard formats for WWW pages. All the new author needs to do is delete the placeholder text and replace it with his own, and a proper WWW page is instantly created.

Moreover, the HTML tags are handled entirely as complete entities by HoTMetaL. They're displayed on-screen as large markers, and it's impossible to delete one half of a tag pair without deleting the other half.

HoTMetaL's import filter is incredibly demanding. You can be sure that if your HTML document passes through this filter that it's without HTML syntax errors. Likewise, the filter doesn't allow you to save a document that has HTML syntax errors in it. If strict adherence to HTML syntax is your goal, HoTMetaL will help you achieve it.

> **Note**
>
> A reduced-function version of HoTMetaL is available as freeware at most utility sites. Look for it at NCSA or CERN. Try the WWW page **http://info.cern.ch/ hypertext/WWW/Tools**, and look for the HoTMetaL.html file.

Converting Documents to HTML

HTML filters are useful tools that let you convert a document produced with any kind of editor (including ASCII text editors) to HTML. Filters are useful when you work in an editor that has its own proprietary format, such as Word, WordPerfect, Rich Text Format (RTF), or nroff.

HTML filters are attractive if you want a utility to convert your document with tags to HTML as you continue to work in your favorite editor. Filters tend to be fast and easy to work with, because they take a file name as input and generate an HTML output file.

Converting Word

Word for Windows and Word for DOS documents can be converted to HTML using the CU_HTML and ANT_HTML extensions mentioned earlier. A few stand-alone conversion utilities have also begun to appear. Because Word can read other word processor formats (including WordPerfect and RTF), you can use these filters when error checking is required or when a dedicated filter for your word processor is not available.

Converting WordPerfect

The utility WPTOHTML converts WordPerfect documents to HTML. WPTOHTML is a set of macros for WordPerfect versions 5.1, 5.2, and 6.0. You can also use the WordPerfect filter with other word processor formats that WordPerfect can import.

> **Note**
>
> WPTOHTML is available through anonymous FTP from **oak.oakland.edu** in the SimTel/msdos/wordperf directory as the wptXXd10.zip file, where XX is the version number of WordPerfect.

Converting FrameMaker and FrameBuilder

You can convert FrameMaker documents to HTML format with the tool FM2HTML. Work was underway to modify the script for FrameBuilder documents, as well, although a working version was not available at the time of this writing. FM2HTML is a set of scripts that converts Frame documents to HTML while preserving hypertext links and tables. It also handles GIF files without a problem.

> **Note**
>
> A copy of FM2HTML is available by anonymous FTP from **bang.nta.no** in the /pub directory. The UNIX set is called "fm2html.tar.v.0.n.m.Z."

Currently, FM2HTML is available for several UNIX systems and an experimental version for Windows is in distribution. Because Frame documents are platform-independent, you can move Frame documents developed on a PC or Macintosh to a supported UNIX platform, where you can then execute FM2HTML.

Converting TeX and LaTeX

You can convert LaTex and TeX files to HTML using several different utilities. There are quite a few UNIX-based utilities available, including LATEXTOHTML, which can even handle inline LaTeX equations and links. For simpler documents, the UNIX utility VULCANIZE is faster, but it can't handle mathematical equations. Both LATEXTOHTML and VULCANIZE are perl scripts.

If you use Windows, convert TeX and LaTeX files to RTF with TEX2RTF. You can convert the file further using one of the other tools that have already been mentioned.

> **Note**
>
> LATEXTOHTML is available through anonymous FTP from **ftp.tex.ac.uk** in the pub/archive/support directory as the latextohtml file. You can obtain VULCANIZE from the Web site **http://www/cis/upenn/edut** in the mjd directory as the vulcanize.html file.

III

Learning HTML

Converting Rich Text Format (RTF)

RTFTOHTML is a common utility that converts RTF documents to HTML. There are versions of RTFTOHTML for some UNIX platforms and Macintosh. An experimental version for DOS/Windows was also briefly available (the file name was truncated to eight letters for DOS). Source code is available for porting to any other platform.

Because many word processors handle RTF formats, you can import an RTF document into your favorite word processor, and then run one of the word processor specific filters. However, RTFTOHTML seems to be faster at performing this conversion.

> **Note**
>
> RTFTOHTML is available through anonymous FTP from **ftp.cray.com** in the src/WWWstuff/RTF directory. Through the Web, try **http://info.cern.ch/hypertext/WWW/Tools** and look for the rtftoftml-2.6.html file (or a later version).

Maintaining HTML

Even though you have written a Web document and it's available to the world, your job isn't over. Unless your document is a simple text file, you will have links to other documents or Web servers embedded. These links must be verified at regular intervals. Also, you should check the integrity of your Web pages periodically to ensure that the flow of the document from your home page is correct.

Spiders

Several utilities are available that help you check links and scan the Web for other sites or documents to which you may want to provide a hyperlink. These utilities tend to go by a number of names, such as *robot, spider,* or *wanderer.* They're all programs that move across the Web automatically, creating a list of Web links that you can access. (Spiders are similar to the Archie and Veronica tools for the Internet, although neither of these cover the Web.)

Although they're often thought of as utilities for users only (to get a list of sites to try), spiders and their kin are used by document authors, too, to show potentially useful and interesting links. One of the best known spiders is the World Wide Web Worm, or WWWW. It won the "Best of the Web '94" award for navigational tools.

WWWW allows you to search for keywords or to create a Boolean search, and can cover titles, documents, and several other search types (including a search of all known HTML pages).

A similarly useful spider is WebCrawler, which is similar to WWWW, except that it can scan entire documents for matches of any key words and display the results in an ordered list from closest match to least match.

> ### Note
>
> You can obtain a copy of World Wide Web Worm from **http:// www.cs.colorado.edu/home/mcbryan/WWWW.html**. WebCrawler is available from **http://www.biotech.washington.edu/WebCrawler/ WebCrawler.html**.

HTML Analyzer

A common problem with HTML documents is that as they age, links that point to files or servers may no longer exist (either because the locations or documents have changed). It is, therefore, good practice to validate the hyperlinks in a document on a regular basis.

A popular hyperlink analyzer is HTML_ANALYZER. It examines each hyperlink and the contents of the hyperlink to ensure that they are consistent. HTML_ANALYZER functions by examining a document to all links, and then creating a text file that has a list of the links in it. HTML_ANALYZER uses the text files to compare the actual link content to what it should be.

HTML_ANALYZER actually does three tests. It validates the availability of the documents pointed to by hyperlinks (called *validation*). It looks for hyperlink contents that occur in the database but are not, themselves, hyperlinks (called *completeness*). And it looks for a one-to-one relation between hyperlinks and the contents of the hyperlink (called *consistency*). Any deviations are listed for the user.

HTML_ANALYZER users should have a good familiarity with HTML, their operating system, and the use of command-line-driven analyzers. HTML_ANALYZER must be compiled using the "make" utility prior to execution. There are several directories that must be created prior to running HTML_ANALYZER, and it creates several temporary files when it runs that are not cleaned up; this is not a good utility for a novice. For more detailed information about HTML_ANALYZER, see the section "HTML Analyzer" in chapter 14, "Usage Statistics and Maintaining HTML."

III

Learning HTML

Note

There are similar products you might want to check out at **http://uts.cc.utexas.edu:80/~churchh/htmlchek.html** and **http://wsk.eit.com/wsk/dist/doc/admin/webtest/verify_links.html.**

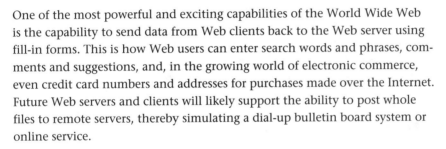

Chapter 11

Forms

One of the most powerful and exciting capabilities of the World Wide Web is the capability to send data from Web clients back to the Web server using fill-in forms. This is how Web users can enter search words and phrases, comments and suggestions, and, in the growing world of electronic commerce, even credit card numbers and addresses for purchases made over the Internet. Future Web servers and clients will likely support the ability to post whole files to remote servers, thereby simulating a dial-up bulletin board system or online service.

At the heart of the Web's interactive capabilities is support for forms and scripts. On the client side, users enter data through fill-in forms that contain familiar graphical elements such as text input fields, check boxes, and push buttons. The browser then sends form data to the server for processing.

In this chapter, you learn

- The elements of HTML fill-in forms

- How form data is passed from client to server

- How to send data to a server without using forms

- How to embed state information in forms

Introduction to Forms and Scripts

When a user submits a form from a browser, the browser encodes the form data into a URL and then sends it to the server like any other document request. Upon receiving the encoded URL, the server passes the form data to a processing script and then starts the specified script. The script reads the form data, completes the required processing, and sends results back to the client. This chapter focuses entirely on the elements of forms. The next chapter focuses on scripts.

Like other elements of HTML, forms have a similar appearance in different browsers, but the appearance is not identical. The appearance of a form always matches the graphical environment in which the form is displayed. For example, Windows pull-down menus and check boxes look significantly different than they do in X Windows. This platform portability is part of the power of forms. Authors of HTML forms do not need to worry about the details of interacting with the user's graphical operating system—the browser handles all the details. This is what allows you to use the same HTML form under Windows, Mac, OS/2, X Windows, and even in text mode with Lynx.

HTML's form support is very simple, and yet surprisingly complete. A handful of HTML tags can create the most popular elements of modern graphical interfaces, including text windows, check boxes and radio buttons, pull-down menus, and push buttons. In fact, using HTML forms in conjunction with server scripts is arguably the fastest and simplest way to create cross-platform graphical applications! The only programming required is the script itself, and the programmer can choose the language.

Creating Forms

The simplest and most natural way to construct a query string for sending data to a server is to use forms. Browsers that support forms use standard GUI elements such as text boxes, menus, buttons, and check boxes to receive data and pass it on to a server.

Note

Even though it is only a text-mode client, the Lynx browser emulates GUI elements to achieve complete support for forms.

You construct HTML forms using tags similar to all other HTML constructs. Forms consist of three elements: a *header* (the FORM tag), *named input fields* (INPUT, SELECT, or TEXTAREA tags), and one or more *action buttons*.

Form Header

When a user submits a form, the browser packages the form data and sends it to the script URL embedded in the form header. The form header tells the browser how to construct the URL to send to the server. It specifies the location of the processing script and the HTTP method used to send the data. The header has the following form:

```
<FORM ACTION="URL" METHOD={GET|POST}>
Form text and elements
</FORM>
```

The ACTION attribute specifies the path to the processing script. This URL can reference any script on any CGI-capable server (any server that can process CGI scripts). The tail end of a URL in an ACTION attribute can contain extra path information. This information is additional data that the browser sends to a script, but it is not included anywhere on the form. A URL with extra path information looks like this:

```
protocol://address:port/filename/extra_path_info
```

You can use extra path information in a URL to pass additional file name or directory information to a script.

> **Note**
>
> The imagemap facility uses extra path information to specify the name of the map file. The name of the map file follows the path to the imagemap script. A sample URL might be **/cgi-bin/imagemap/homepage**. The name of the script is "imagemap," and "homepage" is the name of the map file used by imagemap.

The METHOD attribute determines how the browser sends form data to the server. The POST method causes form data to be sent in a separate transaction, whereas the GET method causes form data to be appended to the script URL. Differences between POST and GET are discussed in the section on "HTTP Methods" later in this chapter.

> **Caution**
>
> Always send form data using the POST method. Otherwise, the length of data appended to the script URL may exceed operating environment limitations on the server.

Use the closing </FORM> tag to show where the form ends. You do not need to include it in HTML documents containing a single form, but you do in HTML documents containing multiple forms.

Input Fields

The form itself consists of standard GUI controls such as text boxes, check boxes, and menus. You give each control a name that eventually becomes a variable name that the processing script uses.

III

Learning HTML

You can use several types of graphical controls to enter information in forms. These include:

Type of Control	Tag
Text box	`<INPUT TYPE="TEXT"...>`
Password box	`<INPUT TYPE="PASSWORD"...>`
Check box	`<INPUT TYPE="CHECKBOX"...>`
Radio button	`<INPUT TYPE="RADIO"...>`
Text window	`<TEXTAREA>...</TEXTAREA>`
Menu	`<SELECT>...<OPTION>...</SELECT>`
Push button	`<INPUT TYPE="{SUBMIT¦RESET}"...>`
Hidden field	`<INPUT TYPE="HIDDEN"...>`

Text and Password Boxes

Text and *password boxes* are simple data entry fields. The only difference between the two is that all text typed in password boxes shows up as asterisks (*). The general form for a text or password field in HTML is:

```
<INPUT TYPE="{TEXT¦PASSWORD}" NAME="name" [VALUE="default_text"]
[SIZE="width,height"] [MAXLENGTH="width"]>
```

Use the SIZE attribute to specify the display size of text and password boxes. The format is SIZE="width,height", and the default size is width 20 and height 1. You can specify a maximum number of characters to enter with the MAXLENGTH attribute, which applies only to single-line entries. For example, a form that accepts a name, phone number, address, and password might look like this:

```
<TITLE>User Registration</TITLE>
<H1>User Registration</H1>
Please enter the following information:<P>
<FORM ACTION="/cgi-bin/newuser" METHOD="POST">
Your Name:  <INPUT TYPE="TEXT" NAME="FullName" SIZE="30"
➥MAXLENGTH="30"><P>
Your Phone:  <INPUT TYPE="TEXT" NAME="Phone" SIZE="10"
➥MAXLENGTH="10"><P>
Street Address:  <INPUT TYPE="TEXT" NAME="Address1" SIZE="30"><P>
City, ST ZIP: <INPUT TYPE="TEXT" NAME="Address2" SIZE="30"><P>
Your Password: <INPUT TYPE="PASSWORD" SIZE="6"><P>
<INPUT TYPE="SUBMIT" VALUE=" Submit "><P>
</FORM>
```

Figure 11.1 shows the form as it appears in Mosaic for Windows. The Submit button shown on the form is an action button. Action buttons are discussed under "Submit and Reset Buttons" below.

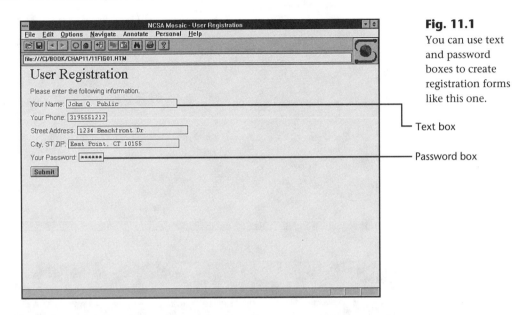

Fig. 11.1
You can use text and password boxes to create registration forms like this one.

— Text box

— Password box

Tip

Because browsers ignore white space, it is difficult to line up the left edges of text input boxes on multiple lines because the text to the left of the boxes is of different lengths. One solution is to put label text to the right of input boxes. Alternatively, you can use the <PRE> tag to force the desired alignment, but this does not work well on all browsers.

Multiline Text Windows

The <TEXTAREA> tag is really just a glorified version of <INPUT TYPE="TEXT">. A *text area* is a multiline text window complete with scroll bars. The format for a text area is:

```
<TEXTAREA NAME="name" [ROWS=rows] [COLS=columns]>
Default_text
</TEXTAREA>
```

Use the ROWS and COLS attributes to specify the number of rows and columns in the text area. You can place the default text between the opening and closing <TEXTAREA> tags. Figure 11.2 shows a multiline text window with 8 rows and 40 columns as it appears in Mosaic for Windows.

III

Learning HTML

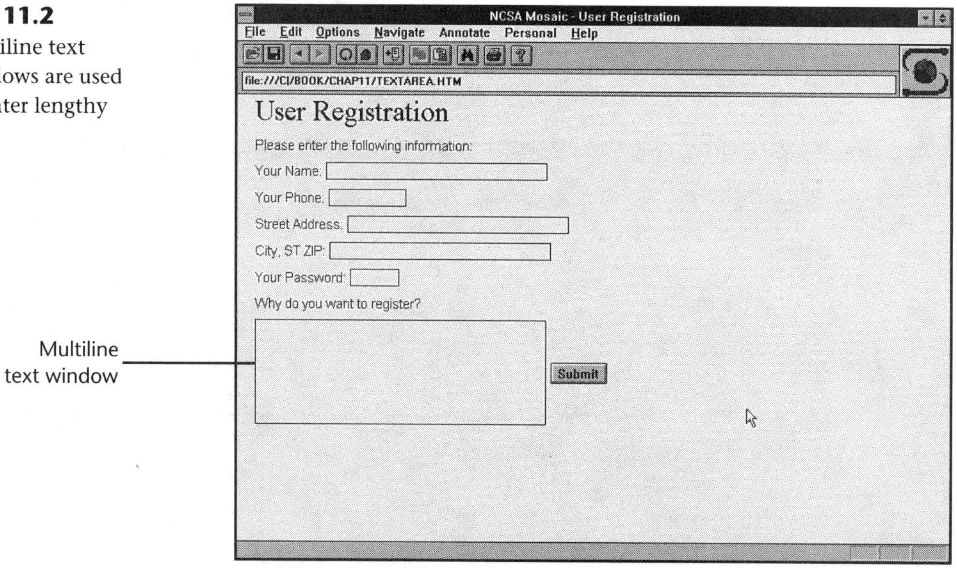

Fig. 11.2
Multiline text
windows are used
to enter lengthy
text.

Multiline
text window

Note

In versions of Mosaic for Windows prior to 2 alpha 8, text areas did not contain scroll bars. In addition, regular text boxes (`<INPUT TYPE="TEXT">`) did not allow multiline entries even though the `SIZE` attribute specified multiple rows.

Check Boxes and Radio Buttons

Check boxes and radio buttons present choices to the reader. The attributes specific to this type are:

```
<INPUT TYPE="{CHECKBOX¦RADIO}" NAME="Name" VALUE="Value" [CHECKED]>
```

Give each check box a unique name to identify it. Multiple check boxes may not have the same name; it would then be impossible to uniquely identify which check box is selected. The VALUE of a check box is not displayed anywhere, but is the value sent back to the server in the form data. For example, in the form below, the field named "Payment" can have a value of "MC,"

"Visa," or "AmEx," depending on which radio button the user selects. If you specify the CHECKED attribute for a check box or radio button, that box or button is selected by default when the form is loaded.

> **Note**
>
> Check boxes only show up in the form data sent to the server if they are selected. Check boxes that are not selected do not appear.

Unlike check boxes, related radio buttons can have the same name because the user can select only one radio button from a group of buttons. The VALUE of radio buttons is not displayed, but it is reported to the server in the form data.

An example of check boxes and radio buttons might be this order form:

```
<TITLE>Order Form</TITLE>
<H1>Order Form</H1>
Please enter your shipping address:<P>
<FORM ACTION="/cgi-bin/newuser" METHOD="POST">
Your Name:  <INPUT TYPE="TEXT" NAME="FullName" SIZE="30"
➡MAXLENGTH="30"><P>
Street Address:  <INPUT TYPE="TEXT" NAME="Address1" SIZE="30"><P>
City, ST ZIP: <INPUT TYPE="TEXT" NAME="Address2" SIZE="30"><P>
<H2>How will you pay for your purchase?</H2>
<INPUT TYPE="RADIO" NAME="Payment" VALUE="MC">MasterCard<P>
<INPUT TYPE="RADIO" NAME="Payment" VALUE="Visa">Visa<P>
<INPUT TYPE="RADIO" NAME="Payment" VALUE="AmEx">American Express<P>
<H2>Check all that apply:</H2>
<INPUT TYPE="CHECKBOX" NAME="Overnight" VALUE="Yes">Ship
➡Overnight<P>
<INPUT TYPE="CHECKBOX" NAME="SameAddress" VALUE="Yes">Ship to Above
➡Address<P>
<INPUT TYPE="CHECKBOX" NAME="CallFirst" VALUE="Yes">Call Before
➡Shipping<P>
<INPUT TYPE="SUBMIT" VALUE=" Submit ">
</FORM>
```

Figure 11.3 shows this form as it appears in Mosaic for Windows.

III

Learning HTML

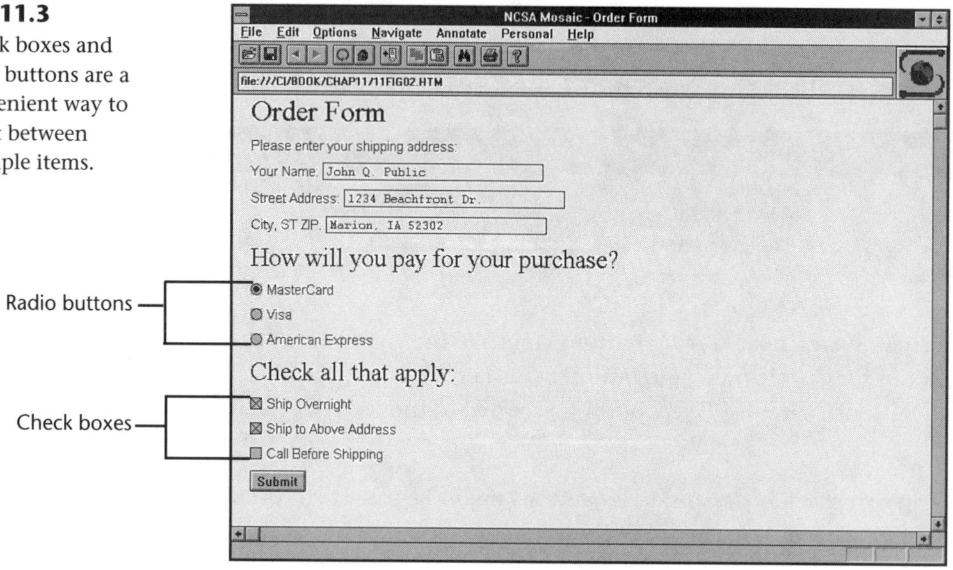

Fig. 11.3

Check boxes and radio buttons are a convenient way to select between multiple items.

Radio buttons ——

Check boxes ——

Submit and Reset Buttons

HTML forms support two types of buttons—reset and submit. A *reset button*, when pressed, sets all the form controls back to their defaults. The *submit button* sends the form data to the server. To create a submit or reset button, add the following lines in HTML:

```
<INPUT TYPE="SUBMIT" VALUE="Send Form">
<INPUT TYPE="RESET" VALUE="Clear Form">
```

The VALUE attribute sets the text that is displayed on the button, and can be any text of your choice. It should, however, clearly indicate the function of the buttons.

All HTML forms must contain a button to submit the form, with one exception: forms that have exactly one text input field do not require a submit button. Pressing Enter in the text input field automatically submits this type of form.

Multiple Submit Buttons

Normally, forms include only one submit button. In some cases, however, you may want to include multiple buttons that take different actions. You can achieve this by naming submit buttons so that the name and value of the button pressed show up in the query string. However, this capability is not yet part of standard HTML. Netscape supports it, but Mosaic for Windows does not, as of version 2 alpha 9.

Hidden Fields

Technically, hidden fields are not meant for data input. However, you can send information to the server about a form without displaying that information anywhere on the form itself. The general format for including hidden fields is:

```
<INPUT TYPE="HIDDEN" NAME="name" VALUE="value">
```

One possible use of hidden fields is to allow a single general script to process data from several different forms. The script would need to know which form is sending the data, and a hidden field could provide this information without requiring anything on the part of the user. For example, all forms processed by the script could have a hidden name of FormID and hidden values of Sales, Order, Followup, NewUser, and so on.

A closely related use of hidden fields is to use a generic script to process several forms that vary only in one or two fields. For example, a generic script to send comments via e-mail might use a hidden field to specify the e-mail address. This way, the user does not have to type an address or even know where the mail is going, but because the form contains the address information in a hidden field, a single script can still be used to send automated feedback to several different e-mail addresses. On an internal Web server, for example, this allows anyone to create his own feedback form just by changing the e-mail address in the hidden field. The back-end script is always the same.

> **Note**
>
> In general, anything you can do with hidden fields, you can do by specifying extra path information in the form's ACTION attribute. However, hidden fields appear as regular data items in a form and may therefore be easier to process, especially if there are multiple hidden items.

A third possible use of hidden fields is to embed state information into forms generated on-the-fly. For example, a form that is generated in response to a previous form can contain the original contents of the first form in a hidden field. This way, when the second form is sent, the data from the first form is sent, too, and the processing script has a complete history of the necessary information. This can be useful in a search for returning preliminary results to the user while still maintaining a record of the original query.

III

Learning HTML

Menus

Option menus can combine some of the features of both radio buttons and check boxes. You can incorporate them into a smaller package by utilizing pull-down menus and scroll bars. The general format for presenting a menu of choices is:

```
<SELECT NAME="name" [SIZE="size"] [MULTIPLE]>
<OPTION [SELECTED]>Option 1
<OPTION [SELECTED]>Option 2
<OPTION [SELECTED]>Option 3
...
<OPTION [SELECTED]>Option n
</SELECT>
```

By default, a menu shows only one entry. A user can select the other entries by clicking the pull-down menu and/or by using the scroll bar. To show more items, use the SIZE attribute. If you specify the MULTIPLE attribute, the user can select more than one item from the menu by holding down the Ctrl key while selecting items. The following HTML allows readers to choose from a menu of pizza toppings:

```
<TITLE>Programmer's Pizza Palace</TITLE>
<H1>Programmer's Pizza Palace</H1>
Welcome to the Programmer's Pizza Palace.  Getting ready for an
overnighter? Simply fill out the following form to order your
delicious virtual pizza.  As soon as your order is received, your
pizza will be UUencoded and sent over the Net from our T1-connected
ovens.  Simply decode and enjoy.<P>
<FORM ACTION="/cgi-bin/form-rpt.bat" METHOD="POST">
<H2>What size of pizza would you like?</H2>
<INPUT TYPE="RADIO" NAME="Size" VALUE="Small">After-Dinner Snack
(enough to sustain you through a new application installation)<P>
<INPUT TYPE="RADIO" NAME="Size" VALUE="Medium">Late-Night Lunch
(will help you put the  finishing touches on a perl script)<P>
<INPUT TYPE="RADIO" NAME="Size" VALUE="Large" CHECKED>Midnight
Marathon (required for installing any Unix system)<P>
<H2>What would you like on it?</H2>
<SELECT NAME="Toppings" MULTIPLE SIZE="5">
<OPTION SELECTED>Cheese
<OPTION>Extra Cheese
<OPTION>Hamburger
<OPTION>Sausage
<OPTION SELECTED>Pepperoni
<OPTION>Canadian Bacon
<OPTION SELECTED>Mushrooms
<OPTION>Onions
<OPTION>Green Olives
<OPTION>Black Olives
<OPTION>Green Peppers
<OPTION>Tomatoes
```

```
<OPTION>Pineapple
</SELECT>
<INPUT TYPE="SUBMIT" VALUE=" Order Now ">
</FORM>
```

Figure 11.4 shows how the form appears in Mosaic for Windows.

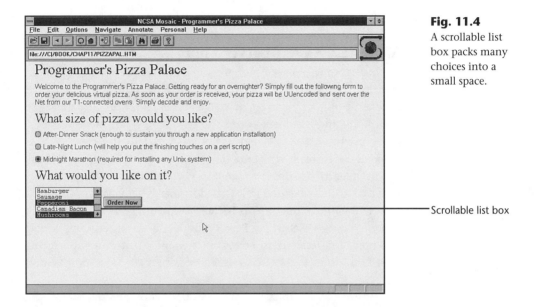

Fig. 11.4
A scrollable list box packs many choices into a small space.

Scrollable list box

Note

If you specify the MULTIPLE keyword and SIZE=1, a one-line scrollable list box is displayed instead of a drop-down list box. This is because you can only select one item (not multiple items) in a drop-down list box.

Unlike most other form elements, the value sent to the server for any menu option is simply the text that appears after the <OPTION> tag. When multiple items are selected, the *name=value* construct simply appears several times in the form data. In figure 11.4, for example, the form data sent to the server would be:

```
Size=Large&Toppings=Cheese&Toppings=Pepperoni&Toppings=Mushrooms
```

III

Learning HTML

> **Tip**
>
> You can replace radio buttons with pull-down menus to save space on-screen. Including the MULTIPLE option in a <SELECT> tag allows menus to replace check boxes, as well.

ISINDEX: A Seven-Letter Form

The <ISINDEX> tag creates a special type of form containing only one text input field. <ISINDEX> fields are typically used to allow users to enter search queries on Gopher servers and in database search scripts. The user types in a search string and then presses Enter to send it. <ISINDEX> tags are difficult to use because the <ISINDEX> tag does not specify a URL to a processing script like forms do. Instead, <ISINDEX> sends the query to the URL of the current page. In order for a script to process an ISINDEX query, this means that <ISINDEX> can only be used in HTML documents generated on-the-fly by a script (or in Gopher documents because Gopher servers are set up to handle such queries). See "Returning Results" under "General Scripting Principles" in chapter 12 to learn to use scripts to create HTML documents on-the-fly. Figure 11.5 shows an ISINDEX query as it appears in Mosaic for Windows.

Fig. 11.5
ISINDEX queries are frequently found on Gopher servers.

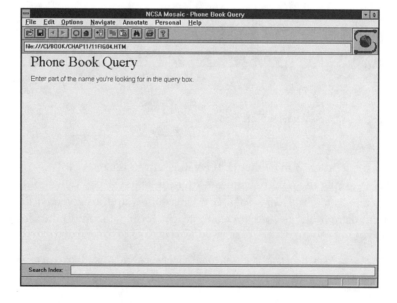

How Browsers Send Form Data

When a user clicks a form's submit button or hits Enter in an ISINDEX query, the form data or query is collected and sent all at once to the server. This data transmission has two aspects. The first is how the data is sent, called the *HTTP method.* The second is the data format, otherwise known as *URL encoding.* All form data is URL encoded, regardless of the HTTP method used to send it from the browser to a server. Once you understand URL encoding, you will also be able to send data to server scripts without using forms at all.

HTTP Methods

An HTTP method is just another name for the type of data transaction that occurs between a Web browser and server. The two most common methods are GET and POST. All form or query data is sent using one of these two methods. You specify the HTTP method for a form submittal in the `<FORM>` tag discussed earlier in the section "Form Header" in this chapter; the following discussion merely explains what happens to form data depending on which method you specify in the `<FORM>` tag.

GET

The GET method is the default method for all normal document requests. You can use the GET method to send form data by specifying it in `<FORM METHOD="{GET¦POST}">`, but this practice is not recommended, as discussed below under "POST."

When form data or a query is sent using the GET method, the data is appended to the URL sent to the server in the manner shown here. The general format for such a URL is:

```
protocol://address:port/filename/extra_path_info?query_string
```

The query string is either the text entered in an ISINDEX window or form data. In either case, the query string is in the data format described below under "URL Encoding."

POST

Browsers currently use the POST method only to send form data, and that only when it is specified in the `<FORM METHOD>` attribute. The POST method is preferred for sending form data because the data is sent as a separate transaction to the server; it isn't appended onto the end of the URL. This separate transaction prevents URLs from becoming too long in the case of forms that contain lots of data. Regulating URL size is important because servers may have size limitations on the length of URLs due to operating environment constraints.

Note that even though POST data is sent as a separate transaction, it still follows the same formatting rules as GET data appended onto a URL.

> **Note**
>
> The HTTP protocol supports the ability to POST data files of any type from browser to server, even outside of a script context. However, this capability has not yet been implemented in any browsers or servers. Form data is of MIME type x-www/url-encoded.

URL Encoding

The browser must somehow convert all data represented graphically in a form to a string of text it can send to the Web server. This involves both packaging the form data and then formatting it for proper transmission to the Web server.

Packaging Form Data

The form designer assigns each field, or graphical control, a name using the NAME attribute, except for submit and reset buttons. This naming provides a way for the server to associate data with where it came from.

The browser translates the entire contents of a form into a single text string using the following format:

```
name1=value1&name2=value2&name3=value3...
```

For example, the URL from a form that adds users' names and phone numbers to a phone book might look like this:

```
http://www.phone.com/cgi-bin/
➡phone_book?name=Call+Me&number=8005551212
```

Because you give each field in a form a unique name, the processing script can figure out what each form entry represents. The type of graphical control in which a user enters a value is not specified directly in the information sent to the server. This lack of specification is okay, though, because the processing script can use each field's unique name to figure out the control type if necessary.

Formatting Rules

Most operating environments interpret spaces in character strings as some type of delimiter indicating the start of a new field, a new parameter, and so on. Consequently, you must remove spaces from all form data and queries in order to ensure that the data is successfully received by the processing script. By convention, all spaces become plus signs (+).

This replacement presents a minor problem. What if a query itself contains a plus sign? Or what if form data contains an equals sign or ampersand, both of which are used to package the form data? There must be some way to distinguish between those characters inside form data versus those characters used to package the data. Consequently, when these characters appear in the form data itself, they are *escaped* by converting them into their hexadecimal ASCII representations, beginning with a percent sign (%). For example, the string "#$%" is converted to "%23%24%25". In hexadecimal ASCII, 23 represents the pound sign (#), 24 represents the dollar sign ($), and so on. For programming convenience, most nonalphanumeric characters are represented in hexadecimal ASCII notation.

> **Note**
>
> The exact range of characters represented in hexadecimal ASCII is not important because the decoding operation converts all character sequences beginning with a percent sign to their hexadecimal ASCII equivalent. Even if letters and numbers in a query string were encoded this way, they would still be decoded properly.

In summary, for both form data and ISINDEX queries, any data inside the form or query itself is converted according to the following rules:

- All spaces in the data are converted to plus signs (+).

- Nonalphanumeric characters are represented by their hexadecimal ASCII equivalents.

Sending a Query without a Form

As you have seen in the previous discussion of URL encoding, packaging form or query data into a single text string follows a few simple formatting rules. Consequently, it is possible to "fake" a script into believing that it is receiving form or query data without using a form. To do this, you simply send the URL that would be constructed if a form were used. This may often be useful for test or demonstration purposes.

For example, suppose you have written a script that accepts as a query several stock ticker symbols and returns their current values. If you are interested in seeing the values of certain stocks every day, you can simply fill out the query form anew each day with the symbols for all your stocks. A more efficient way, however, is to store the query URL and ticker symbols in your browser's hotlist. Each time you select that item on the hotlist, a new query is generated as if you had filled out the form. The query might look like this:

```
http://www.stocks.com/cgi-bin/get_stock_values?MCIC+FON+T
```

Part IV

Applications

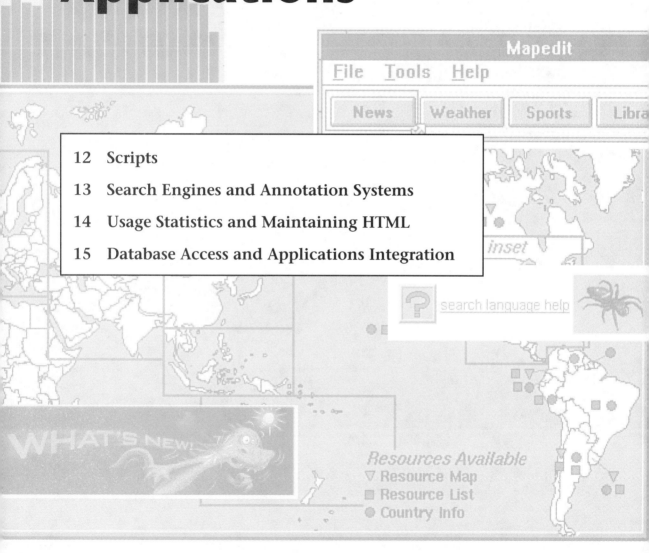

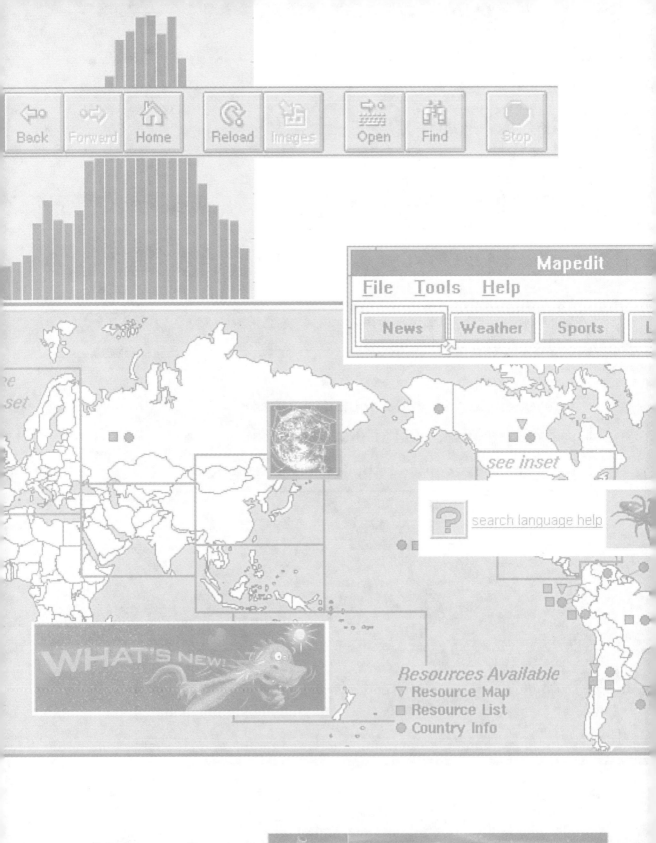

Chapter 12

Scripts

At the heart of the Web's interactive capabilities is the Common Gateway Interface (CGI). Most Web servers and clients have built-in support for the CGI specification, which allows the client to send data from fill-in forms to the server for processing by scripts. Between NCSA's server for UNIX and Windows httpd, it is possible to use almost any programming or macro language to write scripts, including UNIX shells, perl, BASIC and Visual Basic, C++, and application macro languages such as Microsoft Excel's Visual Basic for Applications and Paradox ObjectPAL.

Although this chapter contains an overview of Windows httpd scripting, it is not intended to be a complete reference or tutorial on the topic. Most of the examples focus on UNIX because of the power and simplicity of scripts written for that operating system. To get the most out of this chapter, previous experience writing UNIX shell scripts and perl programs is highly desirable.

In this chapter, you learn how

- The server passes data to processing programs

- To parse and process data in scripts

- To return script results to Web clients

- To write scripts in perl and the Korn shell

- The DOS and Windows CGI gateways work

- To write a feedback form using an e-mail gateway

- To write a simple text database search

Introduction to CGI

The Common Gateway Interface allows a browser on any platform to send data to a server on any platform that supports CGI. The CGI mechanism is relatively simple: the browser encodes data from fill-in forms into a URL and sends it to the server. The server then passes the data to a script or other program to process the data.

Theoretically, you can write CGI scripts in any language on any platform. Practically, however, some languages and platforms are much easier to work with than others. Consequently, it's a good idea to spend some time up front thinking about the platform/language combination you want to use. Depending on the nature of your application, the scripting language may even end up dictating the hardware you buy and the Web server you run.

Both server platforms included with this book support CGI. In addition to NCSA httpd for UNIX, Windows httpd has a DOS-based CGI interface and also experimental Windows CGI support. Most other servers also support CGI (see the comparison of Web servers in chapter 3, "Creating a Home Page on the Internet").

> **Note**
>
> CGI scripts replace the older NCSA-style server scripts, although the NCSA server still supports both.

Choosing a Scripting Platform

Every operating system has unique strengths and weaknesses. Understanding these will help you choose a system that is best-suited for scripting applications. Scripting tasks that are simple in one environment are often remarkably difficult in another. The following sections discuss the strengths and weaknesses of UNIX versus DOS and Windows for specific applications.

Text Manipulation and Searching

If most of your scripting applications involve manipulating ASCII text files (TXT), you likely will find that UNIX is the easiest environment in which to work. UNIX has many high-level commands that make searching, sorting, and other text operations very easy. You can use these commands combined with pipes, filters, and redirection to do almost any common text file operation on a single line.

The DOS environment is the second best for simple text operations. DOS provides a search command (FIND) and file redirection capabilities, although these features are much more limited than in UNIX. The DOS environment is superior to Windows for many basic file operations. Because Windows has no command line, most file operations such as searching and sorting require a significant amount of overhead to open and close files and to read each line individually. The Windows graphical interface is nice, but useless for text-oriented programming.

Non text Data Manipulation

If the data you're working with is not text-based, it is probably closely related to an application such as a word processor or spreadsheet. If this is true, Windows is likely the best operating environment because of its superior capability to exchange data between applications using OLE and DDE. There are many macro languages available in Windows applications, also. Working with ASCII data may be easiest in UNIX, but working with Microsoft Word documents is clearly easiest in Microsoft Word for Windows.

Any Windows program can be run as a script. This enables you to use application macro languages directly to process form data and return results. Using OLE and DDE in conjunction with powerful tools such as Visual Basic, you can string together virtually any combination of Windows programs.

> **Note**
>
> If you're looking for a good reference for Visual Basic uses with OLE and DDE, you can find thorough coverage of Visual Basic along with OLE and DDE in Que's *Using Visual Basic for Applications,* Excel Edition.

> **Tip**
>
> Although launching Windows applications such as word processors and spreadsheets as scripts is possible, the time required to load these programs for each request is significant. A better way is to run the desired applications continually in the background and to communicate with them via small Visual Basic executables that utilize DDE or OLE.

Database Access

The operating system of choice for database access depends largely on which database you're running. Good support for database access exists in both the

UNIX and Windows worlds. In UNIX, many different database gateways have been developed for use with scripts and high-end database servers such as Oracle, SyBase, and Informix. In Windows, you can utilize Visual Basic's built-in database access. In addition, you can access Windows databases directly via their native languages, such as ObjectPAL and AccessBasic.

Choosing a Scripting Language

Just as some operating systems are better suited for certain tasks, so are the programming and scripting languages that can run in a given operating environment. This section presents the merits of each language used to write scripts that appear later in this chapter: a UNIX shell, perl, the MS-DOS shell, and Visual Basic.

UNIX Shells

A UNIX shell, just as the Korn shell, is ideal for short, simple tasks such as searching a text file. Because shell scripts are essentially just batch files that use standard UNIX commands, you don't need to learn an additional command set or language syntax. In addition, you can use UNIX operators, such as redirection, in shell scripts to access the file system. Using these operators is more convenient than opening and closing files, which you have to do in most other languages. Because shell script has all UNIX commands, you also can easily access system functions, such as time and date.

The down side to shell programming is that there is no support for high-level language features such as data abstraction. However, for simple scripting tasks, shell scripting is often the fastest way to get the desired results. Most UNIX systems ship with the C shell (/bin/csh) and Bourne shell (/bin/sh), which is very similar to the Korn shell (/bin/ksh).

Perl

Perl combines many of the best features of both low-level shell scripting languages as well as high-level languages such as C++. Perl stands for Practical Report and Extraction Language, and excels at text parsing and manipulation. Perl can be a very compact language because of its numerous high-level features.

Unlike shell scripts, perl is a compiled language; however, compilation occurs at run-time, so it has the feel of an interpreted language. Compilation occurs automatically each time a program is run, which seems to be a performance hit; however, perl has one of the fastest compilers around. Like other compiled languages, perl has been ported to many platforms. It was originally developed for UNIX, but has been ported to DOS, Macs, OS/2, and Windows NT. Using the DOS version of perl, Windows httpd users can take advantage of the many perl scripts for Web servers available on the Internet. Most of these were originally written for UNIX, but users can easily modify them to work under any other version of perl. VMS platforms can build perl from the standard UNIX distribution. Perl is available for several different platforms in the CD included with this book. The perl FAQ is also included. Updates are available from **ftp://ftp.cis.ufl.edu/pub/perl/doc/FAQ**.

> **Note**
>
> Perl for OS/2 is now included in the official distribution.

DOS Shells

If you are running Windows httpd, you can take advantage of the DOS CGI right away using COMMAND.COM, the default shell supplied with MS-DOS. Unfortunately, however, this shell lacks several features necessary for many Web scripts. File operations are limited and somewhat awkward. It has no support for standard input and output when interacting with Windows. COMMAND.COM does not support advanced program control flow constructs such as if-then-else or while loops. Perhaps worst of all, less-than (<) and greater-than (>) have special meaning to COMMAND.COM. Therefore, you can't use them to produce HTML formatting tags when sending output. However, if all you need to do is rearrange a few variables or copy a text file to the output, COMMAND.COM works fine.

In order to incorporate more advanced features into DOS shell scripts, you can use a replacement command interpreter that supports those features not included in MS-DOS COMMAND.COM. Examples of replacement shells include Norton NDOS, which comes with The Norton Utilities for DOS, and the shareware 4DOS. You can also use other versions of DOS, such as IBM's PC-DOS and Novell DOS, but these have not been tested with Windows httpd.

Another way to overcome the limitations of MS-DOS COMMAND.COM is to run an executable program from within the default DOS shell. An example of this is to run perl, which then compiles and runs a program written in perl. Microsoft QBASIC, which comes with MSDOS, is a simple and powerful language that you can call from inside a DOS batch program. There are dozens of other low-cost BASIC dialects for DOS. Adventurous users can run any executable program from the DOS command line, including those created in C or PASCAL.

Visual Basic

To use the experimental Windows CGI gateway included with Windows httpd, you must be able to execute scripts in the Windows environment. The simplest way to write Windows programs is to use Microsoft Visual Basic for Windows or one of the many other Windows BASIC or scripting dialects available. Because the Windows CGI uses files to pass all data to and from scripts, any language that can read and write files suffices. More experienced programmers may want to use Borland C++ or Visual C++ for Windows.

Scripts written for the Windows CGI in a language like Visual Basic execute somewhat faster than DOS scripts because there is no overhead required to start a DOS shell. Scripts are only concerned with the input or output of text streams or files to Web browsers. This means that using an advanced GUI development tool such as Visual Basic for Windows just to perform simple text operations is somewhat of a waste. On the other hand, because Windows httpd can launch any executable as a script, you can use the macro capabilities of applications such as word processors and spreadsheets to do things that are impossible in a BASIC program. This can be a very powerful way to integrate a database with a Web server.

The remainder of this chapter discusses the exact mechanisms by which script processing takes place. The chapter is organized into three main sections. First, it covers the principles applicable to all platforms. Second, it explains how CGI works on each platform. Finally, it presents some sample scripts with application notes.

General Scripting Principles

When the server receives a query or form data in a URL or POST transaction, the server passes the data to the specified script and starts the script. The script reads the input data, completes the required processing, and sends results back to the server, which adds HTTP header information and sends the data back to the client. From the script's point of view, this process can be broken down into three steps:

1. Receive the data.

2. Parse the data.

3. Return the results.

Many aspects of these three steps are applicable to all platforms. The next few sections cover these steps and are followed by explanations of how they work in NCSA httpd and Windows httpd.

Receiving the Data

Form and query data is made available to scripts in one of three ways, depending on the CGI gateway used (UNIX, DOS, or Windows) and the HTTP method used to send the data. Table 12.1 shows all the possibilities for the platforms considered in this chapter.

Table 12.1	How Data Is Passed to Scripts	
CGI	**GET**	**POST**
UNIX	Environment variables	stdin
DOS	Environment variables, %1%	content file
Windows	CGI data file	content file

Environment variables and their Windows counterpart, the CGI data file, are used to convey information about every data transaction, whether the method was GET or POST. Windows does not support environment variables, but Windows httpd creates a CGI data file to supply the same information. The most important variables are QUERY_STRING, PATH_INFO, and CONTENT_LENGTH because these contain the actual query or form data. The CGI 1.0 specification defines 18 different environment variables that script programs can use for a variety of different purposes. These DOS and UNIX variables are defined below, along with the names of their Windows counterparts in the CGI data file.

The following variables are sent for all requests:

■ SERVER_SOFTWARE (Server Software)

The name and software version of the server.

Example: NCSA/V1.3 (MSWindows)

■ SERVER_NAME (Server Name)

The server's hostname or IP address.

Example: s115.netins.net

■ GATEWAY_INTERFACE (CGI Version)

Which CGI specification the server uses.

Example: CGI/1.1 DOS (experimental)

■ OUTPUT_FILE (Output File) (Windows httpd only)

The name of the temporary file used to pass script output back to the server. The server sets this variable and makes it available to the script.

Example: C:\DOS\HS063D62.ACC

The remaining variables depend on the client and are set accordingly for each request.

■ SERVER_PROTOCOL (Request Protocol)

The protocol used by the client for this request.

Example: HTTP/1.0

■ SERVER_PORT (Server Port)

The port number that received the request.

Example: SERVER_PORT=80

■ REQUEST_METHOD (Request Method)

The HTTP method specified in the request.

Examples: GET, HEAD, PUT, POST

■ HTTP_ACCEPT ([Accept])

The list of MIME types accepted by the client.

Example: text/plain, text/html, image/gif

> **Note**
>
> Under Windows httpd, this variable contains the DOS path to a file that contains the list of acceptable MIME types.

■ PATH_INFO (Logical Path)

The extra path information contained in a URL.

Example: http://myweb/cgi-bin/myscript/homepage

PATH_INFO = "homepage"

- `PATH_TRANSLATED` (Physical Path)

  The extra path information preceded by the physical, rather than the virtual, path to the script.

  Example: `http://myweb/cgi-bin/myscript/homepage`

  `PATH_TRANSLATED = "usr/local/etc/cgi-bin/myscript/homepage"`

  > **Note**
  >
  > Under Windows httpd, the translated path will be in DOS rather than UNIX syntax (\ instead of /).

- `SCRIPT_NAME` (Executable Path)

  The virtual path (URL) to the script being executed.

  Example: `/cgi-dos/test-cgi.bat`

- `QUERY_STRING` (Query String)

  The encoded version of the query data. This data follows the ? in the URL.

  Example: `Smith%27Wesson+OR+security`

- `REMOTE_HOST` (Remote Host)

  The name of the client machine making the request. If this is not available, `REMOTE_ADDR` is set.

  Example: `s115.slipper.net`

- `REMOTE_ADDR` (Remote Address)

  The IP address of the client machine making the request.

  Example: `167.142.100.115`

- `AUTH_TYPE` (Authentication Method)

  The authentication method used to validate the user if the document is protected and the server supports authentication. This corresponds to the `AuthType` directive in NCSA httpd.

- `REMOTE_USER` (Authenticated User name)

  The name of the authenticated user if the document is protected and the server supports authentication. This corresponds to the `AuthUser` directive in NCSA httpd.

■ REMOTE_IDENT (not supported in Windows httpd)

If the server supports remote identity checking via RFC 931 (see NCSA httpd's IdentityCheck directive) and the client is running identd or another program that supports RFC 931, this variable contains the remote user name.

> **Caution**
>
> Use this variable only for logging purposes and not for security purposes.

■ CONTENT_TYPE (Content Type)

The MIME type of data contained in a PUT or POST request.

Example: text/plain

■ CONTENT_LENGTH (Content Length)

The number of bytes of data contained in a PUT or POST request.

Example: 42

■ CONTENT_FILE (Content File) (Windows only)

The DOS path to the server-created temporary file that contains the content (query string) sent by the client in a PUT or POST request.

Parsing the Data

Remember that form data is sent to the server by encoding it into a single query string, in which all spaces have been converted to plus signs and special characters have been escaped (see the section "URL Encoding" in chapter 11, "Forms"). The first step in processing most form data is to decode the query string. Both NCSA httpd for UNIX and Windows httpd include utilities or source code that make light work out of parsing. These are discussed in the tutorials on their respective platforms later in this chapter.

Returning Results

Web server scripts can return three kinds of output—an HTML page or other data type generated on-the-fly, a URL to a new location, or a raw HTTP dialog. The following sections discuss the required format for each type of output.

Returning HTML

All data sent to a Web client from inside a script begins with an HTTP header, followed by the body of the data. To return HTML or any other data type, the HTTP header consists only of two lines: a line stating the MIME type of the data followed by a blank line. The server packages the header and data into standard HTTP and transmits the package directly to the client. The following lines send a simple HTML message back to a Web client.

```
Content-type: text/html

<TITLE>Feedback</TITLE>
<H1>Feedback</H1>
Thank you for your feedback.  Your comments have been forwarded to
the appropriate personnel.
```

To send an HTML message back to the client, the script simply needs to include HTTP header information prior to the HTML text. This consists of a `Content-type: text/html` line followed by a blank line, as illustrated in the preceding sample.

Returning Other Data Types

The previous example sent an HTML message back to the client. If you want to send a file instead, you simply change the content type specified on the first line of the output to match the MIME type of the data being sent. For example, to send a text file from the Korn shell, you send `Content-type: text/plain` followed by the text file itself.

Returning a URL

Rather than send data generated directly inside the script, you can send data from another page on the same server or even another Internet location by specifying a URL. To do this, replace the `Content-type:` line in the output with a `Location:` line. To direct the client to www.somewhere.com, you send `Location: http://www.somewhere.com/`. The Web client receives the URL and attempts to make a connection just as if the URL came from a hypertext link on another page.

Bypassing the Server

Normally, data written to the standard output is intercepted by the server and HTTP header information is added before sending it on to the client. It is possible to bypass the server, however, and to talk to the client directly in HTTP. However, there is little benefit to doing this except for educational or testing purposes.

> **Caution**
>
> You should write scripts that bypass the server and talk in HTTP directly with the client only if you are familiar with the HTTP protocol.

In order to bypass the server, scripts must meet certain conventions. First, the file name must be special. In UNIX, bypass scripts must end in `.nph`. In DOS or Windows, they must begin with `NPH-`. In addition, the first line of the output must begin with `HTTP/1.0`. An example of bypass output taken from Windows httpd's online documentation follows:

```
HTTP/1.0 200 OK
Date: Tuesday, 31-May-94 19:04:30 GMT
Server: NCSA/V1.3Pre/MSWin
MIME-version: 1.0
Content-type: text/html
Last-modified: Sunday, 15-May-94 02:12:32 GMT
Content-length: 4109
<HTML> <HEAD>
<TITLE>A document</TITLE>
```

> **Note**
>
> The previous example includes the status information `200 OK`. This can optionally be included in nonbypass scripts by including the line `Status: 200 OK` along with the `Content-type:` or `Location:` headers. CERN has developed a program called *cgiutils* to assist in the development of nph scripts. For more information, see **http://info.cern.ch/hypertext/WWW/Daemon/User/CGI/cgiutils.html**.

UNIX File Permissions

Before we get into the platform-specific discussion, a word about file permissions on UNIX scripts is applicable. In order for a script to run, it must be executable by the server. Normally, servers process requests as a nonprivileged user such as `nobody` or `daemon`. Consequently, it is common to simply give Web documents world read and execute privileges. In the case of scripts, however, this may not be such a good idea. Scripts that do any kind of database access or file modification, sending mail, or just about anything except returning text output can produce unexpected results if executed out of context.

It is a good idea to set script permission so that only the Web server can execute them. This is easily done by changing the script's owner to the user that processes Web document requests. This way, you can set more restrictive permissions for the world than for the owner and the Web server will still be able to execute the script. As long as the script's author is a member of the group that owns the script, you can use group permissions to give the author execute privileges for test purposes.

> **Tip**
>
> Make sure you change a file's group and group permissions to those desired before you change the file's owner!

In addition to restricting read and execute privileges, it is a good idea to remove all write privileges to scripts. This is to prevent a user who has gained unauthorized access via a script loophole from rewriting or deleting scripts. The drawback to this is that only root can edit or delete scripts. It is also a good idea to deny write privileges to the script directory to the Web server's document request process. See the section "Writing Secure Scripts," later in this chapter.

UNIX CGI

Thus far, this chapter has covered only general scripting principles because the UNIX, DOS, and Windows CGI gateways as implemented by NCSA httpd and Windows httpd are considerably different. The remainder of this chapter presents concrete examples in each environment to help you better understand the principles.

NCSA's Web server for UNIX is the basis for much of Windows httpd. An understanding of how NCSA httpd works will aid you in understanding the DOS and Windows CGI, as well. Essentially, the DOS and Windows CGI gateways simulate the UNIX environment.

On the UNIX platform, data is passed to scripts either through environment variables or the standard input (stdin). UNIX scripts written in any language can access environment variables, which makes this scheme very flexible. To return script output, script simply writes to the standard output (stdout). The server adds HTTP header information to the output and sends it on to the client.

Receiving the Data

Form and query data is made available to scripts in one of two ways, depending on the HTTP method used to send the data. If the GET method was used to send a query string, the query data is available through the environment variable QUERY_STRING. If the HTTP method was POST, the form data is read from the standard input. In addition, the environment variables CONTENT_TYPE and CONTENT_LENGTH contain information about the data on the standard input.

Parsing the Data

On UNIX systems, converting form data to variable assignments using the form field names is relatively simple. A simple program called *cgiparse* decodes the entire query string into a series of lines containing variable assignments. This program comes with CERN's httpd (**http:// info.cern.ch/hypertext/WWW/Daemon/User/Guide.html**). The source code is included with this book. Because cgiparse is an executable program written in C, you can run it from inside any UNIX shell script or other programming language, making it a powerful and versatile tool.

> **Note**
>
> Complete documentation for cgiparse is available from **http://info.cern.ch/ hypertext/WWW/Daemon/User/CGI/cgiparse.html**. A related utility is *unescape,* which you can find in the support directory of your server distribution. Other CGI utilities are available from **ftp://ftp.ncsa.uiuc.edu/Web/httpd/ Unix/ncsa_httpd/cgi/**.

Cgiparse simply takes the contents of the QUERY_STRING environment variable or the standard input and produces a series of variable assignments. To use cgiparse to decode form data, the format is:

```
cgiparse -form -prefix prefix_character
```

The prefix character is the symbol that precedes the variable names. For example, suppose the query string or standard input contained Name=David Jones&Phone=3041391&Email=dmjones and the following line was included at the beginning of a perl script:

```
`cgiparse -form -prefix $`;
```

The result is the following lines written to the standard output:

```
$Name=David Jones
$Phone=3641391
$Email=dmjones
```

Cgiparse removes all the plus signs, decodes the special characters, and separates the input one on each line. In our example, cgiparse has written these lines to the standard output. However, because we used the $ prefix, these lines can appear verbatim in a perl program as variable assignments. Is there a way to treat the output of the cgiparse command as if they were variable assignments? Yes. In perl, the eval command is used to treat a string of characters as if they were part of the perl program. In this case, wrapping the cgiparse command inside the eval command causes the cgiparse output to be treated exactly as if those lines were part of the perl program itself.

```
eval `cgiparse -form -prefix $`;
```

Presto! In one line, all the form data is read and parsed, and variable assignments are made. The remainder of the script can now use the variables $Name, $Phone, and $Email directly. Isn't UNIX great?

The Korn shell can also use cgiparse to automatically decode form data and assign variables, only with slightly different syntax. In the Korn shell, the magic cgiparse line reads:

```
eval `cgiparse -form -prefix ""`
```

The only differences are the prefix character, which is now a blank (indicated by the empty quotes), and the absence of a trailing semicolon, which is not required in the Korn shell. The prefix character is blank because Korn shell variables do not begin with a dollar sign ($) as in perl.

Tip

Many Web servers run as user daemon (see the User directive in chapter 6, "Server Configuration"), which often has no default path specified for security reasons. Consequently, you may need to include the full path to cgiparse in the eval statement.

Returning Results

Under UNIX, data is sent from a script back to a Web client simply by writing to the standard output. This can be done with the print statement in most languages or the UNIX cat command. In many languages, such as the Korn shell and perl, a useful feature for sending several lines of text to the standard output is the *here document* feature.

The here document feature works with redirection to take the input for a given command from inside the script itself. When the script comes to the specified marker (in this case, EOM), normal script processing resumes. In the following excerpt from a Korn shell script, the cat command is used to print lines of text to the standard output, and those lines are sent from directly inside the script using the here document feature.

```
cat << EOM
Content-type: text/html

<TITLE>Feedback</TITLE>
<H1>Feedback</H1>
Thank you for your feedback.  Your comments have been forwarded to
the appropriate personnel.
EOM
```

Tip

You can use the here document feature with any UNIX command that can accept input from the command line. For example, use it in conjunction with mail to send a message to a specified addressee. In the previous example, you replace cat << EOM with mail address << EOM.

Perl also has a here document feature, as demonstrated in the following excerpt from a perl script:

```
print <<EOM;
Content-type: text/html

<TITLE>Feedback</TITLE>
<H1>Feedback</H1>
```

```
Thank you for your feedback.  Your comments have been forwarded to
the appropriate personnel.
EOM
```

> **Note**
>
> A blank line is always required to separate an HTTP header from the body of the
> message.

Any data to be sent back to the client is simply sent to the standard output.
The server automatically picks up this data and adds HTTP header information. As discussed earlier in the chapter, you can use this capability to send
nonHTML data as well as a URL to a new location.

Sample Applications

You've now learned how to get and parse data in the Korn shell and perl, as
well as how to return results. It's time to put it all together in three sample
scripts. The first illustrates a simple feedback gateway that repackages form
data and sends it to an e-mail address. The second is a simple search routine,
and the third improves on the search.

> **Note**
>
> In order to use any of these examples, your server must be running and the URL to
> the example files must begin with "http://<your server address>/." You cannot use
> the "Open Local File" option to view the example forms because the URL to the
> processing script will not be correct when you do this.

Feedback Gateway

A common application of forms on the Web is to forward comments and
suggestions to an e-mail address or database via a feedback form. The following form and script demonstrate how you can reformat form data and send it
to an e-mail address.

> **Note**
>
> Browsers that support the `mailto:` URL do not need to use a form just to send
> feedback to an e-mail address. However, using a form like this one may still be useful
> if you specifically want to see some items in the comments.

Figure 12.1 shows a simple form that you can use to input a name, e-mail address, category of comments, and the comments themselves. Keep in mind that this may look different in different browsers and on different platforms.

Fig. 12.1
This feedback form sends data to a script, which then sends the form data via e-mail.

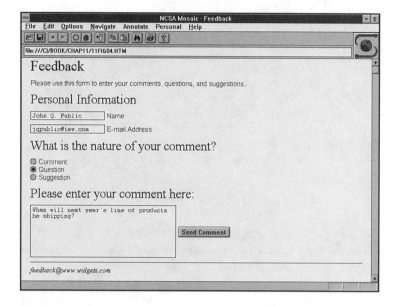

The HTML used to generate this form is included below.

```
# feedback
<TITLE>Feedback</TITLE>
<H1>Feedback</H1>
<FORM ACTION="/cgi-bin/feedback" METHOD="POST">
Please use this form to enter your comments, questions, and
suggestions.
<H2>Personal Information</H2>
<INPUT TYPE="TEXT" NAME="FullName">Name<P>
<INPUT TYPE="TEXT" NAME="Address">E-mail Address<P>
<H2>What is the nature of your comment?</H2>
<INPUT TYPE="RADIO" NAME="Type" VALUE="Comment" CHECKED>Comment<BR>
<INPUT TYPE="RADIO" NAME="Type" VALUE="Question">Question<BR>
<INPUT TYPE="RADIO" NAME="Type" VALUE="Suggestion">Suggestion<BR>
<H2>Please enter your comment here:</H2>
<TEXTAREA ROWS=8 COLS=40 NAME="Comment">
</TEXTAREA>
<INPUT TYPE="SUBMIT" VALUE=" Send Comment ">
</FORM>
<P><HR><P>
<ADDRESS>feedback@www.widgets.com</ADDRESS>
```

When the server receives the form data, it looks for a script named "feedback" in the cgi-bin directory ("FEEDBACK" on WebmasterCD). The purpose of the script is simply to reformat the form contents and send them via e-mail to a specified address. Here's a sample Korn shell script to send the form data to the address "feedback."

> **Note**
>
> In shell scripts, lines beginning with # are comments, except for the first line, which uses the #! convention to point to the shell under which the script runs.

```
#Run under the Korn shell
#!/bin/ksh

# Specify the path to cgiparse
export CGIPATH=/usr/local/etc/httpd/cgi-bin
# Convert form data to variables
eval `$CGIPATH/cgiparse -form -prefix ""`

# Mail the following info. to feedback
mail feedback << EOM
Subject: $Type from $FullName        The message subject line will
                                     include the comment type and
                                     person's name
Comments:  $Comment                  The text of the comment
--------------------
$FullName, $Address                  The user's name and e-mail
                                     address
EOM

# Send the following output back to the browser
cat << EOM
Content-type: text/html

<HEAD>
<TITLE>Automated Feedback Response</TITLE>
</HEAD>
<BODY>
<H2>Thank you for your feedback.</H2>
The following text was received.
<p><hr><p>
2Subject: $Type from $FullName<p> Echo the received comment data
Comments:  $Comment<p>
<address>$FullName, $Address</address>
</BODY>

EOM
```

Figure 12.2 shows the screen that is displayed after our fictitious user clicks the Send Comment button.

Fig. 12.2

After submitting the feedback form, the user receives confirmation that the data has been sent.

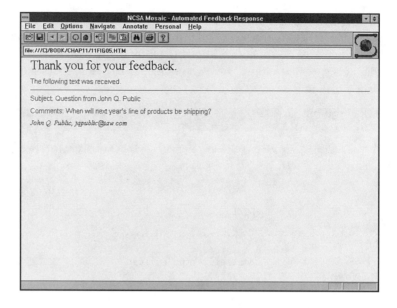

The user whose e-mail address is "feedback" receives the following message:

```
Subject: Question from John Q. Public
Comments: When will next year's line of products be shipping?
--------------------
John Q. Public, jqpublic@iaw.com
```

> **Note**
>
> This example uses the UNIX `mail` command to forward form data to an e-mail address. This is much more difficult on other platforms, which rarely have the capability to send e-mail from the command line. If you plan to forward e-mail through forms, strongly consider using UNIX.

A Simple Search

A common task for Web scripts is to search a simple text file for information. Complex database gateways are not necessary just to search text files for information, but you can learn about advanced databases in chapter 15, "Database Access and Applications Integration."

The example in this section searches an online phone book. The format of the phone book is simply a text file with one person's name and number on each line. The search accepts either a name or number, and returns all matching entries. Here's an example of the phone book file format ("PHONE.TXT" on WebmasterCD):

```
John Q. Public      (555)555-1212    Computer Consultant
Red Haw Realty      (515)774-4242    Southern Iowa Farms
```

The form used for the phone book search is pictured in figure 12.3 and the HTML accompanies it ("PHONE.HTM" on WebmasterCD).

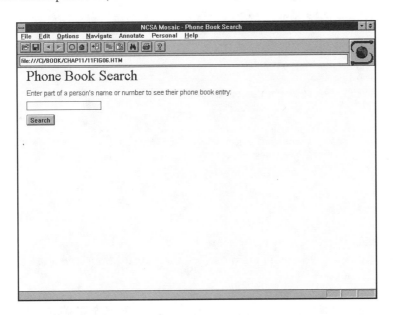

Fig. 12.3

The phone book search form allows you to search an online phone book.

```
<TITLE>Phone Book Search</TITLE>
<H1>Phone Book Search</H1>
<FORM ACTION="/cgi-bin/phone.pl" METHOD="POST">
Enter part of a person's name or number to see their phone book
➥entry:<P>
<INPUT TYPE="TEXT" NAME="Query"><P>
<INPUT TYPE="SUBMIT" VALUE=" Search ">
```

The script referenced in the search form, /cgi-bin/phone.pl, simply needs to search the phone book text file for all occurrences of the query string. Using the UNIX grep command, this is almost a one-liner. The grep command does exactly what is needed: it searches a file for all occurrences of a string of characters and returns all matching lines. Here's a perl script to do the search and return results:

```
# phone.pl
# Invoke the perl compiler
#!/bin/perl

# Define the location of the phone database
$PHONEBOOK="/usr/local/etc/httpd/cgi-bin/phone.txt";

# Define the path to cgiparse
$CGIPATH="/usr/local/etc/httpd/cgi-bin";
# Convert form data to variables
eval `$CGIPATH/test/cgiparse -form -prefix $`;
```

```
# Send results to browser
print <<EOM;
Content-type: text/html

<TITLE>Phone Book Search</TITLE>
<BODY>
<H1>Phone Book Search</H1>
<p><hr><p>
EOM

#Echo the original query
print <<EOM;
Search for <B>$query</B> yields these entries:
<PRE>
EOM

#Do a case-insensitive search and print results
print `grep -i $query $PHONEBOOK`;

print <<EOM;
</PRE>
</BODY>
EOM
```

The actual search is done on one line, which calls the UNIX grep utility and prints the results to the standard output. The format of the search results is shown in figure 12.4.

Fig. 12.4
The simple phone.pl script returns these search results.

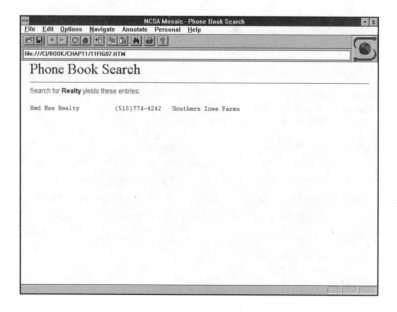

IV

A Better Search

This search can be improved upon by putting the query box and the displayed results on the same page so that the user does not have to continually switch between the query and results pages when conducting a search. To do this, generate the form right inside the script. In the following example, the script automatically generates the form and decides whether or not to do a search based on whether or not a query was entered. This way, all you have to do to get to the phone book search screen is make a hyperlink to the phone book script itself. A form separate from the script is no longer necessary. A second improvement to the phone search is the addition of code to inform the user if the search is unsuccessful.

One final trick: this script includes two additional lines of code to display when the phone book was last updated. This is based on a perl function that returns the number of days since a file was last modified. This is a handy feature, as users often want to know how current the information is.

```
# phone2.pl
#!/bin/perl

$PHONEBOOK="/usr/local/etc/httpd/cgi-bin/phone.txt";

$CGIPATH="/usr/local/etc/httpd/cgi-bin";
eval `$CGIPATH/test/cgiparse -form -prefix $`;

# Determine the age of the phone book
$mod_date=int(-M $PHONEBOOK);

#Display the age of the phone book and generate the search form
print <<EOM;
Content-type: text/html

<TITLE>Phone Book Search</TITLE>
<BODY>
<H1>Phone Book Search</H1>
The phone book was updated $mod_date days ago.<p>
<FORM ACTION="/cgi-bin/phone2.pl" METHOD="POST">
Search for: <INPUT TYPE="TEXT" NAME="QUERY">
<INPUT TYPE="SUBMIT" VALUE="SEARCH">
</FORM>
<p><hr><p>
EOM

# Do the search only if a query was entered
if (length($query)>0) {
  print <<EOM;
Search for <B>$query</B> yields these entries:
<PRE>
EOM
```

```
#Inform user if search is unsuccessful
$answer = `grep -i $query $PHONEBOOK`;
if (!$answer) { print "Search was unsuccessful\n" ;}
else { print $answer\n" ; }

print <<EOM;
</PRE>
</BODY>
EOM
}
```

The beefed-up version of the search now looks like figure 12.5. As soon as the search results are completed, the user is ready for another search on the same page.

Fig. 12.5

By generating the search form inside a script, you can allow users to enter another search on the same page as the search results.

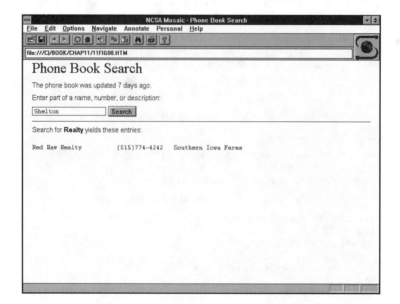

> ## Tip
>
> In scripts like this one that require only one input field, all form elements can be replaced by a single <ISINDEX> tag. The environment variable QUERY_STRING contains the query. A URL to the processing script is not specified anywhere inside the script itself because an <ISINDEX> document automatically includes a reference to itself.

IV

Applications

DOS CGI

Under Windows httpd, you can write scripts in the DOS batch file language or any DOS executable program, including other language interpreters such as perl. This allows you to write scripts in any language, provided a DOS compiler for the language is available. Unfortunately, getting data to and from DOS is a bit trickier than in UNIX. The principles are still the same, but temporary files are used instead of the standard input and output.

Receiving the Data

Windows cannot directly set environment variables in a DOS session running under Windows. To get around this, when Windows httpd receives a URL containing a query (form data), it creates a DOS batch file that sets DOS environment variables and then executes the specified script program. After creating the DOS batch file, it executes it in a DOS session using a Windows PIF file.

> **Note**
>
> You can run any DOS executable from inside the DOS batch file created by the server. Windows httpd allows a high degree of customization for script support, but this requires a very good understanding of DOS and interaction between DOS and Windows.

Because the default command interpreter supplied with DOS (COMMAND.COM) does not support standard input and output when interacting with Windows, the UNIX scheme for accepting POST data and sending output to the client does not work. Instead, the script program must read input data from a temporary file created by the server and write output data to a temporary file created by the server. The names of these files are available to scripts through the environment variables CONTENT_FILE and OUTPUT_FILE. For form data or queries posted with the GET method, the environment variable QUERY_STRING still contains the input data, as well as the parameter %1%.

> **Note**
>
> The default DOS shell, COMMAND.COM, does not support standard input or standard output when interacting with Windows. However, if you are using an alternative DOS shell that supports standard input, POST data is available as standard input as well as in the content file.

Parsing the Data

Unfortunately, DOS has no eval function like perl and many UNIX shells, so you cannot use nifty programs such as cgiparse as readily. It is certainly possible to write a C program like cgiparse to read the QUERY_STRING environment variable or form data from a content file and convert that data to environment variables. However, this is of little benefit for straight DOS programming because the DOS shell was never intended to be a full-featured programming language.

A more powerful way to use the DOS CGI is to call a program written in a BASIC dialect from within a DOS script. In this instance, it is useful to have a program like cgiparse. Windows httpd does not include such a program; however, it does include C functions that you can use in such a program. These are available in C:\HTTPD\HTDOCS\HTTPDDOC\SETUP\SCRIPTS\ UNESCAPE.HTM.

Returning Results

Under the DOS CGI, script output can be sent to the standard output only if the DOS shell being used supports standard output. The default shell supplied with MS-DOS does not. In lieu of writing to the standard output, a DOS script must write to an output file. When the script returns program control to Windows httpd, it will look for this output file and send the contents back to the client. The name of the output file is given by the environment variable OUTPUT_FILE. The following example shows how a simple HTML message is sent to the client from within an MS-DOS script.

```
set OF=%OUTPUT_FILE%
echo Content-type: text/html                    >%OF%
echo.                                           >>%OF%
echo Thank you for using the feedback facility >>%OF%
```

The first line simply defines a shortcut name for the OUTPUT_FILE environment variable. OUTPUT_FILE is defined by the server before the script executes. The second line creates the output file. The third and fourth lines append text to the output file. In a replacement DOS that supports standard output, redirecting the echo statements to a file is not necessary.

Sample Applications

Windows httpd includes a couple of simple DOS scripts that demonstrate the DOS CGI. The examples are not terribly meaningful; however, they do serve to illustrate how DOS scripts work in the default MS-DOS shell. The example found in C:\HTTPD\CGI-DOS\FORM-RPT.BAT simply echoes the contents of a form in an HTML page as part of the server demonstration. This example follows.

```
rem
rem     Used with example forms in the Windows httpd documentation
rem     Too bad angle brackets can't be echoed by COMMAND.COM...
rem     Get a better shell!
rem
set of=%output_file%                    Define shortcut
echo Content-type:text/html > %of%      Send HTTP header
echo. >> %of%                           Send required blank line
type c:\httpd\cgi-bin\form-rpt.pre >> %of% Send top of HTML page
type %CONTENT_FILE% >> %of%             Echo form data
type c:\httpd\cgi-bin\form-rpt.pst >> %of% Send bottom of HTML page
```

Because less-than (<) and greater-than (>) have special meaning to the default DOS shell, HTML formatting tags cannot be sent directly. To get around this, this script echoes two files, "form-rpt.pre" and "form-rpt.pst," to the standard output, one before and one after the form content is sent. These files contain formatted HTML. This is a bit of a pain, as indicated by the initial comment lines.

To see some sample forms in action using the DOS CGI, enter a URL to **http://localhost/httpddoc/info/forms/overview.htm#examples** once your server is up and running. The form examples are useful for learning how forms work and how form data is encoded.

Windows CGI

Windows httpd includes an experimental CGI gateway designed to be used with Visual Basic 3.0. Just as in the DOS version, temporary files are used to pass data to and from scripts instead of standard input and standard output. Because Windows doesn't have its own environment variables like DOS, all data that would normally be written to environment variables is instead written to a *CGI data file,* which uses the same format as common Windows INI files.

Tip

Windows scripts will generally return results more quickly than DOS scripts because there is considerable overhead associated with launching the DOS session to run a DOS script.

In addition to the CGI data file, a content file and output file are created as in DOS. A Windows script reads the CGI data file and content file (depending on the request method) for input and writes to the output file to send data back to the client. The server then repackages the output file in HTTP format and sends it on its way.

> **Note**
>
> Any Windows program can be used as a back-end script. The examples supplied with Windows httpd are written in Visual Basic 3.0 and require VBRUN300.DLL to operate. However, because all communication between scripts and the server is accomplished through temporary files, any Windows programming or scripting language could be used to write scripts. This includes application macro languages such as WordBasic and Paradox ObjectPAL.

Receiving the Data

Because Windows is actually a DOS program rather than a true operating system, there are no such things as Windows environment variables. Instead, Windows frequently uses INI files that store key-value pairs similar to environment variables. GET data is available through the variable Query String in the CGI data file. POST data is available in a separate content file that is described in the CGI data file by the variables Content Type, Content Length, and Content File.

In order to extract these variables from the CGI data file, a program must read each line of the CGI data file, looking for the desired variable names. If you're using Visual Basic, however, you can take advantage of the GetPrivateProfile-String function to do much of the dirty work for you because the CGI data file is in the same format as other Windows INI files. This is illustrated in sample code distributed with Windows httpd. The path to the HTML file containing a sample Visual Basic program to read the CGI data file is located in C:\HTTPD\HTDOCS\HTTPDDOC\INFO\WINCGI.HTM.

Parsing the Data

Windows httpd does not provide a program like cgiparse to parse form or query data into variables. However, C functions that can do the job are provided in C:\HTTPD\HTDOCS\HTTPDDOC\SETUP\SCRIPTS\ UNESCAPE.HTM. These functions can either be compiled into a separate program like cgiparse or translated into the language of your choice for inclusion in Windows scripts.

Returning Results

As for the DOS CGI, Windows output must be written to a temporary file because there is no standard output as in UNIX and some DOS shells. In principle, this works the same as in DOS, except that the name of the output file is specified in the CGI data file as "Output File" rather than the environment variable OUTPUT_FILE.

Sample Applications

Even using Visual Basic, the Windows CGI is fairly complex. Fortunately, sample applications and source code are provided with Windows httpd. The C:\HTTPD\CGI-SRC directory contains the Visual Basic source code and make files for two programs used to demonstrate the Windows CGI interface. To see these programs in action, enter the URL **http://localhost/cgi-win/cgitest.exe** once your server is up and running and try the links on the demo page. You will see that the Windows CGI programs execute considerably faster than DOS scripts.

Writing Secure Scripts

As you have seen, scripts are extremely powerful because they can do a lot with very little code. However, they can also be very dangerous. Because scripts are run in response to client data, a mischievous user can gain unauthorized access to your server by sending it various kinds of bogus data. Here are some tips for making your scripts as secure as possible.

Be Careful with *eval*

The eval command is used in several examples in this chapter to compactly convert form data into variables. However, if a malicious user sends system commands instead of form data in a query, the eval statement might execute the system commands, allowing unauthorized access to your server. Consequently, it is a good idea to check out form data very carefully before using eval to make sure that no system commands will be executed. Good things to watch for would be backquotes (`), which are used in many languages to execute system commands, parentheses (), which might indicate that a system call is being made with arguments inside the parentheses, the semicolon (;), which is the end-of-line separator in many languages, and the backslash (\), which is used to escape other characters. In addition to ensuring the absence of these characters, it would be wise to ensure that each line evaluated is a legitimate variable assignment.

Caution

Of all characters that can have negative consequences when evaluated, backquotes are perhaps the most dangerous. The proper escape characters and backquotes embedded in form data can be used to do almost anything.

The safest way to filter out all potentially dangerous characters in query strings is to take the philosophy that "All that is not expressly permitted is prohibited." In other words, permit only alphanumeric characters and those characters necessary for variable assignments, such as the equals (=) and dollar ($) signs. Depending on the scripting language, even this technique may have pitfalls. A thorough understanding of the methods used to make system calls in your scripting language is essential to preserving security.

Don't Assume Anything

When you write a script, chances are you will design it with a specific form in mind. This is appropriate, but don't forget that clients can send *anything* to your script. Remember that form data is sent like any other URL. It's easy to manually type in a query string appended to a URL and try to fool scripts. Furthermore, you can't assume that a query string will represent special characters in hexadecimal ASCII or follow any other convention because not all clients may do this properly. In addition, more knowledgeable users can connect directly to your server and talk HTTP directly without the aid of any client. Proper data checking is a must.

Don't Let Clients Execute Commands

This one is a real gotcha. You may be tempted to intentionally allow clients to specify a command of some sort, and then use `system()` or another method to execute the command. Don't do this! This is exactly what the other tips are trying to prevent. And don't think you can solve this problem simply by offering only certain choices on a form's menu. Remember—query strings don't have to come from forms. Users can easily add their own items to your menu simply by manually constructing the URL.

Turn Off Server-Side Includes

If you are running NCSA httpd for UNIX or another server that supports server-side includes, be sure to turn them off for your script directories. Includes are dangerous enough in and of themselves, but are especially dangerous in scripts that echo data back to the client as HTML. A mischievous user can intentionally embed a server-side include command in data sent to a script. When the script echoes the data back to the client, the server-side include command is executed with potentially disastrous results.

Pay Attention to File Permissions

A good way to limit the extent of any possible damage from unauthorized access is simply to make sure that document requests (including scripts) from the Web server are processed as a nonprivileged user. This is specified using the User directive in the Server Configuration File (httpd.conf). This way, any client gaining unauthorized access won't gain access to much.

> **Note**
>
> The user name under which document requests are processed is not the same as the user that starts the server. Usually, root starts the server, but individual document requests are processed as a nonprivileged user.

Furthermore, the user that processes document requests should not have write access to much of anything on your server, especially scripts! If the nonprivileged user that processes document requests has write access to a script directory, an intruder could create a new script in that directory and then execute it by sending it the correct URL!

As you can see, there are lots and lots of little gotchas to watch out for when dealing with scripts. Because the Web is relatively new, there are probably dozens of yet-undiscovered ways to do nasty things to other people's computers. As with any new technology or software release, it will probably take a few incidents before all the security holes are plugged. But with a little caution and careful thought, you can prevent the great majority of problems.

Server-Side Includes

Server-side includes have already been mentioned several times in this book as being potentially dangerous, but they can serve a useful purpose and they are worth exploring (for curiosity's sake if nothing else).

> **Note**
>
> Server-side includes are not available in Windows httpd.

What Are Includes?

Perhaps you have a "feature of the day" section on your home page. You would like to be able to create a separate file containing the feature so you don't have to edit the home page every day just to change the feature. You can do this two ways. First, you can write a script that outputs the contents of both the home page and the feature file together. This is simple enough, but the URL to the composite document now points to a script rather than to a document.

An easier way to do this job is to embed a server-side include command in the home page to include the contents of the feature file. When the home page is accessed, the server sends the contents of the included file also. Server-side includes can be used to include any of the following inside an HTML document in real-time:

- Another HTML or text file

- The output of a CGI script

- The output of any command or executable

- Current time and date

- File information such as date last modified

How Includes Work

When a server responds to a normal document request, it simply sends the entire file requested "as is." When a document contains server-side includes, however, the server must read the document and insert the included information first. This is called *parsing.* In order to use server-side includes, you must tell the server that documents contain them so they can be parsed. Usually, this is done by creating a new file extension for parsed files. The commonly used extension for this purpose is SHTML. This extension is then associated with the MIME type `text/x-server-parsed-html` using the `AddType` directive in the server resource map ("srm.conf"). When a document ending in SHTML is requested, the server parses it before sending it.

> **Note**
>
> It would be possible to parse all HTML files by specifying HTML as the parsed exten-
> sion rather than SHTML or some other unique extension. However, this would signifi-
> cantly degrade performance because the server would have to read every file before
> sending it.

Having seen how includes work and what they do, let's move to the commands themselves.

Server-Side Include Commands

Server-side include statements in HTML documents have the general format:

```
<!-- #command attribute1="value1" attribute2="value2" -->
```

IV

Applications

Include statements begin with the same characters as HTML comments. This is so that browsers will ignore include statements as if they were comments. Normally, the server replaces the include statements with the items to be included, but if server-side includes were turned off on the server, the statements are passed along intact.

Including Files

To include another file in an HTML document, the format is:

```
<!-- #include virtual="virtual_path" -->
```

or

```
<!-- #include file="relative_path" -->
```

The `virtual` option specifies a URL-style virtual path to any document on your server. The `file` option specifies a path relative to the current directory. The `file` option may not be an absolute path (beginning with `/`) or contain `../` to reference a higher-lever directory.

Any normal (nonscript) document can be included with the `include` command. Even other parsed documents can be included.

Including Document Information

The `echo` command can be used to display the contents of any CGI environment variable or one of the special variables defined for include statements. The general format is:

```
<!-- #echo var="variable_name" -->
```

Besides CGI environment variables, `variable_name` can be:

- `DOCUMENT_NAME`—The document file name

- `DOCUMENT_URI`—The virtual path to the document

- `DATE_LOCAL`—The current date and time in the local time zone

- `DATE_GMT`—The current Greenwich Mean Time

- `LAST_MODIFIED`—The last modification date of the document

- `QUERY_STRING_UNESCAPED`—The text of any query string sent by the client

Including Information About Other Files

Two commands can be used to include information about files other than the current document. These are `fsize`, which prints the size of any file, and `flastmod`, which prints the last modification date of any file. The format for these commands is:

```
<!-- #fsize file_spec -->
```

and

```
<!-- #flastmod file_spec -->
```

The *file_spec* is either `file="relative_path"` or `virtual="virtual_path"` as in the `include` command.

Including Script and Command Output

You can include the output of any command or CGI script in a parsed document. The general format for this is:

```
<!-- #exec cmd="command_string" -->
```

or

```
<!-- #exec cgi="virtual_path" -->
```

Caution

The `exec` option is the most dangerous server-side include command because it can be used to run any command or program on the server. Among other things, this could rapidly crash your server if a particularly large program were executed every time a certain document was accessed. This option can be restricted while still allowing server-side includes by using the `IncludesNoExec` option in the access configuration file (access.conf).

The `cmd` option will execute the specified command string using /bin/sh (the Bourne shell). The specified command string can be any system command or a path to a user-written program. The `cgi` option allows you to specify a virtual path to a CGI script on your server.

Customizing Output

The `config` command is used to control the output format of other include commands. The format is:

```
<!-- #config [errmsg="error_message"] [sizefmt="{bytes|abbrev}"]
[timefmt="format_string"] -->
```

The `errmsg` tag is used to specify an error message to be sent to the client if there is an error parsing the document. `Sizefmt` specifies whether file size information will appear in bytes (451,233) or in abbreviated format (451K). `Timefmt` specifies the format to be used for all time and date information. The time format string conforms to the `strftime` library call under most versions of UNIX.

Chapter 13

Search Engines and Annotation Systems

The previous chapters covered the basics of setting up a Web server, writing HTML, and creating forms and scripts. The last chapters in this book use the tools acquired in the first part of the book to build or explain several useful applications that can be built with Web servers.

The first section of this chapter deals with search engines that search simple databases and more sophisticated indexing software that searches an entire Web server and presents a hypertext list of documents found. Web technology is a simple and effective way to make data available to a large number of people using a simple interface.

The second part of this chapter presents techniques for using the Web technology as a workgroup tool. Several vehicles for conducting workgroup discussion are presented here, including list servers and newsgroups. Methods of creating annotation capabilities are also discussed.

In this chapter, you learn how to

- Build simple search scripts for simple databases

- Use an advanced search engine to search an entire Web server

- Use Web technology as a workgroup tool, including document annotation capabilities

Searching Simple Databases

The last chapter showed you how to write a simple script to search an online phone book for names or numbers. Although this can be considered a simple database application, it differs from what's normally thought of as a database because users can view but not enter information. Creating relational database applications using Web technology is covered in chapter 15, "Database Access and Applications Integration"; this chapter just looks at simpler, search-only databases.

Even though many types of data in an organization are maintained centrally, they often still need to be made available to hundreds or even thousands of users, either internally or externally. Examples of this type of data include a company phone and address book, a product catalog that maps product numbers to titles, or a list of regional sales offices and contacts. All of these types of information can be stored in a relational database, but there's really no need for anything more than a simple text file. If the goal is simply to quickly and easily make information available, a simple Web search routine can do the trick without a lot of effort.

Grepping for Data

In the previous chapter, the phone book example demonstrated how to search a text file containing names and phone numbers. At the heart of the search is the grep command, which simply looks for pattern matches in a file. One of the benefits of this approach is that the text file need not be in any certain format. Grep just reads each line of the file for a match; it doesn't care how many columns there are or what characters are used to separate fields. Consequently, the phone book script from the previous chapter can be used to search any text file database. That script has been generalized from the phone book example and is reprinted here for convenience. Figure 13.1 shows the resulting search form.

> **Tip**
>
> You can make searches case-sensitive by removing the -i option from the grep command.

```
# search.pl
# Invoke the perl compiler
#!/bin/perl

# Define the location of the database
$DATABASE="/usr/local/etc/httpd/cgi-bin/phone.txt";

# Define the path to cgiparse
$CGIPATH="/usr/local/etc/httpd/cgi-bin";
# Convert form data to variables
```

```
eval `$CGIPATH/test/cgiparse -form -prefix $`;

# Determine the age of the database
$mod_date=int(-M $DATABASE);

#Display the age of the database and generate the search form
print <<EOM;
Content-type: text/html

<TITLE>Database Search</TITLE>
<BODY>
<H1>Database Search</H1>
The database was updated $mod_date days ago.<p>
<FORM ACTION="/cgi-bin/search.pl" METHOD="POST">
Search for: <INPUT TYPE="TEXT" NAME="QUERY">
<INPUT TYPE="SUBMIT" VALUE="SEARCH">
</FORM>
<p><hr><p>
EOM

# Do the search only if a query was entered
if (length($query)>0) {
  print <<EOM;
Search for <B>$query</B> yields these entries:
<PRE>
EOM

#Inform user if search is unsuccessful
$answer =`grep -i $query $DATABASE`;
if (!$answer) { print "Search was unsuccessful\n" ;}
else { print $answer\n" ; }

print <<EOM;
</PRE>
</BODY>
EOM
}
```

To use the script for data other than the phone book, simply change the name and location of the text file containing the desired information. Because the script uses the generic grep command, it can be used with almost any text file for any purpose.

> **Tip**
>
> If the egrep (or grep -e on some systems) command is available on your system, use it instead of grep because it's faster.

Fig. 13.1
This generalized database search form is used with the search script above to search any text file database.

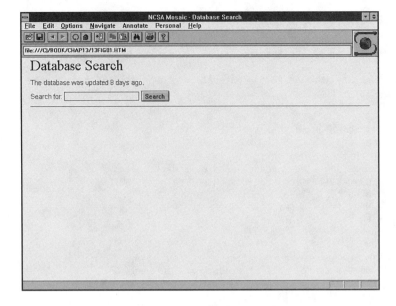

Generating Text Files from Databases

To take advantage of the simple search routine above, you must have some text file data to start with. If your data is currently in another format, such as a Windows database, you must first convert it to an ASCII text file. You can easily create the necessary text file by exporting the data from the native format to ASCII text. Almost all databases include the capability to export text files.

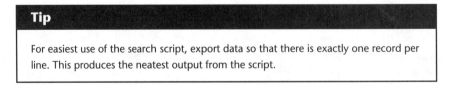

Tip

For easiest use of the search script, export data so that there is exactly one record per line. This produces the neatest output from the script.

After the text file has been created, you simply need to specify its path in the search script.

Choosing between Several Databases

With a few simple modifications, you can use the script generically to search one of many databases that all have different paths. This can be done most efficiently in one of two ways. You can allow the database to be chosen by selecting one of several hyperlinks, in which case extra path information in the URL can be used to specify the database. Or, you can allow the user to choose which database to search in a fill-in form.

Choosing via Hyperlinks

Suppose you want users to be able to choose between several different divisional phone books. One way to do this is to include a pre-search page on which the user selects the database by clicking the appropriate hyperlink. Each link calls the same database search script, but each includes extra path information containing the path to the database. The following HTML demonstrates how the hyperlinks are constructed.

```
<H2>Company Phonebooks</H2>
<A HREF="/cgi-bin/search.pl/db/IAphone.txt">Iowa Locations</A>
<A HREF="/cgi-bin/search.pl/db/CAphone.txt">California Locations</A>
<A HREF="/cgi-bin/search.pl/db/KSphone.txt">Kansas Locations</A>
```

The name of the search script in this example is /cgi-bin/search.pl and the databases are named "/db/IAphone.txt," and so on. The search script itself needs to be modified to use the extra path information.

First, the name of the database to search is now specified in the extra path information rather than hard-coded into the script. Therefore, the line at the top of the script that specifies the path to the data needs to read the extra path information. This is done by reading the PATH_INFO environment variable. In perl, the syntax for this is:

```
$DATABASE=$ENV{"PATH_INFO"};
```

Second, the ACTION attribute of the form, which is generated inside the script, needs to specify the path to the database, as well. This way, after the user performs the initial query, the correct database will still be in use. This is done by changing the <FORM ACTION...> line to:

```
<FORM ACTION="/cgi-bin/search.pl$DATABASE">
```

> **Note**
>
> No slash (/) is necessary to separate the script name (/cgi-bin/search) from the extra path information because $DATABASE already begins with a slash.

These are the two modifications necessary to implement choosing a database via hyperlinks. The hyperlinks to other databases are now included in the search form also. The resulting form is shown in figure 13.2. The complete modified script code follows this paragraph. Only new or changed lines have been commented.

```perl
# search2.pl
#!/bin/perl

# Get database name from extra path info.
$DATABASE=$ENV{"PATH_INFO"};

$CGIPATH="/usr/local/etc/httpd/cgi-bin";
eval `$CGIPATH/test/cgiparse -form -prefix $`;

$mod_date=int(-M $DATABASE);

# Show the current database and list other available databases.
# The <FORM ACTION ...> line now includes the database name as
➥extra path info.
print <<EOM;
Content-type: text/html

<TITLE>Database Search</TITLE>
<BODY>
<H1>Database Search</H1>
Current database is $DATABASE.      Show the current database
It was updated $mod_date days ago.<P>
You can change to one of the following databases at any time:<P>
<A HREF="/cgi-bin/search/db/IAphone.txt">Iowa Location</A><BR>
<A HREF="/cgi-bin/search/db/CAphone.txt">California Locations</A><BR>
<A HREF="/cgi-bin/search/db/KSphone.txt">Kansas Locations</A><P>
<FORM ACTION="/cgi-bin/search2.pl$DATABASE" METHOD="POST">
Search for: <INPUT TYPE="TEXT" NAME="QUERY">
<INPUT TYPE="SUBMIT" VALUE=" Search ">
</FORM>
<p><hr><p>
EOM

if (length($query)>0) {
  print <<EOM;
Search for <B>$query</B> yields these entries:
<PRE>
EOM

$answer = `grep -i $query $DATABASE`;
if (!$answer) { print "Search was unsuccessful\n" ;}
else { print $answer\n" ; }

print <<EOM;
</PRE>
</BODY>
FOM
}
```

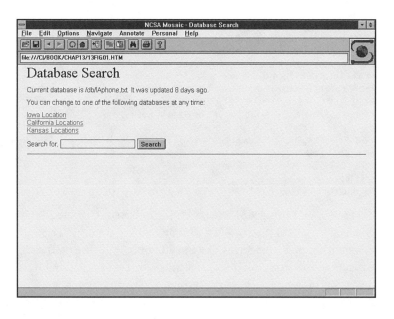

Fig. 13.2
This form uses
hyperlinks to
select a new search
database.

Choosing via a Form

Depending on the application, it may be more convenient for users to choose
their database via a form rather than via hyperlinks. An initial form is used
to specify the database, and after that the chosen database is active for all
searches. Figure 13.3 shows the initial form used to select the database.
The form code follows the figure.

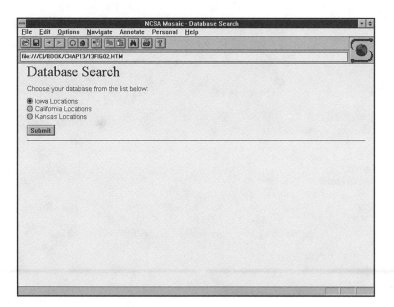

Fig. 13.3
In this form, you
select the search
database and then
proceed to the
search form.

```
<TITLE>Database Search</TITLE>
<BODY>
<H1>Database Search</H1>
Choose your database from the list below:<P>
<FORM ACTION="/cgi-bin/search3.pl" METHOD="POST">
<INPUT TYPE="RADIO" NAME="DATABASE" VALUE="/db/IAphone.txt"
➥CHECKED>Iowa Locations<BR>
<INPUT TYPE="RADIO" NAME="DATABASE" VALUE="/db/
➥CAphone.txt">California Locations<BR>
<INPUT TYPE="RADIO" NAME="DATABASE" VALUE="/db/KSphone.txt">Kansas
➥Locations<P>
<INPUT TYPE="SUBMIT" VALUE=" Submit ">
</FORM>
<p><hr><p>
```

The initial selection form passes the path of the chosen database in the input field named "DATABASE," so only two modifications are necessary to the original search script that receives this information. First, the path to the database is now read from the initial selection form, so a separate line defining $DATABASE is no longer necessary. Second, the search form must have a way to keep track of the current database. This is conveniently accomplished by including a hidden input field in the search form named "DATABASE." This way, whether the search form is called from itself or from the initial selection form, it always knows the path to the correct database. The code for the search script is included below. Only the new or changed lines are commented. The resulting search form appears in figure 13.4.

```
# search3.pl
#!/bin/perl

$CGIPATH="/usr/local/etc/httpd/cgi-bin";
eval `$CGIPATH/test/cgiparse -form -prefix $` ;
# $DATABASE is now defined as a form variable

$mod_date=int(-M $DATABASE);

# A hidden field <INPUT TYPE="HIDDEN" NAME="DATABASE" ...> stores
➥the database path.
print <<EOM;
Content-type: text/html

<TITLE>Database Search</TITLE>
<BODY>
<H1>Database Search</H1>
The current database is $DATABASE.
The database was updated $mod_date days ago.<p>
<FORM ACTION="/cgi-bin/search3.pl" METHOD="POST">
<INPUT TYPE="HIDDEN" NAME="DATABASE" VALUE="$DATABASE">
Search for: <INPUT TYPE="TEXT" NAME="QUERY">
<INPUT TYPE="SUBMIT" VALUE=" Search ">
</FORM>
<p><hr><p>
```

```
EOM

if (length($query)>0) {
  print <<EOM;
Search for <B>$query</B> yields these entries:
<PRE>
EOM

$answer = `grep -i $query $DATABASE`;
if (!$answer) { print "Search was unsuccessful\n" ;}
else { print $answer\n" ; }

print <<EOM;
</PRE>
</BODY>
EOM
}
```

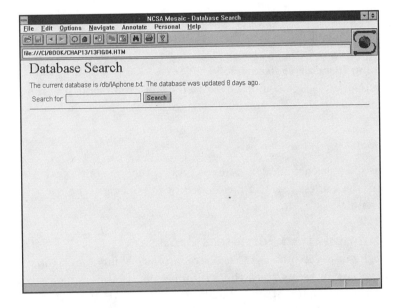

Fig. 13.4
Once the search database is selected in a separate form, this form is used to perform the search.

Searching Multiple Files and Directories

The previous examples searched only one file at a time. However, grep is flexible enough to search multiple files and directories simultaneously.

Searching Multiple Files

In the previous example, the user was allowed to choose between several different phone directories. However, it's also possible to search several files at the same time. The script is easily modified to do this because the grep command can search multiple files simultaneously. Instead of specifying one file in the $DATABASE environment variable, specify a path to the directory containing the phone text files (/db). So, the line beginning $DATABASE= in the original script (search.pl) changes to:

```
$DATABASE="/db/*.txt";
```

The grep command now searches all text files in the /db directory for the desired information.

Searching Multiple Directories

Taking it a step further, the grep command can also accept multiple files in different directories. For example, you can specify the following database files:

```
$DATABASE="/db/phone*.txt /db2/address*.txt"
```

Now, the grep command searches all TXT files in the /db directory beginning with phone and all TXT files in the /db2 directory beginning with address.

Searching Directories Recursively

By combining the grep command with a directory command, it's even possible to recursively search subdirectories. To do this, change the $DATABASE line to:

```
$DATABASE=`find /db -name '*.txt'`;
```

Because the find command operates recursively on directories, $DATABASE contains the names of all TXT files under the /db directory and its subdirectories.

Accommodating Form-less Browsers

Although most Web browsers today have forms capability, not all do. To allow these browsers to search for information, it's common to offer an alphabetical or numerical index of data as an alternative to entering a form-based query. Typically, you create a hyperlink for each letter of the alphabet and specify a URL for each hyperlink that performs the appropriate search. For example, in a phone book listing where last names are listed first, you could search for capital C's at the beginning of a line to get a listing of all last names beginning with C. To create a hypertext index that can submit this type of search automatically, write:

```
<H1>Phone Book Index</H1>
Click on a letter to see last names beginning with that letter.<P>
<A HREF="/cgi-bin/search?A">%26A</A>
<A HREF="/cgi-bin/search?B">%2lb</C>
...
<A HREF="/cgi-bin/search?Z">%26Z</Z>
```

Figure 13.5 shows how this listing appears in Mosaic for Windows if the search script is modified to generate a hypertext index rather than a new search form.

> **Note**
>
> The queries in this example begin with the caret (%26 = "^") to force grep to look for the specified character at the beginning of a line.

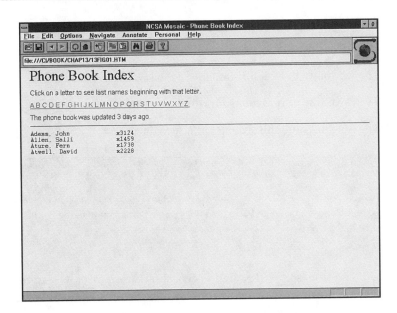

Fig. 13.5
An alphabetical hypertext index allows browsers without forms capability to perform searches.

Searching an Entire Web Server

So far, you have only looked at searching collections of simple text files. However, one of the most useful utilities on any Web server is the capability to search for words anywhere on the server, including plain text and HTML files. It's theoretically possible to simply grep all HTML and TXT files under the document root (and other aliased directories), but this can be very time-consuming if more than a handful of documents are present.

The solution to the problem of searching a large Web server is similar to that used by other types of databases. As data is added to the database, you update a compact index file that summarizes the information contained in the larger database. To do this on a Web server, you run a nightly (or more frequent) indexing program that generates a full-text index of the entire server in a more compact format than the data itself.

Indexing with ICE

A popular indexing and searching solution on the Web is ICE, written in perl by Christian Neuss in Germany. It's freely available on the Internet from **http://www.igd.fhg.de/~neuss/me.html** and is included on the WebmasterCD. The remainder of this section covers ICE, how it works, and how it can be modified to include even more features. By default, ICE includes the following features:

- Whole-word searching using Boolean operators (AND and OR)

- Case-sensitive or case-insensitive searching

- Hypertext presentation of scored results

- The capability to look for similarly spelled words in a dictionary

- The capability to find related words and topics in a thesaurus

- The capability to limit searches to a specified directory tree

> **Note**
>
> Because it's written in perl, ICE can run on any platform for which perl is available, including DOS, Mac, OS/2, and Windows NT. However, some modifications will be required due to the different file systems employed by these operating systems.

Figure 13.6 illustrates the ICE search screen, showing many of its features. By modifying the underlying perl scripts, its appearance and function can be modified to suit the taste of the user.

ICE presents results in a convenient hypertext format. Results are displayed using both document titles (as specified by HTML <TITLE> tags) and physical file names. Search results are scored, or weighted, based on the number of occurrences of the search word or words inside documents. Figure 13.7 illustrates ICE's presentation of results.

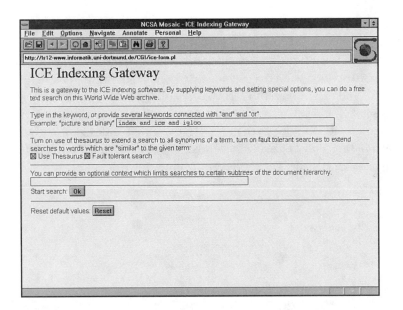

Fig. 13.6
The ICE search screen allows you to specify many options besides simple searching.

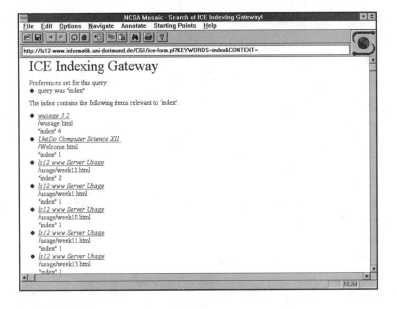

Fig. 13.7
The ICE results screen includes a hypertext list of matching files and the number of occurrences of the search word in each file.

The ICE Index Builder

The heart of ICE is a perl program which reads every file on the Web server and constructs a full-text index. The index builder, named "ice-idx.pl" in the default distribution, works very simply. The server administrator specifies the locations and extensions (TXT, HTML, etc.) of files to be indexed. When you run ice-idx.pl, it reads every file in the specified directories and stores the index information in one large index file (by default, index.idx). The words in each file are alphabetized and counted for use in scoring the search results when a search is made. The format of the index file is simple:

```
@ffilename
@ttitle
word1 count1
word2 count2
word3 count3
...
@ffilename
@ttitle
word1 count1
...
```

Running the Index Builder

The index builder is typically run nightly, or at some other regular interval, so that search results are always based on updated information. Normally, ICE indexes the entire contents of directories specified by the administrator, but it can be modified to index only new or modified files, as determined by the last modification dates on files. This saves a little time, although ICE zips right along as it is. On a fast UNIX workstation, ICE will index 2-5M of files in under 15 seconds, depending on the nature of the files. Assuming an average HTML file size of 10K, that's 200-500 separate documents.

UNIX users can run the index builder nightly using the UNIX cron facility for scheduling regular events. To use the crontab command, a system administrator must add your name to the cron.allow file. Here's a typical cron entry for ICE. This entry runs the index-builder nightly at 9:34 PM (21:34).

```
34 21 * * * /usr/local/etc/index/ice-idx.pl
```

> **Tip**
>
> It's often a good idea to schedule cron jobs at odd times because many other jobs run on the hour by necessity or convention. Running jobs on the hour that don't have to be run this way unnecessarily increases the load on the machine.

Note

Although Windows does not have a native cron facility, Windows users can take advantage of a free program called WinCron included with Windows httpd.

Space Considerations

Searching an index file is much faster than searching an entire Web server using grep or a similar utility; however, there is a definite space/performance tradeoff. Because ICE stores the contents of every document in the index file, the index file could theoretically grow as large as the sum of all the files indexed! The actual "compression" ratio is closer to 2:1 for HTML because ICE ignores HTML formatting tags, numbers, and special characters. In addition, typical documents use many words multiple times, but ICE stores them only once, along with a word count.

Note

When planning your Web server, be sure to include enough space for index files if you plan to offer full-featured searching.

The Search Engine

The HTML which produces the ICE search form is actually generated from within a script (ice-form.pl), but calls the main search engine (ice.pl) to do most of the search work. The search simply reads the index file previously generated by the index builder. As the search engine reads consecutively through the file, it simply outputs the names and titles of all documents containing the search word or words. The search form itself and the search engine can be modified to produce output in any format desired by editing the perl code.

Tips and Tricks

The ICE search engine is powerful and useful by itself. However, there's always room for improvement. This section discusses several modifications you can make to ICE to implement various additional useful features.

Directory Context

A very useful feature of ICE is the ability to specify an optional directory context in the search form. This way, you can use the same ICE code to conduct both local and global searches. For example, suppose you're running an internal server that contains several policy manuals and you want each of them to be searchable individually, as well as together. You could simply require that users of the system enter the optional directory context themselves; however, a more convenient way is to replace the optional directory context box with radio buttons that can be used to select the desired manual.

A more programming-intensive method is to provide a link to the search page on the index page of each manual. The URL in the link can already include the optional directory context so that users don't have to enter this themselves. This way, when a user clicks the link to the search page from within a given manual section, the search form automatically includes the correct directory context. For example, you can tell the ICE search to look only in the /benefits directory by including the following hyperlink on the Benefits page:

```
<A HREF="/cgi-bin/ice-form.pl?context=%2Fbenefits>Search this
➥manual</A>
```

Note

The slash (/) in front of benefits must be encoded in its ASCII representation (%2F) for the link to work properly.

In order for this to work, you'll need to make the following necessary modifications to ice-form.pl:

■ Set the variable $CONTEXT at the beginning of the script (using cgiparse or your favorite parsing utility) based on what was passed in from the search URL.

■ Automatically display the value of $CONTEXT in the optional directory context box (<INPUT TYPE="TEXT" NAME="CONTEXT" VALUE="$CONTEXT">).

Speed Enhancements

If the size of your index file grows larger than two or three megabytes, searches will take several seconds to complete due to the time required to read through the entire index file during each search. A simple way to improve this situation is to build several smaller index files, say, one for each major directory on your server, rather than one large one. However, this means you can no longer conduct a single, global search of your server.

A more attractive way to break up the large index file is to split it up into several smaller ones, where each small index file still contains an index for every file searched, but only those words beginning with certain letters. For example, ice-a.idx contains all words beginning with "a," ice-b.idx contains all words beginning with "b," etc. This way, when a query is entered, the search engine is able to narrow down the search immediately based on the first letter of the query.

> **Note**
>
> In the event that your server outgrows the first-letter indexing scheme, the same technique can be used to further break up files by using unique combinations of the first two letters of a query, and so on.

In order to break up the large index file alphabetically, you need to modify the ICE index builder (ice-idx.pl) to write to multiple index files while building the code. The search engine (ice.pl) also needs to be modified to auto-select the index file based on the first letter of the query.

Searching for Words Near Each Other

Although ICE allows the use of AND and OR operators to modify searches, it only looks for words meeting these requirements anywhere in the same document. It would be nice to be able to specify how close to each other the words must appear, as well. The difficulty with this kind of a search is that the ICE index doesn't specify how close to each other words are in a document. There are two ways to overcome this.

First, you can modify the index builder to store word position information, as well as word count. For example, if the words "bad" and "dog" each occur three times in a file, their index entries might look like this:

```
bad 3 26 42 66

dog 3 4 9 27
```

In this case, 3 is the number of occurrences, and the remaining numbers indicate that "dog" is the 4th, 9th, and 27th word in the file. When a search for "bad dog" is entered, the search engine first checks if both "bad" and "dog" are in any documents, and then whether any of the word positions for "bad" are exactly one less than any of those for "dog." In this case, that is true, as "bad" occurs in position 26 and "dog" occurs in position 27.

There's another way to search for words near each other. After a search is entered and files containing both words are found, those files can simply be read by the search program word-by-word, looking for the target words near each other. Using this method, the index builder itself doesn't have to be modified. However, the first method usually results in faster searches because the extra work is done primarily by the index builder rather than by the search engine in real-time.

Including Content

A further ICE enhancement would be to include some sort of summary of each document presented in the search results. The Lycos Web searcher does exactly this by displaying the first couple of sentences of each document on its search results page (see fig. 13.8). This allows users to quickly find the documents most relevant to their topic of interest.

Tip

The Lycos Web searcher is located at **http://lycos.cs.cmu.edu/**.

Fig. 13.8
The Lycos results page includes summary information for each matching document.

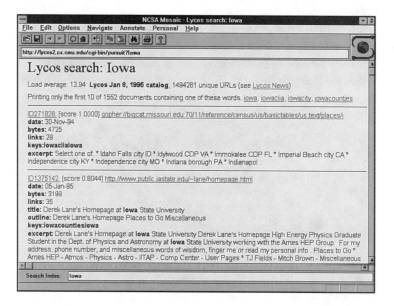

To include summary content, store the first 50-100 words in every document in the index file created by the index builder. Doing this, however, requires yet more storage space for the index file, and therefore may not be desirable.

Discussion and Annotation Systems

The World Wide Web was originally developed as a medium for scientific and technical exchange. One of the important elements of that exchange is the sharing of ideas about other people's work. This has been common on UseNet news for many years now, but articles are limited largely to plain ASCII text. The Web, with its superior hypertext presentation, presents opportunities for richer exchange, but has developed as a remarkably one-sided communications medium thus far. This is unfortunate for those who would like to take advantage of the Web's superior document capabilities along with the flexibility and interactivity of UseNet.

Why Is the Web One-Way?

The Web has developed as a primarily one-way medium simply because the great majority of Web servers and clients have not supported any kind of interactive behavior; Web servers can only serve documents, and Web clients can only browse documents. However, these limitations are not fundamental to either the HTTP protocol or HTML. The ingredients necessary for world-wide annotation of Web documents and posting new documents to servers are already in place, but these have not yet been implemented. There are, however, a few exceptions, which are discussed next.

Group Annotations

The most notable exception is NCSA Mosaic, which supported a feature called *group annotations* in the first few versions. This feature allows users to post text-only annotations to documents by sending annotations to a group annotation server, which NCSA provided with earlier versions of its Web server. Group annotations, however, have been abandoned in later versions of Mosaic in favor of the HTTP 1.0 protocol, which supports group annotations in a different manner.

CGI and HTTP POST

The second exception is CGI scripting, which allows data to be received rather than sent by a server. The data is usually simple text, such as a query or form information, but it can also be an entire document, such as an HTML file, spreadsheet, or even an executable program. The ability to post documents to CGI scripts, however, is not particularly useful, as of yet, because Web clients don't support it. What would be useful is an introduction of a <FILE> element to forms, which, when selected, would ask the user to specify the name of a local file to be sent to the server when the form is submitted.

This would be a convenient way to upload documents to a Web server in the same way that documents are uploaded to CompuServe or bulletin board systems.

Because HTTP and HTML already support most (if not all) of the ingredients necessary for a more interactive Web, it's probably only a matter of time before these will be incorporated into browsers and servers alike. In the meantime, however, prototypes of what the future holds have been constructed using news, e-mail, and CGI scripts.

News and the Web

UseNet news makes available today in plain ASCII text some of what the Web will do tomorrow in HTML. News can effectively be used as both a private or public tool for information exchange. Public newsgroups are the most familiar, with world-wide distribution and the ability for anyone to post articles to these groups. By running your own news server, you can also create entirely private newsgroups (as for an internal bulletin board system) or semiprivate groups, which the public can read but not post to. The ability to control who can read news and who can post to a local server makes news a useful tool for workgroup discussion.

> **Tip**
>
> Many Web browsers can both read and post news. This simplifies the use of both news and hypertext in an organizational context by providing a common interface for viewing both kinds of documents.

While news is an excellent medium for conducting entirely private (inside a corporate network) or entirely public conversations (UseNet), it's not as well suited for allowing discussions between a select group of individuals located all over the world. It's possible to create a special news server for this purpose and use password security to ensure that only the intended group of people can read and/or post news to the server. However, users of the system would be inconvenienced because most newsreaders expect to connect to one news server only. If users were already connecting to another news server to receive public news, they would have to change the news server address in their newsreader in order to connect to the special server. Fortunately, there are other answers to this problem.

Hypermail

E-mail is a more flexible method of having semiprivate discussions among people all around the world. Using a mailing list server (list server), it is possible to create a single Internet e-mail address for a whole group of people. When an item is sent to the mailing list address, it's forwarded to all members of the list. This approach has several advantages over running a news server, in addition to the previously mentioned convenience issue.

> **Note**
>
> A popular UNIX-based list server is majordomo, available from **http://www.greatcircle.com/majordomo/**.

First, e-mail is the most widely accessible of all Internet services. Individuals are more likely to have e-mail access than any other Internet service. Secondly, e-mail is something that users typically check regularly for new messages. Consequently, there is less effort involved in receiving "news" or discussion items from a mailing list than in checking for news in a separate news reader. The same applies to posting news, which tends to encourage use of the system.

> **Tip**
>
> Through various e-mail gateways, it's possible to do almost anything by e-mail that can be done on FTP, Gopher, news, or the Web, only slower.

A very nice complement to a mailing list is a *mailing list archive*, which stores past items on the mailing list. Public mailing list archives are frequently found on FTP sites, but they can also be stored on the Web. A really powerful tool called *hypermail* converts a mailing list archive into a hypertext list of messages, neatly organized to show message threads. Mail archives converted with hypermail can be sorted by author, subject, or date. Figure 13.9 shows the hypermail archive of a public mailing list on WWW literature.

Fig. 13.9
Hypermail
converts mailing
list archives into
a convenient
hypertext list that
can be sorted by
author, subject,
and date.

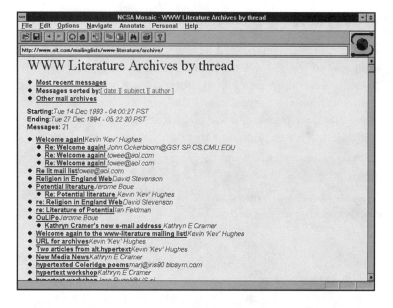

> **Note**
>
> Because hypermail uses the standard UNIX mailbox format, it can even be used to convert your personal mail on a UNIX workstation to hypertext. This allows you to read mail in hypertext, a capability not yet supported by most e-mail readers. The ability to read and write HTML in an e-mail reader would be a useful and interesting addition to e-mail and the Web.

More information on hypermail can be obtained from **http://www.wsr.ac.at/software/hypermail/hypermail.html**. It is reasonably easy to compile and install on any UNIX workstation.

Annotation Systems

While e-mail and news are both valuable tools for workgroup discussion, they still lack an important feature: the ability to make comments on a document in the document itself. In the paper world, this is accomplished with the infamous red pen. However, the equivalent of the red pen in the world of hypertext markup is just beginning to be manifested. The ultimate in annotation would be the ability to attach comments, or even files of any type, anywhere inside an HTML document. For now, however, it's at least possible to add comments to the end of an HTML page. Several people are working on annotation systems using existing Web technology. The following sections take a brief look at a few of them.

HyperNews

Not to be confused with hypermail, HyperNews does not actually use the UseNet news protocol, but it allows a similar discussion format and is patterned after UseNet. You can see examples of HyperNews and find out more about it at **http://union.ncsa.uiuc.edu/HyperNews/get/ hypernews.html**. Figure 13.10 is a list of World Wide Web leased server space providers constructed using HyperNews. At the bottom of the page, there's a link to a form where new service providers can add themselves to the list.

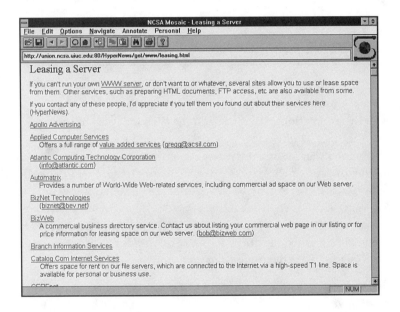

Fig. 13.10
NCSA's list of leased Web space providers uses HyperNews to allow new providers to add themselves to the list.

WWW Interactive Talk (WIT)

A similar system originating at CERN allows new "proposals," or comments, to be submitted in response to a given document. This is a practical way for a group of engineers, for example, to discuss a document. Some degree of security is possible by requiring users to have a valid user name and password before they can post comments. This can be combined with user authorization procedures to control who can see documents, as well. Figure 13.11 shows a WIT page. More information is available from **http:// http3.brunel.ac.uk:10000/wit**.

Fig. 13.11
WWW Interactive Talk (WIT) is similar to HyperNews, and can restrict access through password security.

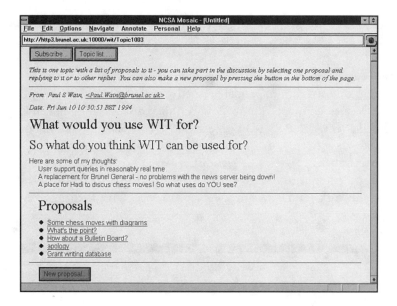

Academic Annotation Systems

Many of the annotation-like systems on the Web today are academic in nature. At Cornell, a test case involving a computer science class allows students to share thoughts and questions about the class via the Web. Documentation on the Cornell system is available from **http://dri.cornell.edu/ pub/davis/annotation.html**. The Cornell site also has useful links to related work on the Web. Some of the related systems that have been developed use custom clients to talk to an annotation database separate from the Web server itself, much like the early versions of Mosaic. This architecture may well be the future of annotations and the Web.

On the lighter side, take a peek at MIT's Discuss->WWW Gateway to get a behind-the-scenes look into an American hall of higher education. For a particularly novel and entertaining use of the Web, take a peek at the Professor's Quote Board at **http://www.mit.edu:8008/bloom-picayune.mit.edu/ pqb/**.

Chapter 14

Usage Statistics and Maintaining HTML

Once your Web server is up and running, there's still a lot of work to do to keep it running smoothly and to maintain a professional image. Ongoing maintenance activities are associated both with the server itself and with the materials on the server. You want to know how often your server is being accessed, what is being accessed most often, and who is accessing your server. You can obtain graphical summaries of all this information quite easily using programs designed to collate server usage statistics.

When the volume of information on your server becomes large, checking all the information to see that all hyperlinks operate correctly and that all intended files have been linked to your server becomes more and more difficult. As the number of related documents grows, the only practical way to do this is to use automated programs that check your documents for you.

In this chapter, you learn

- How to extract and interpret information from the server access and error logs

- What tools are available for analyzing and graphing usage statistics

- What tools are available for ensuring the integrity of your HTML files

- How to automatically find new and changed files on your server

Understanding Usage Logs

When your Web server is running, every document or file request is logged as a separate entry in the server's log file. By default, this file is named "logs/access.log" under the server root directory, as defined in the HTTPD configuration file. Errors are logged separately in "logs/error.log." The access and error logs are very similar but are discussed separately for clarity.

The Log Formats

All major Web servers, including NCSA's and CERN's, produce logs in a common format so that you can use utilities written to analyze these logs on any type of server. The format includes just about every imaginable piece of information about every document request except how long the transfer took.

The Access Log

Most server programs either have a default directory for storing log files, or allow you to configure the server program to indicate where the logs should be kept. In Windows httpd, the files "ACCESS.LOG" and "ERROR.LOG" are kept in a subdirectory under /HTTPD called "/LOGS." Information in the access log includes

- The address of the client that requested the document

- The precise date and time the transfer took place

- The HTTP method and protocol used for the transfer

- The virtual path to the document transferred

- The status of the transfer

- How many bytes were transferred

The following is an excerpt from an access log generated by Windows httpd:

```
s115.infonet.net - - [20/Oct/1994:20:53:17 -0500]
➥"GET / HTTP/1.0" 200 418
s115.infonet.net - - [20/Oct/1994:20:53:37 -0500]
➥"GET /httpddoc/overview.htm HTTP/1.0" 200 3572
s115.infonet.net - - [20/Oct/1994:20:54:00 -0500]
➥"GET /httpddoc/setup/admin/Overview.htm HTTP/1.0" 200 1165
s115.infonet.net - - [20/Oct/1994:20:54:17 -0500]
➥"GET /httpddoc/setup/Configure.html HTTP/1.0" 200 2500
s115.infonet.net - - [20/Oct/1994:20:54:27 -0500]
➥"GET /httpddoc/setup/httpd/Overview.html HTTP/1.0" 200 1121
s115.infonet.net - - [20/Oct/1994:20:54:43 -0500]
➥"GET /httpddoc/setup/srm/Overview.html HTTP/1.0" 200 1334
s115.infonet.net - - [20/Oct/1994:20:54:53 -0500]
➥"GET /httpddoc/setup/srm/Alias.htm HTTP/1.0" 200 1191
```

```
s115.infonet.net - - [20/Oct/1994:20:55:20 -0500]
➥"GET /httpddoc/setup/access/Overview.html HTTP/1.0" 200 3544
s115.infonet.net - - [20/Oct/1994:20:55:40 -0500]
➥"GET /httpddoc/setup/httpd/AccessConfig.html HTTP/1.0" 200 1308
s115.infonet.net - - [20/Oct/1994:20:56:26 -0500]
➥"GET /httpddoc/setup/access/AuthType.html HTTP/1.0" 200 1132
s115.infonet.net - - [20/Oct/1994:20:56:49 -0500]
➥"GET /httpddoc/setup/access/AddEncoding.html HTTP/1.0" 200 721
s115.infonet.net - - [20/Oct/1994:20:56:57 -0500]
➥"GET /httpddoc/setup/srm/AddEncod.htm HTTP/1.0" 200 1058
s115.infonet.net - - [20/Oct/1994:20:57:55 -0500]
➥"GET /httpddoc/setup/access/AddDescription.html HTTP/1.0" 200 709
s115.infonet.net - - [20/Oct/1994:20:58:07 -0500]
➥"GET /httpddoc/setup/srm/AddDescr.htm HTTP/1.0" 200 1270
s115.infonet.net - - [20/Oct/1994:20:58:39 -0500]
➥"GET /httpddoc/setup/Configure.html HTTP/1.0" 200 2500
s115.infonet.net - - [20/Oct/1994:20:58:43 -0500]
➥"GET /httpddoc/setup/admin/Overview.htm HTTP/1.0" 200 1165
s115.infonet.net - - [20/Oct/1994:21:02:20 -0500]
➥"GET /httpddoc/setup/admin/AccessingFiles.html HTTP/1.0" 403 190
```

The first item in each log entry is the address that requested the document, followed by the date and time, the HTTP method (GET in this example), the virtual path to the file, the HTTP protocol level (1.0 in this example), status information (200 means OK), and the number of bytes transferred.

Note

The address of the requesting client is usually in a name format, such as s115.infonet.net in this example, but can also be numerical if the server is unable to look up the name corresponding to the client's numerical IP address.

From these pieces, it is possible to put together a wide variety of statistics on your server usage, including

- Which documents are accessed most frequently

- Which hours of the day, days of the month, and so on are the busiest

- Which domains access your server most (.gov, .edu, .com, and so on)

- The total volume of byte traffic (and percentage of your connection bandwidth) for any given time period

Because every document access is recorded, log files can grow very quickly. This is compounded by the fact that inline GIF files are separate requests, so a request for a document with three inline GIFs actually shows up as four separate requests—one for the document and three for the GIFs.

On a moderately busy server, the access log can grow to over 10M each month. If you want to save historical log data, it is a good idea to periodically compress the current log file and move it to an archive. You might want to do this at the beginning of each month.

Note

If you want to see document requests as they happen rather than after the fact, you can use the UNIX `tail` command to display each new line added to the log file. Simply enter **tail -f *access_log***. To stop this process, enter a break by pressing Ctrl+C.

The Error Log

The format of the error log is very similar to that of the access log. Instead of reporting the number of bytes transferred, however, the error log reports the reason for the error. The following is an excerpt for an error log generated by Windows httpd:

```
[20/Oct/1994:21:02:20 -0500] httpd: access to
➥c:/httpd/htdocs/httpddoc/setup/admin/AccessingFiles.html failed
➥for s115.infonet.net, reason: client denied by server
➥configuration
[20/Oct/1994:21:07:53 -0500]
➥httpd: access to c:/httpd/htdocs/docs failed for
➥s115.infonet.net, reason: file does not exist
[20/Oct/1994:21:08:13 -0500]
➥httpd: access to c:/httpd/htdocs/ failed for s115.infonet.net,
➥reason: client denied by server configuration
[20/Oct/1994:21:10:01 -0500]
➥httpd: access to c:/httpd/htdocs/docs failed for
➥s115.infonet.net, reason: file does not exist
[20/Oct/1994:21:10:25 -0500]
➥httpd: access to c:/httpd/htdocs/.index.html failed for
➥s115.infonet.net, reason: file does not exist
[20/Oct/1994:21:10:35 -0500]
➥httpd: access to c:/httpd/htdocs/index.htm failed for
➥s115.infonet.net, reason: client denied by server configuration
[20/Oct/1994:21:11:13 -0500]
➥httpd: access to c:/httpd/htdocs/index.htm failed for
➥s115.infonet.net, reason: client denied by server configuration
[20/Oct/1994:21:11:44 -0500]
➥httpd: access to c:/httpd/htdocs/docs failed for
➥s115.infonet.net, reason: file does not exist
[20/Oct/1994:21:15:42 -0500]
➥httpd: access to c:/httpd/htdocs/docs failed for
➥s115.infonet.net, reason: file does not exist
[20/Oct/1994:21:17:01 -0500]
➥httpd: access to c:/httpd/htdocs/ failed for s115.infonet.net,
➥reason: client denied by server configuration
```

```
[20/Oct/1994:21:18:31 -0500]
➡httpd: access to c:/httpd/htdocs/demo failed for
➡s115.infonet.net, reason: client denied by server configuration
[20/Oct/1994:21:18:36 -0500]
➡httpd: access to c:/httpd/htdocs/demo/index.htm failed for
➡s115.infonet.net, reason: client denied by server configuration
```

The format of the file is pretty self-evident. The first part of the line indicates the date and time of the error. The second part of the log entry indicates what the client was trying to access when the error occurred. The third part of the log entry explains why the error occurred.

Error logs are valuable for showing attempted access to controlled documents by unauthorized users and reporting server problems. If error logs are monitored frequently, they may be your first clue that a hyperlink is "broken" because a document is missing or has moved. If you see several failed connection attempts to the same document, and the document does not exist, you could find the broken hyperlink (missing link?) by looking in the access log during the same time frame to see where the client was linking from.

Hopefully, your error log doesn't grow nearly as quickly as your access log, so archiving it is not as important for conserving space. However, if there are secure documents on your server, it may not be a bad idea to keep the error log in case it's needed to track down security problems discovered later.

Sifting Usage Data

The access file is a great record of your server's activity, but it's pretty tough to get anything meaningful out of the raw data. Using some simple searches, however, you can find many items you need without having to write a line of code. For starters, look at the basic search tools available under UNIX and DOS.

Searching in UNIX

On a UNIX workstation, the simplest way to search a text file is to use the time-honored grep utility. For example, to find all access log entries containing fred, you enter

```
grep 'fred' access.log
```

> **Tip**
>
> Search strings containing characters that are special to your UNIX shell must be *escaped* by enclosing them in single quotes (for example, 'fred'); you may as well get in the habit of doing this all the time.

grep has many powerful capabilities in addition to basic searching. For example, you could search for all lines except those containing becky using the -v option:

```
grep -v 'becky' access.log
```

Other useful grep options include:

- -i   Turns off case-sensitive searching
- -c   Returns only a count of all matching lines
- -n   Displays the line number of each matching line

You can also use multiple options to help limit your search by putting multiple option flags behind the dash. For example, if you wanted to search for all lines not containing 'becky' and you wanted to shut off case-sensitive searching while looking for 'becky', you would type

```
grep -vi 'becky' access.log
```

Searching in DOS

The DOS FIND command performs nearly the same function as UNIX's grep command. To search for all instances of nasa.gov in the access log, enter

```
FIND "NASA.GOV" ACCESS.LOG
```

> **Note**
>
> With FIND, all search strings must be enclosed in quotes, regardless of whether they contain special characters.

Although the DOS FIND command does not have as many options as grep, it has enough for simple log-file searching, including

- /v   Displays all lines not containing the search string
- /c   Returns only a count of all matching lines
- /n   Displays the line number with each matching line
- /i   Does a case-insensitive search

Because the log files are just ASCII text, you can open your logs in a word processor and use the search features that are part of that particular program. You can also write macros to search for particular strings of text, such as certain error codes, to help you scan through your logs faster.

Useful Search Patterns

Now it's time to put grep and FIND to work looking for useful data in the access log. Without writing a line of programming code, you can see

- A history or count of all accesses from an address or class of addresses

- A history or count of all accesses to any file or directory

- The number of total accesses to your server, excluding inline GIFs

- A history or count of all accesses during a given time period

Sifting by Address

Suppose you get a couple of calls one day from users wanting to know why they can't get to the weather map anymore. You ask for their addresses and discover that they never should have had access in the first place. What do you do now? To verify their claims and assess the damage, you can start by simply searching for their addresses in the log file. Suppose the unauthorized users are from iam.illegal.com and ur.illegal.com. To see what they've looked at besides the weather map, you can simply search for "illegal.com." With trepidation, you enter

```
FIND "illegal.com" access.log
```

The result is a fascinating chronicle of unauthorized activity. If there are too many lines to count, use FIND /C or grep -c to do the dirty work for you, and e-mail the results to your boss on a good day.

This scenario is not all that unlikely, by the way. Web server security itself is good but only as good as the rules that are made for it. More often than not, problems arise when people make assumptions or generalizations that turn out to be false. You may think, for example, that all addresses in a certain subnet (beginning with 127.34.26, for example) are located on your network, only to find out later that the first 20 addresses belonged to another company. The trick here is just to be aware of what you're doing when you're doing it. Taking the "easy way out" can sometimes open up more of a hole in your security than you're really intending.

If you're running a restricted-access Web server, you might want to check now and then to make sure that no one has gotten in from the outside. You can do this easily by looking for all accesses not from your site:

```
FIND /V "widgets.com" ACCESS.LOG
```

In this case, anything returned by the search indicates a possible security breach. If you're running on a UNIX machine, run a grep -v command analogous to the previous DOS FIND command as a cron job every week and mail yourself the results so that you don't forget to check now and then.

Sifting by File or Directory

Perhaps you've recently added a new feature to your Web site and want to see how much attention it's getting. Just search your logs for the directory or file name and you're in business. To see how many times your What's New page has been read in the current logging period, you simply enter

```
FIND "whatsnew.htm" ACCESS.LOG
```

Or if you've added a whole new directory of stuff (called "/stuff"), try

```
FIND "/stuff" ACCESS.LOG
```

> **Note**
>
> The correct URL to get an automatic directory index is the directory name followed by a slash (/). Some servers, like Windows httpd, return an error if the trailing slash is omitted. NCSA httpd for UNIX, however, generates a Redirect URL (status code 302) and then a second request containing the proper URL, causing the document request to show up twice, and thus distorting true usage figures.

> **Tip**
>
> The ease with which simple searches can find all accesses to a given directory is a strong argument for maintaining a close relationship between the hyperlink structure of documents and the physical directory structure.

Computing Total Accesses

One measure of your Web server's utilization or exposure is the number of total document requests. This is not necessarily a measure of effectiveness because many people who visit your site may spend but a few seconds there and travel on. This is especially true now because of the Web's notoriety. In fact, the ratio of tourists to seriously interested patrons of the Web may even be lower than the percentage of sales resulting from direct-mail campaigns. Fortunately, Web space is a lot cheaper.

If nothing else, measuring your server's growth in utilization can give you a good indication of when you'll have to buy more powerful hardware. Without running a more advanced usage statistics program, you can get a good feel for your server's growth simply by counting the number of total document accesses. You want to exclude GIF files, however, because inline GIFs show up as separate document requests, hence distorting the true number of HTML pages accessed. To find out many HTML pages have been accessed on your server, less GIF files, you enter

```
FIND /C /V ".gif" ACCESS.LOG
```

To see how many accesses occur during some specified time period, simply run this command every six hours and compute the difference between each run. For more regular time periods, however, such as days and hours, you can use the next technique.

Computing Accesses During a Given Period

The access log turns out to be in a very convenient format for finding out how many document requests have been processed in most common time periods. For example, if you wanted to find out how many documents were transferred between 3:00 and 4:00 p.m. on October 25, 1994, use

```
FIND /C "25/Oct/1994:15" ACCESS.LOG
```

Using this technique, you can look at total accesses in a given hour, day, month, or year. By piping the output of one FIND or grep command into another, you can obtain even more detailed information. For example, to find all accesses from red.widgets.com in the month of October, use

```
FIND "red.widgets.com" ACCESS.LOG ¦ FIND "/Oct/"
```

The first FIND command finds all occurrences of red.widgets.com, while the second FIND looks only in that data for occurrences of /Oct/. (Of course, if you haven't cleaned up your log files for a while, you end up with data from this and all previous Octobers since you last purged or archived your file.) In UNIX, the same thing can be accomplished using regular expressions in a single grep command. For example,

```
grep 'red.widgets.com.*/Oct/' access.log
```

> **Note**
>
> In UNIX, the dot is part of regular-expression syntax, which means "any character." When followed by an asterisk, it means "a sequence of any characters." Consequently, the expression above actually finds redAwidgetsBcom as well as red.widgets.com.

Usage Utilities

Now for the really neat stuff. A couple of programs have already been written to take all the grunt work out of collating and totaling usage statistics. One of the nicest is *wwwstat*, available from **http://www.ics.uci.edu/WebSoft/ wwwstat/**. Wwwstat is nice because it produces thorough and nicely formatted output and can be used with *gwstat,* which turns the output of wwwstat into attractive usage graphs (in GIF format, of course). Gwstat is available from **ftp://dis.cs.umass.edu/pub/gwstat.tar.gz**, and both wwwstat and gwstat are available on WebmasterCD.

wwwstat

Wwwstat is a perl script that reads the standard access-log file format and produces usage summaries in several categories. Wwwstat produces summary information for each calendar month and can be run for past months as well as the current month. Summary categories include

- Monthly Summary Statistics

- Daily Transmission Statistics

- Hourly Transmission Statistics

- Total Transfers by Client Domain (`.edu`, `.gov`, and so on and country codes)

- Total Transfers by Reversed Subdomain (the address of every computer that accessed the server)

- Total Transfers from each Archive Section (the number of accesses to each file on the server)

Figure 14.1 shows an example of Daily Transmission Statistics generated by wwwstat.

Figure 14.2 shows wwwstat's summary of statistics by client domain, which brings home the truly global nature of the Internet. Part of the wwwstat distribution is a file containing all the country codes in use on the Internet.

Because wwwstat is a perl program, you can port it to other platforms, although no one has, as yet, done that publicly.

gwstat

Gwstat takes the output of wwwstat and turns it into illustrative graphs. Gwstat produces two sizes of GIF files—thumbnail sketches and full-size graphs like the hourly usage graph (see fig. 14.3 and 14.4). You can specify the sizes of both the thumbnail and full-size graphs.

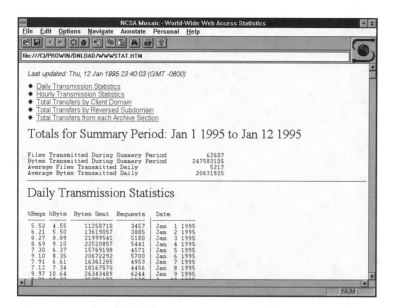

Fig. 14.1
Wwwstat generated these Daily Transmission Statistics.

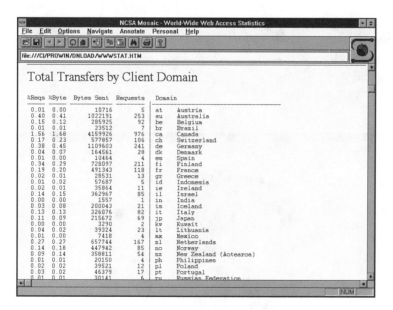

Fig. 14.2
Wwwstat's output of country codes and names.

Fig. 14.3
Gwstat's thumb-
nail sketches.

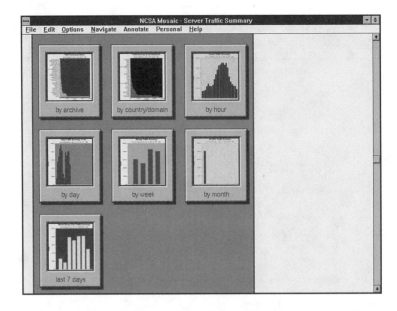

> ### Note
>
> The graphical window-boxes in figure 14.3 are not created by gwstat but can be
> created with the utilities needed to run gwstat. Instructions for doing this are avail-
> able from **http://dis.cs.umass.edu/stats/statsimage.html**.

Fig. 14.4
Hourly usage
graph produced
by gwstat.

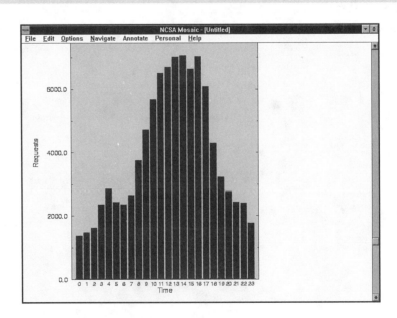

Gwstat requires three other programs to run, so installation can be time-consuming if you don't already have the other programs. However, the results are well worth it. Gwstat is designed to work exclusively under the X Windows system on UNIX workstations, so unfortunately, there is no way to port it to other platforms. Besides wwwstat and perl, gwstat needs Xmgr, ImageMagick, and GhostScript. Information on these programs and hyperlinks to them is available at **http://dis.cs.umass.edu/stats/ gwstat.html**. At that location, there are also instructions for creating a composite imagemap (refer to fig. 14.3).

> **Note**
>
> A list of other programs to analyze log files is available from **http:// union.ncsa.uiuc.edu/HyperNews/get/www/log-analyzers.html**.

Checking HTML

As your server grows, it becomes more and more difficult to find broken hyperlinks, both to documents on your own server as well as documents on other servers. This is especially true if many people are responsible for creating and editing documents on your server. Fortunately, there are two tools to help you analyze the structure of your HTML database and find problems. Both of these tools are freely available on the Internet.

HTML Analyzer

HTML Analyzer is a C program that both finds broken links and attempts to ensure that the HTML database is well-organized and makes sense to users. It is available from **ftp://ftp.ncsa.uiuc.edu** in the /Web/Mosaic/Contrib/ directory. The file name will be something like "html_analyzer-0.30.tar.gz." The documentation for HTML Analyzer is contained in the program's distribution.

The basic philosophy of HTML Analyzer is that the text of any given hyperlink should always point to the same place and that no other text should point to that same place. This is necessary in order for users to get a clear picture of the organization of the HTML database. HTML Analyzer performs three checks on a database of HTML files—validity, completeness, and consistency.

Checking for Validity

The first check performed by HTML Analyzer is for link validity. This ensures that all hyperlinks point to valid locations (that is, no server errors are returned). Empty hyperlinks (such as, HREF=""), local links (such as, HREF="#intro"), and links to interactive services (Telnet and rlogin) are not checked. Even without running the other two checks, validity checking helps to ensure that users of your site won't be frustrated by broken links.

Checking for Completeness

The completeness check ensures that each anchor's contents always occur as a hyperlink. If a hyperlink contained the text Beginner's Guide, for example, and the same text occurred as regular text (not a hyperlink) elsewhere, this is reported. The intent of the completeness check is to improve user-convenience by expecting a hyperlink everywhere there can be, and also to prevent user confusion because the same text sometimes occurs in a hyperlink but not in others.

Checking for Consistency

The final check ensures that every occurrence of a hyperlink anchor points to the same address and that every occurrence of that address is pointed to by the same hyperlink anchor. In other words, HTML Analyzer checks to see that there is a one-to-one correspondence between hyperlink anchors and their respective addresses.

MOMspider

WebmasterCD

MOMspider is a perl program originally written as a class project in distributed information systems at the University of California. MOMspider stands for Multi-Owner Maintenance Spider and is similar to other spiders and robots that traverse the World Wide Web looking for information. MOMspider is available from **http://www.ics.uci.edu/WebSoft/MOMspider/** and requires *libwww-perl*, a library of perl code for the World Wide Web available from the same site.

Because MOMspider is designed to follow hyperlinks anywhere on the Web, it has many features for controlling the depth of searches and is respectful of other sites' wishes not to be visited by automated robots like MOMspider. MOMspider also has an interesting feature that can build a diagram of the structure of the documents it finds. In addition, MOMspider can avoid sites that are known to cause problems for Web-roaming robots. Examples of these kinds of sites are those that use scripts to generate all output rather than static HTML documents.

Finding What's New

When your Web site is being maintained by many people independently, such as an internal server might be in a large organization, it becomes impractical, if not impossible, to require that HTML authors tell you every time they create or modify a page on your server. However, it is highly desirable that server administrators be able to quickly and easily find out what new items have been added each day in order to spot potential problems before they spread too far.

In addition to administrative concerns, information about new or modified documents on the server is helpful for users, who can look on the What's New page and see that the server is continually being updated with valuable information.

In UNIX, it's possible to find all new or modified files in an entire directory tree with a single command:

```
find  directory_name  -mtime  1
```

The `find` command looks recursively down the directory tree specified by `directory_name` to find all files that meet the specified requirements. The `-mtime` option looks for all files that have been modified in the previous number of days, in this case 1. You can narrow the search to include only new files (not directories) using the `-type f` option. You could also look for files of a certain extension using `-name 'search_pattern'`. For example, to find only `.html` files modified in the last week, you enter

```
find  directory_name  -mtime 7  -type f  -name '*.html'
```

By including a `find` command like these examples in a shell or perl script, you can easily generate a list of What's New page, as in the following perl example. The script is available as "whatsnew.pl" on WebmasterCD.

```perl
#!/bin/perl

# whatsnew.pl--David M. Chandler--January 13, 1995
# This program finds all files underneath the search directory
# which have been created or modified within the last day.  The
# output is an HTML # What's New page with hyperlinks to the new pages.

# Invoke the script and redirect the output to your What's New page
# whatsnew.pl >whatsnew.html

#Put your server's document root here
$SEARCHDIR="/httpd/htdocs";
#Create header for What's New document
print "<TITLE>What's New<TITLE>\n";
```

```
print "<H1>What's New!</H1>\n";
print "The following documents were created or modified
➥yesterday:<P>\n";
print "<DL>\n";

#Find all new/modified HTML files in the past day
for each $file (`find $SEARCHDIR -type f -mtime 1 -name '*.html'`)
{
  #Construct the URL from the filename by removing the
# directory path
  if ($file =~ m%$SEARCHDIR/(.*)%) {
  $url = $1; }

  #Find the document title
  chop($title = `grep '<TITLE>' $file`);
  if ($title =~ m%<TITLE>(.*)</TITLE>%i) {
    $anchor = $1; }

  #Create the What's New listing
  print "<DD><A HREF=\"$url\">$anchor</A>\n";
}
print "</DL>\n";
```

Windows for Workgroups users can accomplish this task easily in File Manager by using the Date Sort tool, which lists all files in chronological order. Likewise, many Windows-based shells, such as Norton Desktop or PC Tools for Windows have similar features in their file management utilities. DOS users aren't fortunate enough to have the `-mtime` option available to list only those files modified recently; however, it is possible to see a directory listing sorted by date so that a quick scan reveals any new or modified files. To list a directory with the most recently created or modified files last, use

```
DIR   /OD   directory_name
```

To list a directory with the most recently created or modified files listed first, use

```
DIR   /O-D   directory_name
```

Chapter 15

Database Access and Applications Integration

Because of the Web's ease-of-use and easily programmable user interface, it is an ideal tool for interacting with all kinds of databases. Applications such as genetic databases and helpdesks are already online, with the number growing daily. The potential for financial and business data to be made available over the Web is strong. Researchers now have a way to publish their datasets for public review.

All these applications require more than the text-file searching mechanisms that you've already looked at. In some cases, full relational-database capability is required. The link between the countless types of specific databases and HTML is a common front end called the *Common Graphic Interface,* or CGI. CGI provides a way for browsers on different platforms to interact with databases on equally diverse platforms. Through CGI scripts, nearly every type of data access is possible, though not easy. This chapter discusses some methods for getting to back-end data through CGI scripts. Many of these principles can be generalized to other types of applications, as well.

In this chapter, you learn

- How to access databases using CGI

- How to access databases from UNIX httpd

- How to access databases from Windows httpd

- How to customize Web technology for specific applications

- Where to find more information about developing Web applications

Database Access Using CGI

The general principles of database access are the same for any Web server that supports CGI. At present, CGI scripts are the only way to pass data between Web servers and other applications, so all database gateways use CGI in some fashion or another. In the future, Web servers may be developed that allow the use of DDE (Dynamic Data Exchange) and OLE (Object Linking and Embedding) in the Windows environment to exchange data directly between the Web server and various applications; however, for now this must be accomplished using a language like Visual Basic as the interface.

> **Note**
>
> Microsoft's recent introduction of its Internet Assistant software for Word makes dynamic linking between programs running on a Windows platform seem more likely. Through a freeware special viewer program, Web users may read documents created in Microsoft Word, which could, theoretically, contain links to databases such as Access and spreadsheets such as Excel. While this chapter was being written, this product was still being beta tested, and we were unable to determine the extent to which this interaction between different data formats will actually be integrated in a form that can be used over the Web. For more information on the use of Internet Assistant in the creation of Web pages, please see chapter 10, "HTML Editors and Tools."

The difficulty with CGI is that it always requires programming. CGI is only an interface, or a *front end*. The data is still contained in a database on the *back end*, or the part of the information system that is hidden from the user by the facade of the Interface. In order to link the front and back ends, you will have to write custom scripts to link your specific database to the generic interface. Consequently, getting data into and out of even the easiest-to-use database can be a small chore. It is very likely, however, that products coming out in the near future will make using databases with CGI just as easy as using those databases in their native environment. The next section is a brief overview of the methods that can be used to communicate with a back-end database using CGI.

Retrieving data from a back-end database can be done one of two ways. The simplest is to read the database files directly in their native format. If this is not possible, the CGI script must communicate with the database server.

Reading Database Files Directly

In order for a CGI program to directly read database files, two things must be true. First, the CGI program must have physical access to the files. This means that the CGI program and the database files must be on the same machine or network. Second, the CGI program must be able to read the database file format. This usually requires a special code library of some type. Some languages, like the Professional Edition of Visual Basic for Windows, have built-in access to popular database formats.

Communicating with the Database Server

If the database files cannot be read directly, it is necessary to communicate with the database server, which reads the files and sends the results back to the client (CGI program). This is only possible for databases that implement a standards-based server such as an SQL (Structured Query Language) server or ODBC (Open Database Connectivity) server. This way, any SQL or ODBC client can communicate with the database server. Nearly all databases are either SQL- or ODBC-compatible, including Informix, SyBase, Oracle, Borland Paradox and InterBase, Microsoft Access, and Lotus Approach. The next few sections describe ways to move data between Web servers and databases running on various platforms.

Accessing Databases from UNIX

If you're running the UNIX httpd, there are several ways to get at back-end data. The back-end data most commonly resides on the same or another UNIX machine; however, the data can also reside on other platforms. The following sections cover both possibilities.

Perl's Dialects

Perl seems to be the de facto language for use with Web servers. There are many reasons for this, but one of them is that numerous perl dialects have been developed to assist in working with various databases. These include

- btreeperl—NDBM extensions

- ctreeperl—C-Tree extensions

- duaperl—X.500 Directory User Agent

- ingperl—Ingres

- isqlperl—Informix

- interperl—InterBase

- oraperl—Oracle 6 and 7

- pgperl—Postgres

- sybperl—SyBase 4

- uniperl—Unify 5.0

The perl libraries and extensions included with these database dialects don't do all of the work for you, but they can save you considerable time developing a database gateway. All of the dialects are available from **ftp://ftp.demon.co.uk/pub/perl/db/perl4/** and are mirrored at **ftp://ftp.cis.ufl.edu/pub/perl/scripts/db/**.

GSQL

NCSA has produced an SQL gateway specifically for the World Wide Web. GSQL can be used to generate and send SQL queries to an SQL server. GSQL produces forms based on definition files called *proc files* and then formats the form data into an SQL query for you. GSQL is not, however, a turnkey solution because you still need to write your own code to submit the SQL query to the back-end database. A simple example for SyBase is provided with GSQL.

You can find information on GSQL at **http://www.ncsa.uiuc.edu/SDG/People/jason/pub/gsql/starthere.html**. NCSA's GSQL page contains several demos using InterBase, SyBase, and Oracle, so you can get a feel for what it can do. It is a useful tool but, like the perl dialects, requires strong programming skills to set up.

Windows Database Servers

The traditional approach to client/server databases has been that the database server runs under UNIX or, more recently, under OS/2 or Windows NT. Therefore, if you're running the UNIX httpd and want to access a database, it is easiest to talk to a database server on one of these platforms using SQL or direct file access.

> ### Note
>
> Due to continually increasing processor power, database servers are now available for Windows running NetWare, including Oracle 7 Server for NetWare, SyBase SQL Server for NetWare, and Watcom SQL Network Server for NetWare. Getting these servers to run the TCP/IP protocols so that they can be used with UNIX clients like a CGI script may be possible.

If your data resides in a Windows database like Borland Paradox, Microsoft Access, or Lotus Approach, which are not directly accessible from generic TCP/IP clients, there are still two ways to get to the data from a UNIX CGI script, but doing this is somewhat backwards from the usual client/server topology. Consequently, these techniques are only for the adventurous programmer.

Directory Polling

You can use the *directory polling technique* to exchange any type of data between any two or more platforms on the same network. This technique is based on polling a common file area on the network. For example, if a UNIX script needed to access data in Borland Paradox for Windows, you can set up two directories on a network drive called QUERY and RESULTS. When the UNIX client needs information, it writes a query file to the QUERY directory and gives it a unique number, such as Q0145. A go-between program on the Paradox machine, perhaps written in Visual Basic, continually checks the QUERY directory for new files. When it finds a query, it forwards it to Paradox and then writes the results to the RESULTS directory in a file with the same number as the query (like "R0145"). Figure 15.1 illustrates this process.

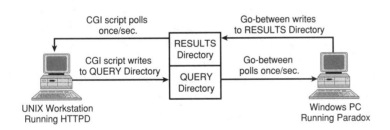

Fig. 15.1
This drawing illustrates the directory polling technique.

A Go-between Server

A second method of sharing data between dissimilar platforms is to write your own server that uses TCP/IP to talk to clients. To use the previous example again, you write a TCP/IP server, perhaps in Visual Basic, that forwards requests to Paradox on the Windows platform via DDE, OLE, or Visual Basic's built-in data access capabilities. A perl script using perl's sockets support can then talk to the Windows server over a TCP/IP network and retrieve data that way. This is a major programming task but is definitely faster than the directory polling technique.

Fortunately, TCP/IP toolkits to assist with server development are available. One is NetManage's NEWT-SDK (**http://www.netmanage.com**), which offers a Visual Basic interface to the TCP/IP API (Applications Programming

Interface). Another is the PC/TCP OnNet Developer's Toolkit for DOS/Windows from FTP Software, Inc. (**http://www.ftp.com**). Dart Communications offers a toolkit called *PowerTCP,* which has the advantage of not being connected to a proprietary WinSock program (the demo version is included on WebmasterCD). These toolkits are certainly not point-and-click solutions, but they can save you considerable time in development.

Accessing Databases from Windows

It's considerably easier to access databases using the Windows httpd than the UNIX httpd because Windows tools for database access are simply easier to work with than dialects of perl or C programs. This is true whether the data is on the same machine or on a network database server like Oracle.

Database Access Through Visual Basic

Visual Basic provides several methods for accessing databases. These include direct access to native formats, ODBC, and SQL, which are specifically database tools, and DDE and OLE, which can be used with any program.

Native Formats, ODBC, and SQL

The Professional Edition of Visual Basic provides built-in access to a number of different database formats, including Microsoft Access, Btrieve, dBASE, FoxPro, and Paradox. Data in these formats can be read directly from the database files on the local machine or a network drive. The Microsoft Access database is probably the easiest of all to work with in Visual Basic because it includes the Access database engine.

> **Note**
>
> Only the Professional Edition of Visual Basic includes database support.

In addition to support for various database formats, Visual Basic provides ODBC and SQL support. Consequently, any databases that support these standards are also accessible from Visual Basic. All major Windows databases, including Borland Paradox, Microsoft Access, and Lotus Approach, support at least one of these standards.

DDE and OLE

In addition to other database access tools, Visual Basic programs can use DDE or OLE to communicate with databases as long as the database program is currently running on the same machine. On network systems that use the NetBIOS protocol (such as LANtastic), NetDDE can be used to access databases on other machines, as well.

Unlike Visual Basic's other database-access tools, DDE and OLE can also be used to access data from any DDE- or OLE-enabled application, including word processors and spreadsheets. These components in all the major office suites (that is, Microsoft Office, Novell PerfectOffice, and Lotus SmartSuite) are OLE- and DDE-enabled. In addition, all of these programs feature their own macro languages, which allows you to create your own highly-specialized applications.

Custom Applications Using the Web

Because of the simplicity of both HTTP and HTML, the Web is a useful tool for creating graphical applications that run on a wide variety of platforms. However, there are definitely limitations to what can be done with forms and scripts in the way of making custom applications.

One of the biggest limitations is that all data and forms are displayed inside a Web browser rather than as a separate application. If your application really needs its own menu bar, spreadsheet interface, or word processor features, you won't be able to create it using a Web browser. You can create an entirely new type of Internet server and a custom client to go with it, but it is nice if you can just put a slightly different face on existing technology. New applications hold the promise of doing just that.

InterAp

InterAp is a suite of Internet applications from California Software, Inc. (**http://www.calsoft.com**). It is different from other Internet application suites because it supports Windows OLE capability and drag and drop. In InterAp's Web browser, Web Navigator, you can drag the text of a Web page right into Microsoft Word (see fig. 15.2). Or you can embed the page in a Word document so that when you click it, it automatically goes out to the Internet to retrieve the updated page. This allows you to create custom applications that use any OLE-capable program of your choice to present data, yet you don't have to worry about the underlying Internet communications.

In addition to OLE capabilities, InterAp features its own scripting language, NetScripts, which can be used as a cross-application macro language for the InterAp applications. NetScripts is compatible with Visual Basic, so your imagination is the limit as far as power and capability. In addition, InterAp features a Scheduler that can be used to automatically perform Internet downloads and searches at predetermined times. For example, you can have InterAp look for a topic of interest each night using the WebCrawler search engine and mail you the results each morning so that you can see whether there are new sites related to your topic.

Fig. 15.2
You can drag
HTML files from
the File Manager
to the InterAp
Web Navigator
to open them.

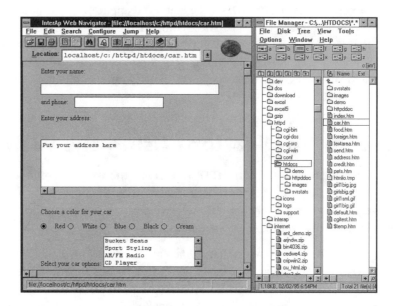

Using InterAp's automation capabilities and compatibility with Visual Basic, you can create a custom application in Visual Basic and rely on InterAp to retrieve the necessary data. For example, suppose your distributors wanted to receive updated price information weekly via the Internet in an easy-to-use interface. An easy way to do this is to write your own custom program to display the data and do the necessary calculations in Visual Basic. Your distributors simply program InterAp's Scheduler to automatically retrieve the price data once a week via your FTP, Web, or Gopher server, and then launch your Visual Basic program to see the updated price info. By incorporating encryption into your Visual Basic program, you protect your data from prying eyes on the Internet.

> **Note**
>
> The description of InterAp here was based on a beta test version of the product; not all of the features were functional and there could be changes before it is finished.

InternetWorks

InternetWorks, from Booklink Technologies (**http://www.booklink.com**), is similar in capability to InterAp. Like InterAp, it is OLE-enabled and supports drag and drop. It can also be used with Visual Basic or Visual C++. InternetWorks has the additional advantage that all Internet activities take place through a single interface, unlike most other Internet application suites, which use different programs for every Internet service. This adds to the program's convenience. In addition, a free InternetWorks Lite version is available on the Internet from Booklink. (AOL recently bought Booklink and the future of this free version is in question.) Figure 15.3 shows a prerelease version of InternetWorks Lite.

IV

Applications

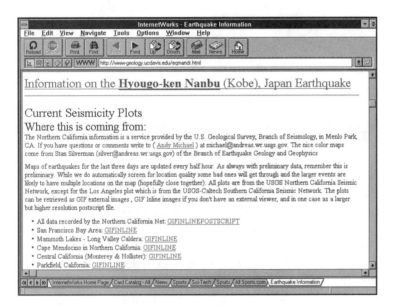

Fig. 15.3
InternetWorks Lite is viewing a Web document.

Figure 15.4 shows InternetWorks' presentation of an FTP site. It combines a Web-like graphical presentation of the directory structure with a listing of the text sent by the server when logging on. This figure also shows the URL hotlist.

Applications such as InterAp and InternetWorks promise to shape much of the future of the Internet by changing the way we use the Internet. Once thought of as a network primarily for public data distribution, the Internet is already heavily used as an internetworking tool for private networks. The more that tools like InterAp and InternetWorks allow programs to break out of the traditional FTP-Gopher-Web mold, the more attractive the Internet becomes for the development of custom applications like the one described previously. In an age of ever-increasing global communications, no one can afford to miss out on the incredible potential offered by the Internet.

Fig. 15.4
InternetWorks Lite viewing an FTP directory.

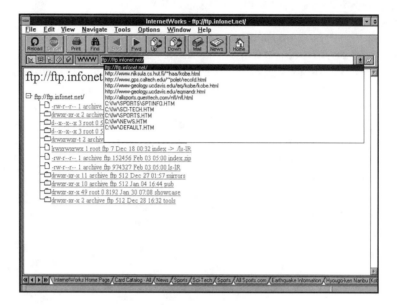

Sources of Additional Information

Before you sit down to write a custom program for your Web server, check the Internet to see if it's already been done. Thousands of organizations around the world probably have needs similar to yours, and chances are you'll find that your topic of interest has been in discussion for quite some time. Here are some good Internet resources to help you develop and keep up to date.

Newsgroups and Mailing Lists

The definitive newsgroup for those running Web servers is **comp.infosystems.www.providers**. This is the appropriate place to post questions about running a Web server. Before you do, however, be sure to check the FAQ, which is included on WebmasterCD.

A mailing list called **www-talk@info.cern.ch** for Web server administrators is also available. To subscribe, send a message containing "SUBSCRIBE" to **www-talk-request@info.cern.ch**. This list is archived in hypermail format at **http://gummo.stanford.edu/html/hypermail/www-talk-1994q3/index.html**.

Documentation on the Web

Several important sites contain documentation on the Web ranging from server installation instructions to protocol specifications. The following are the key sites.

CERN

The home of the Web still has one of the most complete lists of Web tools and documentation found anywhere. Information at **http://info.cern.ch** includes

- A complete list of Web servers for various platforms

- Information about writing your own server

- Information about writing Web robots

- A CGI script library

- The HTT protocol specification

- The HTML specification and information about writing HTML

- HTML editors for various platforms

- Tools for converting and maintaining HTML

NCSA

The home of Mosaic and NCSA's httpd is a good place to look for documentation on these subjects as well as general Web information. Downloadable software is available from **ftp://ftp.ncsa.uiuc.edu/**. Documentation on NCSA httpd and CGI scripts is available from **http://hoohoo.ncsa.uiuc.edu/**. The FTP site also contains HTML editors, sample scripts, and documentation.

Toolkits and Programming Libraries

Several different code libraries are available via the Web or FTP. These contain sample programs or code contributed by authors around the world, as well as the source code used in many Web applications.

libwww-perl

Libwww-perl is a library of perl routines put together by contributors around the globe. The libwww-perl routines are useful for testing Web servers and clients or for just learning more about how the Web works. Libwww-perl is available from **http://www.ics.uci.edu:80/WebSoft/libwww-perl/**.

IV

Applications

The World Wide Web Library of Common Code

CERN's WWW Library of Common Code contains code used by both World Wide Web clients and servers. It contains code for accessing most Internet services, including Telnet, Gopher, FTP, news, and WAIS. You can find out more about the WWW Library of Common Code at **http://www.w3.org/ hypertext/WWW/Library/Status.html**.

The Webmaster's Starter Kit

This useful resource is available from Enterprise Integration Technologies at **http://www.eit.com**. The starter kit includes

- Web construction kit (home pages and so on)

- Virtual document programming tools (libcgi)

- Web maintenance tools (webtest)

- Mail-archive formatter (hypermail)

- Logfile reporting tools (getstats)

Conferences

The definitive conference for World Wide Web developers is the International World Wide Web Conference. The second conference was held in Chicago in the fall of 1994, and was heavily overbooked, so sign up early if you want to go. An upcoming conference is the Fourth International World Wide Web Conference, to be held December 11-14, 1995, in Boston, Massachusetts.

Registration information on this conference, as well as proceedings from past conferences, are available from **http://riwww.osf.org:8001/ri/ announcements/WWW_Conf_upcoming.html**.

Part V

WebmasterCD

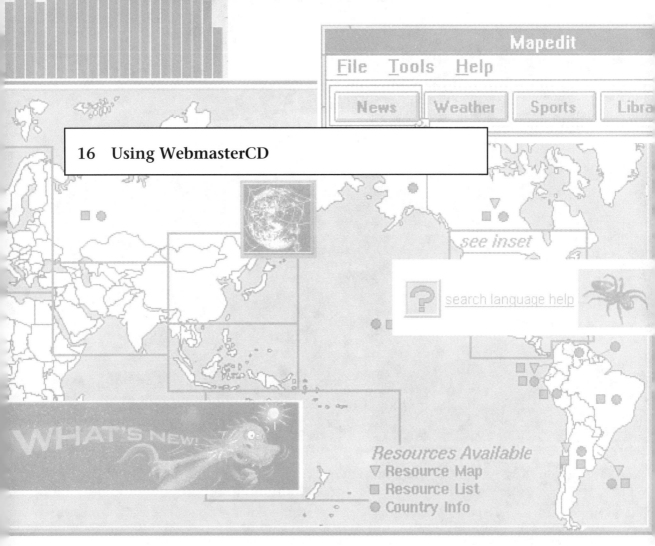

16 Using WebmasterCD

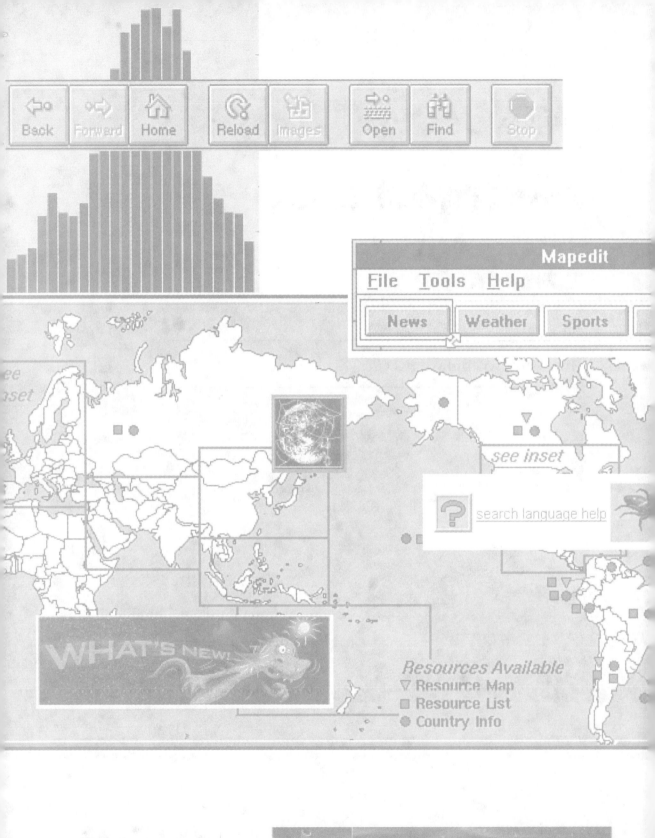

Chapter 16

Using WebmasterCD

If you've read other chapters in this book, you probably read about a program or utility that you are ready to install. Or if you're like many users, this is the first chapter you turned to because you want to see what's on WebmasterCD and dive right in. Regardless of whether you read the book from front to back or are starting at the back, this chapter should help you find the software you need to get your Web site up and running.

You can find a wide variety of software on WebmasterCD for use with the World Wide Web and the rest of the Internet. In addition to software for running your Web server, you'll find software that is useful for Web clients. We hope that having this handy will be useful to site administrators supporting a large number of end users. If you're a consultant or involved in setting up Web clients for others, you'll find this CD handy for most of the software you need. Scores of online hours were spent over the past few months gathering the best freeware, shareware, and public domain software available. Hopefully, these efforts will save you a significant amount of online time and money. Throughout the rest of the book, when you see the WebmasterCD icon (as shown in the margin here) you'll know that the software discussed is on the CD.

WebmasterCD contains software for PCs running DOS or Windows as well as workstations running UNIX. For the convenience of Windows and DOS users, we've expanded the archives for these files so that they are ready to install directly from the CD. Unfortunately, we can't do the same thing for the UNIX software. In order to include DOS and UNIX files on the same CD and preserve the long file names allowed in UNIX, we've kept these archives compressed and given them file names that are legal in DOS.

Finally, a large collection of useful documents about the Internet is included on WebmasterCD. You can find all of the RFCs, STDs, and FYIs. Drop

WebmasterCD in your CD-ROM drive and get ready to load the best collection of Web and Net utilities anywhere.

This chapter covers the following:

- What is shareware?
- How to get new versions of software on WebmasterCD
- How to install programs from WebmasterCD
- Software for connecting to the Net
- World Wide Web software
- Graphics and multimedia viewers for use with Mosaic and other Web Browsers
- Software for UseNet news, FTP, Archie, Gopher, Internet Relay Chat, Telnet, and many other Internet applications and utilities
- UNIX software for the WWW
- Example code from the book
- Internet documents

What Is Shareware?

Much of the software on WebmasterCD is *shareware*. Shareware is software you can try before you buy. It is not free software but it is a neat idea. Shareware software is written by talented and creative individuals. Quite often, their software provides the same power as programs you can purchase at your local computer or software store. However, with shareware you have the advantage of knowing what you are getting before you buy it.

> **Note**
>
> In the case of the Internet, shareware was often the only choice before traditional retail software vendors recognized the large market for products. Shareware software was part of the large driving force in opening up the Internet for your use.

All shareware software on WebmasterCD comes with a text file (or instructions in the software itself) that tells you how to register the software. You are obligated to register any shareware software you plan to use regularly.

What benefits do you gain by registering the shareware? First, you have a clean conscience, knowing that you have paid the author for the many hours spent in creating such a useful program.

Second, registering the software can give you additional benefits, such as technical support from the author, a printed manual, or additional features that are only available to registered users. Consult the individual programs for details about what bonuses you may receive for registering.

Next, registering your shareware usually puts you on the author's mailing list. This enables the author to keep you up-to-date about new versions of the software, bug fixes, compatibility issues, and so on. Again, this varies from product to product. Some authors even include a free update to the next version in the cost of registration.

Finally, if the license agreement states you must pay to continue using the software, you are violating the license if you don't pay. In some cases, this may be a criminal offense. While an individual user is not likely to be arrested or sued over failing to pay registration for shareware, the small possibility of repercussions is no excuse for violating the license. Wise corporations and businesses register shareware to avoid any chance of legal problems.

> **Note**
>
> Several of the authors and companies that provided software for WebmasterCD asked that a notice of their copyright, shareware agreement, or license information be included. However, lack of such a statement printed in this book does not mean that the software is not copyrighted or does not have a license agreement. Please see the text files or help for any of the programs for which you need copyright or licensing information.

Getting Updates for Software on WebmasterCD

The advantage is simple. Putting all this great software on WebmasterCD saves you many hours spent looking for and downloading the software. The only downside is that as new versions of software become available, WebmasterCD stays the same.

V

WebmasterCD

A special FTP site was created for users of this book to get new versions of the software on WebmasterCD. As soon as an update is received, it will be posted on the FTP site. You can download by anonymous FTP. The FTP address for this site is **ftp.mcp.com**. (MCP stands for Macmillan Computer Publishing, the company that owns Que, the publisher of this book.) The directory for software in this book is /pub/que/net-cd.

Anytime you want, you can log onto this FTP site and look for new software. What if you want to be told when there is new software? Your time will be wasted if you look and there's nothing new of interest to you. Well, Que thought about that, too. You can subscribe to the WebmasterCD mailing list by sending an e-mail message to **subscribe@misl.mcp.com**. The body of the message should be

```
subscribe webmastercd
```

> **Note**
>
> You can also subscribe to the WebmasterCD mailing list by visiting the MCP World Wide Web site at **http://www.mcp.com**. From there, choose the Reference Desk. Then click Information Super Library Reports. Enter your name, e-mail address, and company name. Select WebmasterCD. Then click Send.

The Macmillan site and mailing list are not the only ways to keep up-to-date. Many of the programs on WebmasterCD are regularly updated at several of the major software FTP sites. Sites (and directories) to check out for Windows Internet software include:

ftp.cica.indiana.edu in /pub/pc/win3/winsock

archive.orst.edu in /pub/mirrors/ftp.cica.indiana.edu

ftp.ncsa.uiuc.edu in /Web

oak.oakland.edu in /SimTel/win3/winsock

For UNIX software look in:

oak.oakland.cdu in /pub/unix c

ftp.uu.net in /systems/unix

wuarchive.wustl.edu in /systems/unix

> **Note**
>
> Many of the authors and companies asked that an e-mail or postal address where they can be contacted be included. For the ones that don't have an e-mail address listed here, you can find an e-mail address for nearly every program on WebmasterCD in the documentation with the program or in the program.

Installing Windows or DOS Software on WebmasterCD

Before using any of the software on the CD, you need to install it. Many of the programs come with their own installation program. If a program includes an installation program, the description of it in this chapter gives you the directions you need to get started with the installation.

For programs that don't have an installation program, the installation process is straightforward. To install a program that doesn't have an installer, follow these steps:

1. Create a directory on your hard drive for the software.

   > **Note**
   >
   > It's a good idea to create one main directory in the root of your hard drive for all of your Web software, for instance c:\web and then create subdirectories for individual programs in that directory. That keeps the root directory of your hard drive less cluttered.

2. Copy all of the files and subdirectories from the program's directory on WebmasterCD to the directory you created on your hard drive. The easiest way to do this in Windows is to select all of the files and sub-directories to copy in File Manager and drag them from the window for your CD to the directory on your hard drive. This is shown in figure 16.1.

   > **Note**
   >
   > A directory name appears after the name of each program in this chapter. The directory name is where you can find the software on WebmasterCD.

V

WebmasterCD

Fig. 16.1
Drag the selected files from your CD-ROM drive in File Manager to the directory on your hard drive.

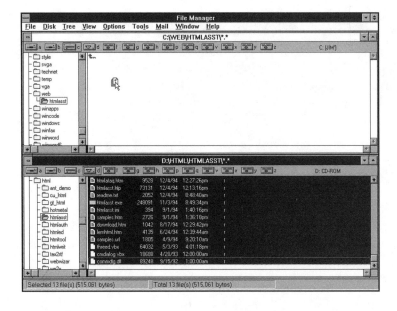

You are prompted to confirm the copy. If you are copying subdirectories, be sure to answer Yes when prompted if you want to create the new subdirectories.

3. If you used File Manager to copy the files, you need to turn off the read only attribute. To do this, select all of the files you copied on your hard drive and choose File, Properties. Deselect Read Only and choose OK (see fig. 16.2).

Fig. 16.2
Click the Read Only box so that no X or shading appears. When you choose OK, the Read Only attribute will be turned off for all files.

Properties
13 Files Selected, Total 515,061 bytes
Attributes
☐ Read Only   ☐ Hidden
☒ Archive   ☐ System

OK
Cancel
Help

> **Note**
>
> It's necessary to do this because File Manager copies the Read Only attribute from the CD when it copies the file. If you copy the files using the DOS copy command, the read only attribute isn't copied. It's your choice which way you would like to do this.

4. After all of the files are copied, you need to create an icon to run the program from Program Manager if you plan to run the program in Windows. The easiest way to do this is to drag the program file from the directory on your hard drive in File Manager to Program Manager and drop it in the program group where you want the icon (see fig. 16.3).

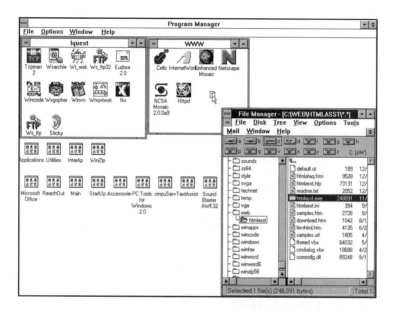

Fig. 16.3
Drag the executable file for the program from File Manager to create a program icon. After you drop it, the program's icon will appear.

V

WebmasterCD

Note

Dragging a file from File Manager to Program Manager doesn't move it, it just creates a program icon in Program Manager.

Tip

It's a good idea to create a new program group to hold all of your Web software program icons. To do this, choose **F**ile, **N**ew and then click Program **G**roup in Program Manager.

That's all there is to it. Repeat these steps for any software you want to install.

Installing UNIX Software on WebmasterCD

To install software for UNIX, you need to first decompress the archives. Most of the UNIX programs are compressed using gzip or Z. Gzip is included on the CD just in case you don't already have it. Most of the compressed files contain the source code for the program in a TAR archive. After restoring the TAR archive, you have to compile a binary for your platform from the included source.

Win32s

\win32s

Several programs on WebmasterCD require Win32 to run. If you are running Windows 3.1, Windows 3.11, or Windows for Workgroups 3.11, you need to install Win32s to make these programs run. The version here is 2.02, which is the correct version to use with NCSA Mosaic version 2 Alpha 9 and other programs requiring Win32.

To install Win32s, it's a good idea to first close any other programs you are working in as the installation will restart Windows after it is done. Then change to the \win32s\disk1 directory on WebmasterCD and run setup.exe. Follow the directions on-screen to complete the installation.

> **Note**
>
> You cannot redistribute Win32s without the permission of Microsoft.

All-in-One Suites

If you are looking for a quick and easy solution to most of your Internet software needs, one of these suites may be exactly what you need. These include software to get connected to the Internet along with good collections of utilities for use once you are connected.

If you are involved in setting up Web software for end users, one of these suites may be your best option, particularly in a corporate setting. If this is your situation, you probably understand the advantages of having everyone you support using the same software. There's also a real-time advantage to a single package that includes most of the pieces you need.

Internet Chameleon with Instant Internet

\suites\chameleo

The Internet Chameleon v4.1 is a complete Internet Windows-based application. It supports FTP transfer, Telnet logins to remote computers over the Internet or standard TCP/IP connection, e-mail sending and receiving, remote pinging of Internet servers, and World Wide Web browsing.

> **Note**
>
> The version included here may be used with a SLIP/ PPP, CSLIP, or ISDN connection. For information on a version that runs on LAN connections, contact NetManage. See their Web page at **http://www.netmanage.com** or send e-mail to **sales@netmanage.com**.

Before installing this, close any other applications you are using. You have to close Windows and restart your machine before using the software after it is installed because it does modify your AUTOEXEC.BAT file. To begin the installation, run setup.exe (in Windows) in the \suites\chameleo\disk1 directory. (When prompted for disks 2 and 3 during installation, enter the path name for these directories on WebmasterCD.)

After you run the installation, you still have to register this software before you can use it. The restoration process is automated and sets up the software immediately. You can register to use the software for a free 30 day trial period or you can purchase a full license to use the software when you register. You can also set it up to work with an existing service provider's account or to register for a new account with one of several providers that have joined with NetManage to provide instant access. Some of these providers offer free trials, others don't. If you are interested, read the information for each provider before proceeding.

> **Note**
>
> To register the software, you must provide a credit card number, even if you are just registering for the trial time period. The registration takes place over phone lines, not over the Internet; you should not worry at all about the safety of your credit card number. If you don't provide a valid card number, you can't use the software.

V

WebmasterCD

Please see the inetcham.wri file in the \disk1 subdirectory for directions on how to complete the installation and register the software.

> **Note**
>
> If you have used an older version of the NetManage Sampler, you will notice some major differences in this version. First, the software now includes all the features of the retail version instead of just some. Second, you can use this trial version for only 30 days. To continue use after that, you must register and purchase the full retail version which you can do by repeating the registration process and choosing to purchase a license. Finally, this software cannot be installed over the older sampler.

Pipeline

\suites\pipeline

This is the software for connecting to The Pipeline, a custom service provider. The Pipeline software provides access to e-mail, Gopher, WWW, FTP, and UseNet News through The Pipeline's service. To install the software, run the setup.exe program from the \suites\pipeline directory. The version included on WebmasterCD is v2.07. (If you get a message that threed.vbx is an old version when you run Pipeline, delete that file from your \windows\system directory and reinstall Pipeline.)

In addition to providing access to the Internet, The Pipeline also allows its users to create Web pages on their systems and provides software for doing this. If you've decided that you don't need a Web server of your own, this is a good option.

> **Note**
>
> The Pipeline also has a Macintosh version of its software. If you have both Windows and Mac users to support, this software may make a good choice for you for that reason. For more information, see the advertisement near the end of this book.

Software for Connecting to the Internet (TCP/IP)

If you want to connect to the Internet, you need software. Whether you use a modem to dial up a SLIP or PPP account, connect from your LAN at work running Windows, or connect from DOS, the software here can make the connection.

Core Internet-Connect 2

\tcpip\inetcon2

This program provides WinSock and TCP/IP for networks. It is designed for an end-user for connection and also for developers who want to build other TCP/IP applications based on it.

Run setup.exe (in Windows) in the \tcpip\inetcon2 directory to run the automatic installation.

> **Note**
>
> This package contains the Internet-Connect Trial Copy program. Internet-Connect is a registered trademark of Core Systems. Internet-Connect is developed and marketed by Core Systems, 245 Firestone Drive, Walnut Creek, CA 94598; 510/943-5765.

Crynwr Packet Drivers

\tcpip\crynwr\pktd11, \tcpip\crynwr\pktd11a,
\tcpip\crynwr\pktd11b, \tcpip\crynwr\pktd11c, \tcpip\crynwr\exp16116

This collection of drivers is required by most DOS-based (and some Windows-based) Internet applications. The collection serves as an interface between established network software and packet-based Internet connections. A wide range of drivers is included in these archive files for most popular network packages such as Novell, LANtastic, and most others. The source code for each driver is also included. If you are experienced enough to alter the code for a driver, you can reassemble these drivers to function differently or better than their current forms.

To install this software, copy only the files you need. You'll find all of the documentation for these in the \pktd11 subdirectory. Please read the documentation for this and your applications to determine which files you need.

NetDial

\tcpip\netdial

NetDial is an Internet dial-up program with many features. NetDial can call, connect to your Internet host, log you in, and run your TCP/IP program at the click of a mouse. Some other features include: baud rate support to 256 kbaud, up to 99 redial attempts, autodial on startup, sound support, up to five separate configurations, cumulative timer window (tracks all time online), built-in call log viewer/editor, up to five startup programs on startup, additional modem support, and more! To install it run \install2\tcpip\ netdial\setup.exe. See the files "read.me" and "install.txt" for more information about the program and installation.

Slipper/Cslipper

\tcpip\slippr

Slipper/CSlipper v1.5 is a DOS-based replacement application for SLIP8250. Slipper and CSlipper were written from scratch in Turbo Pascal. Their purpose is to provide Internet connections through a packet driver interface. Both applications are very small and command-line driven. See the slipper.doc file for information about using Slipper or CSlipper and their options.

Trumpet Winsock 2

\tcpip\twsk20b

This is the most widely used shareware WinSock package. It supports modem and network connections. At this time, twsk20b.zip is the officially released, working version. This version was just released and includes new features such as Firewall Support, improved scripting, routing capabilities, and more. Trumpet also fixes the minor problems in version 1 and fixes a bug with PPP in the first release of version 2.0.

After copying the files in this directory to a directory on your hard drive, create an icon for the tcpman.exe file. The first time you run this you need to provide IP address information. If you are using this over a modem, you need to modify login.cmd to work with your service provider. You also may need to add the directory containing Trumpet to your path statement in AUTOEXEC.BAT. The install.doc file contains installation and configuration information.

> **Note**
>
> The Trumpet Winsock is currently distributed as shareware. You may use the Trumpet Winsock for 30 days to evaluate its usefulness. If at the end of that time you are satisfied with the Trumpet Winsock as a product, you should register it.
>
> Trumpet Winsock Version 2.0 has a "Send Registration" option that will automatically post encrypted credit card details to Trumpet Software International. Choose **F**ile, **R**egister to take advantage of this feature.

World Wide Web

It is amazing how much software is available for use with the World Wide Web. Even though this is one of the newest developments on the Internet, there is more good software relating to it than any other category. So whatever your needs are—a Web browser, a program to help you write Web pages, or even software to start a Web server—there are several choices here for you. We've looked at several of these throughout this book and there are also some here that aren't covered elsewhere. Dig in and enjoy.

Launcher
\www\launcher

This freeware program is a neat utility that allows you to launch a Windows application from a link in a Web browser such as Mosaic. This allows you to open an application, such as WordPerfect or Excel, without having to create a link to a particular document. Source code is also supplied.

See the readme.txt file for directions on how to use this program. You will need to read this carefully because it is not a trivial matter to get this working.

Lynx
\www\lynx

This is a fully working WWW client for DOS machines. Lynx is an alpha release and does not support forms at present. On the positive side, each URL you access is opened in a separate window so you can have several documents open at once. It also has support for displaying inline images. See the readme.txt file for information on configuring DOS Lynx to work with your Internet connection.

perl

\www\dosperl

Throughout the book, the perl scripting language has been used to show how to process requests from forms in HTML. The files in this directory include the binary perl files for DOS and the source code. See chapter 12, "Scripts," for a discussion of the use of perl.

> **Note**
>
> A Windows NT version of perl is also included in \www\winntprl.

SlipKnot

\www\slipknot

SlipKnot is a graphical World Wide Web browser specifically designed for Microsoft Windows users who have UNIX shell accounts with their service providers. SlipKnot's primary feature is that it does not require SLIP or PPP or TCP/IP services. It also allows background retrieval of multiple documents, and storage of complete documents on users' local hard disks.

To install SlipKnot, run \www\slipknot\setup.exe in Windows and follow the directions on-screen. The readme.txt file contains some information about possible installation glitches should you encounter trouble. (There is also an upgrade to version 1.07b, a beta version for the 1.1 release, in the upgrade directory. If you would like to try this beta version, run the snupgr.1exe file.)

> **Note**
>
> There will probably be a new version, SlipKnot 1.1, available by the time you read this. If you use SlipKnot, check the WebmasterCD FTP site for a new version.

URL Grabber Demo

\www\grabdemo

Have you ever read an article in a UseNet newsgroup or an e-mail message and seen a URL that you wanted to save for further reference? Sure, you can copy and paste this into a browser and then save it in a hotlist or bookmark, but this handy little utility makes this even easier. The URL Grabber toolbar lets you grab a URL from documents as you read them and then easily save a collection of addresses as HTML documents that you can open in any WWW browser. You then have a Web document with all of the links to the URL addresses you saved, making it quick and easy to jump to those URLs. In this demo version, you are limited to grabbing three addresses each time you run the program. See the Help file for information about ordering the full version that doesn't have this limit.

Web4ham

\www\web4ham

Web4ham is a World Wide Web server for Windows. This lets your Windows PC act like a World Wide Web Site that other WWW users can access with any Web client software.

Windows httpd 1.4

\www\whttpd

If you're setting up your own Web server in Windows based on the directions in chapters 5 and 6 of this book, this is the software you'll be using. While not as powerful as its UNIX counterpart, it has more than enough capabilities to satisfy most users just starting a basic Web site. Please note that earlier versions of this software were freeware but this version is shareware and requires a payment after a 30 day trial period for continued use. See index.htm for details of this agreement.

For installation instructions, see chapter 5; "Getting Started with Web Servers." To see how to configure this, see chapter 6, "Server Configuration."

HTML

HTML documents are at the heart of the Web. Whether you're creating a Web site for a major corporation or just putting up a few personal pages, you need an HTML editor or translator (unless you plan to hire someone else to do the work for you). This area has seen a flood of good programs and we've got most of them here for you.

ANT_HTML

\html\ant_demo

ANT_DEMO.DOT is a template designed to work in Word for Windows 6.0 and Word for Mac 6.0 to facilitate the creation of hypertext documents. HTML codes can be inserted into any new or previously prepared Word document or any ASCII document. This is a demonstration version of the

ANT_PLUS conversion utility and the ANT_HTML package. This template also works in all international versions of Word 6.

For a more complete description of ANT_DEMO and directions for installation, see chapter 12, "Scripts."

> **Note**
>
> ANT_HTML.DOT and ANT_DEMO.DOC are Copyright © 1994 by Jill Swift. For more information, contact
>
> Jill Swift
> P.O. Box 213
> Montgomery, TX 77356
> **jswift@freenet.fsu.edu**

CU_HTML
\html\cu_html

This template is for writing hypertext (HTML) documents in Word for Windows 2.0 and 6.0. The version included here is 1.5. This package is described in some detail in chapter 12, "Scripts"; installation instructions are also given there.

> **Note**
>
> CU_HTML is developed by Kenneth Wong Y.P. and Anton Lam S.Y. of the Computer Services Centre of The Chinese University of Hong Kong. The package can be distributed freely except in conjunction with any commercial or for-fee product. Prior permission from the authors must be obtained if the package is to be included in any commercial or for-fee product. You must distribute this copyright notice together with the software.
>
> The software is provided *as is*. Currently, there is no warranty, and no support in any form will be entertained. You use this software at your own risk. However, you can send comments and wish lists to **anton-lam@cuhk.hk**.

GT_HTML
\html\gt_html

This is another Word 6 template for creating HTML documents. Currently, only a small number of HTML tags are supported. But the ones included are the most common tags and should be useful for many basic HTML documents.

For installation instructions and a more complete description, please see chapter 12, "Scripts."

HTML Assistant for Windows

\html\htmlasst

This is a simple shareware HTML document editor. Most commands are implemented via a huge button bar. This is a good editor for small documents, but there is a 32K file size limit in this version. (There is also a Pro version available that loads larger documents. See the Help file for ordering information.) One neat feature of note is the ability to convert files containing URLs, like Cello bookmarks and Mosaic INI files to HTML documents that can then be read with any Web browser.

For installation instructions and a more complete description, please see chapter 12, "Scripts."

HTML Author

\html\htmlauth

This is another template for creating HTML documents in Word 6 for Windows. This latest version adds support for international versions of Word.

To use HTML Author, copy all of the files from this directory to a directory on your hard drive as explained in the section "Installing Windows or DOS Software on WebmasterCD," then copy the HTMLAUTH.DOT template into your Microsoft Word for Windows templates directory. (This is usually the directory "C:\WINWORD\TEMPLATE"). To create an HTML source document, just start up Microsoft Word for Windows, and create a new document, selecting HTMLAUTH.DOT as the template. For more complete directions see the manual, which is included in Word and HTML formats.

HTML Writer

\html\htmlwrit

HTML Writer is a stand-alone HTML authoring program. Most HTML tags can be inserted via an extensive set of menu choices. It has a nice toolbar for implementing many HTML tags. Another good feature is the support of templates. You can use templates to help design and create HTML documents with a consistent look and feel.

To install HTML Writer, copy all of the files from the \html\htmlwrit directory to a directory on your hard drive. Then move cmdialog.vbx, commdlg.dll, emedit.vbx, and toolbars.vbx to your \windows directory. Then, you can create an icon for the htmlwrit.exe file and start the program. See readme.txt for more details.

HTMLed

\html\htmled

This is a powerful shareware HTML document editor. The interface features a button bar for ease-of-use and the abundant and clear menus make it easy to find the features you need.

For installation instructions and a more complete description, please see chapter 12, "Scripts."

RTF To HTML

\html\rtf2html

This is a utility for converting documents from the RTF format to HTML. RTF (Rich Text Format) is a format that many word processors, including Word for Windows, can import and export. The package also includes a Word 2 for Windows template for writing HTML.

After copying this program from WebmasterCD to a directory on your hard drive, you should move RTFTOHTM.DLL to somewhere in your path. The best place for it is your \windows directory. You should also move HTML.DOT to your Word template directory, usually \winword\template. You can then open a new document in WinWord using HTML.DOT as template.

SoftQuad HoTMetaL

\html\hotmetal

This is a full-featured, freeware, professional-quality, HTML editor for Windows. You can edit multiple documents at the same time, use templates to ensure consistency between documents, and use the powerful word-processor-like features to do such things as search and replace.

Note

The commercial version, HoTMetaL PRO, includes the following new features:

- A clean-up filter called "TIDY" for any invalid legacy HTML files

- Bit-mapped graphics inline in your documents

- Macros to automate repetitive tasks and reduce errors

- Rules Checking and Validation to ensure correct HTML markup

- Built-in graphical table editor

- Capability to fix invalid HTML documents and import them with the `Interpret Document` command.

- URL editor

- Full table and forms support

- Macro creation and editing support

- Document validations commands

- Supports Microsoft Windows help

- Includes printed manual and access to support personnel

- Homepage templates

- Editing Tools

- Spell checking

- Thesaurus

- Full Search and Replace is context-sensitive

You can order a copy of HoTMetaL PRO from SoftQuad. See their ad in the back of this book for contact and pricing information. There is also a Macintosh commercial version and freeware and commercial UNIX versions. The freeware UNIX version is covered later in this chapter.

For installation instructions and a more complete description, please see chapter 12, "Scripts."

Tex2RTF

/html/tex2rtf

This program converts LaTeX files to RTF (Rich Text Format) and HTML. (There's also a UNIX version of this discussed in the HTML section earlier in this chapter.)

WebWizard

\html\webwizard

This is another HTML authoring system that works as a template in Word 6 for Windows. It adds a new toolbar with some HTML commands and a new WebWizard menu to the Word 6 menu bar when loaded.

To install WebWizard, run the \html\webwiza\setup.exe file in Windows and follow the directions on-screen. Once loaded, you can use it by opening a new file and selecting web.wiz (which should be in the Word templates directory) as the template. Note that since this template name does not end with DOT extension, you'll have to select to show all files in the Attach Templates dialog box to see this in the list.

The documentation provided here (in the \html\webwiza\doc directory on WebmasterCD) is for a larger commercial version of this called SGML TagWizard, but the two products function in the same way. HTML is a subset of the SGML markup language so WebWizard is a subset of the SGML product. If you need an SGML document creator, see the readme.txt file for information about contacting the creator of this product.

WP2X

\html\wp2x

This program translates WP files (from the old WP 4.2 format) to HTML. In the event that you have some WP 4.2 files you need to convert, this is probably your only option. There are also UNIX versions of this discussed later in the "UNIX" portion of this chapter.

Viewers

If you will be including graphics, sound, or movies as part of your Web site, you need software for editing, viewing, and converting the various formats. Or, if you are setting up Web clients for customers or employees you support, they'll need some of the utilities here to view or listen to download multimedia files. While a commercial graphics program may have more power and versatility than the programs here, sometimes you'd rather use a smaller, simpler program. In addition to programs for graphics and sound, you'll find text editors and other file-viewing programs here.

While no one is likely to use all of these programs, we have included quite a few with similar features to give you more choices. What is right in one situation may not be right in others.

GhostView

\viewers\gsview

You can use GhostView v1.0, a Windows 3.1 application, to view printer files that conform to GhostScript 2.6 or later standards. GhostScript is an interpreter for the PostScript, page-description language used by many laser printers. You can also use GhostView to print GhostScript embedded documents. Source code for this application is part of the archive. GhostView is the interpreter that NCSA recommends for use with Mosaic for viewing PostScript files with GhostScript. See gsview.doc for installation and setup directions. (You also will need the GhostScript 2.61 files. These are on WebmasterCD in the \viewers\gsview\gscript directory. See use.doc for installation and setup directions.)

GrabIt Pro

\viewers\grabpro

This is a Windows screen capture utility. If you are putting together Web pages for software documentation, you'll find this an invaluable aid in creating pages with embedded screen shots. (It does not save files in GIF format. If you want to use saved images as inline images, you need to convert them using one of the other utilities discussed here.) There is a Windows 3.1 and Windows NT version, both of which are included here.

To install this utility, run the gpsetup.exe program in Windows from either the win31 or winnt directory and follow the directions on-screen.

Image'n'Bits

\viewers\ima

This is a graphics manipulation and conversion utility. Among the formats support are BMP and GIF. Some of the special effects it includes are dithering, pixelize, and solarize. If you are working with artistic images or photographs as Web images, this utility is very useful.

To install this utility, run \viewers\ima\setup.exe in Windows and follow the directions on-screen.

Jasc Media Center
\viewers\jascmedi

If you have a large collection of multimedia files you have collected from the Web, you will find this utility useful for keeping them organized. It supports 37 file formats including GIF, JPEG, MIDI, WAV, and AVI. Formats that aren't supported can still be used if you have an external file filter for them.

To install Jasc Media Center, run \viewers\jascmedi\setup.exe in Windows.

LView
\viewers\lview

This is one of the best all around graphics viewers and utilities. NCSA recommends this viewer for both GIF and JPEG images with Mosaic. It also supports TIFF, PCX, and several other image formats. In addition to viewing these files, you can retouch images by adjusting their color balance, contrast, plus many other attributes.

Media Blastoff
\viewers\blastoff

This viewer provides support for several popular graphics formats as well as sound and movies. The file formats that will probably be of most use to you with the Internet are GIF, AVI, and WAV.

To install this, run \viewers\blastoff\setup.exe in Windows and follow the directions on-screen.

MegaEdit
\viewers\megaedit

MegaEdit v2.08 is a Windows text file editor with many of the standard features you might find in a DOS-based text editor. This application works for multiple or large files. MegaEdit has internal support for the original IBM OEM (Original Equipment Manufacturer) font set. This means it has the capability to correctly display extended IBM characters, such as the line sets with which other Windows-based editors have problems.

> **Note**
>
> This is a shareware version limited to files of 5,000 lines or fewer. The full version has no limit on file size except for the limits placed on it by the amount of virtual memory you have in Windows.

MPEGPLAY

\viewers\mpegwin

This MPEG movie player for Windows currently requires Win32 to run. MPEGPLAY is the viewer recommended by NCSA for use with Mosaic. This latest version adds a Save As feature so that there is now a way to save movies downloaded by Mosaic. If you've used older versions of this with Mosaic, you'll appreciate this. This is an unregistered shareware version and does not play files larger than 1M. This limitation is removed if you register.

To install, run \viewers\mpegwin\setup.exe in Windows and follow the directions on-screen.

Paint Shop Pro

\viewers\paintshp

This powerful graphics viewing and editing utility supports around 20 different graphics file formats including the common GIF and GPEG formats found on the Web. It has a host of features for editing and manipulating graphics and rivals commercial packages with its number and variety of filters and special effects. It also includes a screen capture program.

To install, run \viewers\paintshp\setup.exe in Windows and follow the directions on-screen.

PlayWave

\viewers\playwav

This simple Windows application for playing WAV sound files requires fewer mouse clicks for playing waves and you can set it to loop a WAV file continuously. The author states that this application may not work on all systems. To use it, just use the File Manager to "associate" WAV files with PlayWave, not the Sound Recorder. Then, when you double-click WAV file names, PlayWave will come up, not the Sound Recorder. To use it with Mosaic, just designate it as the viewer for WAV files and when you download a WAV format sound, PlayWave will start.

Video for Windows

\viewers\vid4win

This is the Microsoft Video for Windows runtime version that you need to view Video for Windows (AVI) files. This is the latest version, 1.1d. Even if you have Video for Windows installed, you should check the version to see if it is older. This newer version runs significantly faster and better than some older versions.

The installation program will restart Windows when done; save anything you are working on and exit all applications before starting. To install Video for Windows, run \viewers\vid4win\setup.exe in Windows and follow the directions on-screen.

WinJPEG

\viewers\winjpg

Windows JPEG is a Windows-based, graphics file viewer and converter. You can read and save TIFF, GIF, JPG, TGA, BMP, and PCX file formats with this viewer/converter. Windows JPEG has several color-enhancement and dithering features that allow the user to alter a graphics file slightly. Batch conversions and screen capturing are also features of this program.

WinECJ

\viewers\winecj

This fast JPEG viewer has the capability to open multiple files. It also has a slide show presentation mode.

WinLab

\viewers\winlab

In addition to image processing features, this powerful graphics viewer and editor has built-in twain and network support. It also has a WinSock-compliant application for sending and receiving images.

WPlany

\viewers\wplany

WPlany is a sound utility that plays sound files through a Windows Wave output device (like a Sound Blaster). It is recommended by NCSA for use with Mosaic. It supports a number of sound file formats, including most formats that are encountered on the Net, and it is very easy to use.

E-Mail

E-mail is one of the most popular applications on the Internet. A freeware version of Eudora and several other popular programs are included on WebmasterCD.

Eudora

\email\eudora

Eudora v1.4.4 is an e-mail package that offers many features. Eudora supports private mail boxes, reply functions, periodic mail checking, and many more features that make this software one of the best mail packages on the market.

> **Note**
>
> You can get information about Eudora 2, the commercial version, on the Web page for Qualcomm's QUEST group. The URL is **http://www.qualcomm.com/quest/QuestMain.html**. Or you can get information about the commercial version by e-mail to **eudora-sales@qualcomm.com**, or call (800) 2-EUDORA (that's 1-800-238-3672). You can find the latest version of the freeware version at **ftp.qualcomm.com**, in the directory "quest/eudora/windows/1.4."

Pegasus Mail

\email\pegasus

Pegasus Mail is a powerful and easy to use e-mail program. There are several add-ins for Pegasus that make it easier to send attachments of popular document types, such as Ami Pro and Word for Windows. One of these add-ins, Mercury (a mail transport system), is included in the install2\email\pegasus\mercury directory. Pegasus is free software that you can use without restriction.

RFD MAIL

\email\rfdmail

RFD MAIL is an MS Windows shareware offline mail reader that supports many Internet sites, including CompuServe, DELPHI, GEnie, MCI Mail, World UNIX, The Direct Connection, MV Communications, Panix, The Well, The Portal System, NETCOM, CRL, INS, and The Internet Access Company. Its other features are as follows: support for additional services through scripts; Address Book; Folders with drag, drop, and searching; Backup and Restore; Polling; and multiple signature blocks. Registration grants code to unlock shareware version, free update, and tech support via e-mail. To install it, run \email\rfdmail\install.exe in Windows.

Transfer Pro

\email\xferpro

Transfer Pro is a shareware, Windows-based software tool that allows users to send text, application data, messages, images, audio, video, executable files, and other data types via e-mail using the latest MIME 1.0 standards according to RFC1341. It supports UU and XX encoding and decoding. To install it, run \install2\email\xferpro\setup.exe in Windows.

Windows SMTP Server

\email\wsmtp

If you want to run more than just a Web site in Windows and are considering setting up your own mail server, examine this option. It includes source code that may be handy if you are inclined to write your own mail server. There are installation and configuration directions as well as bug reports in the readme.txt file.

UseNet News

If you plan to read UseNet News on a regular basis, you'll want to use one of the excellent newsreaders included here. There are newsreaders for Windows as well as DOS.

NewsXpress

\news\nxpress

This is one of the newest Windows newsreaders but it is quickly becoming very popular. It has all of the features found in the traditional leaders in this category and adds a more pleasant interface. Early feedback on it has been positive about its speed and functionality.

Trumpet News Reader

\news\wt_wsk

This is a full-featured shareware WinSock newsreader for Windows. You can do all of the expected functions such as reading, posting, and replying (as a follow up post or by e-mail). You can also save messages and decode attached files. After copying this to your hard drive, you have to provide information about your news server and your Internet account the first time you run it.

> **Note**
>
> There are three other versions of this software for other types of Internet connections. WT_LWP requires Novell LWP DOS/Windows; you can find it in the \news\wt_lwp directory. WT_ABI requires the Trumpet TSR TCP stack; you can find it in the \news\wt_abi directory. WT_PKT works with direct to packet driver (internal TCP stack); you can find it in the \news\wt_pkt directory. All of these versions are similar in function to the WinSock version.

WinVN Newsreader

\news\winvn

This is a full-featured public domain WinSock newsreader. As with the Trumpet program, you'll find all of the expected features. You'll need to provide information about your news server and Internet account the first time you run it.

> **Note**
>
> You'll find new versions of this program at **ftp.ksc.nasa.gov** in the /pub/win3/ winvn directory. New releases are posted there rather frequently.

YARN

\news\yarn

YARN is a freeware, offline reader program for UseNet mail and news. It runs in DOS 3.0 or higher. It does not run in Windows. YARN accepts "packets" created by a host program such as uqwk in the Simple Offline Usenet Packet format (SOUP). It is better than the common QWK format readers for UseNet use because it preserves more of the unique UseNet header information when posting replies.

To install, exit Windows, change to the news\yarn directory, and then run install.bat.

V

WebmasterCD

Gopher

A number of good Gopher clients are available. You can find varying degrees of features implemented and varying degrees of complexity. You are sure to find one that suits your needs. (Unfortunately for us, some of the popular free Gopher clients have recently been commercialized and we can't include them here although they are still freely available on the Net.) While you can access all of GopherSpace through the World Wide Web with a Web browser, you'll want to use a dedicated Gopher application if you send a lot of time gophering.

Gopher for Windows

\gopher\wgopher

The Chinese University of Hong Kong has presented us with this simple little Gopher client. If you are looking for something fancy, this may not be the ticket for you. But if you want something fast and simple, this is the perfect Gopher client.

FTP and Archie

If you plan to do a lot of file transfers on the Internet, you want to find an FTP client that you like. You also need a good Archie client to help you find the files you want to transfer. While you can use just about any Web browser for FTP and there are Web pages that perform Archie searches, if you download many files, an Archie program and FTP client are must-haves.

WinFTP

\ftp\winftp

If you have used WS_FTP, you'll recognize WinFTP as the author based his work on the source code from WS_FTP. For the most part, the operation is the same. You'll find a few nice additional features such as a history dialog so that you can pick a directory you have already visited, without having to traverse the entire directory tree, filters to allow you to look for specific, file types such as *.txt, or a*.zip in the local and remote hosts, and more. This directory contains a 16-bit and 32-bit version.

Windows FTP Daemon
\ftp\wftpd

This may be useful to you if you would like to run an FTP site in Windows in addition to your Web site. This shareware, WinSock-compliant server for FTP enables you to use your Windows PC as an FTP server. It allows both anonymous FTP and FTP using accounts with login names and passwords. There are some security features, and you can keep a log of logins and activity. This version will respond to FTP requests from Mosaic, Cello, and Netscape.

WSArchie
\ftp\wsarchie

This WinSock-compliant Archie program enables you to connect to an Archie server and search for a file using the familiar Windows interface. It comes preconfigured with the locations of several Archie servers. You can configure WSArchie to transfer files you find directly from the list of found files without having to manually open your FTP client and reenter the address and directory information. However, this software doesn't work this way with the current version of WS_FTP32.

WS_FTP
\ftp\ws_ftp16

This is the very popular WS_FTP FTP freeware client for Windows. WS_FTP makes it very easy to use FTP in a Windows point-and-click fashion that is as easy to understand as File Manager. It comes with configurations for connection to several popular FTP sites and you can add more to the list. It also has support for advanced features such as firewalls. There is also a 32-bit version in the \ftp\viewers\ws_ftp32 directory.

Internet Relay Chat

Internet Relay Chat is a real time way to carry on a conversation with one or several people via your computer over the Internet. Whatever, you type, everyone else will see. There isn't much software available for the PC for IRC. But the program included here is very good.

WSIRC
\irc\wsirc

This product comes in several different styles. There is a freeware version, a shareware version that opens up more functionality to you when registered, and retail versions for personal and corporate use. The author can also custom design an IRC client for special needs. The freeware and shareware versions are both included here. In this release, the shareware version has all the features enabled, but only for a limited time. After 30 days, you must register the shareware version to continue using it. The freeware version has no such limitations.

Other Internet Applications and Useful Utilities

This chapter has covered all of the main categories, but there is still a lot of software left over that doesn't fit into any one of the big categories. So this section deals with the programs that just don't fit anywhere else.

ArcMaster

\other\arcmastr

This is a handy utility for compressing and decompressing files using many popular compression formats. Support formats include ZIP, LHZ, and ARJ. You need to have the file compression/decompression utilities for each of these as this is just a front end to make it easier to use the DOS utilities. It supports drag and drop, allows you to conveniently manipulate compressed files, and converts files from one compression format to another.

ArcShell

\other\arcshell

ArcShell is a Windows shell for ZIP, LHZ, ARC, and ARJ compression files. You need to have the file compression/decompression utilities for each of these formats. ArcShell makes it easier to use the DOS utilities, but this is just a front end and won't work without PKZIP, LHArc, or another compression utility.

Batch UUD for DOS

\other\batchuud

As the name implies, this batch UUDecoder runs in DOS. With UUD, all you have to do is a UUD *.* and all saved files in UUEncoded format are decoded! It's smart as well: by alphabetizing all entries, UUD can make a logical guess at the order of split files!

COMt

\other\comt

COMt is a shareware program that allows a standard Windows-based communication program to act as a Telnet client in a TCP/IP environment. It allows you to use the more powerful features of your communication program in a Telnet session.

Run \other\comt\ install.exe (in Windows) to run the automatic installation or read the readme.txt file to install the program manually.

Crip for Windows

\other\cripwin

This Windows-based text encryption program was designed for use over the Internet. It has options for dealing with PC linefeeds in files that will be sent over the Internet. (See the readme.txt file for information.)

Drag And Zip

\other\dragzip

Drag And Zip is a set of utilities that makes Windows 3.1 File Manager into a file manager for creating and managing ZIP, LZH and GZ files. Drag And Zip is a set of utilities that makes Windows 3.1 With its built-in routines to zip and unzip files, Drag And Zip makes it very easy to compress files into ZIP files and to extract files from ZIP files from any Windows file manager that supports drag and drop. Drag And Zip also supports use of your copies of PKZIP, LHA and GUNZIP, to manage compressed files. Drag And Zip has a built-in virus scanner that you can use to scan the files in the compressed file for possible viruses.

To install Drag and Zip, run \other\dragzip\dzseup.exe in Windows and follow the directions on-screen.

Enigma for Windows

\other\enigma

This file encryption program supports the DES encryption standard used by many US government agencies. While it isn't designed for sending encrypted messages via Internet e-mail, you can use it for transferring files through any protocol that supports binary transfer. So you can encrypt files on an FTP site, you can send encrypted files as attachments to e-mail using UUEncode or MIME, or you can make encrypted files available via the WWW as links from an HTML document. This is not a public key system; the same password is used to encode and decode files. This limits its security for Internet usage because anyone who receives a file will need your password.

To install this program, run \other\enigma\install.exe in Windows.

EWAN—Emulator Without A good Name
\install1\other\ewan

Despite the fact that this emulator does not have a good name, it is a good product. The main use for this, in a typical setting, is for Telnet. You can save configurations for several different Telnet sites. It allows a capture log and the usual copying and pasting from the text in the capture log. To install, run \other\ewan\install.exe in Windows.

Extract
\other\extract

Extract v3.04 is a Windows application for encoding and decoding UU embedded files.

> **Note**
>
> The documentation with this software is a little out of date. The author requests that you send e-mail regarding the product to **dpenner@msi.cuug.ab.ca**; his surface mail address is
>
> Eau Claire Place II
> 650, 521 — 3rd Avenue S.W.
> Calgary, Alberta
> T2P 3T3

Finger 1.0
\other\finger10

Finger 1.0 is a simple, but functional, Finger client. Enter a host and user name and it reports back with information about the user as determined by the host.

IP Manager
\other\ipmgr

Do you have trouble keeping track of IP addresses? If this is something you need help with, IP Manager is the solution. It helps you keep track of IP addresses and ensures that you don't have duplicate addresses; you can even launch FTP and Telnet sessions from it.

This trial version is limited to only 25 devices. You may try IP Manager for 21 days. If at the end of the trial period you decide not to purchase IP Manager, you should delete it.

Name Server Lookup Utility

\other\nslookup

This simple, but powerful, little utility looks up information about a specific machine or domain on the Internet. It reports the numeric IP address and other information based on the site or machine name.

Sticky

\other\sticky

This interesting application enables you to post messages that look like "sticky notes" on other user's computers via the Internet. You can create a small database of other users to send these notes to.

To install Sticky, run \other\sticky\sticky.exe in Windows to begin the installation.

TekTel

\other\tektel

TekTel is a simple Telnet application with Tektronix T4010 and VT100 emulation. It is still a little rough around the edges. The source code is included and it is written in Visual Basic.

Time Sync

\other\tsync

Time Sync v1.4 is a Windows-based application designed to synchronize your PC clock to the same time as a UNIX host. This program relies on an established WinSock connection to function and it's written in Visual Basic.

To install Time Sync, run \other\tsync\setup.exe in Windows.

Triple DES

\other\tripldes

This is a collection of Windows DLLs and DOS libraries for the DES (Data Encryption Standard) encryption algorithm.

U2D

\other\u2d

This handy program converts UNIX text file line endings to DOS text file format. All you have to do is drag a file (or files) from File Manager to the U2D icon to process them.

UUCode

\other\uucode

UUCode is a Windows-based application used to decode UUEncoded files sent over the Internet in messages. This application also encodes a binary file in UUCode so it can be inserted into a message and sent over the Internet in this manner. Configuration options such as file overwriting, default file names, and enabling or disabling status messages are aspects of this program.

To install UUCode, run \other\uucode\setup.exe in Windows.

Visual Basic Run Time DLLs

\other\vbrun

Many of the Windows programs included on WebmasterCD are written in Visual Basic and require one of these files to run. Most of the time, these files will be installed by the program or will have been installed by something else. But, if you ever get an error message that says something like Cannot run, cannot find vbrunx00.dll, just copy the missing VB Run Time file from here to your \windows\system directory.

VoiceChat

\other\ivc

VoiceChat is a great example of a cutting-edge Internet application. This program enables two users connected to the Internet to talk to each other via their PCs. It requires both PCs to have a sound card and speaker. If you have a fast Internet connection (Ethernet for instance) the conversation is in real time. If you have a slower connection (like SLIP) the program still works, but there are delays in transmission of the audio. Audio quality is not affected by a SLIP connection, but you can choose a lower sampling rate to speed up transmission. Even so, the quality should be as good as or better than a telephone. If you register this, you get additional features such as answering machine and fax modes. See the file readme.n0w for installation directions.

> **Note**
>
> Internet VoiceChat is Copyright © 1994, Richard L. Ahrens. You can use the unregistered version of IVC on an evaluation basis for no more than thirty days. Continued use after the thirty-day trial period requires registration, which is $20 for individual users. Site licenses are negotiable. You can contact the author at:
>
> Richard L. Ahrens
> 7 Omega Ct.
> Middletown, NJ 07748

WinCode
\other\wincode

This is a great utility for UUEncoding and UUDecoding files. A couple of really nice features are the way it handles multiple files effortlessly and its ability to tie its menus in to other programs. You'll also find that this program decodes many poorly encoded files that other decoders can't handle. Run the install.exe file in this directory in Windows to begin the installation process.

Windows Sockets Host
\other\wshost

Windows Sockets Host is a simple utility that determines a host computer's name based on a numeric IP address or vice versa.

Windows Sockets Net Watch
\other\ws_watch

This program makes active checks on hosts that are listed in its database file. This program is designed to work on any WinSock DLL, but the documentation has some notes about the compatible and the problematic WinSocks.

Windows Sockets Ping

\other\ws_ping

Ping is an uncomplicated Windows application used to test an Internet connection. The author wrote this application to test whether his two computers were connected on the Internet, You can use it to do the same thing. The source code is included in the archive and the author has granted for alteration if needed. There are Windows 3.1 and Windows NT versions included here.

> **Note**
>
> Because Ping uses nonstandard WinSock calls, this application may not run on every WinSock stack.

WinZip

\install1\other\winzip

WinZip version 5.6 is a fantastic Windows ZIP archive-managing program that no Internet user should be without. This application provides a pleasant graphical interface for managing many archive-file formats, such as ZIP, ARJ, ARC, and LZH. WinZip allows you to extract text files from an archive directly to the screen, so that you can read a file in an archive without actually extracting it. Another feature in this version enables you to uninstall a program soon after you install it.

Version 5.6 has added support of archives that use the GZIP, TAR, and Z formats that are very common on the Internet. You can now manage these files just as easily as ZIP files. It is common to find files on the Internet that have been stored as TAR files and then compressed with GZIP or Z. WinZip handles these multiple formats with no problems. This support is unique amongst the other ZIP file utilities discussed in this chapter.

WinZip is shareware and well worth the $29 registration fee for an individual user.

To install WinZip, run \other\winzip\setup.exe in Windows.

YAWTELNET

\install1\other\yawtel

YAWTELNET (Yet Another Windows Socket Telnet) is a freeware Telnet client designed specifically to work well with Mosaic. Many of the menu commands are not functional, but you can select text in the active window and copy it to another application.

> **Note**
>
> YAWTELNET is Copyright © 1994, Hans van Oostrom. Please refer to the license.txt file in the yawtel directory.

Zip Master

\other\zipmastr

ZMW is a stand-alone Windows 3.1 ZIP utility. PKZIP and PKZUNZIP are not required to use this, which sets it apart from most other Windows based ZIP utilities. You can use it to add to, freshen, or update existing ZIP files, create new ZIP files, extract from or test existing ZIP files, view existing ZIP file contents, and to perform many other functions.

Zip Manager

\other\zipmgr

This is another Windows ZIP utility that doesn't require you to also have PKZIP or PKUNZIP. It is 100 percent PKZIP 2.04 compatible and the compression utilities are designed especially for Windows. Zipping and unzipping functions (ZMZIP and ZMUNZIP) are built in to Zip Manager.

To install this, run \other\zipmgr\zmsetup.exe in Program Manager.

> **Note**
>
> You must run ZMSETUP.EXE from the Windows Program Manager. Other shells such as the Norton Desktop or PC Tools for Windows are not 100 percent compatible with our setup program and may cause it to fail when you attempt to create the Zip Manager Group.

UNIX

We've pulled together a few programs and utilities to make setting up a UNIX Web server easier. All of the UNIX programs included on the CD are included in the /unix directory.

V

WebmasterCD

Because we wanted to make WebmasterCD compatible with the DOS and UNIX file structure, we've had to leave all of the UNIX files compressed. Each program's compression file has been renamed with a DOS legal file name. When you decompress the archives on a UNIX machine, the full UNIX file names should be properly restored from the compression file.

Most of the UNIX programs are compressed in either the gzip or Z format indicated by a GZ or Z extension. Within most of those, you will find a TAR file. Use gzip (which is included on the CD) to decompress files with a GZ extension and the UNIX `unpack` command to decompress files with a Z extension. After that, use the UNIX `tar` command with the x option to extract the contents from the TAR file.

Most of the programs here are distributed as source code that you'll need to compile for your OS. Where a compiled version of a program for a common OS exists that we could get, we've included it, too.

CERN httpd

/unix/wwwdaemo.z

NCSA's Web server (which is discussed throughout this book) isn't the only game in town for setting up a Web server in UNIX. The creators of the Web, CERN, also have released CERN httpd, their Web server, into the public domain. The source code for version 3 is included here. For more information on this and for some precompiled versions see **http://info.cern.ch/ hypertext/WWW/Daemon/Status.html**.

DocFinder

/unix/docfinde.tar

Doc Finder is a suite of scripts and programs based on freeWAIS that are used to create indexes HTML documents and then to do searches against this index database to locate the HTML documents. It requires freeWAIS which is also included as freewais.gz.

Frame to HTML

/unix/frame2ht.z

This HTML filter converts Framemaker documents to HTML.

Note

Frame to HTML is used by permission of Telenor Research and Jon Stephenson von Tetzcherner. Telenor Research owns the rights to the software, but MacDonald Dettwiler and Duncan Fraser have contributed substantially.

gwstat

/unix/gwstat.gz

This program processes the output from wwwstat as discussed in chapter 14, "Usage Statistics and Maintaining HTML." Gwstat generates GIF graphs of your server traffic data. In order to run it, you need the following programs, which are also included on WebmasterCD (the file name on WebmasterCD follows the program name):

> Perl5 (perl5000.gz)
>
> wwwstat (wwwstat-.z)
>
> ImageMagick (imagemag.gz)
>
> GhostScript (ghostscr.gz)

You'll also need Xmgr, which is not on WebmasterCD. You can get it by FTP at **ftp.ccalmr.ogi.edu/CCALMR/pub/acegr/xmgr-3.01.tar.Z**

The TAR file you should expand from the gz file is named gwstat1.12.tar. After that, look at **http://dis.cs.umass.edu/stats/gwstat.html** for detailed installation directions.

Note

There's a precompiled version of Gwstat for Linux in the gwstat-l.gz file. To use it, you'll also need the files in libjpeg-.gz

gzip

/unix/gzip124.tar

You need this program to uncompress all of the gzip files on WebmasterCD, just in case you don't already have it. This is version 1.2.4, which was the latest version at the time we went to press.

LaTeX2HTML

/unix/latex2ht.tar

This translator converts LaTeX documents to HTML. It can break documents into pieces as you specify, handle equations, footnotes, tables and other elements frequently found in technical LaTeX documents, and translate cross-references into hyperlinks.

MOMspider

/unix/momspide.z

This program for checking hyperlinks is a perl script. It roams the Web, following each link. It can build a map of the links it follows. See chapter 14, "Usage Statistics and Maintaining HTML," for more information.

> **Note**
>
> This software has been developed by Roy Fielding as part of the Arcadia project at the University of California, Irvine. Copyright © 1994 Regents of the University of California. All rights reserved. Redistribution and use in source and binary forms are permitted, subject to the restriction noted below, provided that the above copyright notice and this paragraph and the following paragraphs are duplicated in all such forms and that any documentation, advertising materials, and other materials related to such distribution and use acknowledge that the software was developed in part by the University of California, Irvine. The name of the University may not be used to endorse or promote products derived from this software without specific prior written permission. THIS SOFTWARE IS PROVIDED *AS IS* AND WITHOUT ANY EXPRESS OR IMPLIED WARRANTIES, INCLUDING, WITHOUT LIMITATION, THE IMPLIED WARRANTIES OF MERCHANTABILITY AND FITNESS FOR A PARTICULAR PURPOSE.

NCSA Web Server

/unix/ncsahttp/source.z

This is the Web server for UNIX that is discussed in chapter 5 and throughout most of the rest of the book. Please see the directions in chapter 5, "Getting Started with Web Servers," to install this server. To configure it, see chapter 6, "Server Configuration."

All of the file names in this directory have been shortened by removing the httpd_ that precedes the given name at the NCSA site. In addition to the source files, WebmasterCD includes documentation and binaries for the following platforms:

DECAXP

DECMIPS

HP

RS6000

SGI

SUN4

perl
/unix/perl5000.gz

This, version 5 of the perl script processing language for UNIX, is discussed throughout the book. For more information on perl, see chapter 12 "Scripts."

SoftQuad HoTMetaL
/unix/sq-hotme.z

This is the UNIX version of the freeware HTML editor from SoftQuad. This UNIX version is similar in features to the Windows version discussed earlier in "SoftQuad HoTMetaL" in this chapter.

Tex2RTF
/unix/tex2rtfs.z

This program converts LaTeX files to RTF (Rich Text Format) and HTML. (There's also a Windows version of this discussed in "Tex2RTF" in the HTML section earlier in this chapter.) This file contains the source code. Precompiled versions for Sun Motiff (tex2rtsm.z) and HP (tex2rtfh.z) are also included.

tkHTML
/unix/tkhtml22.gz

In order to use this WYSIWYG HTML editor you also need wwwish (wwwish.gz), which is included on WebmasterCD. You should also see the tkhtml.rea file (which is the author's tkHTML.README file) and the change.log file (the author's ChangeLog file) for information on contacting the author and a pointer to the WWW homepage.

txt2html

/unix/txt2html.pl

This is a perl script for converting existing UNIX text documents into HTML. The author states that there are probably better programs for creating new HTML. (Because this is a perl script, you can also use it with the DOS version of perl to convert DOS text files to HTML.)

WP2x

/unix/wp2x_23.gz

This program converts WordPerfect documents created on the UNIX platform to HTML.

wwwstat

/unix/wwwstat-.z

This program keeps statistics about accesses to your Web site and is discussed in chapter 14, "Usage Statistics and Maintaining HTML."

Examples from *Running A Perfect Web Site*

\examples

Throughout the book, there are examples of HTML code. All of the longer examples and code used for figures is included in this directory. You'll also find many of the scripts used throughout the book.

Internet Documents

The final group of files on WebmasterCD is a large collection of documents about the Internet. I hope you find it useful to have this information at your fingertips rather than having to find it yourself on the Net. WebmasterCD doesn't install any of these documents. Any documents that were zipped are now unzipped, so you can read them all in a text viewer or word processor directly from the CD or you can easily copy them.

FYIs

\docs\fyi

FYIs (For Your Information) are a subset of the RFCs and they tend to be more informational and less technical. An index file is also included.

Internet Provider Lists

\docs\lists\provider

This directory contains several text files that list many companies and providers on the Internet that supply a constant Internet connection. Many of the sites listed in this text file also have dial-up access to the Internet. Information such as contact name, phone number, Internet address, and system information are all listed for each site in the Provider lists. These lists are broken up by geographic region. They are compiled and maintained by InterNIC.

RFCs

\docs\rfc

WebmasterCD includes well over 1,000 RFCs (Request for Comments). These are the working notes of the committees that develop the protocols and standards for the Internet. They are numbered in the order that they were released. (Zeros were added to the beginning of the number part of the file names for the ones numbered below 1000 so that they display in numerical order in File Manager.) You will notice that there are some numbers that are skipped. These are RFCs that are outdated or were made obsolete by a newer one. An index file is also included.

STDs

\docs\std

If an RFC becomes fully accepted, it becomes a standard and is designated an STD (Internet Activities Board Standards). These tend to be technical. An index file is also included.

V

WebmasterCD

Index

J-K

L

T

T1-T3 (leased line speeds), 52
tables, creating (HTML), 231-235
tags
  <A HREF>, 241
  <ADDRESS>, 230
  <BASE>, 227

 (line break), 232
  <CITE>, 230
  <CODE>, 230
  <DFN>, 230
  <DIR>, 233
  <DL>, 233
  <EM>, 230
  <FORM>, 303
  <HEAD>/<BODY>, 226
  <HR> (horizontal rule), 232
  <IMG>, 238
  <INPUT TYPE> tags, 294
  <ISINDEX>, 302
  <KBD>, 230
  <MENU>, 233
  <OL>, 233
  <OPTION>, 301
  <P>, 232
  <PRE>, 231
  <SAMP>, 230
  <SELECT>...<OPTION>...
    </SELECT>, 294
  <STRONG>, 230
  <TEXTAREA>, 295
  <TEXTAREA>...
    </TEXTAREA>, 294
  <TITLE>, 227
  <UL>, 233
  <VAR>, 230
  ALT, 172-173
  Directory, 151
  HTML, 258
  Limit, 153
  nested, 284
tar command (NCSA httpd
  server installation), 109
TCP/IP, 54, 387
  internal Web servers
    commercial products,
      82-86
    network requirements,
      79-82
  Internet connection
    software, 406-409
TekTel program
  (WebmasterCD), 429

templates
  ANT, 268-273
  ANT_HTML, 271, 411-412
  CU_HTML, 274-276, 412
  GT_HTML, 276-277, 412-413
Test HTML Document
  command (File menu), 283
TeX documents, converting to
  HTML, 287
Tex2RTF
  HTML programs, 416
  UNIX software, 437
text
  bold, 228-229
  italicized, 228-229
  nontext data
    manipulation, 311
  preformatted, 231-235
  tables, creating (HTML),
    231-235
  underlined, 228-229
  UUEncoded, 215
text alignment (HTML),
  231-235
text anchors, creating
  (hypertext), 241-242
text boxes (graphical
  controls), 294-295
text file databases, searching
  (grep command), 344-345
text files
  converting from search-only
    databases, 346
  searching
    DOS, 372
    UNIX, 371-372
text formatting (browsers),
  24-25
text operations (CGI scripting
  platforms), 310-311
text styles (HTML text/
  graphics features), 231
  logical styles, 229-230
  physical styles, 228-229
text-only browsers (Web
  servers), 172-173
Time Sync program
  (WebmasterCD), 429
time zone variable
  settings, 104
time zones, troubleshooting
  (Windows httpd), 107
TimeOut directive, 122
timeouts, see server timeouts
Title (Internet Assistant
  tools), 258

titles (HTML header
  elements), 227
tkHTML (UNIX software), 437
toolbars
  ANT, 269-270
  Forms, 260
  HTML Assistant, 279
  HTMLed, 282-283
toolkits, 393-394
tools
  Internet Assistant, 258
  Web Author, 265
Tools menu commands
  (HTML Authoring), 262
tooltips, 264
trade-offs, establishing Web
  presence
  creating Web server, 40
  leasing space, 42
  using FTP/Gopher servers, 44
traditional print catalogs, see
  print catalogs
traffic, 12-14
Transfer Pro (e-mail
  programs), 422
TransferLog directive, 127
Transmission Control
  Protocol/Internet Protocol,
  see TCP/IP
Triple DES program
  (WebmasterCD), 430
troubleshooting Windows
  httpd server
  DOS scripts, running, 108
  time zones, setting, 107
  WinSock software,
    running, 107
Trumpet News Reader,
  422-423
Trumpet Winsock (TCP/IP
  commercial products), 84
Trumpet Winsock 2.0
  (Internet connection
  software), 408-409
tutorials/how-to information
  (Web server publicity
  issues), 182
txt2html (UNIX software), 438
TypesConfig directive, 126
typewriter (HTML physical
  styles), 228-229

X–Y–Z

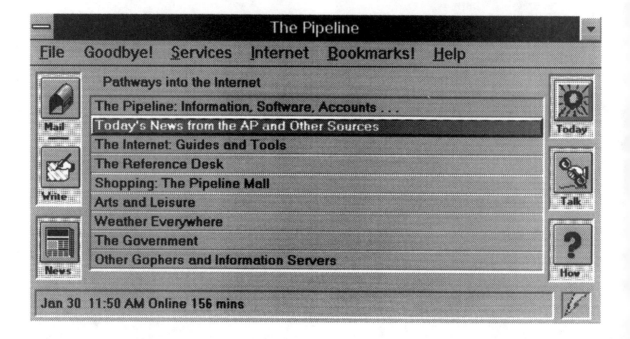

WebWizard™

The World-Wide Web authoring system that works with your word processor

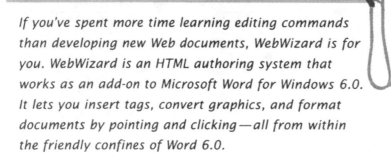

If you've spent more time learning editing commands than developing new Web documents, WebWizard is for you. WebWizard is an HTML authoring system that works as an add-on to Microsoft Word for Windows 6.0. It lets you insert tags, convert graphics, and format documents by pointing and clicking—all from within the friendly confines of Word 6.0.

WebWizard delivers these features and benefits:

★ Creates fully-formatted HTML and Word documents in a single file

WebWizard uses standard Word files, letting you insert HTML tags that can be hidden. Now you can create documents that can be viewed on the Web and formatted and printed like any other Word files.

★ Provides "Assisted Tagging"

When you click to insert HTML tags, WebWizard provides a dialog box that shows which tags can be inserted in that specific context. Tags are clearly distinguishable, and you have full access to all HTML attributes.

★ Automatically works with any HTML DTD

Because WebWizard has a full SGML parser built in, you can use any HTML DTD. So when standards change, or when companies like NetScape™ extend the standards, WebWizard continues to work uninterrupted.

★ Automatically translates any graphic to GIF format

With WebWizard, any graphic that can be pasted into Word can be converted to GIF format simply by pointing and clicking.

Here's what the experts have to say:

"For those authoring HTML, it takes away the guesswork associated with filtering files from Microsoft Word."

The Seybold Report, July 1994

"NICE Technologies' Word for Windows add-on...has a simple yet well-designed toolbar that will help you build error-free HTML Level 2 compliant documents."

PC Magazine, February 1995

For more information, or to order WebWizard, contact:

NICE Technologies
2121 41st Avenue, Suite 303
Capitola, CA 95010
Phone: (408) 476-7850
Fax: (408) 476-0910
Email: nicetech@netcom.com

WebWizard and NICE Technologies are trademarks of NICE Technologies.
All other trademarks are the properties of their respective owners.

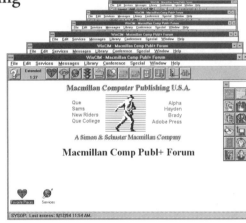

Before using any of the software on this disc, you need to install the software you plan to use. See chapters 5 and 16 for directions. If you have problems with WebmasterCD, please contact Macmillan Technical Support at (317) 581-3833. We can be reached by e-mail at support@mcp.com or by CompuServe at GO QUEBOOKS.

Read This before Opening Software

By opening this package, you are agreeing to be bound by the following:

This software is copyrighted and all rights are reserved by the publisher and its licensers. You are licensed to use this software on a single computer. You may copy the software for backup or archival purposes only. Making copies of the software for any other purpose is a violation of United States copyright laws. THIS SOFTWARE IS SOLD AS IS, WITHOUT WARRANTY OF ANY KIND, EITHER EXPRESSED OR IMPLIED, INCLUDING BUT NOT LIMITED TO THE IMPLIED WARRANTIES OF MERCHANTABILITY AND FITNESS FOR A PARTICULAR PURPOSE. Neither the publisher nor its dealers and distributors nor its licensers assume any liability for any alleged or actual damages arising from the use of this software. (Some states do not allow exclusion of implied warranties, so the exclusion may not apply to you.)

The entire contents of this disc and the compilation of the software are copyrighted and protected by United States copyright laws. The individual programs on the disc are copyrighted by the authors or owners of each program. Each program has its own use permissions and limitations. To use each program, you must follow the individual requirements and restrictions detailed for each. Do not use a program if you do not agree to follow its licensing agreement.

This package contains the Internet-Connect™ Trial Copy program. Internet-Connect is a registered trademark of Core Systems. Internet-Connect is developed and marketed by Core Systems.